RIGHTSTART MATHEMATICS

by Joan A. Cotter, Ph.D.
with Kathleen Cotter Lawler

LEVEL D LESSONS
Second Edition

A *Activities for Learning, Inc.*

A special thank you to Maren Ehley and Rebecca Walsh for their work on the final preparation of this manual.

Note: Levels are used rather than grades. For example, Level A is kindergarten and Level B is first grade and so forth.

Copyright © 2015 by Activities for Learning, Inc.

All rights reserved. No part of this publication may be reproduced, stored in a retrieval system, or transmitted, in any form or by any means, electronic, mechanical, photocopying, recording, or otherwise, without written permission of Activities for Learning, Inc.

The publisher hereby grants permission to reproduce the appendix for a single family's use only.

Printed in the United States of America

www.RightStartMath.com

For more information: info@RightStartMath.com
Supplies may be ordered from: www.RightStartMath.com

Activities for Learning, Inc.
321 Hill Street
Hazelton, ND 58544-0468
United States of America
888-775-6284 or 701-782-2000
701-782-2007 fax

ISBN 978-1-942943-03-7

January 2018

RightStart™ Mathematics Objectives for Level D

	Quarter 1	Quarter 2	Quarter 3	Quarter 4
Numeration				
Rounds numbers to the nearest 10, 100, and 1000	N/A			
Reads, writes, and compares numbers to the millions	N/A			
Addition				
Adds 2-digit numbers mentally				
Adds 4-digit numbers				
Subtraction				
Understands subtraction as a missing addend				
Subtracts 2-digit numbers mentally				
Subtracts 4-digit numbers				
Multiplication				
Understands 5 × 7 as 5 multiplied by 7	N/A			
Knows multiplication facts to 10 × 10	N/A	N/A	N/A	
Applies commutative, associative, and distribute properties	N/A			
Multiplies multiples of 10, e.g. 80 × 7	N/A	N/A		
Multiplies a 4-digit number by a 1-digit number	N/A	N/A		
Division				
Understands division as the number of groups or size of a group	N/A			
Understands division as finding a missing factor	N/A			
Knows division facts	N/A	N/A	N/A	
Problem Solving				
Solves two-step problems involving four operations				
Solves problems in more than one way				
Persists in solving problems				
Identifies and explains patterns				
Time and Money				
Tells time to the minute	N/A	N/A		
Solves elapsed time problems	N/A	N/A		
Adds and subtracts with dollars and cents	N/A	N/A	N/A	
Measurement				
Understands square units, cm², sq ft, and sq miles	N/A	N/A		
Finds perimeter and area in customary and metric units	N/A	N/A		
Measures in grams, kilograms, and liters	N/A	N/A	N/A	
Fractions				
Understands fraction a/b as a divided by b	N/A			
Understands a/b as $1/b$ multiplied by a	N/A			
Understands $n\frac{a}{b}$ as a whole number plus a fraction	N/A			
Compares and finds equivalences on the fraction chart	N/A	N/A		
Data				
Gathers and interprets data with charts and graphs	N/A	N/A		
Geometry				
Knows angles 30°, 45°, 60°, 90°, 180°, and 360°	N/A	N/A	N/A	
Categorizes shapes by attributes, e.g., square is a rectangle	N/A	N/A	N/A	
Partitions shapes into simple fractions	N/A	N/A	N/A	
Constructs equilateral triangle and other shapes with drawing tools	N/A	N/A	N/A	

© Activities for Learning, Inc. 2015

Materials needed that are not included in the RightStart™ Supplies

Occasionally, the materials needed for a lesson have items listed in boldface type, indicating that these items are not included in the RightStart™ materials list. Below is a list of theses items and the lesson number where they are needed.

Lesson 12   Chinese checkers game board, if available

Lesson 15   Two sticky notes or cards, one with "4" and the other with "=" for every two children

Lesson 30   Colored pencil or marker per child

Lesson 57   Scissors and glue or tape

Lesson 58   Colored pencils or markers

Lesson 68   Scissors and tape

Lesson 75   1 gallon container, filled with water, 2 half-gallon containers, at least 2 quart containers and a funnel

Lesson 87   Chinese checkers game board, if available

Lesson 91   Colored pencil or marker for each child

Lesson 93   Colored marker for each child

Lesson 95   Map of the U.S. showing the states

Lesson 100   2 sheets of construction paper (9 inches by 12 inches) per child

Lesson 111   Two 9-ounce clear plastic cups* and two pieces of string 8" (20 cm) long per math balance and small objects to weigh**

> * Paper cups would work, but clear plastic cups allow the child to see the contents of the cups more easily, but use only cups with plastic code 1. The code is found in the recycling triangle on the bottom. A cup with plastic code 6 is brittle and often breaks when making the hole, leaving sharp edges.
> ** Some suggestions for objects for weighing include: coins, erasers, toys, teaspoon of sugar, piece of folded paper, and paper clips.

Lesson 112   1-quart (4 cups or 1 liter) clear measuring cup, water, and empty container *

> * An empty half-gallon (two liter) container from milk or juice is ideal.

Lesson 114   Two rulers or pencils for showing angles

Lesson 121   Tape *, sharp pencil (preferably mechanical), and eraser for each child

> * The best tape is "removable" tape, which can be reused several times and doesn't tear the corners of the paper.

Lesson 124   Colored pencils or markers

Lesson 126   Colored pencils or markers

Lesson 129   Colored pencils or markers

Lesson 132   Colored pencils or markers

How This Program Was Developed

We have been hearing for years that Japanese students do better than U.S. students in math in Japan. The Asian students are ahead by the middle of first grade. And the gap widens every year thereafter.

Many explanations have been given, including less diversity and a longer school year. Japanese students attend school 240 days a year.

A third explanation given is that the Asian public values and supports education more than we do. A first grade teacher has the same status as a university professor. If a student falls behind, the family, not the school, helps the child or hires a tutor. Students often attend after-school classes.

A fourth explanation involves the philosophy of learning. Asians and Europeans believe anyone can learn mathematics or even play the violin. It is not a matter of talent, but of good teaching and hard work.

Although these explanations are valid, I decided to take a careful look at how mathematics is taught in Japanese first grades. Japan has a national curriculum, so there is little variation among teachers.

I found some important differences. One of these is the way the Asians name their numbers. In English we count ten, eleven, twelve, thirteen, and so on, which doesn't give the child a clue about tens and ones. But in Asian languages, one counts by saying ten-1, ten-2, ten-3 for the teens, and 2-ten 1, 2-ten 2, and 2-ten 3 for the twenties.

Still another difference is their criteria for manipulatives. Americans think the more the better. Asians prefer very few, but insist that they be imaginable, that is, visualizable. That is one reason they do not use colored rods. You can imagine the one and the three, but try imagining a brown eight–the quantity eight, not the color. It cannot be done without grouping.

Another important difference is the emphasis on non-counting strategies for computation. Japanese children are discouraged from counting; rather they are taught to see quantities in groups of fives and tens.

For example, when an American child wants to know 9 + 4, most likely the child will start with 9 and count up 4. In contrast, the Asian child will think that if he takes 1 from the 4 and puts it with the 9, then he will have 10 and 3, or 13. Unfortunately, very few American first-graders at the end of the year even know that 10 + 3 is 13.

I decided to conduct research using some of these ideas in two similar first grade classrooms. The control group studied math in the traditional workbook-based manner. The other class used the lesson plans I developed. The children used that special number naming for three months.

They also used a special abacus I designed, based on fives and tens. I asked 5-year-old Stan how much is 11 + 6. Then I asked him how he knew. He replied, "I have the abacus in my mind."

The children were working with thousands by the sixth week. They figured out how to add 4-digit numbers on paper after learning how on the abacus.

Every child in the experimental class, including those enrolled in special education classes, could add numbers like 9 + 4, by changing it to 10 + 3.

I asked the children to explain what the 6 and 2 mean in the number 26. Ninety-three percent of the children in the experimental group explained it correctly while only 50% of third graders did so in another study.

I gave the children some base ten rods (none of them had seen them before) that looked like ones and tens and asked them to make 48. Then I asked them to subtract 14. The children in the control group counted 14 ones, while the experimental class removed 1 ten and 4 ones. This indicated that they saw 14 as 1 ten and 4 ones and not as 14 ones. This view of numbers is vital to understanding algorithms, or procedures, for doing arithmetic.

I asked the experimental class to mentally add 64 + 20, which only 52% of nine-year-olds on the 1986 National test did correctly; 56% of those in the experimental class could do it.

Since children often confuse columns when taught traditionally, I wrote 2304 + 86 = horizontally and asked them to find the sum any way they liked. Fifty-six percent did so correctly, including one child who did it in his head.

The following year I revised the lesson plans and both first grade classes used these methods. I am delighted to report that on a national standardized test, both classes scored at the 98th percentile.

Joan A. Cotter, Ph.D.

© Activities for Learning, Inc. 2017

Some General Thoughts on Teaching Mathematics

1. Only five percent of mathematics should be learned by rote; 95 percent should be understood.

2. Real learning builds on what the child already knows. Rote teaching ignores it.

3. Contrary to the common myth, "young children can think both concretely and abstractly. Development is not a kind of inevitable unfolding in which one simply waits until a child is cognitively 'ready.'" —*Foundations for Success* NMAP

4. What is developmentally appropriate is not a simple function of age or grade, but rather is largely contingent on prior opportunities to learn." —Duschl & others

5. Understanding a new model is easier if you have made one yourself. So, a child needs to construct a graph before attempting to read a ready-made graph.

6. Good manipulatives cause confusion at first. If a new manipulative makes perfect sense at first sight, it is not needed. Trying to understand and relate it to previous knowledge is what leads to greater learning. —Richard Behr & others.

7. According to Arthur Baroody, "Teaching mathematics is essentially a process of translating mathematics into a form children can comprehend, providing experiences that enable children to discover relationships and construct meanings, and creating opportunities to develop and exercise mathematical reasoning."

8. Lauren Resnick says, "Good mathematics learners expect to be able to make sense out of rules they are taught, and they apply some energy and time to the task of making sense. By contrast, those less adept in mathematics try to memorize and apply the rules that are taught, but do not attempt to relate these rules to what they know about mathematics at a more intuitive level."

9. Mindy Holte puts learning the facts in proper perspective when she says, "In our concern about the memorization of math facts or solving problems, we must not forget that the root of mathematical study is the creation of mental pictures in the imagination and manipulating those images and relationships using the power of reason and logic." She also emphasizes the ability to imagine or visualize, an important skill in mathematics and other areas.

10. The only students who like flash cards are those who do not need them.

11. Mathematics is not a solitary pursuit. According to Richard Skemp, solitary math on paper is like reading music, rather than listening to it: "Mathematics, like music, needs to be expressed in physical actions and human interactions before its symbols can evoke the silent patterns of mathematical ideas (like musical notes), simultaneous relationships (like harmonies) and expositions or proofs (like melodies)."

12. "More than most other school subjects, mathematics offers special opportunities for children to learn the power of thought as distinct from the power of authority. This is a very important lesson to learn, an essential step in the emergence of independent thinking." —*Everybody Counts*

© Activities for Learning, Inc. 2017

13. The role of the teacher is to encourage thinking by asking questions, not giving answers. Once you give an answer, thinking usually stops.

14. Putting thoughts into words helps the learning process.

15. Help the children realize that it is their responsibility to ask questions when they do not understand. Do not settle for "I don't get it."

16. The difference between a novice and an expert is that an expert catches errors much more quickly. A violinist adjusts pitch so quickly that the audience does not hear it.

17. Europeans and Asians believe learning occurs not because of ability, but primarily because of effort. In the ability model of learning, errors are a sign of failure. In the effort model, errors are natural. In Japanese classrooms, the teachers discuss errors with the whole class.

18. For teaching vocabulary, be sure either the word or the concept is known. For example, if a child is familiar with six-sided figures, we can give him the word, hexagon. Or, if he has heard the word, multiply, we can tell him what it means. It is difficult to learn a new concept and the term simultaneously.

19. Introduce new concepts globally before details. This lets the children know where they are headed.

20. Informal mathematics should precede paper and pencil work. Long before a child learns how to add fractions with unlike denominators, she should be able to add one half and one fourth mentally.

21. Some pairs of concepts are easier to remember if one of them is thought of as dominant. Then the non-dominant concept is simply the other one. For example, if even is dominant over odd, an odd number is one that is not even.

22. Worksheets should also make the child think. Therefore, they should not be a large collection of similar exercises, but should present a variety. In RightStart™ Mathematics, they are designed to be done independently.

23. Keep math time enjoyable. We store our emotional state along with what we have learned. A person who dislikes math will avoid it and a child under stress stops learning. If a lesson is too hard, stop and play a game. Try the lesson again later.

24. In Japan students spend more time on fewer problems. Teachers do not concern themselves with attention spans as is done in the U.S.

25. In Japan the goal of the math lesson is that the student has understood a concept, not necessarily has done something (a worksheet).

26. The calendar must show the entire month, so the children can plan ahead. The days passed can be crossed out or the current day circled.

27. A real mathematical problem is one in which the procedures to find the answer are not obvious. It is like a puzzle, needing trial and error. Emphasize the satisfaction of solving problems and like puzzles, of not giving away the solution to others.

© Activities for Learning, Inc. 2017

RightStart™ Mathematics

Ten major characteristics make this research-based program effective:

1. Refers to quantities of up to 5 as a group; discourages counting individually. Uses fingers and tally sticks to show quantities up to 10; teaches quantities 6 to 10 as 5 plus a quantity, for example 6 = 5 + 1.

2. Avoids counting procedures for finding sums and differences. Teaches five- and ten-based strategies for the facts that are both visual and visualizable.

3. Employs games, not flash cards, for practice.

4. Once quantities 1 to 10 are known, proceeds to 10 as a unit. Temporarily uses the "math way" of naming numbers; for example, "1 ten-1" (or "ten-1") for eleven, "1-ten 2" for twelve, "2-ten" for twenty, and "2-ten 5" for twenty-five.

5. Uses expanded notation (overlapping) place-value cards for recording tens and ones; the ones card is placed on the zero of the tens card. Encourages a child to read numbers starting at the left and not backward by starting at the ones.

6. Proceeds rapidly to hundreds and thousands using manipulatives and place-value cards. Provides opportunities for trading between ones and tens, tens and hundreds, and hundreds and thousands with manipulatives.

7. Teaches mental computation. Investigates informal solutions, often through story problems, before learning procedures.

8. Teaches four-digit addition on the abacus, letting the child discover the paper and pencil algorithm.

9. Introduces fractions with a linear visual model, including all fractions from 1/2 to 1/10. "Pies" are not used initially because they cannot show fractions greater than 1. Later, the tenths will become the basis for decimals.

10. Teaches short division (where only the answer is written down) for single-digit divisors, before long division.

Second Edition

Many changes have occurred since the first RightStart™ lessons were begun in 1994. First, mathematics is used more widely in many fields, for example, architecture, science, technology, and medicine. Today, many careers require math beyond basic arithmetic. Second, research has given us new insights into how children learn mathematics. Third, kindergarten has become much more academic, and fourth, most children are tested to ensure their preparedness for the next step.

This second edition is updated to reflect new research and applications. Topics within each level are always taught with the most appropriate method using the best approach with the child and teacher in mind.

Daily Lessons

Objectives. The objectives outline the purpose and goal of the lesson. Some possibilities are to introduce, to build, to learn a term, to practice, or to review.

Materials. The Math Set of manipulatives includes the specially crafted items needed to teach RightStart™ Mathematics. Occasionally, common objects such as scissors will be needed. These items are indicated by boldface type.

Warm-up. The warm-up time is the time for quick review, memory work, and sometimes an introduction to the day's topics. The dry erase board makes an ideal slate for quick responses.

Activities. The Activities for Teaching section is the heart of the lesson; it starts on the left page and continues to the right page. These are the instructions for teaching the lesson. The expected answers from the child are given in square brackets.

Establish with the children some indication when you want a quick response and when you want a more thoughtful response. Research shows that the quiet time for thoughtful response should be about three seconds. Avoid talking during this quiet time; resist the temptation to rephrase the question. This quiet time gives the slower child time to think and the quicker child time to think more deeply.

Encourage the child to develop persistence and perseverance. Avoid giving hints or explanations too quickly. Children tend to stop thinking once they hear the answer.

Explanations. Special background notes for the teacher are given in Explanations.

Worksheets. The worksheets are designed to give the children a chance to think about and to practice the day's lesson. The children are to do them independently. Some lessons, especially in the early levels, have no worksheet.

Games. Games, not worksheets or flash cards, provide practice. The games, found in the *Math Card Games* book, can be played as many times as necessary until proficiency or memorization takes place. They are as important to learning math as books are to reading. The *Math Card Games* book also includes extra games for the child needing more help, and some more challenging games for the advanced child.

In conclusion. Each lesson ends with a short summary called, "In conclusion," where the child answers a few short questions based on the day's learning.

Number of lessons. Generally, each lesson is to be done in one day and each manual, in one school year. Complete each manual before going on to the next level.

Comments. We really want to hear how this program is working. Please let us know any improvements and suggestions that you may have.

Joan A. Cotter, Ph.D.

info@RightStartMath.com
www.RightStartMath.com

© Activities for Learning, Inc. 2017

LEVEL D TABLE OF CONTENTS

Lesson 1	Review Entering Quantities on the Abacus
Lesson 2	Review Addition Strategies
Lesson 3	Review Hundreds with Place-Value Cards
Lesson 4	Review Thousands and Side 2 of the Abacus
Lesson 5	Review Trading on Side 2 of the Abacus
Lesson 6	Review Mental Adding
Lesson 7	Review Subtraction Strategies
Lesson 8	Review Subtracting on Side 2 of the Abacus
Lesson 9	Review Traditional Subtracting on the Abacus
Lesson 10	Review Arrays
Lesson 11	Review Multiplication in Arrays
Lesson 12	Chinese Checkerboard Problem
Lesson 13	Multiplying by Two
Lesson 14	More Multiplying by Two
Lesson 15	Multiples of Two and Four
Lesson 16	Multiples of One
Lesson 17	Multiples of Eight
Lesson 18	The Commutative Property
Lesson 19	Multiples of Ten and Nine
Lesson 20	Multiples of Five
Lesson 21	Multiples of Three
Lesson 22	Multiples of Six
Lesson 23	Multiples of Seven
Lesson 24	The Associative Property for Multiplication
Lesson 25	Shortcut Multiplying
Lesson 26	Review and Games 1
Lesson 27	Multiplication Problems
Lesson 28	The Multiplication Table
Lesson 29	Area on the Multiplication Table
Lesson 30	Evens and Odds on the Multiplication Table
Lesson 31	Comparing Addition and Multiplication Tables
Lesson 32	The Short Multiplication Table
Lesson 33	Using the Short Multiplication Table
Lesson 34	Finding Missing Factors
Lesson 35	Division Problems

© Activities for Learning, Inc. 2015

LEVEL D TABLE OF CONTENTS

Lesson 36	Introducing Parentheses
Lesson 37	Assessment Review 1
Lesson 38	Review Games
Lesson 39	Assessment 1
Lesson 40	Multiplying on the Math Balance
Lesson 41	Distributive Property on the Math Balance
Lesson 42	Order of Operations with a Calculator
Lesson 43	Reviewing Place Value with a Calculator
Lesson 44	Estimating by Rounding to Tens
Lesson 45	More Rounding
Lesson 46	Story Problems with Rounding
Lesson 47	Review and Games 2
Lesson 48	Composing 6-Digit Numbers
Lesson 49	Composing Larger Numbers
Lesson 50	Comparing Larger Numbers
Lesson 51	Enrichment The Billions
Lesson 52	Introducing Remainders
Lesson 53	Remainders after Dividing by Nine
Lesson 54	Check Numbers
Lesson 55	Identifying Multiples
Lesson 56	Review and Games 3
Lesson 57	Enrichment Building Pascal's Triangle
Lesson 58	Enrichment Pascal's Triangle Patterns
Lesson 59	Checking Subtraction by Adding Up
Lesson 60	Checking Subtraction with Check Numbers
Lesson 61	Multiplying with Multiples of Tens
Lesson 62	More Multiplying with Multiples of Tens
Lesson 63	Multiplying Multi-Digit Numbers Horizontally
Lesson 64	Multi-Digit Multiplication
Lesson 65	Using Check Numbers with Multiplication
Lesson 66	Review and Games 4
Lesson 67	Unit Fractions
Lesson 68	Fractions as Division
Lesson 69	Non-Unit Fractions
Lesson 70	Fraction Pairs That Total One

© Activities for Learning, Inc. 2015

LEVEL D TABLE OF CONTENTS

Lesson 71	The Ruler Chart
Lesson 72	Adding Halves and Fourths
Lesson 73	Quarters of an Hour
Lesson 74	Fractions of a Dollar
Lesson 75	Gallons and Quarts
Lesson 76	Enrichment Musical Notes
Lesson 77	Assessment Review 2
Lesson 78	Review Games
Lesson 79	Assessment 2
Lesson 80	Making One with Fractions
Lesson 81	Comparing Fractions
Lesson 82	Fraction Line
Lesson 83	Multiples Patterns
Lesson 84	More Multiples Patterns
Lesson 85	Growing Geometric Patterns
Lesson 86	Numeric Patterns
Lesson 87	Chinese Checkerboard Revisited
Lesson 88	Review and Games 5
Lesson 89	Months of the Year
Lesson 90	Calendar for One Year
Lesson 91	Calendars for Two Years
Lesson 92	Measuring and Graphing Lengths
Lesson 93	Scoring Corners™ with a Bar Graph
Lesson 94	Reading a Bar Graph
Lesson 95	Constructing a Bar Graph
Lesson 96	Review and Games 6
Lesson 97	Time to the Minute
Lesson 98	Adding Minutes
Lesson 99	Time Problems
Lesson 100	Finding Perimeter in Feet and Inches
Lesson 101	Square Miles
Lesson 102	Measuring Areas
Lesson 103	Finding Areas
Lesson 104	Area of Tangram Pieces
Lesson 105	Area and Perimeter Comparisons

LEVEL D TABLE OF CONTENTS

Lesson 106   Finding Perimeter and Area of Squares

Lesson 107   Enrichment Graphing Perimeter and Area

Lesson 108   Review and Games 7

Lesson 109   Finding Factors

Lesson 110   Area and Perimeter Problems

Lesson 111   Measuring in Grams

Lesson 112   Liters and Kilograms

Lesson 113   Measurement Problems

Lesson 114   Naming Angles

Lesson 115   Measuring Sides in Triangles

Lesson 116   Measuring Angles in Triangles

Lesson 117   Dollars and Cents

Lesson 118   More Dollars and Cents

Lesson 119   Money Problems

Lesson 120   Review and Games 8

Lesson 121   Review Drawing Horizontal Lines

Lesson 122   Review Drawing Lines with a 30-60 Triangle

Lesson 123   Drawing Shapes in a Hexagon

Lesson 124   Drawing 30° and 60° Lines in a Circle

Lesson 125   Drawing 45° Lines in a Square

Lesson 126   Drawing 45° Lines in a Circle

Lesson 127   Drawing Congruent Figures

Lesson 128   Completing the Whole

Lesson 129   Finding a Fraction of a Figure

Lesson 130   Organizing Quadrilaterals

Lesson 131   Drawing Symmetrical Figures

Lesson 132   Congruent Shapes

Lesson 133   Arithmetic Review

Lesson 134   Arithmetic Games

Lesson 135   Time, Money, and Problem Solving Review

Lesson 136   Time, Money, and Problem Solving Games

Lesson 137   Data, Fraction, and Geometry Review

Lesson 138   Fraction Games

Lesson 139   Final Assessment

Lesson 140   Geometry Panels

© Activities for Learning, Inc. 2015

Review Lesson 1: Entering Quantities on the Abacus

OBJECTIVES:
1. To construct quantities 1 to 10 on fingers
2. To enter quantities 1 to 10 on the abacus
3. To identify quantities 1 to 10 on the abacus
4. To review facts that equal 10

MATERIALS:
1. Yellow is the Sun CD, optional
2. AL Abacus
3. *Math Card Games* book *, A3

ACTIVITIES FOR TEACHING:

Warm-up. Ask the child to repeat or sing the following rhyme while raising the appropriate fingers:

Yellow is the Sun
Yellow is the sun.
Six is five and one. (5 on left hand; 1 on right.)

Why is the sky so blue?
Seven is five and two. (5 on left; 2 on right.)

Salty is the sea.
Eight is five and three. (5 on left; 3 on right.)

Hear the thunder roar.
Nine is five and four. (5 on left; 4 on right.)

Ducks will swim and dive.
Ten is five and five. (5 on left; 5 on right.)

Exploring the AL Abacus. Give the child the abacus. Ask: Are the two sides of the abacus the same? [no] How are the sides different? [One side has the AL logo and the other side has 1000, 100, 10, and 1 along the top.]

Tell her to lay her abacus flat with the wires horizontal and the logo in the top right. Then tell her to "clear" her abacus by lifting the left edge and allowing the beads to slide to the right. See the figure on the right.

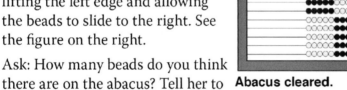

Abacus cleared.

Ask: How many beads do you think there are on the abacus? Tell her to find the exact number. [100 beads]
Ask the child how she found her answers. [count by ones, fives, or tens, or other ways]

Quantities 1 to 5. Tell the child to show 2 with her fingers on her left hand and then enter 2 on the abacus by moving both beads together. See the figure on the next page. Tell her to clear her abacus.

Tell her to show 3 with her fingers and enter 3 on the abacus by sliding all 3 beads together to the left edge as shown on the next page. Repeat for 4, 5, and 1. Explain: Naming quantities without counting is called *subitizing*.

EXPLANATIONS:

These review lessons are designed for children who have had no previous RightStart™ instruction or for a child needing a quick review.

The child can use any fingers on her left hands to show the quantity.

Use your right hand when you are across from the child so she sees the quantity on her "left."

* The Fifth Edition of the *Math Card Games* book is needed for this manual.

The book is arranged in chapters as follows:
1. Number Sense (N)
2. Addition (A)
3. Clocks (C)
4. Multiplication (P)
5. Money (M)
6. Subtraction (S)
7. Division (D)
8. Fractions (F)

The games are numbered sequentially within each chapter. For example, A2 is the second game in the Addition chapter and N3 is the third game in the previous chapter, Number Sense.

Within each chapter the games get progressively harder.

Subitizing (SOO bih tighz ing) is perceiving at a glance the number of items without counting. Five-month-old babies can subitize up to three objects and many 12-month old babies up to four objects. It is easier for children (and adults) to subitize quantities than to count them.

RightStart™ Mathematics Level D Second Edition © Activities for Learning, Inc. 2015

ACTIVITIES FOR TEACHING:

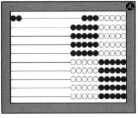
Two.

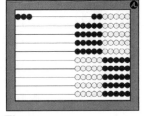
Three.

Quantities 6 to 10. Tell the child to show 6 with her fingers, 5 with the left hand and 1 with the right hand, as shown below on the left. Then ask her to enter 6 on her abacus as one group. Repeat the above activities for 7 through 10.

Six.

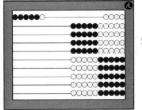
Six.

Practice with her to construct quantities from 6 to 10. Next, practice with quantities 1 to 10 on the abacus; tell her she needs to only change the quantity to show the new number without clearing the previous number.

The stairs. Tell the child to build the stairs by entering 1 on the first wire, 2 on the second wire, and so forth. See the figure at the right. Ask her to read the quantities from top to bottom. [1, 2, 3, . . . , 10] Ask her to point to 8, to 10, to 6, to 9, and other quantities.

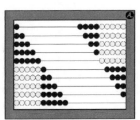
The stairs.

Tell her to look at the row where 8 is entered and ask: How many beads are on the right side of the wire? [2] What do you get when you add 8 and 2? [10] Tell her to find 4 on the abacus and ask: What do you need with 4 to equal 10? [6] Repeat for other quantities.

Go to the Dump game. Play the Go to the Dump game found in *Math Card Games* book, A3. Tell the child to use the stairs on the abacus to find pairs.

In conclusion. Ask: What are the ways to make 10? [9 & 1, 8 & 2, 7 & 3, 6 & 4, 5 & 5, 4 & 6, 3 & 7, 2 & 8, and 1 & 9]

EXPLANATIONS:

Be sure the child uses her left hand for five and her right hand for amounts over five. This way her hands will match the abacus.

Subitizing beyond five by grouping is called *conceptual subitizing*.

Often the quantity of eight is the hardest for a child to recognize.

Some children will need to clear the abacus to enter a new quantity. Work towards changing the current number to the new number.

The beads must be moved together as a unit, not one by one.

Conclusions may be a summary of the day's lesson or an expansion of the lesson to challenge higher level thinking.

© Activities for Learning, Inc. 2015

Review Lesson 2: Addition Strategies

OBJECTIVES:
1. To review addition strategies
2. To practice using the strategies

MATERIALS:
1. AL Abacus
2. Worksheet 1, Addition Strategies
3. *Math Card Games* book, A44

ACTIVITIES FOR TEACHING:

Warm-up. Ask the child to recite or sing the rhyme "Yellow is the Sun" while raising the appropriate fingers.

Say numbers 6 to 10 and ask the child to show the quantities with her fingers. Do the inverse: Show the child quantities 6 to 10 with your fingers and ask her to name them.

Ask: What are the ways to make 10? [9 & 1, 8 & 2, 7 & 3, 6 & 4, 5 & 5, 4 & 6, 3 & 7, 2 & 8, and 1 & 9]

Tens and Near Tens Strategies. Say: A strategy is a good way to remember facts. In the last lesson you used the Tens Strategy to find the facts that equal 10. Ask: If you know 3 + 7, how could you find 3 + 8? [It is 1 more than 10, or 11.] Say: We can call that the Near Tens Strategy.

Ones and Twos Strategies. Ask: What strategy could you use for facts like 7 + 1 or 9 + 1? [the next number] Say: We can call that the Ones Strategies. Ask: What about 5 + 2? [the next number two times] Say: We can call that the Twos Strategies.

Doubles and Near Doubles Strategies. Give the child the abacus. Ask: Can you name a doubles fact? [2 + 2, 8 + 8, and so forth] Tell her to enter 8 on the first and second rows of the abacus. See the figure at the right. Ask: How many blue beads are entered? [10] How many yellow beads are entered? [6] What is 10 + 6? [16] If 8 + 8 = 16, what is 8 + 9? [17] Say: We can call these the Doubles and Near Doubles Strategies.

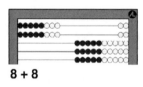
8 + 8

Two-Fives Strategy. Tell her that there is a strategy for adding facts when both numbers are 5 or more. Tell her to enter 9 and 6 on the top two wires of the abacus as shown in the left figure on the next page. Ask: Can you see the 10? [the two groups of five beads] See the right figure on the next page. Ask: How much is left over?

EXPLANATIONS:

Yellow is the Sun

Yellow is the sun.
Six is five and one. (5 on left; 1 on right.)

Why is the sky so blue?
Seven is five and two. (5 on left; 2 on right.)

Salty is the sea.
Eight is five and three. (5 on left; 3 on right.)

Hear the thunder roar.
Nine is five and four. (5 on left; 4 on right.)

Ducks will swim and dive.
Ten is five and five. (5 on left; 5 on right.)

The child can use any fingers on her left hands to show the quantity.

The first half of these RightStart™ Mathematics lessons refers to the child as a female and the second half refers to the child as a male.

ACTIVITIES FOR TEACHING:

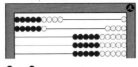 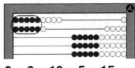

9 + 6   9 + 6 = 10 + 5 = 15

[4 + 1] So, how much is 9 + 6? [15] Tell her: We can call that the Two-Fives Strategy. Repeat for 5 + 8. [13]

Make Ten Strategy. Tell her there is one more strategy, the Make Ten Strategy. Tell the child to enter 9 on the first wire and 4 on the next wire. Say: We want to make a 10, so take 1 bead from the 4 and give it to the 9. See the figures below.

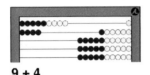 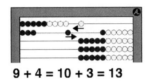

9 + 4   9 + 4 = 10 + 3 = 13

Tell her to add 7 + 8: 2 is taken from 7 to make 10.

Worksheet 1. Give the child the worksheet. Tell her it will be used for the Addition War game. Tell her to look at the left side of the worksheet for the strategy names.

Write: 8 + 3

and ask: In what two rectangles could you write this fact? [Tens and Near Tens and Make Ten]

Write: 7 + 9

and ask: In what two rectangles could you write this fact? [Two Fives and Make Ten]

Repeat for: 6 + 7

and ask: In what two rectangles could you write this fact? [Near Doubles and Two-Fives]

Addition War game. Play the following variation of Addition War game found in *Math Card Games* book, A44. When the players turn over two cards, she writes their fact in all the rectangles that have a strategy for finding that sum. Then the player with the greater sum takes all four cards. When necessary, use the abacus and appropriate strategy to find the sum.

At the end of the game, there are two winners: the player with the most cards (higher stack) and the player with the highest number of facts written on the worksheet.

In conclusion. Ask: What strategies could you use to find 8 + 7? [Two Fives, Near Doubles, and Make Ten] What strategies could you use to find 9 + 7? [Two Fives and Make Ten]

EXPLANATIONS:

Trading is best done using both hands simultaneously. One hand removes the bead(s) from the second wire while the other hand adds the same number of bead(s) to the first wire.

See page iii, numbers 15 and 23 of "Some General Thoughts on Teaching Mathematics," for additional information.

Generally, worksheets are to be done during the lesson.

Play the Addition War game as needed to increase confidence with the addition strategies.

To assist the child, family members need to play games with the child—at least three games a week.

© Activities for Learning, Inc. 2015

Review Lesson 3: Hundreds with Place-Value Cards

OBJECTIVES:
1. To review place value with place-value cards
2. To practice composing numbers to 999

MATERIALS:
1. AL Abacus
2. Place-value cards, 1 to 900
3. Abacus Tiles
4. *Math Card Games* book, N43

ACTIVITIES FOR TEACHING:	EXPLANATIONS:

Warm-up. Ask the child to recite or sing the rhyme "Yellow is the Sun" while raising the appropriate fingers.

Say numbers 6 to 10 and ask the child to show the quantities with her fingers. Do the inverse: Show the child the quantities 6 to 10 with your fingers and ask her to name them.

Tens on the abacus. Give the child the abacus. Tell her to enter 10 on her abacus. Then tell her to enter another 10 on the second wire. Ask: How many beads are entered? [twenty] Say: If you lived in Asia, you would call it 2-ten. So, today we will use these Asian names for the numbers.

Tell her to enter another 2-ten. Ask: How much do you have now? [4-ten] Tell her to enter another 2-ten. Ask: How much do you have now? [6-ten] See the figure on the right. How can you tell it is 6-ten without counting? [Five rows are one color pattern and one is reversed.] Repeat for 8-ten.

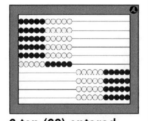
6-ten (60) entered.

Next, enter various tens on the abacus and ask the child to name them. Focus especially on 6-ten to 10-ten.

Place-value cards. Give the child the place-value cards. Write 20 and tell her this is how we record, or write, 2-ten; point to the 2 while saying "two" and to the 0 while saying "ten." See the figure on the right. Tell her to find her 2-ten card.

Ask her to find her 4-ten, 9-ten, and 7-ten cards. Then show her the 3-ten card and tell her to enter it on the abacus. Repeat for 2-ten and 6-ten.

Place-value cards with tens and ones. Tell her: Enter 3-ten and 6 on the abacus. See top figure on the right. Find the place-value cards for 3-ten and 6. Then ask the child to watch while you stack the 6 on top of the 3-ten as shown on the right. Ask her to read it. [3-ten 6] Repeat for 1-ten 2, 6-ten 1 and 4-ten 8.

Yellow is the Sun
Yellow is the sun.
Six is five and one. (5 on left; 1 on right.)
Why is the sky so blue?
Seven is five and two. (5 on left; 2 on right.)
Salty is the sea.
Eight is five and three. (5 on left; 3 on right.)
Hear the thunder roar.
Nine is five and four. (5 on left; 4 on right.)
Ducks will swim and dive.
Ten is five and five. (5 on left; 5 on right.)

If possible, use the name of an Asian country the child is familiar with.

It is more difficult for a child to see the beads changing colors after 5-ten than changing colors after five in a row.

It is important that the child identifies a "ten" by noting that a digit follows it. This allows her to read numbers from left to right, the normal order. Later it will help her see 120 as 12 tens.

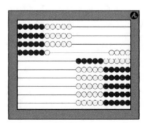
3-ten 6 (36) entered.

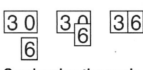
Overlapping the cards to compose 3-ten 6.

ACTIVITIES FOR TEACHING:

Hundreds. Tell the child to enter 10 tens on her abacus. Remind her it has another name, *one hundred*. Ask: How could you show 2 hundred with an abacus? [stack two abacuses] Tell the child we will use two abacus tiles, which are pictures of 100 on the abacus. See the right figure. Ask her to make 7 hundred. [7 abacus tiles]

2 hundred.

Recording hundreds. Write 200 and say: This is how we write 200. Point to the 2 while saying two; point to the first 0 while saying "hun"; and point to the second 0 while saying "dred." See the figure on the right. Tell her this number has 3 digits: 2, 0, and 0.

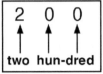

Ask the child to enter 48 on an abacus and set it next to seven abacus tiles. See the figures below. Ask: How many beads are entered? [748] Tell the child to find the place-value cards for the quantity. Demonstrate how to stack the cards. Ask: How many digits are in 748? [3]

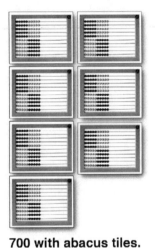

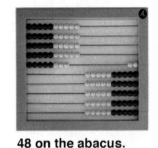
48 on the abacus.

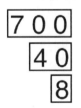
700 with abacus tiles.

Stacking the cards to compose 748.

Can You Find game. Play the Can You Find game in the *Math Card Games* book, N43, using the ones, tens, and hundreds place-value cards. The following numbers includes all the cards.

1. Can you find 400?
2. Can you find 43?
3. Can you find 104?
4. Can you find 57?
5. Can you find 629?
6. Can you find 760?
7. Can you find 215?
8. Can you find 998?
9. Can you find 371?
10. Can you find 502?
11. Can you find 86?
12. Can you find 830?

In conclusion. Ask: How many digits do you need after the 4 to write 400? [2] How many digits do you need after the 4 to write 40? [1] How many digits do you need after the 4 to write 4? [0]

EXPLANATIONS:

The seventh abacus tile can be on either the left or right side.

Following the game, if time permits, tell the child to put her 12 numbers in order from least to greatest.

Remember to play the Addition War game as needed to increase confidence with the addition strategies from Lesson 2.

See page ii, number 11 of "Some General Thoughts on Teaching Mathematics," for additional information.

© Activities for Learning, Inc. 2015

Review Lesson 4: Thousands and Side 2 of the Abacus

OBJECTIVES:
1. To review place value with place-value cards
2. To practice composing numbers to 9999
3. To review side 2 of the abacus

MATERIALS:
1. Place-value cards
2. AL Abacus
3. Abacus Tiles
4. *Math Card Games* book, N43
5. Worksheet 2, Thousands and Side 2 of the Abacus

ACTIVITIES FOR TEACHING:

Warm-up. Ask the child to recite or sing the rhyme "Yellow is the Sun" while raising the appropriate fingers.

Ask: How many digits do you need after the 7 to write 700? [2] How many digits do you need after the 7 to write 70? [1] How many digits do you need after the 7 to write 7? [0]

Ask: How many digits do you need after the 5 to write 500? [2] How many digits do you need after the 5 to write 50? [1] How many digits do you need after the 5 to write 5? [0]

Thousands with the place-value cards. Give the child the place-value cards, abacus, and abacus tiles. Tell the child to show 10 hundreds with the abacus tiles. See the figure on the right. Tell her it has another name, *one thousand*.

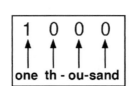

ten hundred

Tell the child to find the 1 thousand place-value card; tell her it has a 1 and three zeros. Write 1000 as shown on the right and say: This is how we read 1 thousand. Point to the 1 while saying "one"; point to the first 0 while saying "th"; point to the second 0 while saying "ou"; and point to the third 0 while saying "sand." Ask: How many digits do you need after 1 to make a thousand? [3]

one th - ou - sand

Ask her to find the 2 thousand card and to point to each digit in turn while saying its name. Repeat for 9 thousand.

Can You Find game. Play the Can You Find game, found in the *Math Card Games* book, N43. Ask the child to use all the place-value cards. As you name a quantity, the child looks for the corresponding cards, stacks them, and sets them aside near the bottom of her workspace.

EXPLANATIONS:

While pronouncing "thousand" with three syllables is phonetically incorrect, it is the best that can be done.

Noting the number of digits following the left-most digit(s) in a number is a more accurate determination of place value than the total number of digits. For example, 2700 can be read correctly as "27 hundred" by observing the two digits following the 27.

ACTIVITIES FOR TEACHING:

The following numbers will include all the cards:

6-ten	5 thousand 8 hundred 4
2 hundred	7 hundred 8-ten 1
6 thousand 3 hundred	3 thousand and 23
9 thousand 3-ten	4 thousand and 7-ten 6
5 hundred and 7	2 thousand 4 hundred 58
7 thousand 5	8 thousand 6 hundred 42
1 hundred 90	1 thousand 9 hundred 19

Tell the child to keep the numbers she has made. She will need them again in a few minutes.

Side 2 of the abacus. Tell the child to turn her abacus to side 2, with 1000, 100, 10, 1 on top. Ask: How many wires do you see under the 1000? [2] How many wires for the hundreds? [2] The tens? [2] The ones? [2]

Say: Find the place-value card that says 60 and place it above your abacus. Demonstrate entering 60 and tell her to enter it on her abacus. See the left figure below. Tell her to keep the beads on the tens wires as even as possible.

Stress that on this side of the abacus we do not enter actual tens, but only the number of tens. This is also true with the hundreds and thousands. Repeat for 200 and 7005.

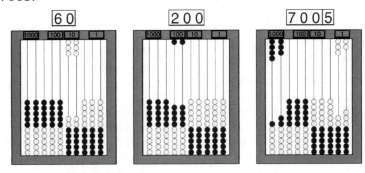

Continue with the remaining numbers made with the place-value cards during the Can You Find game.

Worksheet 2. Ask the child to do the worksheet. The answers are as follows.

4000	50	800
9010	79	7080
7347	3256	6730

In conclusion. Ask: On side 1 of the abacus, how many beads do you enter to make 20? [20] On side 2 of the abacus, how many beads do you enter to make 20? [2] On side 1 of the abacus, how many beads do you enter to make 50? [50] On side 2 of the abacus, how many beads do you enter to make 50? [5]

EXPLANATIONS:

It is acceptable to say "one hundred *and* one."

6300 5804   507 2458
 781 8642 4076   200
7005 1919 9030   60
       190 3023

Quantities are entered from left to right for several reasons. We read from left to right, do mental arithmetic from left to right, and enter quantities on a calculator from left to right. It also is the way we say numbers (except the teens).

See page ii, number 1, and page iii, number 24 of "Some General Thoughts on Teaching Mathematics," for additional information.

Review Lesson 5: Trading on Side 2 of the Abacus

OBJECTIVES:
1. To review trading on side 2 of the abacus

MATERIALS:
1. Place-value cards
2. AL Abacus
3. *Math Card Games* book, A7.1

ACTIVITIES FOR TEACHING:

Warm-up. Ask: How many digits do you need after the 3 to write 300? [2] How many digits do you need after the 3 to write 30? [1] How many digits do you need after the 3 to write 3? [0]

Ask: On side 1 of the abacus, how many beads do you enter to make 30? [30] On side 2 of the abacus, how many beads do you enter to make 30? [3]

Ask: On side 1 of the abacus, how many beads do you enter to make 100? [100] On side 2 of the abacus, how many beads do you enter to make 100? [1]

Trading ones on the abacus. Give the child the place-value cards and abacus. Tell her to find the place-value cards for 8 and 6 and set them aside. Tell her to enter 8 on side 2 of the abacus and then to add 6. See the left figure below. Ask: What is the sum? [14] Say: We have a problem: we cannot have more than 10 ones. We need to trade 10 ones for 1 ten.

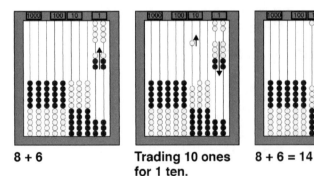

8 + 6   Trading 10 ones   8 + 6 = 14
              for 1 ten.

Demonstrate trading as shown in the second figure above, using the left hand for the ten and the right hand for the ones. The final sum is shown in the third figure. Tell her to do the trading on her abacus.

Trading tens on the abacus. Tell the child to find 80 and 60 from her place-value cards. Tell her to add them as shown in the left figure on the next page. Ask: How many tens do you have? [14 tens] What do you need to do?

EXPLANATIONS:

It is important to keep the two wires as even as possible to make trading easier. See the figures below, both showing 12 ones entered. The right figure clearly identifies the sum is over 10, therefore needs trading.

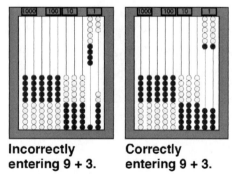

Incorrectly entering 9 + 3.   **Correctly entering 9 + 3.**

Remember, trading is best done using both hands simultaneously.

ACTIVITIES FOR TEACHING:

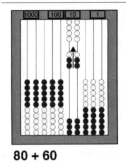 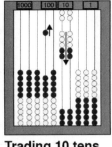 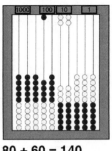

80 + 60   Trading 10 tens for 1 hundred.   80 + 60 = 140

EXPLANATIONS:

[Trade 10 tens for 1 hundred.] Tell her to do the trading. Then ask: Now what is the sum? [140]

Trading hundreds on the abacus. Tell the child to find the place-value cards for 800 and 600. Tell her to add them on her abacus. Ask the child to explain how to do it. [8 hundred and 6 hundred is 14 hundred, then trade 10 hundreds for 1 thousand. Sum is 1 thousand 4 hundred.]

Bead Trading game. Play this variation of the Bead Trading game found in *Math Card Games*, A7.1. Tell her she will need the place-value cards that are less than 4000 to play the game. She is to add the value of all the remaining place-value cards on her abacus.

To play, she picks up any one of the remaining place-value cards and enter that quantity on the abacus, trading if necessary. Next she picks up another card and adds it to the amount on the abacus. Continue until all the place-value cards have been added. The final sum will be 10,995.

In conclusion. Ask: How much is 30 + 70? [100] Eighty plus what equals 100? [20] Forty plus what equals 100? [60] How much is 500 + 500? [1000] How much is 300 + 700? [1000] Eight hundred plus what equals 1000? [200]

See page iii, number 25 of "Some General Thoughts on Teaching Mathematics," for additional information.

12

REVIEW LESSON 6: MENTAL ADDING

OBJECTIVES:
1. To practice mental addition
2. To learn to play the Corners™ game

MATERIALS:
1. AL Abacus, if needed
2. Dry erase board, optional
3. Math journal, found in the back of the child's worksheets
4. *Math Card Games* book, A9

ACTIVITIES FOR TEACHING:	EXPLANATIONS:
Warm-up. Ask: On side 1 of the abacus, how many beads do you enter to make 70? [70] On side 2 of the abacus, how many beads do you enter to make 70? [7]	
Ask: What is 4 + 1? [5] What is 40 + 10? [50] What is 8 + 1? [9] What is 80 + 10? [90] What is 6 + 1? [7] What is 60 + 10? [70] What is 9 + 1? [10] What is 90 + 10? [100]	
Mentally adding 5, 10, and 15. Tell the child that today she will be playing the game Corners™. First she needs to practice mental adding. Ask the following:	
What is 60 + 10? [70]	If the child is struggling with mental addition, use side 2 of the abacus.
What is 75 + 10? [85]	
What is 105 + 10? [115]	
What is 60 + 15? [75] Tell her a good way to add 15 is to first add the 10 and then the 5, 60 + 10 = 70 + 5 = 75.	
What is 85 + 15? [100]	
What is 135 + 15? [150]	
Add It Up game. Give the child the dry erase board or math journal. Play the following Add It Up game: Call out one of the three numbers, 5, 10, or 15, which the child writes down at the top of a column on her dry erase board or in her math journal. Call out another one of the three numbers. The child mentally adds the new number to the number written down and writes only the sum below the first number. Continue until 15 sums are written.	
The figure at the right shows the results when the following numbers are called in succession: 10, 5, 10, 5, 15, 10, 15, and 10.	This type of scoring will be needed for the upcoming Corners™ game.

<table>
<tr><td>10</td></tr>
<tr><td>15</td></tr>
<tr><td>25</td></tr>
<tr><td>30</td></tr>
<tr><td>45</td></tr>
<tr><td>55</td></tr>
<tr><td>70</td></tr>
<tr><td>80</td></tr>
</table>

Scoring mentally.

RightStart™ Mathematics Level D Second Edition

© Activities for Learning, Inc. 2015

ACTIVITIES FOR TEACHING:

Corners™ game. Play the Corners™ game found in *Math Card Games* book, A9.

Tell the child to write her scores in her math journal. She is two write down only the result of the latest addition with no intermediate step.

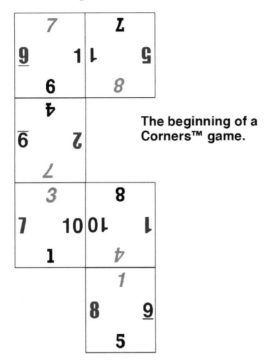

The beginning of a Corners™ game.

Follow-up activity 1. At the end of the game, ask the child to write her scores. Then have her read it so that she can practice reading larger numbers.

In conclusion. Ask: In the Corners™ game, what three numbers can you join with 9? [1, 6, and 9] How many points would a 1 give you? [10] How many points would a 6 give you? [15] How many points would a 9 give you? [0]

EXPLANATIONS:

Instructions for the Corners™ game can also be found on the DVD inside the back cover of the *Math Card Games* book or at RightStartMath.com.

Note that the numbers touching must either be the same or have a sum of 5, 10, 15, or 20. However, only the sums that are a multiple of 5 are added to the score. In other words, matching numbers, such as 3 + 3, that are not a multiple of 5 are valid plays, but result in no points.

Other Corners™ games will be played throughout the year.

© Activities for Learning, Inc. 2015

Review Lesson 7: Subtraction Strategies

OBJECTIVES:
1. To review part-whole circles
2. To review subtraction strategies
3. To practice the strategies

MATERIALS:
1. AL Abacus
2. *Math Card Games* book, S24

ACTIVITIES FOR TEACHING:	EXPLANATIONS:

Warm-up. Ask: On side 1 of the abacus, how many beads do you enter to make 80? [80] On side 2 of the abacus, how many beads do you enter to make 80? [8]

Ask: What is 9 + 6? [15] What is 8 + 7? [15] What do you need with 6 to make 10? [4] With 6 to make 15? [9] What do you need with 8 to make 10? [2] With 8 to make 15? [7] What do you need with 7 to make 10? [3] With 7 to make 15? [8]

Part-whole circles. Draw a part-whole circle, shown below on the left. Write "whole" in the large circle and "part" in the smaller circles.

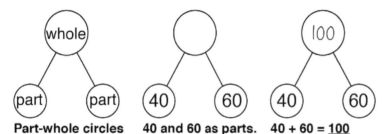

Part-whole circles   **40 and 60 as parts.**   **40 + 60 = 100**

See page ii, numbers 7 and 8 of "Some General Thoughts on Teaching Mathematics," for additional information.

Write 40 and 60 in the smaller circles as shown in the second figure above. Ask: If 40 and 60 are parts, what is the whole? [100] Write 100 in the large circle. See the right figure above.

Going Up Strategy. Write 14 in the whole-circle and 9 in a part-circle as shown below on the left. Ask: How

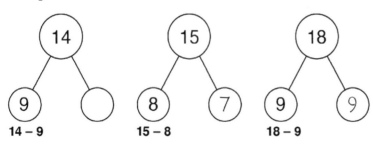

14 − 9   15 − 8   18 − 9

can you find the other part? [subtract] Can you think of a strategy to find the answer if you didn't know it? Ask: What do you need to get up to 10? [1] Then how many

It is best to avoid the term "take away" when referring to subtraction. It is not listed in the dictionary. The term emphasizes the going back aspect of subtraction, ignoring other meanings such as going up and differences, making it difficult for the child to develop a deeper understanding of subtraction.

ACTIVITIES FOR TEACHING:

EXPLANATIONS:

more to 14? [4] How much is needed to go from 9 to 14? [5] Tell her: This is the Going Up Strategy. Repeat for 14 – 8, [6] and 18 – 9. [9]

Subtracting Part from Ten Strategy. Give the child the abacus and write:

$$15 - 7$$

Tell the child: Enter 15 on your abacus. Ask: How could you subtract 7? [Subtract 5 from second wire and 2 from first wire.] See the figures below. Say: So to subtract the 7,

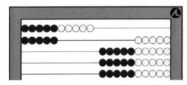 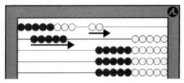

Subtracting 15 – 7 by taking 5 from 5 and 2 from 10.

you subtract 5 from the 5 and 2 from the 10, giving 8. We can call this Subtracting Part from Ten Strategy. Repeat for 13 – 4, [9] and 16 – 9. [7]

Subtracting All from Ten Strategy. Say: There is another strategy for subtracting 15 – 7. Tell her to enter 15 on the abacus. Next tell her to subtract the whole 7 from the 10, as shown in the right figure below.

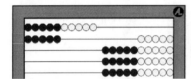 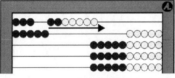

15 – 7 by subtracting 7 from the 10 and adding 5 + 3 = 8.

Ask: What is left? [3 plus 5, 8] Tell her: We can call this the Subtracting All from Ten Strategy. Repeat for 11 – 4, [7] and 13 – 5. [8]

Subtraction Bingo game. Play the Subtraction Bingo game, found in the *Math Card Games* book, S24. Tell her to use her abacus.

In conclusion. Say: Explain several ways to subtract 14 – 8. [Going Up: 2 to get to 10; 2 + 4 = 6. Taking Part from Ten: 4 from 4 and 4 from 10 gives 6. Taking All from Ten: 8 from 10 is 2; 2 + 4 = 6.]

© Activities for Learning, Inc. 2015

Review Lesson 8: Subtracting on Side 2 of the Abacus

OBJECTIVES:
1. To learn (or review) subtraction from left to right on side 2 of the AL Abacus

MATERIALS:
1. AL Abacus
2. Worksheet 3, Subtracting on Side 2 of the Abacus

ACTIVITIES FOR TEACHING:	EXPLANATIONS:

Warm-up. Ask: On side 1 of the abacus, how many beads do you enter to make 60? [60] On side 2 of the abacus, how many beads do you enter to make 60? [6]

Ask: On side 2 of the abacus, how many beads do you enter to make 4? [4] How many beads do you enter to make 40? [4] How many beads do you enter to make 400? [4] How many beads do you enter to make 4000? [4]

Subtracting on side 2. Give the child the abacus. Say: Today you will be subtracting large numbers on side 2 of your abacus. Write the following subtraction in the vertical format:

$$\begin{array}{r} 6829 \\ -\ 2637 \end{array}$$

Tell the child to enter the larger number, 6829, on her abacus. See the left figure below. Say: First subtract the thousands. See the second figure below.

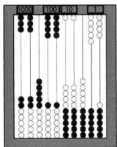 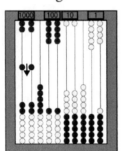 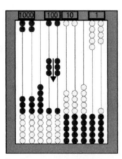

6829 entered.   **Subtracting 2000.**   **Subtracting 600.**

Ask: What do we subtract next? [6 hundred] See the right figure above.

Ask: What do you subtract next? [3 tens] Do you have enough tens to do the subtraction? [no] How can you get more tens? [Trade 1 hundred for 10 tens.] Tell her to do the trade. See the left figure on the next page. Ask: How many tens do you have now? [12] See the second figure on the next page. Tell her to subtract 30. See the right two figures on the next page.

Tell her to finish the subtraction of the ones and read the difference. [4192]

There are at least eight different ways to subtract multi-digit numbers. Even though a person has learned one method, it is good to explore other methods to enhance understanding.

See page iii, number 13 of "Some General Thoughts on Teaching Mathematics," for additional information.

The subtraction shown here proceeds from left to right like division. It was taught in RightStart Mathematics Second Grade.

If the child has an accurate and efficient method of subtraction, do not insist that the child change to a new method.

ACTIVITIES FOR TEACHING:	EXPLANATIONS:

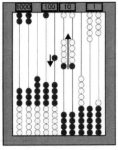 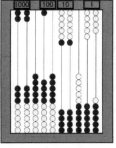 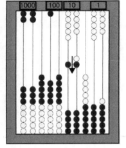 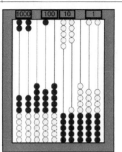

Trading 1 hundred for 10 tens.   After the trade.   Subtracting 30.   Difference 4192.

Second example. Write:

$$\begin{array}{r} 7094 \\ -\ 3528 \\ \hline [3566] \end{array}$$

Tell her to do the subtraction problem on her abacus. The steps are shown in the figures below.

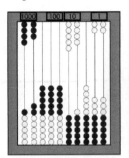 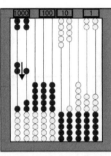 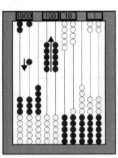 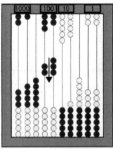

7094 entered.   Subtracting 3000.   Trading 1 thousand for 10 hundreds.   Subtracting 500.

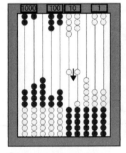 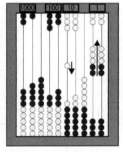 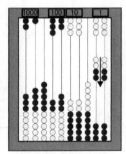 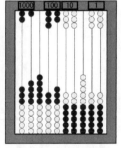

Subtracting 20.   Trading 1 ten for 10 ones.   Subtracting 8.   Difference 3566.

Worksheet 3. Tell the child to do the first six subtraction problems, up to the first dotted line. The problems and solutions are:

$$\begin{array}{r} 8445 \\ -\ 5372 \\ \hline 3073 \end{array} \quad \begin{array}{r} 3189 \\ -\ 1734 \\ \hline 1455 \end{array} \quad \begin{array}{r} 7240 \\ -\ 5808 \\ \hline 1432 \end{array}$$

$$\begin{array}{r} 2159 \\ -\ 451 \\ \hline 1708 \end{array} \quad \begin{array}{r} 2573 \\ -\ 1094 \\ \hline 1479 \end{array} \quad \begin{array}{r} 9162 \\ -\ 4585 \\ \hline 4577 \end{array}$$

In conclusion. Ask: How do know when you need to trade? [when the number being subtracted is less than the top number]

Grid lines are provided to help the child align the numbers.

The rest of this worksheet will be completed in future lessons.

Continue playing games on a regular basis. If there is additional time following this lesson or more practice is needed, play the Subtraction Bingo game, found in *Math Card Games* book, S24.

© Activities for Learning, Inc. 2015

Review Lesson 9: Traditional Subtracting on the Abacus

OBJECTIVES:
1. To learn (or review) subtraction from left to right on side 2 of the AL Abacus

MATERIALS:
1. AL Abacus
2. Worksheet 3, Subtracting on Side 2 of the Abacus

ACTIVITIES FOR TEACHING:	**EXPLANATIONS:**

Warm-up. Ask: On side 2 of the abacus, how many beads do you enter to make 6? [6] How many beads do you enter to make 60? [6] How many beads do you enter to make 600? [6] How many beads do you enter to make 6000? [6]

Give the child the abacus and Worksheet 3. Tell her to do problems 7 to 9 on the worksheet, using her abacus.

```
  3079     8625     9062
 -1836    -6632    -5146
  1243     1993     3916
```

Subtracting on side 2. Say: Today you will be subtracting large numbers, but starting at the right. Write the following subtraction in the vertical format:

```
  9062
 -5146
```

Tell the child to enter the larger number, 9062, on her abacus. See the left figure below.

Here subtraction proceeds from right to left, as in the traditional method used in the U.S. and Canada.

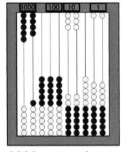 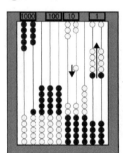 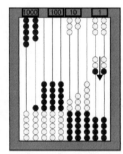

9062 entered.   **Trading 1 ten for 10 ones.**   **Subtracting 6.**

Say: First subtract the ones. Ask: Do you have enough ones to do the subtraction? [no] How can you get more ones? [Trade 1 ten for 10 ones.] Tell her to do the trade and subtraction. See the second and third figures above.

Tell her to finish the subtraction. See the figures on the next page. Tell her to read the difference. [3916] Tell her to compare her answer to Problem 9 on her worksheet. [same]

Subtracting on side 2 of the abacus makes it virtually impossible to subtract 2 from 6 as some children want to do in the following example:

```
  62
 -46
```

ACTIVITIES FOR TEACHING:

EXPLANATIONS:

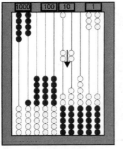
Subtracting 40.

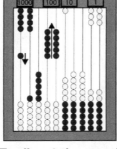
Trading 1 thousand for 10 hundreds.

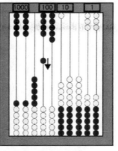
Subtracting 100.

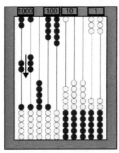
Subtracting 5000.

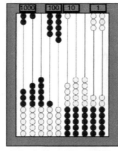
Difference 3916.

Double trade. Write:

$$\begin{array}{r} 400 \\ -222 \\ \hline [178] \end{array}$$

Tell her to enter 400 on her abacus. Ask: How can you get the ones you need to subtract? [trade twice] The trading steps are shown in the figures below.

See page ii, number 12 of "Some General Thoughts on Teaching Mathematics," for additional information.

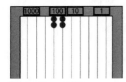
Entering 400.

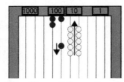
Trading 1 hundred for 10 tens.

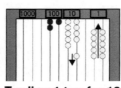
Trading 1 ten for 10 ones.

Worksheet 3. Tell the child to do the last nine subtraction problems. The problems and solutions are given below.

$$\begin{array}{r} 9468 \\ -8273 \\ \hline \mathbf{1195} \end{array} \quad \begin{array}{r} 4883 \\ -1709 \\ \hline \mathbf{3174} \end{array} \quad \begin{array}{r} 2728 \\ -1859 \\ \hline \mathbf{869} \end{array}$$

$$\begin{array}{r} 6283 \\ -2657 \\ \hline \mathbf{3626} \end{array} \quad \begin{array}{r} 7570 \\ -4094 \\ \hline \mathbf{3476} \end{array} \quad \begin{array}{r} 7608 \\ -4059 \\ \hline \mathbf{3549} \end{array}$$

$$\begin{array}{r} 8945 \\ -1388 \\ \hline \mathbf{7557} \end{array} \quad \begin{array}{r} 8600 \\ -3893 \\ \hline \mathbf{4707} \end{array} \quad \begin{array}{r} 2068 \\ -1493 \\ \hline \mathbf{575} \end{array}$$

In conclusion. Ask: How much is 100 – 37? [63]

Continue playing games on a regular basis. If there is additional time following this lesson or more practice is needed, play the On the Number Ten game, found in *Math Card Games* book, S25.

© Activities for Learning, Inc. 2015

Review Lesson 10: Arrays

OBJECTIVES:
1. To build and name arrays
2. To find the values of arrays
3. To review that a square is a special rectangle

MATERIALS:
1. Tiles, about 20
2. *Math Card Games* book, P3
3. AL Abacus
4. Math Journal

ACTIVITIES FOR TEACHING:

EXPLANATIONS:

Warm-up. Ask: On side 1 of the abacus, how many beads do you enter to make 20? [20] On side 2 of the abacus, how many beads do you enter to make 20? [2] How many beads do you enter to make 200? [2] How many beads do you enter to make 2000? [2]

Ask: How much is 100 – 49? [51] How much 100 – 51? [49] How much is 50 – 39? [11] How much is 50 – 38? [12] How much is 80 – 15? [65] How much is 75 – 15? [60]

Building a 4 by 3 array. Give the child about 20 tiles. Tell her to build a row with four tiles. Ask her to build two more rows with four tiles directly below the first row. See the figure below. Say: This is an *array*, which is an arrangement of rows and columns.

4 by 3 array.

Ask: What shape is the outline of your array? [rectangle] How many rows in the array? [3] How many columns in the array? [4] How many tiles are in this array? [12] Say: The name for this array is 4 *by* 3 and is written like this:

4 by 3

Building more arrays. Tell the child to build a 3 by 4 array. See the figure below. Ask: What shape is the outline of your array? [rectangle] How many rows in the array? [4] How many columns in the array? [3] How many tiles in your array? [12] Why do you think it has the same number of tiles as the 4 by 3 array? [It is the same array turned.]

3 by 4 array.

ACTIVITIES FOR TEACHING:	EXPLANATIONS:

Tell her to make a 4 by 4 array. See the figure below. Ask: What shape is the outline of your array? [square, rectangle] Discuss that a square is a rectangle – a special rectangle.

A rectangle has four sides and right angles.

4 by 4 array.

Tell her to turn her 4 by 4 array into a 5 by 3 array. See the figure below. Ask: What shape is the outline of your array? [rectangle] Why is it not a square? [Not all four sides are congruent.] Ask: How many rows in the array? [3] How many columns in the array? [5] How many tiles in your array? [15] How did you find the number of tiles?

Congruent is defined as fitting exactly on top.

This last question is open ended and is intended to encourage multiple solutions and problem solving.

5 by 3 array.

Sum Rummy game. Show the child how to play the Sum Rummy game, found in the *Math Card Games* book, P3. Provide an abacus for the child to use. Let her figure out how to find her scores, the sum of all her cards. Tell her to write her work in her math journal.

In conclusion. Ask: What is an array? [things arranged in rows and columns] Ask her to find arrays in the room. [possibly book shelves, tiles on floor or ceiling]

Ask: How many objects are in a 2 by 2 array? [4] Does a 2 by 2 array made with tiles have the shape of a rectangle or square? [both] How many objects in a 10 by 4 array? [40] How many objects in a 4 by 10 array? [40]

The mathematics in this game is the child determining her scores, that is, the value of all her cards at the end of the game. Let her decide how to do this for her first game; be sure the abacus is available.

The child will play this game again in the next lesson.

See page ii, number 9 of "Some General Thoughts on Teaching Mathematics," for additional information.

© Activities for Learning, Inc. 2015

Review Lesson 11: Multiplication in Arrays

OBJECTIVES:
1. To build arrays on the AL Abacus
2. To understand multiplication as arrays
3. To review (or learn) the symbol for multiplication, ×
4. To learn different ways to find the value of an array

MATERIALS:
1. Tiles, about 25
2. AL Abacus
3. Math journal
4. *Math Card Games* book, P3

ACTIVITIES FOR TEACHING:	EXPLANATIONS:

Warm-up. Ask: How many objects are in a 3 by 2 array? [6] Does a 3 by 2 array made with tiles have the shape of a rectangle or square? [rectangle] How many objects are in a 3 by 3 array? [9] Does a 3 by 3 array made with tiles have the shape of a rectangle or square? [both] How many objects in a 10 by 5 array? [50] How many objects in a 5 by 10 array? [50]

Arrays on the abacus. Give the child the tiles, abacus, and the math journal. Ask the child to build a 6 by 3 array with her tiles, using two colors to group by fives, as shown below on the left. Tell her to make the same array on her abacus as shown below on the right.

6 by 3 array.

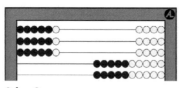
6 by 3 array.

Ask: How many tiles are in your array? [18] How many beads are in your array? [18] Ask the child to write the array name and the addition equation in her math journal.

$$6 \text{ by } 3$$
$$6 + 6 + 6 = 18$$

The multiplication symbol. Say: As you may know, there is a simpler way to write the amount of the array by using a math symbol for the word *by*. Write:

$$6 \times 3 = 18$$

Say: We can read it as 6 *multiplied by* 3 equals 18. Some people say it is 6 taken 3 times. Some other people say 6 times 3. It is still the 6 by 3 array.

Sometimes 6 × 3 is thought of as "6 groups of 3." However, consistency with the other arithmetic operations requires a second look. When adding 6 + 3, we start with 6 and transform it by adding 3. When subtracting 6 – 3, we start with 6 and transform it by removing 3. When dividing 6 ÷ 3, we start with 6 and transform it by dividing it into 3 groups or into groups of 3s. Likewise, 6 × 3 means we start with 6 and transform it by duplicating it 3 times.

In the array (an arrangement of quantities in rows and columns) model, 6 × 3, 6 represents the horizontal quantity and 3 the vertical quantity. This is also consistent with the coordinate system; in (6, 3), the first number, 6, indicates the horizontal number and 3, the vertical number.

ACTIVITIES FOR TEACHING:	EXPLANATIONS:

Explain that the multiplication sign is made like the diagonals in a square, as shown below.

Note that the multiplication sign, ×, is not an "x," which is an unknown or a variable in algebra. A good model for writing the multiplication sign is the diagonals in a square as discussed in the lesson.

Finding 9 × 4. Tell the child to enter the 9 by 4 array on the abacus. See below.

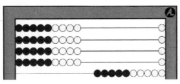

9 multiplied by 4.

Ask her to think of as many ways as possible to find the amount. [36] Some possibilities include:

1. The dark-colored beads are 2 tens, or 20, and the light-colored beads are 8 + 8 = 16; 20 + 16 is 36.
2. The first two rows are 18; 18 + 18 is 36.
3. Four 10s is 40; 40 − 4 is 36.
4. Take and Give, shown below, ends up with 36.

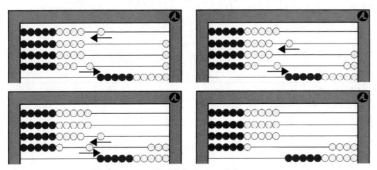

Using Take and Give to find 9 × 4 = 36.

In Take and Give, beads from one row are "moved" to another row. Simultaneously, one hand "takes" while the other hand "gives." Several beads may be traded during a Take and Give operation.

Sum Rummy game. Play the Sum Rummy game, found in the *Math Card Games* book, P3. Suggest she uses multiplication equations to record her scores. Tell her to write her work in her math journal. One way is shown at the right.

$6 \times 4 = 24$
$1 \times 6 = 6$
$5 \times 3 = 15$
$4 \times 5 = \underline{20}$
65

See page ii, number 10 of "Some General Thoughts on Teaching Mathematics," for additional information.

In conclusion. Ask: If you are playing Sum Rummy and you have ten cards that have a five, what is the multiplication equation? [five multiplied by ten is 50] What is the multiplication equation for four cards with threes? [three multiplied by four is 12] What is the multiplication equation for seven cards with twos? [two multiplied by seven is 14]

© Activities for Learning, Inc. 2015

LESSON 12: CHINESE CHECKERBOARD PROBLEM

OBJECTIVES:
1. To practice counting by various numbers
2. To count objects in several ways

MATERIALS:
1. AL Abacus
2. **A Chinese checkers game board, if available**
3. Worksheet 4, Chinese Checkerboard Problem

ACTIVITIES FOR TEACHING:

Warm-up. Ask: If you are playing Sum Rummy and you have five cards that have a five, what is the multiplication equation? [five multiplied by five is 25] What is the multiplication equation for three cards with fours? [three multiplied by four is 12] What is the multiplication equation for eight cards with twos? [eight multiplied by two is 16]

Counting by twos on the abacus. Give the child the abacus. Tell the child to count aloud by twos on her abacus. See the figure at the right. Continue to 100. Ask: Which of the numbers that you said were even numbers? [all of them] Which were odd numbers? [none] Say: When

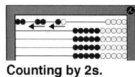
Counting by 2s.

you count by twos starting at zero, you are naming some multiples of two. Ask: What are the first three multiples of two? [2, 4, 6]

Counting by tens on the abacus. Tell her to clear her abacus and count aloud by tens. See the left figure below. Ask: How many multiples of ten are there up to 100? [ten] Is ten also a multiple of two? [yes]

Counting by fives on the abacus. Tell her to count by fives to 100. See the right figure below. Ask: Are the multiples of five even or odd numbers? [both] When might you need to count by fives? [telling time and counting nickels]

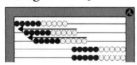
Counting by tens.

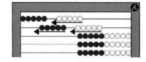
Counting by fives.

Counting by fours on the abacus. Tell the child to count by fours on her abacus. Adding the second four, 8, is shown in the left figure on the next page. The third four, 12, requires adding two beads on two wires. See the right figure on the next page. Continue to 100.

EXPLANATIONS:

When introducing new topics, avoid asking the child to guess the answer. Children with poor memories tend to remember the first response, even when it is wrong.

See page ii, numbers 1 and 2 of "Some General Thoughts on Teaching Mathematics," for additional information.

ACTIVITIES FOR TEACHING:

Counting by fours.

Ask: Are the multiples of four even or odd numbers? [even numbers] Is 20 a multiple of four? [yes] Is 10 a multiple of four? [no] Are all the multiples of four also multiples of two? [yes]

Worksheet 4. Give the child the worksheet. Show the child a Chinese checkerboard, if available. Tell her to read the instructions:

Find how many dots there are on a Chinese checkerboard. Do not count by ones. Circle your groups. Explain your work.

Ask: What do the instructions ask you to do? [Find the number of dots.] Is there only one way to do it? [no, many ways] Two possible solutions are shown below.

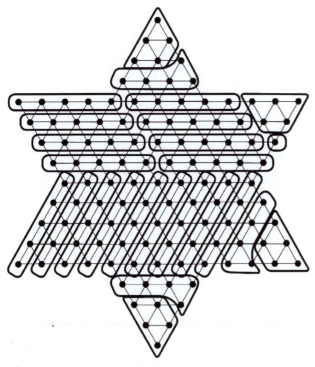

Counting by 5s gives 121.

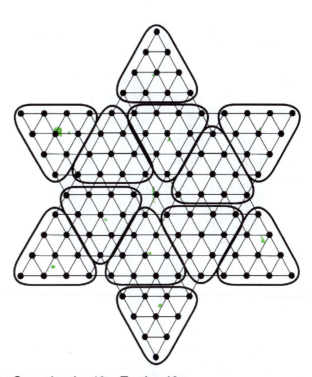

Counting by 10s: Twelve 10s plus 1 in the middle gives 121.

In conclusion. Ask: When counting to 100, do you say more numbers when you count by twos or count by fives? [twos] Do you say more numbers when you count by fours or count by threes? [threes] Do you say fewer numbers when you count by twelves or count by sixes? [twelves]

EXPLANATIONS:

Generally, worksheets are to be done during the lesson.

Chinese Checkers is a game in which the players move 10 marbles from one point of the star to the opposite star with moves and jumps. A player can jump over their own or other players' marbles, but all the marbles stay on the board.

Continue playing games on a regular basis. If there is additional time following this lesson or more practice is needed, play the Go to the Dump game, found in *Math Card Games* book, A3.

© Activities for Learning, Inc. 2015

Lesson 13: Multiplying by Two

OBJECTIVES:
1. To learn the term *times*
2. To practice doubling on the abacus
3. To practice writing multiplication equations

MATERIALS:
1. AL Abacus
2. Worksheet 5, Multiplying by Two
3. Math journal
4. *Math Card Games* book, A9

ACTIVITIES FOR TEACHING:

EXPLANATIONS:

Warm-up. Give the child the abacus and worksheet. Tell her the warm-up today will be on her worksheet. Have her read the instructions, then count by 2 to 20 using her abacus and write the numbers on the spaces provided. Do the same with 4 to 40. Solutions are shown below.

 2 4 6 8 10 12 14 16 18 20
 4 8 12 16 20 24 28 32 36 40

Multiplying by two. Give the child the math journal. Tell the child to enter two eights on her abacus. See the figure at the right. Tell her to write the addition and multiplication equations:

$8 + 8 = 16$
$8 \times 2 = 16$

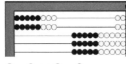

$8 + 8$ or 8×2

Ask the following:
 What is 5 multiplied by 2? [10]
 What is 9 multiplied by 2? [18]
 What is 10 multiplied by 2? [20]
 What is 6 multiplied by 2? [12]

Tell her the word *times* means multiplied by. Continue by asking:
 What is 9 times 2? [18]
 What is 7 times 2? [14]
 What is 30 times 2? [60]
 What is 12 times 2? [24]

Worksheet 5. Say: Enter 2 on side 2 of your abacus. Double that number and write the equation:

$2 \times 2 = 4$

See the left figure on the next page.

Tell her to double the 4 on her abacus and write that equation: $4 \times 2 = 8$

See the second figure on the next page.

RightStart™ Mathematics Level D Second Edition © Activities for Learning, Inc. 2015

ACTIVITIES FOR TEACHING:

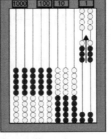

Doubling 2.   Doubling 4.   Doubling 8.

Tell her to double the 8 and write the equation:

$$8 \times 2 = 16$$

See the right figure above. Tell her to continue for 13 doublings. The solutions are shown below.

2 × 2 = 4
4 × 2 = **8**
8 × 2 = **16**
16 × 2 = **32**
32 × 2 = **64**
64 × 2 = **128**
128 × 2 = **256**
256 × 2 = **512**
512 × 2 = **1024**
1024 × 2 = **2048**
2048 × 2 = **4096**
4096 × 2 = **8192**
8192 × 2 = **16,384**

Corners™ with Double Score game. Play the Corners™ with Double Score game, a variation of the Corners™ game found in the *Math Card Games* book, A9. In this variation, whenever a player joins a 2 with another 2, their current total score is doubled. (Usually, playing a 2 to a 2 results in no points.) Tell her to circle her score when the doubling occurs. See the sample scoring on the right where the 30 is circled and doubled.

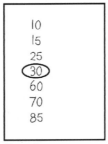

Scoring.

In conclusion. Ask: What is 80 multiplied by 2? [160] What is 900 doubled? [18 hundred or 1 thousand 8 hundred] What is 7 times 2? [14]

EXPLANATIONS:

Some children may recognize these numbers as special to electronic devices. (They are the powers of 2.)

You might want to tell the child the following norm for including a comma in a number: If a number is more than 9 thousand, we put a comma where the word thousand is spoken. (In some countries a period or a space is used in lieu of a comma.)

To assist the child at home, family members need to play games with the child—at least three games a week.

© Activities for Learning, Inc. 2015

LESSON 14: MORE MULTIPLYING BY TWO

OBJECTIVES:

1. To solve problems involving multiplying by 2

MATERIALS:

1. AL Abacus
2. Worksheet 6, More Multiplying by Two
3. *Math Card Games* book, A9

ACTIVITIES FOR TEACHING:

Warm-up. Give the child the abacus and worksheet. Have her read the instructions, then count by 5 to 50 using her abacus and write the numbers on the spaces provided. Do the same with 10 to 100. Solutions are shown below.

| 5 | 10 | **15** | **20** | **25** | **30** | **35** | **40** | **45** | **50** |

| 10 | **20** | **30** | **40** | **50** | **60** | **70** | **80** | **90** | **100** |

Tell the child to look at her completed work and ask: What is 5×2? [10] What is 10×2? [20] What is 15×2? [30] What is 30×2? [60] What is 45×2? [90] What pattern do you see? [the second row is double the first row]

Worksheet 6. These problems are to be solved during the lesson.

Problem 1. Say: The first problem on the worksheet is about a brother and sister. You may change the characters' names to that of your family or friend, if you want.

The problem is:

Nathan is twice as old as his sister, who is 4 years old. How old is Nathan? [8 years old]

How old will they be in one year? [Nathan, 9; sister, 5]

Will Nathan still be twice as old as his sister? [no]

After the child has solved the problem individually, tell her to read the problem to be sure she has answered all the questions. Ask: Do your answers make sense? Ask her if there is another way to find the answers. The equations are:

Nathan's age: $4 \times 2 = 8$
Nathan's age 1 year later: $8 + 1 = 9$
Sister's age 1 year later: $4 + 1 = 5$
No, 9 is not twice 5

Problem 2. Say: Drawing a figure often helps to solve the problem. In Problem 2, the figure is drawn for you, but you need to write the measurements on it.

EXPLANATIONS:

See page ii, numbers 10 and 14 of "Some General Thoughts on Teaching Mathematics," for additional information.

At this level, children are beginning to "read to learn."

Encourage the child to write short phrases explaining what the equation shows.

RightStart™ Mathematics Level D Second Edition

© Activities for Learning, Inc. 2015

ACTIVITIES FOR TEACHING:

Tell her to read and solve the second problem:

The width of a rectangular garden is 14 ft.
The length of the garden is double the width.
What is the perimeter of the garden? [84 ft]
(Perimeter is distance around a figure.)

After the child has solved the problem, tell her to read the problem again to be sure she answered the question. Ask: Does your answer make sense?

Discuss the solution. The equations are:

  Garden length: 14 × 2 = 28
  Perimeter: 14 + 28 + 14 + 28 = 84 ft

or

  Perimeter: 14 + 28 = 42 and 42 × 2 = 84 ft

Problem 3. Ask the child to read the third problem:

A school has 206 boys. It has two more girls than boys. How many children does the school have altogether? [414]

After the child has solved the problem, tell her to read the problem again to be sure she answered the question. Ask: Does your answer make sense?

Discuss the solution. A possible equation is:

  Number children: 206 + 206 + 2 = 206 × 2 + 2 = 414

Corners™ with Double Score game. Play the same game as the previous lesson: Corners™ with Double Score game, a variation of the Corners™ game found in the *Math Card Games* book, A9. In this variation, whenever a player joins a 2 with another 2, their current total score is doubled. (Usually, playing a 2 and 2 results in no points.) Tell her to circle her score when the doubling occurs. See the figure on the right where the 45 is circled and doubled.

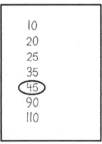
Scoring.

In conclusion. Ask: What is 8 times 2? [16] What is 60 doubled? [1 hundred twenty] What is another way of saying 90 + 90? [90 × 2] How much is it? [180]

EXPLANATIONS:

If there are two children, it is best if the child using the simplest method to solve the problem share their solution first. Then a child using more sophisticated methods can share their solution.

The unfortunate children who have been taught to look for "key" words might add 206 and 2 because the word "altogether" means add. Rather than being distracted by searching for certain words, good problem solvers work at understanding the situation.

For children needing extra help, the following may work:

Ask: How can you find the number of children? [Add the number of boys and girls.] Do you know the number of boys? [206] Do you know the number of girls? [206 + 2]

© Activities for Learning, Inc. 2015

Lesson 15: Multiples of Two and Four

OBJECTIVES:
1. To learn the term *product*
2. To practice the multiples of 2 and 4

MATERIALS:
1. AL Abacus
2. Worksheet 7, Multiples-1
3. *Math Card Games* book, P10 *
4. **Two sticky notes or cards, one with "4" and the other with "="**

ACTIVITIES FOR TEACHING:

Warm-up. Ask: What is 9 times 2? [18] What is 7 times 2? [14] What is 50 doubled? [1 hundred] What is 40 doubled? [80] What is another way of saying 80 + 80? [80 × 2] How much is it? [160] What is another way of saying 60 + 60? [60 × 2] How much is it? [120]

Worksheet 7. Give the child the abacus and worksheet.

Multiplying twos. Say: Enter 2 on the first wire of your abacus and say the equation. [2 × 1 = 2] Enter another 2 on the next wire and say the equation. [2 × 2 = 4] Tell her to continue to 2 × 10 = 20. See the figure at the right.

Tell her the answer in multiplication is called the *product*. Tell her to write the products for multiplying two on the worksheet. The solutions are shown below.

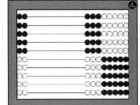
Multiples of 2.

2 × 1 = [2]   2 × 2 = [4]   2 × 3 = [6]   2 × 4 = [8]   2 × 5 = [10]
2 × 6 = [12] 2 × 7 = [14] 2 × 8 = [16] 2 × 9 = [18] 2 × 10 = [20]

Multiplying fours. Say: Now we will do the fours. Enter 4 on the top wire and say the equation. [4 × 1 = 4] Enter another 4 in the next row and say the equation. [4 × 2 = 8] Enter another 4. Now separate two beads on each wire, leaving a tiny space. See the left figure below. Ask: Do you see 2 × 3 doubled? How much is it? [6 + 6 = 12] Tell her to say the equation. [4 × 3 = 12]

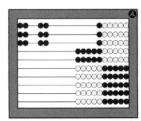
4 × 3 is 2 × 3 doubled.

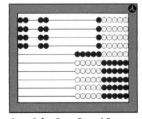
4 × 4 is 8 + 8 = 16.

EXPLANATIONS:

* Included with the multiplication cards are 10 envelopes, each printed with the multiples of a number from 1–10. Insert into each envelope 10 multiplication cards matching the numbers listed on the front of the envelope. A new deck of multiplication cards is collated to make this task easy: the first 10 cards go into the 1s envelope; the next 10 cards go into the 2s envelope; and so forth.

Learning multiples is necessary for work with fractions and in algebra. Skip counting should *not* be used to find a product.

ACTIVITIES FOR TEACHING:	EXPLANATIONS:

Tell her to enter another 4 on the fourth row, broken into twos. How much is it? [8 + 8 = 16] See the right figure on the previous page. Tell her to say the equation. [4 × 4 = 16] Repeat for 4 × 5. [4 × 5 = 20]

Tell her to enter 4 × 6 and to find another way to find the product. See the figure below; there are 20 dark-colored beads and 4 light-colored beads. Continue to 4 × 10.

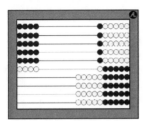

4 × 6 is 20 + 4.

Tell her to write the products for multiplying four on the worksheet. Tell her to find the products by any method she like. The solutions are shown below.

4 × 1 = [4]   4 × 2 = [8]   4 × 3 = [12]   4 × 4 = [16]   4 × 5 = [20]
4 × 6 = [24]   4 × 7 = [28]   4 × 8 = [32]   4 × 9 = [36]   4 × 10 = [40]

See page iii, number 24 of "Some General Thoughts on Teaching Mathematics," for additional information.

The rest of this worksheet will be completed in future lessons.

Patterns in multiples. Tell the child to look at her multiples of two. Ask: What patterns do you see? If necessary, ask: How does the second row compare to the first row? [Each multiple is 10 more than the one above it. Also, the ones are the same.] Are there any odd numbers? [no]

The child might discover that the multiples are 20 more in the second row because the light color starts with the second row.

Tell her to find patterns in the multiples of four. [even numbers, first row is every other multiple of two, second row is 20 more than the first row.]

Multiplication Memory game. Play the Multiplication Memory game found in the *Math Card Games* book, P10. Use one set of the basic number cards from 1–10 and the multiplication cards from the 4s envelopes. Tell her to use her abacus to find the products. Tell her play several times.

Some children may benefit from playing the Multiplication Memory game with the 2s envelopes.

Instead of the basic number cards, the cards from the 1s envelope can be used.

In conclusion. Ask: If you know that 4 times 5 is 20, how much more is 4 times 6? [4 more] What is 4 times 6? [24] What is 4 times 10? [40] What is 4 times 9? [36] What is 4 times 8? [32]

© Activities for Learning, Inc. 2015

Lesson 16: Multiples of One

OBJECTIVES:
1. To learn the multiples of 1
2. To practice the multiples of 4

MATERIALS:
1. AL Abacus
2. Worksheet 7, Multiples-1 (used in the previous lesson)
3. *Math Card Games* book, P12
4. Colored tiles

ACTIVITIES FOR TEACHING:

Warm-up. Ask: What is 4 times 2? [8] What is 4 times 3? [12] What is 4 times 4? [16] What is 4 times 5? [20]

Ask: What is 4 doubled? [8] What is 40 doubled? [80] What is 400 doubled? [800] What is another way of saying 400 + 400? [400 × 2]

Multiplying twos. Give the child the abacus. Say: Enter twos on the wires of your abacus and say the equations like you did in the last lesson. See the left figure below.

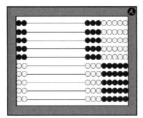

Multiples of 2.　　　Multiples of 2.

Say: There is another way to do the multiples on the abacus. Enter as many 2s on the first wire as possible and then go to the next wire. Leave a little space between each 2. See the right figure above. Tell her to enter the 2s and say the equations. [2 × 1 = 2, ..., 2 × 10]

Multiplying fours. Say: Now we will do the fours. First practice saying the equations using your abacus. See the left figure below.

Say: Now do the 4s the other way on the abacus. Enter as many fours on the first wire as possible. Enter another 4 by entering part on the first wire and the rest on the second wire. See the right figure below.

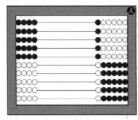 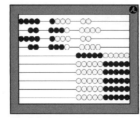

Multiples of 4.　　　Multiples of 4.

EXPLANATIONS:

In the first method from the previous lesson, the multiplier is easy to see, but the product is harder to determine. In the second method given here, the product is easy to see, but the multiplier is harder to see.

ACTIVITIES FOR TEACHING:	EXPLANATIONS:

Multiplying ones. Say: Enter 1 multiplied by 4. Ask: How much is it? [4] See the figures below. Ask: What is the product of 1 multiplied by 7? [7] What is 1 multiplied by 10? [10] What is 1 times 6? [6] What is 1 times 8? [8] What pattern do you see when you multiply 1 times a number? [The product is the same number.]

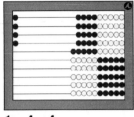   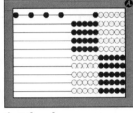

1 × 4 = 4   1 × 4 = 4

The child should not be taught any rules about 1 multiplied by a number or a number multiplied by 1. A mental image is far superior.

Worksheet 7. Give the child the worksheet. Tell the child to write the products for multiplying one on the worksheet. The solutions are shown below.

1 × 1 = [1]   1 × 2 = [2]   1 × 3 = [3]   1 × 4 = [4]   1 × 5 = [5]
1 × 6 = [6]   1 × 7 = [7]   1 × 8 = [8]   1 × 9 = [9]   1 × 10 = [10]

The rest of this worksheet will be completed in a future lesson.

What's on Top game. Play the What's on Top game found in the *Math Card Games* book, P12. Use 4 as the multiplier and use the colored tiles as the markers.

The What's on Top game, P12, was previously called "Who's on Top."

For the first game, tell her to lay out 4s in two rows like her worksheet (or the envelope). For subsequent games, tell her to lay the 4s in a single row like the instructions in the *Math Card Games* book.

In conclusion. Ask: What is 1 times 8? [8] What is 1 times 6? [6] What is 1 times 47? [47] What is 4 times 4? [16] What is 4 times 9? [36] What is 4 times 7? [28] What is 4 times 8? [32]

© Activities for Learning, Inc. 2015

Lesson 17: Multiples of Eight

OBJECTIVES:
1. To find the multiples of 8

MATERIALS:
1. A set of 4s and 8s multiplication cards and envelopes
2. AL Abacus
3. Worksheet 7, Multiples-1 (used in the previous lessons)
4. *Math Card Games* book, P12

ACTIVITIES FOR TEACHING:

Warm-up. Ask: What is 1 times 4? [4] What is 1 times 7? [7] What is 1 times 32? [32] What is 1 times 700? [700]

Ask: What is 4 times 5? [20] What is 4 times 6? [24] What is 4 times 7? [28] What is 4 times 8? [32] What is 4 times 9? [36] What is 4 times 10? [40]

Double the Product Memory game. Show the child how to play a new game, Double the Product Memory. Remove the cards from the 4s envelope and place them face down in two rows of five each. A short ways away, place the cards from the 8s envelope in the same arrangement. See the figure below.

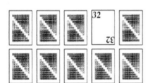
Multiples of 4.

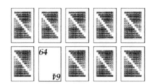
Multiples of 8.

To play, the first player turns over a 4s card, doubles it, and says for example, "32 doubled is 64." She then decides where the 64 could be among the 8s cards. If she is correct, she collects both cards and takes another turn. If she is not correct, both cards are returned face down in their original place, and the other player takes his turn. The winner is the player with the most 4s cards.

Play the game at least twice. Tell her to be sure to return the cards to the correct envelopes.

Multiplying eights. Give the child the abacus and say: Now you will multiply the eights. Enter 8 times 1 and say the equation. [8 × 1 = 8] See the left figure below. Enter another 8 and say the equation. [8 × 2 = 16] See the right figure below.

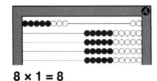
8 × 1 = 8

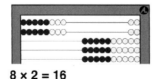
8 × 2 = 16

EXPLANATIONS:

Some children may need to use the abacus for some of these warm-up questions.

The objective of this game is to make the child familiar with doubling the 4s in preparation for multiplying the 8s by doubling the 4s.

ACTIVITIES FOR TEACHING:	EXPLANATIONS:

Tell her: Enter another 8 and find different ways to find the product. See the left figure below.

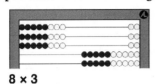 

8 × 3   8 × 3 is 4 × 3 doubled.

One way is to see it as 4 × 3 doubled as shown in the right figure above: 4 × 3 = 12, 12 doubled is 24. Another way is to see the dark-colored beads as 15 and the light-colored beads as 9; 15 + 9 = 24. See the left figure below. A third way is to see it 30 − 6 as in the right figure below.

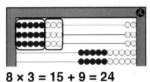 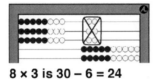

8 × 3 = 15 + 9 = 24   8 × 3 is 30 − 6 = 24

Continue with 8 × 4 through 8 × 10.

Worksheet 7. Give the child the worksheet. Tell the child to write the products for multiplying eight on the worksheet. The solutions are shown below.

8 × 1 = [8]   8 × 2 = [16]   8 × 3 = [24]   8 × 4 = [32]   8 × 5 = [40]
8 × 6 = [48]   8 × 7 = [56]   8 × 8 = [64]   8 × 9 = [72]   8 × 10 = [80]

The child is not expected to have these facts memorized at this time. Rather, at this point, she is seeing 8 × 7 as a process, which can be approached in several ways.

Patterns in multiples. Tell the child to look at her multiples of eights on her worksheet. Ask: What patterns do you see? If necessary, ask: How do the two rows compare? [In each column the second row is 40 more than the first row. The ones are the same in each column.] How do the tens change in the first row? [They increase from zero to four.] How do the tens change in the second row? [They increase from four to eight.]

What's on Top game. Play the What's on Top game found in the *Math Card Games* book, P12. Use 8 as the multiplier. For the first game, tell her to lay out the 8s in two rows like her worksheet (or the envelope). For subsequent games, tell her to lay the 8s in a single row like the instructions in the *Math Card Games* book.

The What's on Top game, P12, was previously called "Who's on Top."

In conclusion. Ask: What is 8 times 2? [16] What is 8 times 3? [24] What is 8 times 8? [64] What is 8 times 10? [80] What is 8 times 4? [32]

© Activities for Learning, Inc. 2015

Lesson 18: The Commutative Property

OBJECTIVES:
1. To learn the term *factor*
2. To introduce the commutative property
3. To learn the term *commutative*

MATERIALS:
1. AL Abacus
2. Dry erase board
3. *Math Card Games* book, P10

ACTIVITIES FOR TEACHING:

Warm-up. Ask: What is 4 times 1? [4] What is 8 times 1? [8] What is 4 times 2? [8] What is 8 times 2? [16] What is 4 times 3? [12] 8 times 3? [24] What 4 times 4? [16] 8 times 4? [32] What is 4 times 5? [20] 8 times 5? [40]

Ask: What is 4 times 6? [24] 8 times 6? [48] What is 4 times 7? [28] 8 times 7? [56] What is 4 times 8? [32] 8 times 8? [64] What is 4 times 9? [36] 8 times 9? [72] What is 4 times 10? [40] 8 times 10? [80]

The commutative property on the abacus. Give the child the abacus and dry erase board. Tell the child: Enter 4 multiplied by 2 on the top two rows of your abacus. Also enter 2 multiplied by 4 on the bottom four rows of your abacus. See the left figure below. Ask: What are the equations? [$4 \times 2 = 8$ and $2 \times 4 = 8$]

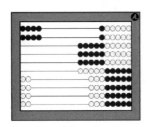

4×2 and 2×4

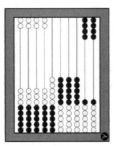

4×2 and 2×4

Now tell her to turn her abacus clockwise, that is, in the same direction the hands turn on a clock. See the right figure above. Tell her to write the equations on her white board. [$4 \times 2 = 8$ and $2 \times 4 = 8$]

Say: The number we multiply and the number we multiplied by are called *factors*. In the equations just written, 2 and 4 are the factors.

Tell her to enter 8 multiplied by 4 on her abacus and to write the equation. [$8 \times 4 = 32$] Then tell her to turn her abacus clockwise and write that equation. [$4 \times 8 = 32$] Did the order of the factors make a difference? [no]

Commutative examples. Make two columns. Label the left column "Makes a Difference" and the right side

EXPLANATIONS:

Some children may need to use the abacus for some of these warm-up questions.

The commutative property was formerly called the commutative *law*. A property is an attribute or quality.

ACTIVITIES FOR TEACHING:	EXPLANATIONS:

"Makes No Difference." See the figure below.

Ask: Does it make any difference at a meal whether you eat beans or corn first? [no] Write it in the left column.

Ask: Does it matter if you mix the batter or bake the cake first? [yes] Write it in the right column.

Makes No Difference	Makes a Difference
Eat beans or corn	Mix the batter or bake the cake
Put on left or right shoe	
	Eat or peel banana

Ask: Does the order matter for peeling and eating a banana? [yes]

Ask: Do you get the same results if you first put on your left shoe or your right shoe? [yes]

Tell her to think of some examples to be recorded.

Ask: Is 89 + 3 equal to 3 + 89? [yes] Does the order make a difference in adding? [no] Write it in the left column.

Ask: In subtraction, is 5 – 3 equal to 3 – 5? [no] Put it in the right column.

Ask: For multiplication, is 5 multiplied by 2 the same as 2 multiplied by 5? [yes] Does the order make a difference in multiplying? [no] Put in the left column.

See page iii, number 18 of "Some General Thoughts on Teaching Mathematics," for additional information.

Tell her: The mathematical word for getting the same results when the order of the numbers is changed is _commutative_. Write "Commutative" above the left column and "Not commutative" above the right column as shown below.

Commutative	Not commutative
Makes No Difference	Makes a Difference
Eat beans or corn	Mix the batter or bake the cake
Put on left or right shoe	
Foot to pedal on bike	Eat or peel banana
Mittens on hands	Put on shoes or socks
89 + 3 or 3 + 89	Dry or wash hair
2 × 5 or 5 × 2	5 – 3 or 3 – 5

Multiplication Memory game. Play the Multiplication Memory game from the _Math Card Games_ book, P10, using the 8s.

In conclusion. Ask: What is 8 times 3? [24] What is 3 times 8? [24] What is 8 times 7? [56] What is 7 times 8? [56] What is 9 times 8? [72]

© Activities for Learning, Inc. 2015

Lesson 19: Multiples of Ten and Nine

OBJECTIVES:
1. To practice the multiples of 10
2. To practice the multiples of 9

MATERIALS:
1. AL Abacus
2. Worksheet 8, Multiples-2
3. *Math Card Games* book, P10

ACTIVITIES FOR TEACHING:

Warm-up. Ask: What is 8 times 4? [32] What is 4 times 8? [32] What is 8 times 6? [48] What is 6 times 8? [48] What is 7 times 8? [56] What is 8 times 9? [72]

Ask: What is 1 times 4? [4] What is 1 times 7? [7] What is 8 times 1? [8] What is 56 times 1? [56]

Multiplying tens. Give the child the abacus and say: Now we will multiply ten. Enter 10 times 1 and say the equation. [10 × 1 = 10] Enter another 10 and say the equation. [10 × 2 = 20] See the left figure below.

Continue to 10 × 10. [100] See the right figure below.

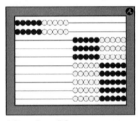
10 × 2 = 20

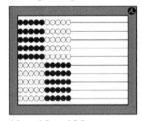
10 × 10 = 100

Worksheet 8. Give the child the worksheet and tell the child to write the products for multiplying ten on the worksheet. The solutions are shown below.

10 × 1 = [10] 10 × 2 = [20] 10 × 3 = [30] 10 × 4 = [40] 10 × 5 = [50]
10 × 6 = [60] 10 × 7 = [70] 10 × 8 = [80] 10 × 9 = [90] 10 × 10 = [100]

Then ask: What other multiples are similar to the tens multiples? [the ones]

Multiplying nines. Say: Now we will do the nines. Enter 9 on the top wire and say the equation. [9 × 1 = 9] See the left figure below. Enter another 9 in the next row and say the equation. [9 × 2 = 18] See the right figure below.

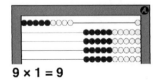
9 × 1 = 9

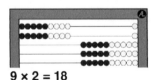
9 × 2 = 18

EXPLANATIONS:

Some children may need to use the abacus for some of these warm-up questions.

See page ii, number 10 of "Some General Thoughts on Teaching Mathematics," for additional information.

ACTIVITIES FOR TEACHING:	EXPLANATIONS:

Tell her to enter a third 9 and to find the product. See left figure below. Tell her to explain how she found the product. One way is to see it as 30 – 3. See the right figure below.

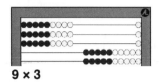
9 × 3

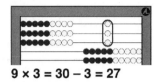
9 × 3 = 30 – 3 = 27

Another way is to use Take and Give as shown in the figures below. Tell her to say the equation. [9 × 3 = 27]

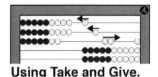
Using Take and Give.

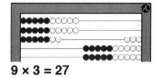
9 × 3 = 27

The Take and Give procedure was shown in Lesson 11.

Continue with the remaining 9s products.

Worksheet 8. Tell the child to write the products for multiplying nine on the worksheet. The solutions are shown below.

9 × 1 = [9]   9 × 2 = [18]   9 × 3 = [27]   9 × 4 = [36]   9 × 5 = [45]
9 × 6 = [54]   9 × 7 = [63]   9 × 8 = [72]   9 × 9 = [81]   9 × 10 = [90]

The rest of this worksheet will be completed in a future lesson.

Patterns in multiples. Tell the child to look at her multiples of nines on her worksheet. Ask: What patterns do you see? If necessary, ask: What happens to the ones? [They decrease from nine to zero.] What happens to the tens? [They increase from zero to nine.] What happens when you add the digits for each product? [They total 9.]

Tell her to compare 10 × 1 and 9 × 1. [9 × 1 is 1 less]
Tell her to compare 10 × 2 and 9 × 2. [9 × 2 is 2 less]
Tell her to compare 10 × 3 and 9 × 3. [9 × 3 is 3 less]
Continue to 10 × 10 and 9 × 10.

The child is not expected to have these facts memorized at this time. Rather, at this point, she is seeing 9 × 6 as a process, which can be approached in several ways.

Multiplication Memory game. Play the Multiplication Memory game found in the *Math Card Games* book, P10. Use one set of the basic number cards from 1–10 and the multiplication cards from the 9s envelopes. Tell her to use her abacus to find the products. Tell her play several times.

The 9s envelope has the 9s pattern in reverse order to emphasize how the digits reverse. This will be addressed later.

In conclusion. Ask: What is 9 + 9? [18] What is 18 + 9? [27] 27 + 9? [36] 36 + 9? [45] 45 + 9? [54] 54 + 9? [63] 63 + 9? [72] 72 + 9? [81] 81 + 9? [90]

© Activities for Learning, Inc. 2015

Lesson 20: Multiples of Five

OBJECTIVES:
1. To practice the multiples of 5
2. To review minute numbers on a clock

MATERIALS:
1. AL Abacus
2. Worksheet 8, Multiples-2 (used in the previous lesson)
3. Geared clock
4. *Math Card Games* book, P13.1

ACTIVITIES FOR TEACHING:

Warm-up. Ask: What is 9 + 9? [18] What is 18 + 9? [27] 27 + 9? [36] 36 + 9? [45] 45 + 9? [54] 54 + 9? [63] 63 + 9? [72] 72 + 9? [81] 81 + 9? [90]

Ask: What is 8 + 8? [16] What is 16 + 8? [24] 24 + 8? [32] 32 + 8? [40] 40 + 8? [48] 48 + 8? [56] 56 + 8? [64] 64 + 8? [72] 72 + 8? [80]

Multiplying fives. Give the child the abacus and say: Now we will multiply the fives. Enter 5 times 1 and say the equation. [5 × 1 = 5] Enter another 5 in the same row with a little space. Say the equation. [5 × 2 = 10] See the left figure below.

Tell her to continue entering fives and saying the equations. See the right figure below.

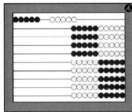
5 × 2

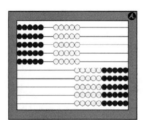
Multiples of 5.

Worksheet 8. Give the child the worksheet. Tell the child to write the products for multiplying five on the worksheet. The solutions are shown below.

5 × 1 = [5]   5 × 2 = [10]
5 × 3 = [15] 5 × 4 = [20]
5 × 5 = [25] 5 × 6 = [30]
5 × 7 = [35] 5 × 8 = [40]
5 × 9 = [45] 5 × 10 = [50]

Patterns in multiples. Tell the child to look at her multiples of fives on her worksheet. Ask: What patterns do you see? If necessary, ask: What happens when you multiply five by an odd number? [The product ends with a five in the ones place.] What happens when you multiply

EXPLANATIONS:

Some children may need to use the abacus for some of these warm-up questions.

ACTIVITIES FOR TEACHING:

five by an even number? [The product ends with a zero in the ones place and the tens number is half of the factor that is multiplied by five.]

Minutes on a clock. Show the child the geared clock. Ask: Which hand is the hour hand? [the shorter hand] What do we call the longer hand? [the minute hand] How many minutes are there between each number of the clock? [five]

Worksheet 8. Tell the child to write the minute numbers around the clock. The finished clock is shown below.

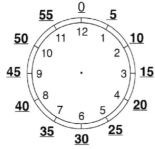

Then ask: How are the minute numbers related to the fives? [Five times an hour number equals the minute number.]

Mixed-Up Products game. Play the Mixed-Up Products game found in the *Math Card Games* book, P13.1. Use cards from the 1s and 5s envelopes.

In conclusion. Ask: What is 5 times 8? [40] What is 6 times 5? [30] What is 5 times 5? [25] What is 7 times 5? [35] What is 5 times 4? [20]

EXPLANATIONS:

See page iii, number 22 of "Some General Thoughts on Teaching Mathematics," for additional information.

© Activities for Learning, Inc. 2015

Lesson 21: Multiples of Three

OBJECTIVES:
1. To practice the multiples of 3

MATERIALS:
1. AL Abacus
2. Worksheet 9, Multiples-3
3. *Math Card Games* book, P2

ACTIVITIES FOR TEACHING:

Warm-up. Ask: What is 5 times 9? [45] What is 7 times 5? [35] What is 5 times 4? [20] What is 6 times 5? [30] What is 5 times 5? [25]

Ask: What is 9 + 9? [18] What is 18 + 9? [27] 27 + 9? [36] 36 + 9? [45] 45 + 9? [54] 54 + 9? [63] 63 + 9? [72] 72 + 9? [81] 81 + 9? [90]

Multiplying threes. Give the child the abacus. Say: Now we will multiply the threes. Enter 3 times 1 on your abacus and say the equation. [3 × 1 = 3] Leave a space of 2 centimeters and enter another 3 on the same wire. Each bead is 1 centimeter wide. Say the equation. [3 × 2 = 6] See the left figure below.

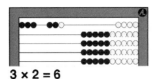

3 × 2 = 6

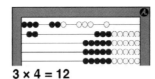

3 × 4 = 12

Tell her: Enter another 3 and say the equation. [3 × 3 = 9] Enter another 3 by entering part on the first wire and the rest on the second wire. See the right figure above. Say the equation. [3 × 4 = 12]

Continue with 3 × 5 through 3 × 10. See the left figure below. Tell the child to recite all the 3s.

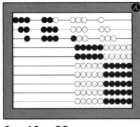

3 × 10 = 30

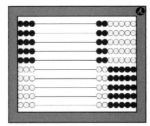

The threes.

Now tell her to enter the 3s again in each of the 10 rows and recite the 3s. See right figure above. Ask: What is another way to find 3 × 8? [Think of 8 × 3.]

EXPLANATIONS:

Some children may need to use the abacus for some of these warm-up questions.

ACTIVITIES FOR TEACHING:

Worksheet 9. Give the child the worksheet. Tell the child to write the products for multiplying three on the worksheet. Remind the child to use her abacus. The solutions are shown below.

$3 \times 1 = \boxed{3}$ $3 \times 2 = \boxed{6}$ $3 \times 3 = \boxed{9}$

$3 \times 4 = \boxed{12}$ $3 \times 5 = \boxed{15}$ $3 \times 6 = \boxed{18}$

$3 \times 7 = \boxed{21}$ $3 \times 8 = \boxed{24}$ $3 \times 9 = \boxed{27}$

$3 \times 10 = \boxed{30}$

Patterns in multiples. Tell the child to look at the patterns in the multiples of threes on her worksheet. Ask: What patterns do you see? If necessary, ask: What happens to the ones? [The ones go from 0–9 by starting at the bottom of the first column and going up and then continuing with the other two columns.] What pattern do the tens make? [The tens are 0 in the first row, 1 in second row, and 2 in the third row.] What happens when you add the digits in the first column, [3] the second column, [6] and the third column? [9] Is there an even-odd pattern? [Yes, they alternate.]

Multiples Memory game. Play the Multiples Memory game found in the *Math Card Games* book, P2. Use the 3s envelope and one of the other multiples she has worked with, the 4s, 5s, 8s, or 9s. Have her play several games.

In conclusion. Ask: What is 3 times 6? [18] What is 7 times 3? [21] What is 3 times 8? [24] What is 5 times 3? [15] What is 3 times 9? [27]

EXPLANATIONS:

The rest of this worksheet will be completed in future lessons.

© Activities for Learning, Inc. 2015

Lesson 22: Multiples of Six

OBJECTIVES:

1. To practice the multiples of 6

MATERIALS:

1. AL Abacus
2. Worksheet 9, Multiples-3 (used in the previous lesson)
3. *Math Card Games* book, P2 and P10

ACTIVITIES FOR TEACHING:

Warm-up. Ask: What is 5 + 5? [10] What is 10 + 5? [15] 15 + 5? [20] 20 + 5? [25] 25 + 5? [30] 30 + 5? [35] 35 + 5? [40] 40 + 5? [45] 45 + 5? [50]

Ask: What is 3 + 3? [6] What is 6 + 3? [9] 9 + 3? [12] 12 + 3? [15] 15 + 3? [18] 18 + 3? [21] 21 + 3? [24] 24 + 3? [27] 27 + 3? [30]

Multiplying sixes. Give the child the abacus and say: Now we will multiply the sixes. Enter 6 times 1 and say the equation. [6 × 1 = 6] Say: Enter another 6 in the next row and say the equation. [6 × 2 = 12] See the left figure below.

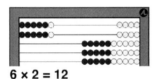
6 × 2 = 12

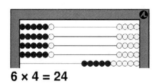
6 × 4 = 24

Tell her: Enter a third 6 and say the equation. [6 × 3 = 18] Add another 6 and find different ways to find the product. See the right figure above. One way is to see it as two 10s and 4 as shown in the left figure below. Another way is to see 3 × 4 doubled as in the right figure below.

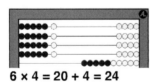
6 × 4 = 20 + 4 = 24

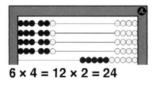
6 × 4 = 12 × 2 = 24

Continue with 6 × 5, which can be see as three 10s.

Tell her to find 6 × 6. The large group of dark-colored beads is 25 and the two groups of light-colored beads are 10, making the product 25 + 10 + 1 = 36. See the figure on the right. It can also be seen as 30 from the first five rows plus 6.

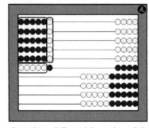
6 × 6 = 25 + 10 + 1 = 36

EXPLANATIONS:

Some children may need to use the abacus for some of these warm-up questions.

See page iii, number 13 of "Some General Thoughts on Teaching Mathematics," for additional information.

ACTIVITIES FOR TEACHING:

Continue with 6 × 7. Seeing the multiples of 6 as the multiples of 5 plus the multiples of 1 is shown below in the left figure. See the multiples as two groups of 3s is shown in the right figure below.

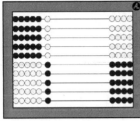
Multiples of 6.

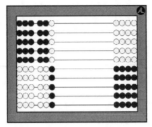
Multiples of 6.

Worksheet 9. Give the child the worksheet and tell her to write the products for multiplying six. The solutions are shown below.

6 × 1 = 6   6 × 2 = 12   6 × 3 = 18   6 × 4 = 24   6 × 5 = 30
6 × 6 = 36   6 × 7 = 42   6 × 8 = 48   6 × 9 = 54   6 × 10 = 60

Patterns in multiples. Tell the child to look at her multiples of sixes on her worksheet. What patterns do you see? If necessary, ask: Are the numbers even or odd? [even] How much more is the second row compared to the first row? [30 more] How does the first row compare to the threes? [the even threes, also every other 3]

Multiples Memory game. Play the Multiples Memory game found in the *Math Card Games* book, P2. Use the 6s envelope and one of the other multiples she has worked with, the 3s, 4s, 5s, 8s, or 9s. Have her play several games.

Multiplication Memory game. Play the Multiplication Memory game from the *Math Card Games* book, P10, using the 6s.

In conclusion. Ask: What is 6 times 6? [36] What is 8 times 6? [48] What is 6 times 5? [30] What is 9 times 6? [54] What is 6 times 7? [42]

EXPLANATIONS:

The child is not expected to have these facts memorized at this time. Rather, at this point, she is seeing 6 × 8 as a process, which can be approached in several ways.

The rest of this worksheet will be completed in a future lesson.

© Activities for Learning, Inc. 2015

Lesson 23: Multiples of Seven

OBJECTIVES:
1. To practice the multiples of 7

MATERIALS:
1. AL Abacus
2. Worksheet 9, Multiples-3 (used in prior lessons)
3. *Math Card Games* book, P2 and P12

ACTIVITIES FOR TEACHING:

Warm-up. Ask: What is 6 + 6? [12] What is 12 + 6? [18] 18 + 6? [24] 24 + 6? [30] 30 + 6? [36] 36 + 6? [42] 42 + 6? [48] 48 + 6? [54] 54 + 6? [60]

Ask: What is 3 + 3? [6] What is 6 + 3? [9] 9 + 3? [12] 12 + 3? [15] 15 + 3? [18] 18 + 3? [21] 21 + 3? [24] 24 + 3? [27] 27 + 3? [30]

Multiplying sevens. Give the child the abacus. Say: Now we will multiply the sevens. Enter 7 times 1 and say the equation. [7 × 1 = 7] Enter another 7 in the next row and say the equation. [7 × 2 = 14] See the left figure below.

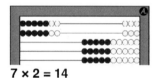
7 × 2 = 14

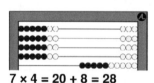
7 × 4 = 20 + 8 = 28

Say: Enter a third 7 and say the equation. [7 × 3 = 21] Add another 7. See the right figure above. Ask: How can you find the product? One way is to see the two groups of 10 and 8 more. Tell her to say the equation. [7 × 4 = 28]

Tell her to enter 7 × 5 and ask: How do you find the product? [There are 25 dark-colored beads and 10 light-colored beads, making 35 in all.] See the left figure below.

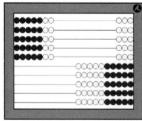
7 × 5 = 25 + 10 = 35

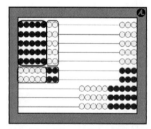
7 × 7 = 25 + 10 + 10 + 4 = 49

Continue with 7 × 6 through 7 × 10. The abacus with 7 × 7 is shown in the right figure above.

The product for 7 × 8 can be seen as 5 × 8 plus 2 × 8 = 56. See the left figure on the next page.

EXPLANATIONS:

ACTIVITIES FOR TEACHING:

The product for 7 × 9 can be seen as 7 × 9 = 70 − 7 = 63. If the last 7 were added, it would be 7 × 10. Since it is 7 × 9, the product will be 70 − 7, or 63. See the right figure below.

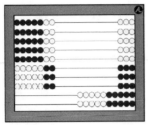
7 × 8 = 5 × 8 + 2 × 8 = 56

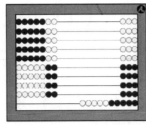
7 × 9 = 70 − 7 = 63

Worksheet 9. Give the child the worksheet. Tell her to write the products for multiplying seven on the worksheet. The solutions are shown below.

7 × 1 = ⬚7   7 × 2 = ⬚14   7 × 3 = ⬚21
7 × 4 = ⬚28   7 × 5 = ⬚35   7 × 6 = ⬚42
7 × 7 = ⬚49   7 × 8 = ⬚56   7 × 9 = ⬚63
7 × 10 = ⬚70

Patterns in multiples. Tell the child to look at her multiples of sevens on her worksheet. What patterns do you see? If necessary, ask: Are the numbers even or odd? [Both. They alternate.] What happens to the ones? [The ones go from 0–9 by starting at the top of the third column and going down and then continuing with the other two columns.] Is that the same as the 3s pattern? [No, it is the opposite.]

Ask: What pattern do the tens make? [The tens in the first row are 0, 1, 2. The tens in the second row are 2, 3, 4. The tens in the third row are 4, 5, 6.]

Multiples Memory game. Play the Multiples Memory game found in the *Math Card Games* book, P2. Use the 7s envelope and any other envelope. Have her play several games.

What's on Top game. Play the What's on Top game found in the *Math Card Games* book, P12. Use 7 as the multiplier. For the first game, tell her to lay out the 7s in rows like her worksheet (or the envelope). For subsequent games, tell her to lay the 7s in a single row.

In conclusion. Ask: What is 5 × 7? [35] What is 7 × 5? [35] What is 7 × 9? [63] What is 9 × 7? [63] What is 2 × 7? [14] What is 4 × 7? [28]

EXPLANATIONS:

The child is not expected to have these facts memorized at this time. Rather, at this point, she is seeing 7 × 8 as a process, which can be approached in several ways.

Lesson 24: The Associative Property for Multiplication

OBJECTIVES:
1. To understand the associative property for multiplication
2. To apply the associative property
3. To work with the 8s multiples

MATERIALS:
1. Worksheet 10, The Associative Property for Multiplication
2. AL Abacus
3. *Math Card Games* book, P12 or P13

ACTIVITIES FOR TEACHING:

Warm-up. Give the child the worksheet and abacus. Tell her to do just the warm-up equations. Solutions are:

45 + 35 = **80**   100 − 14 = **86**   3 × 9 = **27**   6 × 5 = **30**
53 + 29 = **82**   43 × 1 = **43**   8 × 4 = **32**   7 × 8 = **56**

The associative property on the abacus. Tell the child: On your abacus enter 2 × 3 on the first row, keeping spaces between the twos. Now multiply that 2 × 3 four times. See the left figure below.

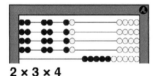   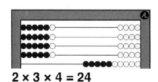

2 × 3 × 4   2 × 3 × 4 = 24

Write the equation: 2 × 3 × 4 =

and ask: What is the product? [24] See the right figure above.

Below the first equation write:

4 × 2 × 3 =

and tell her to first enter 4 × 2 on the first row and then multiply it by 3. See the left figure below. Ask: What is the product? [24] Repeat for 3 × 2 × 4. [24] See the right figure below.

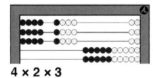   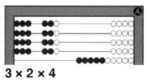

4 × 2 × 3   3 × 2 × 4

Ask: What do you notice about the left side of the three equations? [They have the same three numbers, but in a different order.] What about the products? [the same]

Tell her: The mathematical word for getting the same results when the numbers are multiplied in any order is called the *associative property*.

EXPLANATIONS:

ACTIVITIES FOR TEACHING:	EXPLANATIONS:

Applying the associative property. Write:

$$2 \times 4 \times 5 = \underline{\quad}$$

and ask: How many different ways could you find the product? One way is 2×4 is 8 and $8 \times 5 = 40$. Another way is 5×4 is 20 and $20 \times 2 = 40$. Still another way is $2 \times 5 = 10$ and $10 \times 4 = 40$. Ask: Which way do you think is easiest?

Repeat for: $4 \times 4 \times 2 = \underline{\quad}$ [32]

Worksheet 10. Say: Today's worksheet is like a puzzle. First guess at an answer and then see if it works.

See page iii, number 27 of "Some General Thoughts on Teaching Mathematics," for additional information.

Write: $8 =$

and tell the child to find three factors that when multiplied together will equal 8 without using a 1. [$8 = 2 \times 2 \times 2$] Ask: Do you think there could be another answer? [No, a 3 would make the product more than 8.] Tell her to write the answer on her worksheet.

Next ask her to find the factors for 16 before discussing it. Remind her she can use only three factors. [$16 = 4 \times 2 \times 2$] Repeat for find the factors for 24; tell her there is more than one answer. [$4 \times 3 \times 2$ and $6 \times 2 \times 2$]

Factors were discussed in Lesson 18.

Tell her to find the remaining factors. Then discuss her solutions. Solutions are:

$8 = 2 \times 2 \times 2$
$16 = 4 \times 2 \times 2$
$24 = 4 \times 3 \times 2$ or $6 \times 2 \times 2$
$32 = 8 \times 2 \times 2$ or $4 \times 4 \times 2$
$40 = 5 \times 4 \times 2$ or $10 \times 2 \times 2$
$48 = 8 \times 3 \times 2$ or $4 \times 4 \times 3$ or $12 \times 2 \times 2$ or $6 \times 4 \times 2$
$56 = 7 \times 4 \times 2$ or $14 \times 2 \times 2$
$64 = 8 \times 4 \times 2$ or $16 \times 2 \times 2$
$72 = 8 \times 3 \times 3$ or $18 \times 2 \times 2$
$80 = 8 \times 2 \times 5$ or $10 \times 4 \times 2$ or $20 \times 2 \times 2$

Wynter Frenette, age 10, found another solution: $72 = 4 \times 3 \times 6$.

What's on Top or What's on Top Now game. Play either the What's on Top or What's on Top Now game found in the *Math Card Games* book, P12 or P13. Use 8 as the multiplier.

In conclusion. Ask: What is $8 \times 2 \times 3$? [48] What is $8 \times 3 \times 2$? [48] What is $2 \times 3 \times 8$? [48] Why are these answers the same? [associative property]

© Activities for Learning, Inc. 2015

LESSON 25: SHORTCUT MULTIPLYING

OBJECTIVES:

1. To learn to multiply by zero
2. To learn to multiply zero by other numbers
3. To learn *Shortcut Multiplying*

MATERIALS:

1. Worksheet 11, Shortcut Multiplying
2. AL Abacus
3. Basic number cards

ACTIVITIES FOR TEACHING:

Warm-up. Give the child the worksheet and abacus. Tell her to do just the warm-up equations. Solutions are:

$67 + 19 = $ **86** $100 - 61 = $ **39** $4 \times 8 = $ **32** $7 \times 6 = $ **42**

$65 + 25 = $ **90** $0 \times 23 = $ **0** $9 \times 5 = $ **45** $8 \times 6 = $ **48**

Zero. Ask: Can you think of some ways we use zero? [thermometer, ruler, writing numbers like 10, 20, 100]

Write: $\qquad\qquad 8 + 0$

$\qquad\qquad\qquad 9 - 0$

Ask: What happens when you add or subtract zero? [The number stays the same.]

Multiplying with 0s. Write:

$$0 \times 4 =$$

and ask what it means. [0 multiplied 4 times] Ask: Enter 0 on your abacus [nothing entered] and pretend to multiply 0 four times. What is your answer? [0] What is 0×9? [0] What is 0×2? [0] What is 0×4000? [0]

Next write: $\qquad\qquad 4 \times 0 =$

and ask what this means. [4 taken 0 times] Tell the child to enter it on the abacus. [nothing entered] To demonstrate take 4 beads and show that you cannot enter them because you have to do it 0 times. Ask: What is 5×0? [0] What is 0×0? [0] What is 27×0? [0] What is 478×0? [0]

Shortcut Multiplying. Tell the child that you are going to show her a shortcut way of finding products for numbers between five and ten. Say: The method is called *Shortcut Multiplying*. It is done on only the last two rows of the abacus.

Write: $\qquad\qquad 8 \times 6$

then say: Enter 8 and 6 on the last two rows on your abacus. See the left figure on the next page. Say: To find number of tens, *add* the number of dark-colored beads on the left representing ten. See the second figure. Ask: How many tens are there? [4 tens] Say: To find number of ones,

EXPLANATIONS:

Shortcut Multiplying is a quick method for finding products when both factors are between five and ten. It has been known for hundreds of years and is often done with fingers.

Using the abacus makes the process more visualizable.

RightStart™ Mathematics Level D Second Edition

© Activities for Learning, Inc. 2015

ACTIVITIES FOR TEACHING:

multiply the number of dark-colored beads in each row on the right. See the third figure. Ask: How many ones are there? [8, 2 × 4 = 8] What is 8 × 6? [48, 40 + 8 = 48]

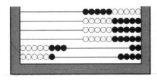

8 × 6   Tens are 30 + 10 = 40   Ones are 2 × 4 = 8

Repeat for: 8 × 7 [56]

See the figures below.

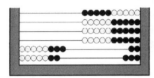  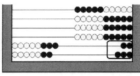

8 × 7   Tens are 30 + 20 = 50   Ones are 2 × 3 = 6; 50 + 6 = 56

Continue with: 6 × 7

Here the tens are 30 and the ones are 12. Adding them together gives 42.

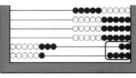

6 × 7 = 30 + 12 = 42

Worksheet 11. Tell the child to do the six equations under the abacus pictures. Solutions are below.

9 × 5 = 40 + 5 = 45   9 × 6 = 50 + 4 = 54   9 × 7 = 60 + 3 = 63
9 × 8 = 70 + 2 = 72   9 × 9 = 80 + 1 = 81   9 × 10 = 90 + 0 = 90

Multiplication War game. Play the Multiplication War game using the deck of basic number cards 1 to 10. Players turn over two cards. If the two cards are both 5 or more, the player uses Shortcut Multiplying and writes the product on the worksheet, unless it is already written. If the two cards are less than 5, the players multiply them any way they choose.

The players say the product and the player with the greater product takes all four cards. There are two winners: the player who first completes their worksheet and the player who has the most cards when both worksheets are completed. Worksheet solutions are:

```
25
30   36
35   42   49
40   48   56   64
45   54   63   72   81
50   60   70   80   90   100
```

In conclusion. Ask: What is 9 × 5? [45] What is 9 × 6? [54] What is 9 × 7? [63] What is 9 × 8? [72] What is 9 × 9? [81] What is 9 × 10? [90]

EXPLANATIONS:

See page ii, number 7 of "Some General Thoughts on Teaching Mathematics," for additional information.

When calculating the Shortcut Multiplication equations, note that as each bead is moved to the left for the next equation, the number of tens increases by one and the number of ones decreases by 1. Indeed, adding 9 is equal to 10 − 1.

For basic instructions on playing War games, see Addition War game found in *Math Card Games* book, A44.

LESSON 26: REVIEW AND GAMES 1

OBJECTIVES:
1. To review recent topics
2. To develop skills through playing math card games

MATERIALS:
1. Worksheet 12-A or 12-B, Review 1
2. *Math Card Games* book, P2

ACTIVITIES FOR TEACHING:

Worksheet 12-A. Give the child the worksheet. Tell her to listen to the problems and write the answers. Read each problem twice.

$$109 + 10 \qquad 69 + 22 \qquad 5 \times 6$$

Tell her to complete the worksheet. Solutions are below.

Write only the answers.

$$\underline{119}$$
$$\underline{91}$$
$$\underline{30}$$

Write the answers.

$38 + 87 = \underline{125}$

$43 + \underline{57} = 100$

$6 \times 3 = \underline{18}$

Add.
496 + 5781

6277

Fill in the blanks.

$4 \times 1 = \underline{4} \quad 4 \times 2 = \underline{8} \quad 4 \times 3 = \underline{12} \quad 4 \times 4 = \underline{16} \quad 4 \times 5 = \underline{20}$
$4 \times 6 = \underline{24} \quad 4 \times 7 = \underline{28} \quad 4 \times 8 = \underline{32} \quad 4 \times 9 = \underline{36} \quad 4 \times 10 = \underline{40}$

What pattern do you see?_____

Second row is 20 more than top row.
Numbers are all even.

Solve the problem.

Peyton has a rectangular scarf. A shorter side measures 9 cm. The longer side is 4 times longer than the shorter side. What is the perimeter of Peyton's scarf?

36 cm

9 cm

$P = 36 + 9 + 36 + 9 = 90$ cm

Write >, <, or = on the lines.

$47 + 53 \underline{<} 53 + 48$

$8 \times 3 \underline{=} 4 \times 2 \times 3$

$100 - 29 \underline{<} 100 - 28$

$4 \times 9 \underline{=} 6 \times 6$

$3 \times 2 \times 1 \underline{>} 8 \times 0 \times 9$

Complete the equations.

$4 \times 7 = \underline{28}$

$6 \times 10 = \underline{60}$

$2 \times 2 \times 8 = \underline{32}$

$1 \times 12 \times 0 = \underline{0}$

$9 \times 9 \times 1 = \underline{81}$

EXPLANATIONS:

The Review worksheets each have two versions. The second version can be used in various ways: as a quiz, as a test, as a check after tutoring, and so forth.

Ask the child to correct any errors during the lesson.

Grid lines are provided on the worksheet to help the child align the numbers.

There are a variety of possible answers.

See page iii, number 17 of "Some General Thoughts on Teaching Mathematics," for additional information.

ACTIVITIES FOR TEACHING:

Multiples Memory game. Play the Multiples Memory game found in the *Math Card Games* book, P2. Tell her to use envelopes with multiples she does not know. Tell her to play several games.

Worksheet 12-B. Give the child the worksheet. Tell her to listen to the problems and write the answers. Read each problem twice.

107 + 10   76 + 15   8 × 5

Tell her to complete the worksheet. Solutions are below.

Write only the answers.
117
91
40

Write the answers.
49 + 94 = 143
69 + 31 = 100
5 × 5 = 25

Add.
828 + 6805
7633

Fill in the blanks.
9 × 1 = 9   9 × 2 = 18   9 × 3 = 27   9 × 4 = 36   9 × 5 = 45
9 × 10 = 90   9 × 9 = 81   9 × 8 = 72   9 × 7 = 63   9 × 6 = 54

What pattern do you see? The digits in each product equals 9. Digits are reversed in the two rows.

Solve the problem.
Isaac drew an equilateral triangle with sides 4 cm long. Lily drew an equilateral triangle with sides four times greater. What is the perimeter of each triangle?

4 cm

I's P = 12 cm; L's P = 48 cm

Write >, <, or = on the lines.
74 + 53 __>__ 53 + 73
9 × 3 __=__ 3 × 3 × 3
100 − 61 __>__ 100 − 62
4 × 10 __=__ 8 × 5
9 × 0 × 8 __<__ 6 × 5 × 3

Complete the equations.
9 × 5 = 45
8 × 10 = 80
2 × 2 × 6 = 24
2 × 14 × 0 = 0
4 × 9 × 1 = 36

EXPLANATIONS:

Lesson 27: Multiplication Problems

OBJECTIVES:
1. To solve story problems involving multiplication
2. To write multiplication equations using letters for unknowns

MATERIALS:
1. Worksheet 13, Multiplication Problems
2. AL Abacus
3. *Math Card Games* book, P2

ACTIVITIES FOR TEACHING:

Warm-up. Give the child the worksheet and abacus. Tell her to do just the warm-up equations. Solutions are:

8 × 4 = **32**   4 × 8 = **32**   7 × 2 × 3 = **42**   3 × 7 × 2 = **42**
6 × 7 = **42**   7 × 6 = **42**   4 × 2 × 4 = **32**   4 × 4 × 2 = **32**

Worksheet 13. These problems are to be solved during the lesson.

Problem 1. Tell the child to read the first problem:

A small restaurant has 9 tables with each table having 4 chairs. How many chairs does the restaurant have? [36]

Say: Read the problem again. See the room in your mind and draw a picture if it helps you. Ask: What are you looking for? [number of chairs] How can you find the number of chairs? [Multiply the number of tables by the number of chairs.]

Tell her we can write the equation like this:

   c = number of chairs
   c = 9 × 4
   c = 36 chairs

Also ask her to show the problem on her abacus as shown below. Tell her to write the equations on her worksheet.

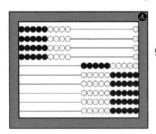

9 × 4 = 36 chairs

Problem 2. Tell the child to read the second problem:

Quinn is paid $3 for walking a dog. How much money will Quinn receive altogether after he has walked 7 dogs? [$21]

Ask: What do we need to find out? [amount of money, number of dollars] Give her several minutes to solve the

EXPLANATIONS:

Do *not* teach the child to look for "key" words in solving problems. Her attention then becomes focused on the words and not the logic and mathematics of the story problem.

See page ii, numbers 3 and 5 of "Some General Thoughts on Teaching Mathematics," for additional information.

ACTIVITIES FOR TEACHING:	EXPLANATIONS:

problem independently before sharing with you. The equations are:

$$d = dollars$$
$$d = 7 \times 3$$
$$d = \$21$$

Problem 3. Tell the child to read the third problem:

Cole goes to bed every night at 8 o'clock and sleeps ten hours. How many hours does he sleep in a week? [70 hours]

Tell the child to solve this story problem as before. The equations are:

$$h = hours$$
$$h = 10 \times 7$$
$$h = 70 \ hours$$

Ask: What did you need to know in order to solve this problem? [number of days in a week] Does the 8 o'clock time help you solve the problem? [no] Does your answer make sense?

Problem 4. Tell the child to read the fourth problem:

Zoey is buying 4 gifts that cost $5 each. Trey is buying 6 gifts that cost $3 each. Who is spending more money and how much more? [Zoey is spending $2 more.]

Tell her: Read the story twice and solve it as before. The equations are:

$$Z = cost \ of \ Zoey's \ gifts$$
$$T = cost \ of \ Trey's \ gifts$$
$$Z = 4 \times 5 = \$20$$
$$T = 6 \times 3 = \$18$$
$$Z - T = \$20 - \$18 = \$2$$
Zoey spent $2 more than Trey.

Multiples Memory game. Play the Multiples Memory game found in the *Math Card Games* book, P2. Tell her to use envelopes with multiples she does not know. Tell her to play several games.

In conclusion. Say: Make up a story problem for the equation, $9 \times 7 = 63$.

© Activities for Learning, Inc. 2015

LESSON 28: THE MULTIPLICATION TABLE

OBJECTIVES:
1. To construct the multiplication table
2. To use the multiplication table for finding products

MATERIALS:
1. Worksheet 14, The Multiplication Table
2. AL Abacus
3. *Math Card Games* book, P8 and P15

ACTIVITIES FOR TEACHING:

Warm-up. Give the child the worksheet and abacus. Tell her to do just the warm-up equations. Solutions are:

$8 \times 7 = 56$ $7 \times 8 = 56$ $3 \times 2 \times 9 = 54$ $9 \times 3 \times 2 = 54$

$9 \times 6 = 54$ $6 \times 9 = 54$ $4 \times 7 \times 2 = 56$ $2 \times 4 \times 7 = 56$

Build a Table game. Tell the child that she will play the Build a Table game, which is found in the *Math Card Games* book, P8.

1	2	3	4	5	6	7	8	9	10
2	4	6	8	10	12	14	16	18	20
3	6	9	12	15	18	21	24	27	30
4	8	12	16	20	24	28	32	36	40
5	10	15	20	25	30	35	40	45	50
6	12	18	24	30	36	42	48	54	60
7	14	21	28	35	42	49	56	63	70
8	16	24	32	40	48	56	64	72	80
9	18	27	36	45	54	63	72	81	90
10	20	30	40	50	60	70	80	90	100

When she has completed it, tell her it is called the *multiplication table*.

Ask: How could you find 3×4 on the multiplication table? [In the third row, go over to the fourth column.] Tell the child to find 3×8. Ask: How could you tell it was the eighth column without counting? [by looking at the top row]

EXPLANATIONS:

See page iii, number 19 of "Some General Thoughts on Teaching Mathematics," for additional information.

Sometimes multiplication tables go to 12 by 12. However, the 11s and 12s are not basic facts. There really is no good reason to burden the child with memorizing 44% more facts.

The 12s can be quickly calculated when the child understands that 12 is 10 plus 2. 12×9 is the same as 10×9 plus 2×9, which is $90 + 18 = 108$.

RightStart™ Mathematics Level D Second Edition

© Activities for Learning, Inc. 2015

ACTIVITIES FOR TEACHING:	EXPLANATIONS:

Tell her to find other products, such as 7×8, [56] 8×7, [56] 6×6, [36] 9×7, [63] and 7×9. [63]

Say: Find two factors that equal 54. [6 and 9] Write two equations to show this. [$54 = 9 \times 6$ and $54 = 6 \times 9$] Find the factors that equal 36 and write the three equations. [$36 = 9 \times 4$, $36 = 4 \times 9$, and $36 = 6 \times 6$]

To return the cards to the envelopes, ask the child to collect the cards by columns.

Show Your Product game. Play the Show Your Product game, which is found in the *Math Card Games* book, P15.

Worksheet 14. Tell the child to complete the worksheet. The solutions are as follows:

$3 \times 9 = \textbf{27}$ $6 \times 8 = \textbf{48}$
$7 \times 7 = \textbf{49}$ $9 \times 9 = \textbf{81}$
$5 \times 7 = \textbf{35}$ $4 \times 4 = \textbf{16}$
$9 \times 6 = \textbf{54}$ $8 \times 3 = \textbf{24}$
$7 \times 4 = \textbf{28}$ $10 \times 1 = \textbf{10}$

$28 = \textbf{7} \times \textbf{4}$ $28 = \textbf{4} \times \textbf{7}$ $72 = \textbf{9} \times \textbf{8}$ $72 = \textbf{8} \times \textbf{9}$
$8 = \textbf{8} \times \textbf{1}$ $8 = \textbf{1} \times \textbf{8}$ $8 = \textbf{4} \times \textbf{2}$ $8 = \textbf{2} \times \textbf{4}$
$20 = \textbf{10} \times \textbf{2}$ $20 = \textbf{2} \times \textbf{10}$ $20 = \textbf{5} \times \textbf{4}$ $20 = \textbf{4} \times \textbf{5}$

Which numbers in the table are used only once? **1, 25, 49, 64, 81, 100**

1	2	3	4	5	6	7	8	9	10
2	4	6	8	10	12	14	16	18	20
3	6	9	12	15	18	21	24	27	30
4	8	12	16	20	24	28	32	36	40
5	10	15	20	25	30	35	40	45	50
6	12	18	24	30	36	42	48	54	60
7	14	21	28	35	42	49	56	63	70
8	16	24	32	40	48	56	64	72	80
9	18	27	36	45	54	63	72	81	90
10	20	30	40	50	60	70	80	90	100

In conclusion. Ask: How many numbers are on the multiplication table? [100] What is the size of the array? [10 by 10] Can you use the multiplication table for adding? [no] Can you use it for multiplying? [yes]

Lesson 29: Area on the Multiplication Table

OBJECTIVES:
1. To review *perimeter* and *area*
2. To see area on the multiplication table
3. To introduce exponents
4. To see the symmetry of the multiplication table

MATERIALS:
1. Worksheet 15, Area on the Multiplication Table
2. Tiles
3. *Math Card Games* book, P21

ACTIVITIES FOR TEACHING:

Warm-up. Ask: How many numbers are on the addition table? [100] How many numbers are on the multiplication table? [100] What is the size of the arrays? [10 by 10] Can you use the multiplication table for adding? [no] Can you use it for multiplying? [yes]

Worksheet 15. Give the child the worksheet and tiles.

Reviewing perimeter. Show a tile and say: The length of an edge of a tile is 1 inch. The distance around an object is called the *perimeter*. Ask: What is the perimeter of a tile? [4 in.]

Area. Say: How much space something takes up is called *area*. Show the tile and say: The area of a tile is 1 square inch. Tell her to make a 6 by 4 array with the tiles as shown.

6 × 4 array

Ask: What is the perimeter of your array in inches? [20 in.] What is the area of your array in square inches? [24 sq. in.] Tell the child to start at the dot on her worksheet and draw this rectangle. Tell her to write the area at the opposite corner. See the left figure below.

Tell her to repeat for a 4 × 6 array. See right figure below.

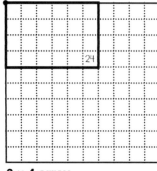

6 × 4 array

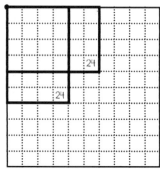

4 × 6 array added

EXPLANATIONS:

RightStart™ Mathematics Level D Second Edition © Activities for Learning, Inc. 2015

ACTIVITIES FOR TEACHING:	EXPLANATIONS:

Tell her to do the arrays for the second and third tables on her worksheet. The solutions are shown below.

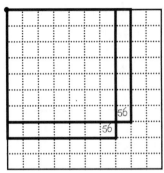
8 × 7 and 7 × 8 arrays

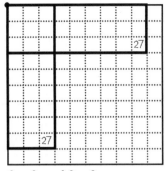
9 × 3 and 3 × 9 arrays

Squares on the multiplication table. For the last table on the worksheet, ask the child to construct several squares with the tiles and draw all the squares on the fourth multiplication table. See below.

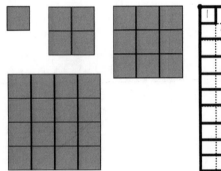
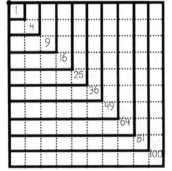
The square arrays.

Writing squares with exponents. Write:

$$3 \times 3 = 3^2$$

and explain this is a shortcut for writing squares. Say: We write 3 times 3 by writing only one 3 with a little 2 after it. The little 2 means we are multiplying 3 by itself twice. Read it as "3 squared".

Write: $5^2 = \_\_\_$

and ask: What does this mean? [5 × 5] How much is it? [25] Repeat for 8^2 [8 × 8 = 64] and 1^2. [1 × 1 = 1]

Square Memory game. Play the Square Memory game, which is found in the *Math Card Games* book, P21. Say: You will need one card from each envelope. Take the 1-card from 1s envelope, the 4-card from the 2s envelope, and so forth up to the 100-card from the 10s envelope. Tell her to play the game twice and return the cards to the correct envelopes.

By removing these cards from the envelopes, the child may become more aware of the square numbers that are indicated on the outside of the envelopes.

In conclusion. Ask: What numbers are on the diagonal in the multiplication table? [squares] Why is 56 on the multiplication table twice? [56 is 8 × 7 and 7 × 8]

© Activities for Learning, Inc. 2015

LESSON 30: EVENS AND ODDS ON THE MULTIPLICATION TABLE

OBJECTIVES:
1. To review evens and odds
2. To review adding and subtracting evens and odds
3. To extend evens and odds to products

MATERIALS:
1. AL Abacus
2. Worksheet 16, Evens and Odds on the Multiplication Table
3. **Colored pencil or marker**

ACTIVITIES FOR TEACHING:	EXPLANATIONS:
Warm-up. Ask: When two numbers are added together, what do we call the answer? [sum] What do you call a subtraction answer? [difference] What do you call the answer when you multiply? [product]	

Ask: What is the sum of 8 and 6? [14] What is the difference of 8 and 6? [2] What is the product? [48]

Reviewing even and odd numbers. Give the child the abacus. Ask the following: What is an even number and how do you know? [a number with a partner, a multiple of 2] Is 14 an even number? [yes] Ask the child to show it using the abacus. See the left figure below.

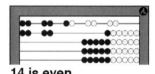
14 is even.

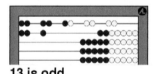
13 is odd.

Ask: What do you call a number that is not even? [odd] Is 13 an even number? [No, it is odd.] Ask the child to show it using the abacus. See the right figure above.

It also interesting to note that the number of syllables in "even" is even and the number of syllables in "odd" is odd.

Ask: How many letters are in the word even? [4] Is it even or odd? [even] How many letters are in the word odd? [3] Is it even or odd? [odd]

Tell her to use side 2 of her abacus and add two even numbers, such as 8 and 4. Ask: Is the sum even or odd? [even] See the left figure below.

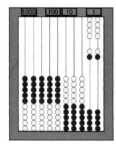
Even + even.

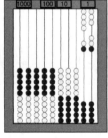
Odd + odd.

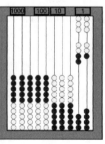
Even + odd.

Ask: What happens when you add two odd numbers, such as 7 and 5? [Even, the two extras form a group of

ACTIVITIES FOR TEACHING:

two.] See the second figure on the previous page.

Ask: What happens when you add an odd number and an even number, such as 6 and 7? [odd] See the third figure on the previous page.

Multiplying even and odd numbers. Tell the child to enter 6 × 6 on her abacus. Ask: Is the product even or odd? [even] Why? [Even numbers are being added.]

Ask: What happens when you multiply 8 × 3? [still adding even numbers although an odd number of times] Tell her to enter 7 × 7 on the abacus. See the figure below. Ask: Is the product even or odd? [odd] Tell her to explain it to you.

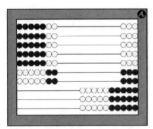
Odd × odd.

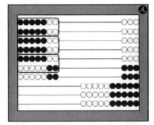
Odd × odd = odd.

Worksheet 16. Give the child the worksheet. Solutions are:

even + even = **even**
even + odd = **odd**
odd + odd = **even**
even − even = **even**
odd − even = **odd**

+	even	odd
even	**even**	**odd**
odd	**odd**	**even**

−	even	odd
even	**even**	**odd**
odd	**odd**	**even**

Using evens and odds, what kinds of numbers do you need to get an even sum? **even + even, odd + odd**

Using evens and odds, what kinds of numbers do you need to get an odd difference? **even − odd, odd − even**

Color all the squares with even numbers.

1	2	3	4	5	6	7	8	9	10
2	4	6	8	10	12	14	16	18	20
3	6	9	12	15	18	21	24	27	30
4	8	12	16	20	24	28	32	36	40
5	10	15	20	25	30	35	40	45	50
6	12	18	24	30	36	42	48	54	60
7	14	21	28	35	42	49	56	63	70
8	16	24	32	40	48	56	64	72	80
9	18	27	36	45	54	63	72	81	90
10	20	30	40	50	60	70	80	90	100

In the multiplication table, how many numbers are odd? **25** How many are even? **75**

even × even = **even** odd × odd = **odd**
even × odd = **even** odd × even = **even**

×	even	odd
even	**even**	**even**
odd	**even**	**odd**

When an even number is multiplied by another number, is the product even or odd? **even**

When an odd number is multiplied by another number, is the product even or odd? **If number is odd, odd; if number is even, even.**

In conclusion. Ask: Is the product of 99 × 99 even or odd? [odd] Is the sum of 99 + 99 even or odd? [even]

EXPLANATIONS:

To find the number of even numbers, subtract 25 from 100.

Continue playing games on a regular basis. If there is additional time following this lesson, have the child choose a game to play.

62

LESSON 31: COMPARING ADDITION AND MULTIPLICATION TABLES

OBJECTIVES:

1. To learn the term *cell*
2. To discover patterns on the addition and multiplication tables

MATERIALS:

1. Worksheet 17, Comparing Addition and Multiplication Tables
2. AL Abacus
3. *Math Card Games* book, P20

ACTIVITIES FOR TEACHING:	EXPLANATIONS:
Warm-up. Write: 52 27 89 306	
Ask: Which of those numbers are even? [52 and 306] How do you know 306 is an even number? [3 hundred is even and 6 is even] Can you look at the ones digit in a number and tell if it is even? [If the ones digit is even, the number is even.]	Although we "know" that a number is even if the digit in the ones place is even, children need to understand why this is true.
Worksheet 17. Give the child the worksheet and abacus. Ask: What is different about the two tables on your worksheet? [One is an addition table and the other is a multiplication table.]	
Say: A *cell* is a small rectangle in a table. Ask: How many cells does the multiplication table have? [100]	
Ask: What are doubles? [1 + 1 = 2 and so on] Where are the doubles on the addition table? [the diagonal cells starting at the top left corner] Where are the doubles on the multiplication table? [in the second row and in the second column]	
Ask: On the multiplication table what numbers are on the diagonal starting at the top left? [the square numbers] Where can you find 8 + 7? [on the addition table in the row starting with 8 and over 7 spaces] Where can find 8 × 7? [on the multiplication table in the row starting with 8 and over 7 spaces]	Square number were addressed in Lesson 29.
Ask: In the addition table, what happens when you move one cell to the right? [1 more] Why is that? [One addend is 1 more.] What happens when you move one cell to the left? [1 less] What happens when you move one cell up? [1 less] What happens when you move one cell down? [1 more] Does this happen on the multiplication table? [no] Why not? [The next cell is the next multiple.]	
Ask: What happens when you move one cell to the right and one cell up on the addition table? [same number]	

RightStart™ Mathematics Level D Second Edition

© Activities for Learning, Inc. 2015

ACTIVITIES FOR TEACHING:	EXPLANATIONS:

Squares and near squares. Say: Find 5 × 5 on the multiplication table. Ask: What happens when you move one cell to the right and one cell up? [one number less] Starting at 5 × 5 again, what happens when you move one cell down and one cell to the left? [one number less]

Tell her: Enter 5 × 5 on her abacus. Now use Take and Give to change it to 4 times a number. See the figures below. Ask: How does 5 × 5 compare to 4 × 6? [4 × 6 is one less]

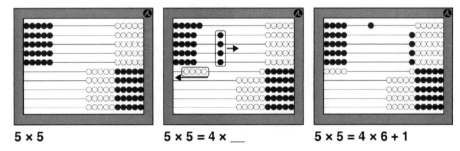

5 × 5   5 × 5 = 4 × __   5 × 5 = 4 × 6 + 1

Tell her to find 9 × 9 and 10 × 8 on the multiplication table. Ask: How do they compare? [9 × 9 is one greater] Tell her to show it on her abacus. See below.

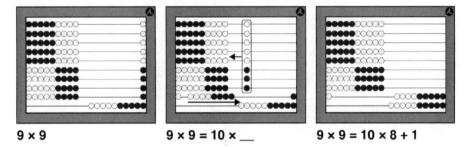

9 × 9   9 × 9 = 10 × __   9 × 9 = 10 × 8 + 1

Worksheet 17. Tell the child to complete the worksheet. Solutions are below.

5 + 5 = **10**   7 + 7 = **14**   11 + 11 = **22**   30 + 30 = **60**   100 + 100 = **200**
4 + 6 = **10**   6 + 8 = **14**   10 + 12 = **22**   29 + 31 = **60**   101 + 99 = **200**
5 × 5 = **25**   8 × 8 = **64**   4 × 4 = **16**   6 × 6 = **36**   7 × 7 = **49**
4 × 6 = **24**   9 × 7 = **63**   3 × 5 = **15**   5 × 7 = **35**   8 × 6 = **48**
11 × 13 = **143**   19 × 21 = **399**   31 × 29 = **899**

See page ii, number 4 of "Some General Thoughts on Teaching Mathematics," for additional information.

Multi-Fun game. Play the Multi-Fun game, found in *Math Card Games* book, P20. Tell her she gets an extra point for a card with an odd number.

After the game tell the child she will play the game in the next lesson. Therefore, she needs to pick up and keep the cards in the top row and left column separate.

Scoring can be done on the dry erase board or at the bottom of the worksheet.

In conclusion. Ask: What is 8 × 8? [64] What is 7 × 9? [63] What is 7 × 7? [49] What is 8 × 6? [48]

© Activities for Learning, Inc. 2015

Lesson 32: The Short Multiplication Table

OBJECTIVES:
1. To construct the short multiplication table
2. To use the short multiplication table

MATERIALS:
1. *Math Card Games* book, P28
2. Math journal
3. Worksheet 18, The Short Multiplication Table

ACTIVITIES FOR TEACHING:

Warm-up. Ask: What is 8 × 8? [64] What is 7 × 9? [63] What is 9 × 7? [63]

Ask: What is 7 × 7? [49] What is 8 × 6? [48] 6 × 8? [48]

Ask: What is 6 × 6? [36] What is 7 × 5? [35] 5 × 7? [35]

Ask: What is 9 × 9? [81] What is 8 × 10? [80] 10 × 8? [80]

Weighted Multi-Fun game. Play the Weighted Multi-Fun game, found in *Math Card Games* book, P28. Tell her to write her scores in her math journal, in the same way she did for the Sum Rummy game, P3. See the example on the right. The first equation, 5 × 4, shows 5 cards played in the fourth row or column; the second equation, 4 cards in the eighth row or column. She can write several equations before summing as shown.

```
5 × 4 = 20
4 × 8 = 32
7 × 5 = 35
       87
3 × 6 = 18
3 × 10 = 30
        135
```

EXPLANATIONS:

Maintain the card layout for the next activity.

The short multiplication table. Say: There is one more activity to do with the cards at the end of the game. Tell the child to find 2 × 7 and 7 × 2. Find the duplicate products. [14] Turn face down the 14-card in the column with the higher factor. Continue with 3 × 1 and 1 × 3, also with 5 × 8 and 8 × 5. See the figure below.

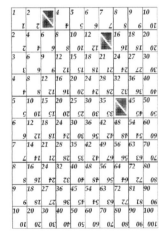

The duplicate products of 7 × 2, 3 × 1, and 8 × 5 turned face down.

Tell her to repeat for all duplicate products. See figure on the next page. Tell her this is the *short multiplication table*.

ACTIVITIES FOR TEACHING:

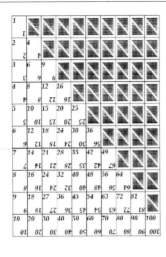

The multiplication table with the duplicates face down, resulting in the short multiplication table.

Worksheet 18. Give the child the worksheet. Tell her to find the 6 row. Say: The first six multiples are in the 6 row. Ask: Where are the rest of the 6s? [She continues down in the 36 column to 60.] See the left figure below.

Tell her to find 6 × 8. See the left figure below. Then tell her to find 8 × 6. See the right figure. Ask: What do you notice? [The product is in the same cell.]

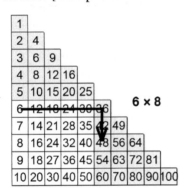

Tell her to complete the worksheet. The solutions are below.

4 × 4 = **16**	4 × 5 = **20**
9 × 4 = **36**	2 × 5 = **10**
8 × 7 = **56**	7 × 8 = **56**
5 × 7 = **35**	3 × 9 = **27**
9 × 6 = **54**	6 × 9 = **54**
7 × 4 = **28**	10 × 1 = **10**

3	8	6	4	9	2	10	7	5	9	8
×4	×9	×8	×6	×7	×7	×4	×6	×8	×9	×8
12	**72**	**48**	**24**	**63**	**14**	**40**	**42**	**40**	**81**	**64**

The last number in a row **is a square number.**
Number of cells in row 7 is **7**; 8 is **8**; 5 is **5**; 10 is **10**.

In conclusion. Tell her to say the facts for the square numbers: [1 × 1 = 1, 2 × 2 = 4, . . . , 10 × 10 = 100]

EXPLANATIONS:

The short multiplication table is shown in the first printed arithmetic book, *Treviso Arithmetic*, printed in 1478.

Gather the cards that are face down into one pile and the face-up cards into another pile. Then combine the two piles so that all the cards are face up. There is no need to put the cards in the envelopes as the next games need all the cards.

No counting is necessary because the cells are grouped by fives.

© Activities for Learning, Inc. 2015

Lesson 33: Using the Short Multiplication Table

OBJECTIVES:
1. To practice the multiplication facts using the short multiplication table

MATERIALS:
1. Worksheet 19, Using the Short Multiplication Table
2. AL Abacus
3. Basic number cards and multiplication cards
4. Centimeter cubes for markers

ACTIVITIES FOR TEACHING:

Warm-up. Ask: When two numbers are added together, what do we call the answer? [sum] What do you call a subtraction answer? [difference] What do you call the answer when you multiply? [product]

Give the child the worksheet and abacus. Tell the child to just do the warm-up equations. Solutions are:

Sum of 8 and 7: **15**	Difference between 8 and 7: **1**	Product of 8 and 7: **56**
Sum of 9 and 6: **15**	Difference between 9 and 6: **3**	Product of 9 and 6: **54**
Sum of 7 and 4: **11**	Difference between 7 and 4: **3**	Product of 7 and 4: **28**

Worksheet 19. Tell the child to read the instructions on her worksheet and do Problems 1 and 2.

The solution for the short multiplication table is shown on the right.

Ask the child to explain her ideas for the 8 × 7 question on the worksheet. Some possible methods are the following.

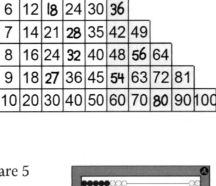

Since 8 × 5 = 40 and two more 8s are 16, 8 × 7 is 40 + 16 = 56.

On the abacus, there are 5 groups of 10 and 6 more, making 56.

7 × 10 is 70, so 7 × 8 must be 7 × 2 less: 70 − 14 = 56.

Using Shortcut Multiplying: tens are 50 and ones are 6. So 7 × 8 = 56.

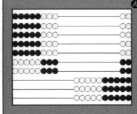

8 × 7 = 10 × 5 + 6 = 56
or 70 − 14 = 56.

Tell her to answer Question 3 and discuss solutions.

EXPLANATIONS:

See page ii, number 9 of "Some General Thoughts on Teaching Mathematics," for additional information.

Although it is not mathematical, there is another way to remember 8 × 7:
56 = 7 × 8 (5, 6, 7, 8).

Notice the similarity to
12 = 3 × 4 (1, 2, 3, 4).

ACTIVITIES FOR TEACHING:

Ring around the Factors game. Play the Ring around the Factors game. In the center, place six basic number cards face up, in two rows of three each. Around these cards, place 14 multiplication cards, also face up. Place the stocks nearby. See the figure below.

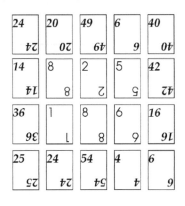

The first player checks the inside cards for pairs with a product that equals an outside card. The player removes the corresponding cards and stacks them on three piles face up. More than one group may be collected during a turn. In the figure above, the player can collect three facts: 6 × 1 = 6, 8 × 5 = 40, and 2 × 8 = 16. The player then places a centimeter cube in the matching cell of the short multiplication table on the worksheet. See the left figure below.

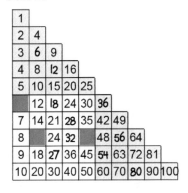

This table has four completed rows (the 1s and 4s) and columns (5s and 10s).

For the next turn, fill in the missing cards from the respective card stocks. Play continue until the basic number card stock is exhausted. If a player is unable to play, she loses her turn. The next player may replace either two basic number cards or up to three multiplication cards. He then takes his turn. The winner is the player with the most completed rows or columns on the short multiplication table. See the right figure above.

In conclusion. Ask: Do you prefer the short multiplication table or the whole multiplication table?

EXPLANATIONS:

This game is similar to Ring around the Products game, found in *Math Card Games* book, P32.

LESSON 34: FINDING MISSING FACTORS

OBJECTIVES:
1. To practice finding a missing factor in a multiplication equation

MATERIALS:
1. Worksheet 20, Finding Missing Factors
2. *Math Card Games* book, P29

ACTIVITIES FOR TEACHING:	EXPLANATIONS:
Warm-up. Ask: What is the sum of 9 and 5? [14] What is the difference of 9 and 5? [4] What is the product of 9 and 5? [45] What are the factors in the equation $9 \times 5 = 45$? [9 and 5] If necessary, remind the child that the number we multiply and the number we multiplied by are called factors. Ask: What is the sum of 8 and 7? [15] What is the difference of 8 and 7? [1] What is the product of 8 and 7? [56] What are the factors in the equation $8 \times 7 = 56$? [8 and 7]	
Worksheet 20. Give the child the worksheet. Tell the child that today she will use the short multiplication table to find a missing factor. Write: $\qquad 5 \times \underline{} = 15$ Ask: 5 times what is equal to 15? [3] Tell her to look at the short multiplication table on her worksheet. Ask: How can you find the other factor from using the table? [In the 5-row, notice that 15 is in the third column.] Is 5 times 3 equal to 15? [yes] Write: $\qquad 8 \times z = 56$ Ask: How can you find z? [In the 8-row, 56 is in the 7-column.] What is z? [7] Tell her to say the final equation. [8 times 7 equals 56] Write: $\qquad 7 \times y = 56$ Ask: How can you find y? [56 is not in the 7-row, so go to the end of the 7-row and down one. It is in the 8-column.] What is y? [8] What is the final equation? [7 times 8 = 56] Write: $\qquad 16 = \underline{} \times \underline{}$ Ask: Can you find more than one solution for this equation? [yes; $16 = 4 \times 4$, $16 = 8 \times 2$, $16 = 2 \times 8$]	See page ii, number 3 of "Some General Thoughts on Teaching Mathematics," for additional information.

RightStart™ Mathematics Level D Second Edition

© Activities for Learning, Inc. 2015

ACTIVITIES FOR TEACHING:	EXPLANATIONS:

Tell the child to complete the worksheet. The solutions are below.

$5 \times m = 25$ $\quad$ $8 \times i = 16$
$m = 5$ $\qquad$ $i = 2$

$s \times 9 = 90$ $\quad$ $s \times 6 = 54$
$s = 10$ $\qquad$ $s = 9$

$i \times 9 = 27$ $\quad$ $n \times 6 = 6$
$i = 3$ $\qquad$ $n = 1$

$4 \times g = 36$ $\quad$ $7 \times f = 28$
$g = 9$ $\qquad$ $f = 4$

$3 = 1 \times a$ $\quad$ $48 = 8 \times c$ $\quad$ $72 = t \times 9$ $\quad$ $49 = o \times 7$ $\quad$ $32 = r \times 8$ $\quad$ $35 = 7 \times s$
$a = 3$ $\qquad$ $c = 6$ $\qquad$ $t = 8$ $\qquad$ $o = 7$ $\qquad$ $r = 4$ $\qquad$ $s = 5$

$40 = 10 \times 4$ $\quad$ $24 = 8 \times 3$ $\quad$ $18 = 9 \times 2$ $\quad$ $36 = 6 \times 6$
$40 = 4 \times 10$ $\quad$ $24 = 3 \times 8$ $\quad$ $18 = 2 \times 9$ $\quad$ $36 = 9 \times 4$
$40 = 8 \times 5$ $\quad$ $24 = 6 \times 4$ $\quad$ $18 = 6 \times 3$ $\quad$ $36 = 4 \times 9$
$40 = 5 \times 8$ $\quad$ $24 = 4 \times 6$ $\quad$ $18 = 3 \times 6$

Find the Two Factors game. Play the Find the Two Factors game, found in *Math Card Games* book, P29.

In conclusion. Ask: 10 times what is 70? [7] 5 times what is 40? [8] 7 times what is 28? [4] What times 4 is 28? [7]

LESSON 35: DIVISION PROBLEMS

OBJECTIVES:
1. To introduce the division sign
2. To introduce the term *quotient*
3. To solve division problems
4. To solve division equations

MATERIALS:
1. Worksheet 21, Division Problems
2. AL Abacus
3. Short Multiplication Table, Appendix p. 1

ACTIVITIES FOR TEACHING:

Warm-up. Give the child the worksheet, abacus, and the short multiplication table. Tell her to do just the warm-up equations, using her abacus or short multiplication table if needed. Solutions are:

$32 = 8 \times 4$ $16 = 2 \times 8$ $7 \times 5 = 35$ $7 \times 2 \times 3 = 42$

$6 \times 3 = 18$ $7 \times 7 = 49$ $63 = 7 \times 9$ $4 \times 4 \times 2 = 32$

Worksheet 21. These problems are to be solved during the lesson.

Problem 1. Tell the child to read the first problem:

Oranges are packed with six in a bag. How many bags are needed for 48 oranges? [8 bags]

Demonstrate dividing on the abacus as follows: Enter 48, the number of oranges as shown below in the left figure. Since we need 6 in a bag, slide the amounts over 6 a short

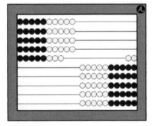

48 oranges.

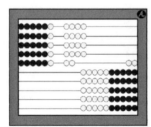

Forming groups of 6.

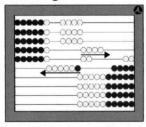

Using Take and Give.

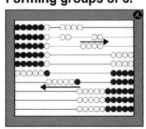

Using Take and Give.

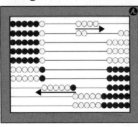

Using Take and Give.

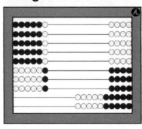

8 bags needed.

EXPLANATIONS:

Give the child a copy of the short multiplication table for her personal use. The table will not become a "crutch," but will help the child see relationships in multiplication and division, similar to a dictionary.

Some children will see the answer immediately after forming the groups and will not need to use the Take and Give procedure.

There are a variety of ways to use Take and Give to get the quotient.

ACTIVITIES FOR TEACHING:	EXPLANATIONS:

ways away as shown on the previous page on the right.

Then use Take and Give to find the solution of 8 bags. See the remaining figures on the previous page.

Ask the child to write an equation to show the problem.

$$6 \times b = 48$$
$$b = 8$$

Say: There is another way to write the equation. Since we are dividing the 48 oranges into groups of sixes, we can write:

$$48 \div 6 = b$$
$$b = 8$$

Division terms. Explain that the symbol, ÷, is called the *division sign* and it means *divided by*. Tell her there are other division symbols that will be discussed later.

Tell her the answer in division is called the *quotient*. Write the word for her.

Problem 2. Tell the child to read Problem 2:

Thirty-five tiles are in the shape of a rectangle. There are seven in a row. How many rows are there? [5]

Tell her to solve it independently then discuss it. The equations are:

$$7 \times r = 35$$
$$r = 5$$
$$35 \div 7 = r$$
$$r = 5$$

The missing factor equation can also be written as:
$$35 = 7 \times r$$
$$r = 5$$

Problem 3. Tell the child to read Problem 3:

There are 9 activity centers for 27 children. Each center has the same number of children. How many children will be at each center?

Tell her to solve it independently then discuss it. The equations are as follows:

$$n \times 9 = 27$$
$$n = 3$$
$$27 \div 9 = n$$
$$n = 3$$

The first two problems gave the size of a group and asked for the number of groups. This problem asks for the size of a group.

Tell her to finish the worksheet. The solutions are:

$40 \div 8 = \mathbf{5}$	$45 \div 9 = \mathbf{5}$	$16 \div 8 = \mathbf{2}$	$8 \div 8 = \mathbf{1}$
$40 \div 10 = \mathbf{4}$	$45 \div 5 = \mathbf{9}$	$16 \div 4 = \mathbf{4}$	$8 \div 1 = \mathbf{8}$
$40 \div 4 = \mathbf{10}$	$49 \div 7 = \mathbf{7}$	$16 \div 2 = \mathbf{8}$	$8 \div 2 = \mathbf{4}$

In conclusion. Ask: What is opposite of addition? [subtraction] What is opposite of subtraction? [addition] What is opposite of multiplication? [division] What is opposite of division? [multiplication]

If there is additional time following this lesson, play the Ring Around the Factors game from Lesson 33.

© Activities for Learning, Inc. 2015

LESSON 36: INTRODUCING PARENTHESES

OBJECTIVES:
1. To introduce parentheses for grouping
2. To introduce the order of operation

MATERIALS:
1. Worksheet 22, Introducing Parentheses
2. AL Abacus
3. Short Multiplication Table, Appendix p. 1

ACTIVITIES FOR TEACHING:

Warm-up. Give the child the worksheet and abacus. Tell the child to get her short multiplication table. Tell her to do just the warm-up equations. Solutions are:

8 + 7 = **15**	15 = **7 + 8**	15 − 8 = **7**	15 − 7 = **8**
8 × 7 = **56**	56 ÷ 8 = **7**	56 ÷ 7 = **8**	7 × 4 × 2 = **56**

Ask: Which operation calls the answer a sum? [addition] Which operation calls the answer a difference? [subtraction] Which operation calls the answer a product? [multiplication] Which operation calls the answer a quotient? [division]

Worksheet 22. These problems are to be solved during the lesson.

Problem 1. Tell the child to read the first problem:

> Madison is buying balloons for a party. Each package has 4 red balloons and 3 blue balloons. She buys 2 packages. How many balloons does she get? [14]

Tell her to read the story twice and solve it. The child might write the following equations:

$$4 \times 2 + 3 \times 2 = b$$
$$b = 14 \text{ balloons}$$

Parentheses. Say: There is a pair of mathematical symbols that show grouping. They look somewhat like our hands and are called *parentheses*. See the figure on the right.

Say: We can think of adding the balloons together and then multiplying by 2. The equation looks like this:

$$(4 + 3) \times 2 = 14 \text{ balloons}$$

Tell her to do what is inside the parentheses first.

Ask: How could you show that on the abacus? One way is shown on the right.

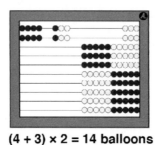

(4 + 3) × 2 = 14 balloons

EXPLANATIONS:

The short multiplication table will help the child see relationships in multiplication and division, similar to a dictionary, and will not become a "crutch."

See page ii, number 12 of "Some General Thoughts on Teaching Mathematics," for additional information.

The singular form is *parenthesis*; the plural form is *parentheses*.

RightStart™ Mathematics Level D Second Edition © Activities for Learning, Inc. 2015

ACTIVITIES FOR TEACHING:	EXPLANATIONS:

Problem 2. Tell her to read the second problem:

> The Yang family drove 44 miles north to their cousins' house. Then they drove 38 miles farther north to the lake. How many miles did they drive before reaching home?

Tell her to solve it independently then discuss it. The equation is follows:

$$(44 + 38) \times 2 = m$$
$$m = 164 \text{ miles}$$

Ask for another way to write the equation:

$$44 \times 2 + 38 \times 2 = m$$

Say: When an equation has more than one operation, multiplication and division must be done first before addition and subtraction. Write:

$$y = 2 + 3 \times 4$$

and ask: What is y? [14] Explain: It is wrong to add $2 + 3 = 5$ and $5 \times 4 = 20$. First do $3 \times 4 = 12$ and then $12 + 2 = 14$.

Ask: Is it correct to write the first equation as:

$$44 + 38 \times 2 = m$$

[No, the answer would be $38 \times 2 = 76$ and $76 + 44 = 120$]

Problem 3. Tell her to read the third problem:

> The Hansen family drove 56 kilometers to a camp. While at the camp they drove 17 kilometers. How far did they drive when they arrived home? [129 kilometers]

A kilometer is a little more than half the distance of a mile.

Although many people pronounce *kilometer* with the accent on the second syllable, to be consistent with other metric lengths, (centimeter and millimeter) *kilometer* should be pronounced KIL-o-me-ter.

Tell her to solve the problem as before. The equation is:

$$56 \times 2 + 17 = k$$
$$k = 129 \text{ kilometers}$$

Write and ask: Is this equation correct? [yes]

$$56 + 17 + 56 = k$$

On the other hand, measuring tools, such as odometer, thermometer, speedometer, and goniometer have their accents on the third to the last syllable, for example, o-DOM-e-ter.

Practice. Write: $4 + 6 \times 3 = \underline{\quad}$

and ask the child how she could solve it. [Multiply 6 by 3 and then add 4 to get 22.] Repeat for:

$$(4 + 6) \times 3 = \underline{\quad} \quad [4 + 6 = 10 \text{ and } 10 \times 3 = 30]$$

Tell her to finish the worksheet. The solutions are:

$(3 + 7) \times 4 = \mathbf{40}$	$3 \times (4 + 1) = \mathbf{15}$	$(24 \div 8) - 2 = \mathbf{1}$
$3 + 7 \times 4 = \mathbf{31}$	$(45 \div 5) - 9 = \mathbf{0}$	$(7 \times 5) + (7 \times 2) = \mathbf{49}$
$(40 \div 4) + 9 = \mathbf{19}$	$8 + 2 \times 5 = \mathbf{18}$	$(8 + 2) \times 5 = \mathbf{50}$

In conclusion. Ask: What are symbols that group numbers called? [parentheses] If an equation has addition and multiplication, what do you do first? [multiplication]

If there is additional time following this lesson, play the Corners™ game, found in *Math Card Games* book, A9.

© Activities for Learning, Inc. 2015

LESSON 37: ASSESSMENT REVIEW 1

OBJECTIVES:
1. To review concepts learned in previous lessons

MATERIALS:
1. Worksheet 23, Assessment Review 1
2. AL Abacus, if needed

ACTIVITIES FOR TEACHING:

Worksheet 23. Give the child the worksheet. Tell her that today will be a review for the upcoming assessment. She will complete the two-page worksheet, then discuss the solutions.

Tell the child to listen to the problems and write the answers. Read each problem twice.

$109 - 10$ $\qquad$ 9×6 $\qquad$ $42 \div 6$

Tell her to complete the worksheet. Solutions are below and on the next page.

EXPLANATIONS:

This lesson is a review of concepts learned so far. It is designed to prepare the child for the upcoming assessment lesson.

The child may use the abacus where needed.

1-3. Write only the answers.

  99
  54
  7

4-9. Write the answers.

$75 + 25 = 100$ $70 - 58 = 12$

$47 + 58 = 105$ $82 - 49 = 33$

$37 + 63 = 100$ $100 - 57 = 43$

10-11. Find the sums.

$$4678 + 2712$$

  4678
$+ 2712$
  7390

$$3367 + 678$$

  3367
$+ 678$
  4045

12-13. Find the differences.

$$8054 - 2731$$

  8054
$- 2731$
  5323

$$6731 - 2856$$

  6731
$- 2856$
  3875

14-23. Fill in the blanks.

$4 + 1 = 5$ $4 - 1 = 3$ $4 \times 1 = 4$ $4 \div 1 = 4$ $4 + 1 - 1 = 4$

$8 \times 8 = 64$ $9 \times 7 = 63$ $7 \times 9 = 63$ $64 \div 8 = 8$ $7 \times 9 = 63$

24. Fill in the missing numbers in the short multiplication table.

1									
2	4								
3	6	9							
4	8	12	16						
5	10	15	20	25					
6	12	18	24	30	36				
7	14	21	28	35	42	49			
8	16	24	32	40	48	56	64		
9	18	27	36	45	54	63	72	81	
10	20	30	40	50	60	70	80	90	100

25-28. Write four different equations using factors between 1 and 9.

$12 = 2 \times 6$

$12 = 6 \times 2$

$12 = 3 \times 4$

$12 = 4 \times 3$

29. Circle the even numbers that are greater than 50.

RightStart™ Mathematics Level D Second Edition

© Activities for Learning, Inc. 2015

ACTIVITIES FOR TEACHING:

EXPLANATIONS:

30-38. Complete the equations.

$8 \times \underline{5} = 40$

$6 \times \underline{7} = 42$

$56 \div 8 = \underline{7}$

$4 \times 5 \times \underline{2} = 40$

$6 \times 10 + 17 = \underline{77}$

$\underline{0} = 2 \times 0 \times 8$

$1 + 4 \times 9 = \underline{37}$

$(9 \times 9) + (1 \times 9) = \underline{90}$

$(9 + 1) \times (1 + 9) = \underline{100}$

39-47. Write <, >, or = in the blank.

$8 \times 0 \underline{<} 8 + 0$

$16 \times 8 \underline{=} 16 \times (4 + 4)$

$56 \div 8 \underline{<} 56 \div 7$

$4 \times 5 \times 2 \underline{=} 40$

$5 \times 10 \times 6 \underline{<} 6 \times 10 \times 6$

$78 + 29 \underline{>} 100$

$2 \times 0 \times 8 \underline{=} 0$

$(9 \times 6) + (9 \times 3) \underline{=} 9 \times 9$

$234 + 82 - 234 \underline{<} 90$

48-50. Solve the problems.

Alaina made a square with five tiles in a row. Luke made a rectangle with six rows with each row having four tiles. Whose rectangle had more tiles? How many more?

Alaina's square takes 5×5 tiles = 25.
Luke's is $6 \times 4 = 24$.
Alaina has 1 more tile.

Rebecca's family drove 379 miles on the first day of a trip. They drove 259 miles on the second day and 87 miles on the third day. How long was the trip?

$T = 379 + 259 + 87$
$T = 725$ miles

The width of a rectangular garden is 16 ft. The length of the garden is double the width. What is the perimeter of the garden?

16

32

$P = (32 + 16) \times 2$
$P = 96$ ft

Worksheet solutions. Check the answers to the review worksheet with the child. Discuss the various methods for the solutions.

The next day will be a day of games. Games review and practice facts and skills in an enjoyable environment.

© Activities for Learning, Inc. 2015

Lesson 38: Review Games

OBJECTIVES:
1. To review recent topics by playing math card games

MATERIALS:
1. *Math Card Games* book, A46, S9, and P29
2. AL Abacus, if needed
3. Math journal
4. Short Multiplication Table, Appendix p. 1

ACTIVITIES FOR TEACHING:	EXPLANATIONS:
Warm-up. Ask: Which operation calls the answer a sum? [addition] Which operation calls the answer a difference? [subtraction] Which operation calls the answer a product? [multiplication] Which operation calls the answer a quotient? [division]	This lesson is a review of concepts learned so far by playing games. It is designed to prepare the child for the assessment in the next lesson.
Ask: What is the sum of 8 and 5? [13] What is the difference of 8 and 5? [3] What is the product of 8 and 5? [40]	
Addition War with Three Cards game. Play the Addition War with Three Cards game found in the *Math Card Games* book, A46. This variation of Addition War requires the players to find the sum of three cards for each hand.	The child may use the abacus if needed.
Zero Corners™ game. Ask: What is 25 – 5? [20] What is 105 – 5? [100] What is 70 – 5? [65] What is 130 – 5? [125] What is 190 – 10? [180] What is 25 – 10? [15] What is 175 – 10? [165] What is 105 – 10? [95]	
Ask: What is 25 – 15? [10] If needed, remind the child to first subtract the 10 and then the 5. Ask: What is 45 – 15? [30] What is 195 – 15? [180] What is 40 – 15? [25] What is 90 – 15? [75] What is 170 – 15? [155]	
Give the child the math journal and play the Zero Corners™ game found in the *Math Card Games* book, S9. This Corners™ game differs in the method of scoring. Players work their way toward zero by subtracting their points from a starting score of 500. All subtraction is to be done mentally as shown on the right. Tell the child to use the abacus when necessary.	

500
485
475
455
450
435

ACTIVITIES FOR TEACHING:	EXPLANATIONS:

Find the Two Factors game. Ask: What is 6 × 6? [36] What is 7 × 5? [35] 5 × 7? [35]

Ask: What is 7 × 7? [49] What is 8 × 6? [48] 6 × 8? [48]

Ask: What is 8 × 8? [64] What is 7 × 9? [63] 9 × 7? [63]

Ask: What is 9 × 9? [81] What is 8 × 10? [80] 10 × 8? [80]

Play the Find the Two Factors game found in the *Math Card Games* book, P29.

In conclusion. Ask: What is opposite of addition? [subtraction] What is opposite of subtraction? [addition] What is opposite of multiplication? [division] What is opposite of division? [multiplication]

© Activities for Learning, Inc. 2015

78

LESSON 39: ASSESSMENT 1

OBJECTIVES:

1. To assess concepts learned in previous lessons

MATERIALS:

1. Worksheet 24, Assessment 1

ACTIVITIES FOR TEACHING:	EXPLANATIONS:

Worksheet 24. Give the child the worksheet.

Tell her to listen to the problems and write the answers. Read each problem twice.

$$107 - 10 \qquad 9 \times 8 \qquad 45 \div 9$$

Tell her to complete the worksheet. Solutions are below and on the next page.

The child may use the abacus where needed.

1-3. Write only the answers.

<u> 97 </u>

<u> 72 </u>

<u> 5 </u>

4-9. Write the answers.

$65 + 35 = \underline{100}$ $63 - 29 = \underline{34}$

$38 + 47 = \underline{85}$ $25 - 17 = \underline{8}$

$53 + \underline{47} = 100$ $100 - \underline{62} = 38$

10-11. Find the sums.

3768 + 4839	8356 + 839

$$3768 \ (6)$$
$$+ \ 4839 \ (6)$$
$$8607 \ (3)$$

$$8356 \ (4)$$
$$+ \ 839 \ (2)$$
$$9195 \ (6)$$

12-13. Find the differences.

4828 – 3795	9124 – 4680

$$4828 \ (4)$$
$$- \ 3795 \ (6)$$
$$1033 \ (7)$$

$$9124 \ (7)$$
$$- \ 4680 \ (0)$$
$$4444 \ (7)$$

14-23. Fill in the blanks.

$5 + 1 = \underline{6}$ $5 - 1 = \underline{4}$ $5 \times 1 = \underline{5}$ $5 \div 5 = \underline{1}$ $5 - 1 \times 1 = \underline{4}$

$9 \times 9 = \underline{81}$ $7 \times 9 = \underline{63}$ $9 \times 7 = \underline{63}$ $81 \div \underline{9} = 9$ $\underline{9} \times 7 = 63$

24. Fill in the missing numbers in the short multiplication table.

①									
2	4								
③	6	⑨							
4	8	12	16						
⑤	10	⑮	20	㉕					
6	12	18	24	30	36				
⑦	14	㉑	28	35	42	49			
8	16	24	32	40	48	56	64		
⑨	18	27	36	45	54	63	72	81	
10	20	30	40	50	60	70	80	90	100

25-28. Write four different equations using factors between 1 and 9.

$24 = \underline{3} \times \underline{8}$

$24 = \underline{8} \times \underline{3}$

$24 = \underline{6} \times \underline{4}$

$24 = \underline{4} \times \underline{6}$

29. Circle the odd numbers that are less than 26.

RightStart™ Mathematics Level D Second Edition

© Activities for Learning, Inc. 2015

ACTIVITIES FOR TEACHING:

EXPLANATIONS:

30-38. Complete the equations.

$9 \times \underline{4} = 36$

$5 \times \underline{9} = 45$

$54 \div 9 = \underline{6}$

$6 \times 5 \times \underline{2} = 60$

$5 \times 10 + 16 = \underline{66}$

$\underline{0} = 4 \times 0 \times 7$

$1 + 3 \times 8 = \underline{25}$

$(8 + 2) \times (2 + 8) = \underline{100}$

$4 \times 7 + 12 = \underline{40}$

39-47. Write <, >, or = in the blank.

$0 \times 7 \underline{<} 0 + 7$

$12 \times 9 \underline{=} 12 \times (5 + 4)$

$35 \div 5 \underline{>} 35 \div 7$

$5 \times 8 \times 2 \underline{=} 80$

$4 \times 9 \times 6 \underline{>} 3 \times 6 \times 9$

$57 \times 2 \underline{>} 100$

$49 \times 38 \times 0 \underline{=} 0$

$(8 \times 4) + (8 \times 6) \underline{=} 8 \times 10$

$17 + 82 - 17 \underline{<} 117$

48-50. Solve the problems.

Aspen walked seven blocks every day for a week. Maren walked eight blocks for six days. Who walked the farther? How much farther?

Aspen: $7 \times 7 = 49$ blocks

Maren: $8 \times 6 = 48$ blocks

Aspen walked 1 more block.

A farmer planted 95 acres on Monday. She planted 256 acres on Tuesday and 479 acres on Wednesday. How many acres did she plant?

$F = 95 + 256 + 479$

$F = 830$ acres

The perimeter of a rectangular garden is 64 ft. One side is 18 ft. How long is the other side?

18

$64 = (s + 18) \times 2$

$s = 14$ ft

© Activities for Learning, Inc. 2015

Lesson 40: Multiplying on the Math Balance

OBJECTIVES:
1. To multiply on the math balance
2. To write equations represented on the math balance

MATERIALS:
1. Worksheet 25, Multiplying on the Math Balance
2. AL Abacus, if needed
3. Short Multiplication Table, Appendix p. 1
4. Math balance
5. Dry erase board

ACTIVITIES FOR TEACHING:	EXPLANATIONS:

Warm-up. Give the child the worksheet. Tell her to do just the warm-up equations and to use her abacus or short multiplication table where needed. Solutions are:

$(24 \div 6) - 2 = \mathbf{2}$ $9 + 8 \times 4 = \mathbf{41}$ $(45 \div 9) + 7 = \mathbf{12}$
$8 \times 5 + 2 \times 8 = \mathbf{56}$ $6 + 2 \times 5 = \mathbf{16}$ $(6 + 2) \times 5 = \mathbf{40}$

Reviewing the math balance. Give the child a dry erase board and the math balance.

Tell her to put a weight on the left 10 and use two weights to find several ways to make the beam balance. Tell her to end with two weights on the same peg. See below.

Tell her to write the addition equation on her board:

$10 = 5 + 5$

Now tell her to write it as a multiplication equation:

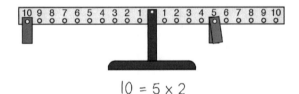

$10 = 5 \times 2$

Multiplying on the math balance. Tell the child to put one more weight on the right 5. Ask: How can you make it balance with another weight? [put the weight on the left 5] See below.

Tell her to write the new multiplication equation:

$15 = 5 \times 3$

If the child has not used the math balance before, give her some time to explore.

See page ii, number 6 of "Some General Thoughts on Teaching Mathematics," for additional information.

ACTIVITIES FOR TEACHING:	EXPLANATIONS:

Practice. Write: $7 + 4 \times 2 = 10 + \underline{}$

and ask her to solve it and then check it on her math balance. [5] Remind her, if necessary, to do the multiplying before the adding. See the figure below.

Worksheet 25. Tell the child to do the first problem on the worksheet then discuss it.

Tell her to complete the worksheet. The solutions are shown below.

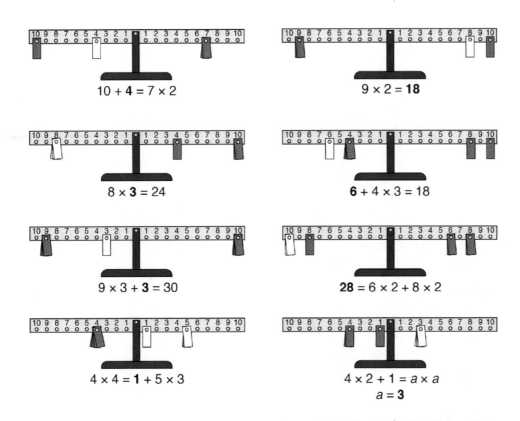

$10 + \mathbf{4} = 7 \times 2$

$9 \times 2 = \mathbf{18}$

$8 \times \mathbf{3} = 24$

$\mathbf{6} + 4 \times 3 = 18$

$9 \times 3 + \mathbf{3} = 30$

$28 = 6 \times 2 + 8 \times 2$

$4 \times 4 = \mathbf{1} + 5 \times 3$

$4 \times 2 + 1 = a \times a$
$a = \mathbf{3}$

In conclusion. Ask: What symbol means to put quantities together? [plus sign] What symbol means to separate quantities? [minus sign] What symbol means to put quantities together in groups? [multiplication sign] What symbol means two quantities are the same? [equal sign]

If there is additional time following this lesson, play the Lowest in the Corners game, found in *Math Card Games* book, P18.

Lesson 41: Distributive Property on the Math Balance

OBJECTIVES:
1. To review the commutative and associative properties
2. To introduce the distributive property
3. To solve equations with several operations

MATERIALS:
1. Dry erase board
2. Math balance
3. Worksheet 26, Distributive Property on the Math Balance

ACTIVITIES FOR TEACHING:

Warm-up. Ask: What symbol means to put quantities together? [plus sign] What symbol means to separate quantities? [minus sign] What symbol means to put quantities together in groups? [multiplication sign] What symbol means two quantities are the same? [equal sign]

Ask: What are the symbols that group numbers called? [parentheses] If an equation has addition and multiplication and no parentheses, what do you do first? [multiplication]

Multiplying on the math balance. Give the child a dry erase board and the math balance. Write:

$$6 + 4 = 10$$

and tell her to show it on her math balance. See the figure below.

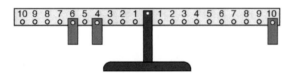

Next tell her to multiply each number in the equation by 3 and to write the equation on her board.

$$6 \times 3 + 4 \times 3 = 10 \times 3$$

Ask: Would it balance if you multiplied each number by 4 instead of 3? [yes] How about multiplying by 100? [yes]

Write: $(3 + 5) \times 4 = 3 \times 4 + \underline{} \times 4$ [5]

and tell her to show it on the math balance. Remind her to do the adding in the parentheses first.

EXPLANATIONS:

Parentheses are optional in this example.

ACTIVITIES FOR TEACHING:	EXPLANATIONS:

Properties of multiplication. Write:

$$8 \times 7 = 7 \times 8$$

and ask: Is this true? [yes] Say: It is true in multiplication that we can change the numbers around without changing the answer. This is the *commutative property*.

Write: $(2 \times 4) \times 5 = (5 \times 2) \times 4$

and ask: Is this true? [yes] Say: It is true in multiplication that we can group the numbers any way we like. This is called the *associative property*.

Write: $(4 + 2) \times 5 = (4 \times 5) + (2 \times 5)$

and ask: Is this true? [yes] Say: It is true that when we add two numbers and then multiply, that we can multiply each number and then add. This is called the *distributive property*.

Write: $(4 - 2) \times 5 = (4 \times 5) - (2 \times 5)$

and ask: Does the distributive property work for subtraction and multiplication? [yes] Say: The distributive property works for numbers being added or subtracted and then multiplied.

Worksheet 26. Give the child the worksheet and tell her to complete it. The solutions are:

7 × 4 = 28   25 = 1 + 8 × 3

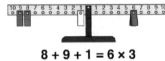 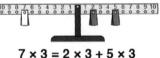

8 + 9 + 1 = 6 × 3   7 × 3 = 2 × 3 + 5 × 3

 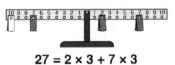

9 × 2 + 7 × 2 = 32   27 = 2 × 3 + 7 × 3

(3 + 7) × **6** = 60   6 × 4 + 6 × 6 = **60**   (**16** ÷ 8) + 2 = 4
3 + (12 ÷ 4) = **6**   (15 − 5) × 9 = **90**   8 × 3 + 8 × 7 = **80**
(**50** ÷ 5) + 7 = 17   9 + 7 × 9 = **72**   (1 + 8) × **7** = 63

In conclusion. Ask: Does 67 + 29 = 29 + 67? [yes] Say: The commutative property works for addition. Ask: Does 7 × 9 = 9 × 7? [yes] Say: The commutative property works for multiplication. Ask: Does 9 − 7 = 7 − 9? [no] Say: The commutative property does not work for subtraction.

Commutative property was discussed in Lesson 18.

Associative property was discussed in Lesson 24.

Although it is helpful for the child to know these names, it is not necessary to specifically identify each property. The concepts are essential to understand.

If there is additional time following this lesson, play the Lowest in the Corners game, found in *Math Card Games* book, P18.

© Activities for Learning, Inc. 2015

84

LESSON 42: ORDER OF OPERATIONS WITH A CALCULATOR

OBJECTIVES:

1. To follow the order of operations while using a calculator
2. To introduce the memory functions on a calculation

MATERIALS:

1. Worksheet 27, Order of Operations with a Calculator
2. Casio SL-450S calculator

ACTIVITIES FOR TEACHING:

Warm-up. Give the child the worksheet. Tell her to do just the warm-up equations. Solutions are:

6	12	18	24	**30**	36	42	48	**54**	60
7	14	**21**	28	35	42	49	**56**	**63**	70
8	16	24	**32**	40	**48**	**56**	64	72	80
9	18	27	36	45	54	**63**	**72**	81	90

Order of operations. Write:

$$n = 2 + (3 \times 4)$$
$$m = 2 + 3 \times 4$$

If necessary, remind her that what is inside the parentheses is done first, then multiplication is done before addition. Ask: What is n and m? [14]

Give the child the calculator and tell her to try it on the calculator. Ask: What answer do you get when you add 2 + 3 and then multiply by 4? [20] What happens when you multiply 3 by 4 and then add 2? [14] Say: These basic calculators do not follow the rules for order of operations. More expensive calculators, such as scientific calculators, will give the right answer because they will multiply first and then add.

Write: $8 + 7 \times 5 = $ [43]

Tell her to use her calculator to find the answer.

Calculator memory. Change the problem to:

$$8 \times 8 + 7 \times 5 = $$

and ask her how she could do it. Let her think for a few minutes. Say: To solve this equation on your calculator without writing down numbers, you need to use calculator memory.

Tell her: If you see an *M* in the upper left corner, press (MRC) (MRC) to clear memory. Then press (8) (×) (8) (M+). The *M* will show. It is not necessary to press the (=) key. Continue with 7 × 5: press (7) (×) (5) (M+). To get the answer to the equation, press (MRC), which will show 99.

EXPLANATIONS:

See page iii, numbers 13 and 16 of "Some General Thoughts on Teaching Mathematics," for additional information.

Calculator basics: Tell the child to turn the calculator on by pressing the (AC) key. Tell her to use it to add 36 + 85, [121] then subtract 85, [36] then multiply by 2. [72]

Scientific calculators will give the correct answer for 2 + 3 × 4 when adding 2 + 3 first and then multiplying by 4. They are programmed to follow the order of operations when the equal sign is pressed; whereas, basic calculators usually are not.

Encourage the child to learn about the calculator intuitively.

Intuition is a method of learning that is becoming increasingly more important in our technological world. To learn intuitively is to try new procedures by combining common sense with a willingness to take a risk. It implies the hope that what is learned is worth the inevitable frustration.

RightStart™ Mathematics Level D Second Edition

© Activities for Learning, Inc. 2015

ACTIVITIES FOR TEACHING:	EXPLANATIONS:

Repeat for: $6 \times 9 + 5 \times 8 = [94]$

Ask: What does the (M+) key do? [adds to memory] What do you think the (M−) key does? [subtracts from memory]

Change the problem to:

$6 \times 9 - 5 \times 8 = [14]$

and ask: How can you do it now? [Use the (M−) key instead of the (M+) key to subtract the second expression.]

Allow the child to explore and develop her intuitive learning. Encourage her to try various processes, to risk frustration, then to continue to success.

Worksheet 27. Tell the child to do the first three problems in the first column on her worksheet then discuss it.

$6 + 17 \times 8 = \textbf{142}$

$34 \times 8 + 52 \times 4 = \textbf{480}$

$34 \times 78 - 773 \times 3 = \textbf{333}$

Continue with the next three:

$(17 + 35) \times 8 = \textbf{416}$

$7 \times 6 + 7 \times 3 + 7 \times 11 = \textbf{140}$

$7 \times (6 + 3 + 11) = \textbf{140}$

Ask: Why do the last two have the same answer? [the distributive property]

Tell her to look at the last four equations in that column and ask: How are they different? [only the parentheses] Do you think the answers are the same? Tell her to find the answers.

$(3 + 5) \times (4 + 7) = \textbf{88}$

$3 + 5 \times (4 + 7) = \textbf{58}$

$3 + 5 \times 4 + 7 = \textbf{30}$

$(3 + 5) \times 4 + 7 = \textbf{39}$

Tell her to complete the worksheet. The remaining solutions are:

182
80
144
144
1701
2520
1660
2458
$10 + 7 \times 4 + 12 \times 3 = \textbf{\$74}$
$5 \times 20 + 2 \times 30 = \textbf{160}$

If there is additional time following this lesson, play the Square Memory game, found in *Math Card Games* book, P21.

In conclusion. Ask: What feature of a calculator remembers numbers while you are calculating other numbers? [memory] What key do you press to add to memory? [(M+)] What key do you press to subtract from memory? [(M−)] What key do you press to clear memory? [(MRC) (MRC)]

© Activities for Learning, Inc. 2015

LESSON 43: REVIEWING PLACE VALUE WITH A CALCULATOR

OBJECTIVES:
1. To review place value
2. To practice facts using a calculator

MATERIALS:
1. Worksheet 28, Reviewing Place Value with a Calculator
2. Casio SL-450S calculator

ACTIVITIES FOR TEACHING:

EXPLANATIONS:

Warm-up. Ask: What feature of a calculator remembers numbers while you are calculating other numbers? [memory] What key do you press to add to memory? [M+] What key do you press to subtract from memory? [M−] What do you press to clear memory? [MRC MRC]

Give the child the worksheet. Tell her to do just the warm-up equations. Solutions are:

6	12	18	**24**	30	36	**42**	48	54	60
7	**14**	21	28	35	**42**	**49**	56	63	70
8	16	**24**	32	40	**48**	56	64	**72**	80
9	18	27	**36**	45	54	63	72	81	90

Reviewing place value. Write:

> 36
> 368
> 3682

Ask: What do we call the 3 in 36, thousands, ones, or what? [tens] How do you know? [One digit after the 3 tells us that it is a ten.] Point to 368 and ask: What is the 3 in this number? [hundred] How do you know? [Two digits after a number means it is hundred.] Point to 3682 and ask: What is the 3 in this number? [thousand] How do you know? [Three digits after a number means it is thousand.]

Partitioning numbers. Draw two part-whole sets with three parts as shown below. Write 123 in a whole-circle. Ask: How many hundreds are in 123? [1] How many tens? [2] How many ones? [3] Write it as shown in the left figure below.

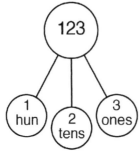
Partitioning 123.

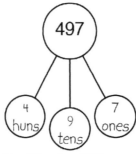
Partitioning 497.

ACTIVITIES FOR TEACHING:	EXPLANATIONS:

Repeat for 497 in the second part-whole set. Ask the child to write numbers in the parts-circles. See the right figure on the previous page.

Erase the 123 in the first whole-circle and change the numbers in the part-circles to 6 ones, 2 huns, and 4 tens, as shown below. Tell the child that the numbers are mixed up. Ask: What is the number? [246] Write 246 in the whole-circle.

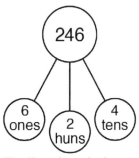

Finding the whole.

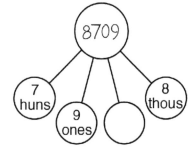

Finding the whole.

Erase the 497 in the second whole-circle and add a fourth part-circle. Write 7 huns, 9 ones, and 8 thous in the parts-circles, leaving one part-circle blank as shown above. Ask: What is the number? [8709] Ask the child to write the number in the whole-circle.

Leaving a blank part-circle indicates that there are no tens in the number 8709; therefore, is it not necessary to write 0 tens in the part-circle.

Place value on the calculator. Give the child the calculator. Ask her to enter 588 on her calculator and then change the result to 888 without clearing with the (AC) button. [add 300]

Tell the child to clear. Say: Enter 5642 and change to 5648. [add 6] Clear, enter 946, and change to 906. [subtract 40]

Worksheet 28. Tell the child to complete the worksheet. The solutions are:

532	subtract 4
3422	subtract 600
3654	add 90
2005	add 300
345	subtract 3000
3240	add 99
3324	add 440
3502	
2023	

In conclusion. Ask: How many digits do you need after the 7 to write 700? [2] How many digits do you need after the 7 to write 70? [1] How many digits do you need after the 7 to write 7? [0]

If there is additional time following this lesson, play the Find the Factors game, found in *Math Card Games* book, P29.

© Activities for Learning, Inc. 2015

Lesson 44: Estimating by Rounding to Tens

OBJECTIVES:
1. To introduce estimating
2. To learn the term *rounding*
3. To learn rounding to the nearest 10

MATERIALS:
1. Place-value cards, tens only
2. AL Abacus
3. *Math Card Games* book, N46

ACTIVITIES FOR TEACHING:	EXPLANATIONS:
Warm-up. Ask: What are symbols that group numbers called? [parentheses] If an equation has addition and multiplication without parentheses, what do you do first? [multiplication]	

Ask: 27 and what equals 30? [3] What is 30 – 3? [27] 46 and what equals 50? [4] What is 50 – 46? [4] 94 and what equal 100? [6] 94 and what equal 110? [16] What is 120 – 94? [26]

Estimating. Say: You might have heard someone say, "Dinner will be ready in about 10 minutes." Ask: Does that mean dinner will be ready in exactly 10 minutes, or could it be in 8 or 9 minutes, or maybe 11 or 12 minutes? Say: Today you will learn about estimating, when numbers are not exact. One way to estimate is called *rounding*.

Rounding to tens. Give the child the place-value cards and the abacus. Tell the child to lay out the tens from her place-value cards. Say: Enter 32 on your abacus. See the left figure below. Ask: Which place-value card, 30 or 40, is closest to 32? [30]

Tell her to change 32 to 30 on her abacus. See the right figure below. Say: You have just *rounded* 32 to the nearest 10.

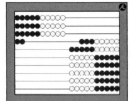  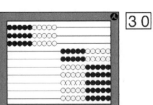

ACTIVITIES FOR TEACHING:	EXPLANATIONS:

Say: Now enter 59 on your abacus. See the left figure below. Ask: Which place-value card is closest to 59? [60] Tell her to change her abacus to show the nearest 10. See the right figure below. Say: This time you rounded 59 to the nearest 10.

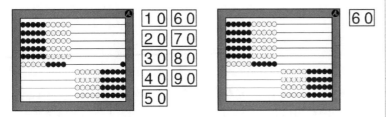

Repeat for 87 [90] and 14. [10] Ask: How would you round 25? Tell her: It is in the middle and could go either way, but most of the time people round it up, to 30.

Practice. Write the following and ask the the child to show the rounded number with the place-value cards:

   23 [20]   77 [80]   18 [20]   64 [60]   45 [50]

Rounding War game. Play the Rounding War game found in the *Math Card Games* book, N46.

In conclusion. Ask: If 80 represents a number that has been rounded, what could the original number have been? [75, 76, 77, 78, 79, 80, 81, 82, 83, or 84]

90

LESSON 45: MORE ROUNDING

OBJECTIVES:
1. To round to the nearest 100 and 1000

MATERIALS:
1. Worksheet 29, More Rounding
2. Place-value cards

ACTIVITIES FOR TEACHING:

Warm-up. Give the child the worksheet. Tell her to do just the warm-up section. She is to read the instructions and fill in the missing blanks. Remind her to check her work when she is done. Solution is shown on the right.

3	5	1	9
6	2	4	12
3	8	5	16
12	15	10	37

Ask: If 70 represents a number that has been rounded, what could the original number have been? [65, 66, 67, 68, 69, 70, 71, 72, 73, or 74]

Rounding to tens. Give the child the place-value cards and tell her to spread out the ones, tens, and hundreds.

Tell her to compose 73 with her place-value cards. Then tell her to round the number to the nearest 10. See the left figure below.

7|3 → 7 0   2|7|3 → 2|7 0
Rounding to tens.   **Rounding to tens.**

Say: Now compose 273 with your place-value cards. Round it to the nearest 10 by doing it the same way as you did 73. Ask: What would the rounded number be? [270] Tell her to change her place-value cards. See the right figure above.

Repeat for rounding to the nearest 10 the numbers 48 [50] and 648. [650] See the figures below.

4|8 → 5 0   6|4|8 → 6|5 0
Rounding to tens.   **Rounding to tens.**

Rounding to hundreds. Explain that sometimes we need to round to 100s instead of 10s. Tell the child to compose 584 with her place-value cards. Say: To round to the nearest 100, decide whether 584 is closer to 500 or 600. Ask: Which place-value card shows the nearest 100? [600] See the figure on the next page.

EXPLANATIONS:

See page iii, number 27 of "Some General Thoughts on Teaching Mathematics," for additional information.

Instructions are as follows:

The sum of the first three numbers in a row equals the last number in that row. The sum of the first three numbers in a column equals the last number in that column.

Check your puzzle when you are done by adding all the rows and columns.

RightStart™ Mathematics Level D Second Edition   © Activities for Learning, Inc. 2015

ACTIVITIES FOR TEACHING:

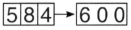
Rounding to hundreds

Next tell her to compose 129 and round it to the nearest hundred. [100]

$$129 \rightarrow 100$$
Rounding to hundreds.

Tell her to round 548 to the nearest 10 [550] and the nearest 100. [500] See the figures below.

$$548 \rightarrow 550 \qquad 548 \rightarrow 500$$
Rounding to tens. **Rounding to hundreds.**

Rounding to thousands. Tell her to compose 6129 and round it to the nearest 1000. [6000]

$$6129 \rightarrow 6000$$
Rounding to thousands.

Repeat for rounding 2901. [3000]

$$2901 \rightarrow 3000$$
Rounding to thousands.

Worksheet 29. Give the child the worksheet and tell her to complete it. The solutions are:

65 **70**	257 **260**	257 **300**	2467 **2000**
19 **20**	345 **350**	345 **300**	3840 **4000**
85 **90**	552 **550**	552 **600**	3041 **3000**
46 **50**	136 **140**	136 **100**	8304 **8000**
88 **90**	5372 **5370**	2563 **2600**	4729 **5000**
30 **30**	9605 **9610**	4705 **4700**	13472 **13000**

649 ≈ 1500
1509 ≈ 2000
289 ≈ 300
1946 ≈ 80
77 ≈ 650
99 ≈ 100

82 + 86 + 38 ≈ 120
72 + 15 + 84 ≈ 210
34 + 39 + 18 ≈ 300
142 − 59 + 43 ≈ 170
563 + 195 + 268 ≈ 90
793 − 312 − 187 ≈ 1000

In conclusion. Ask: What is 4444 rounded to the nearest 10? [4440] What is 4444 rounded to the nearest 100? [4400] What is 4444 rounded to the nearest 1000? [4000]

EXPLANATIONS:

The child should not think that rounding to the nearest 100 requires rounding first to the nearest 10 and then rounding that number to the nearest 100.

The child can read for herself the meaning of the symbol ≈ in her worksheet instructions.

If there is additional time following this lesson, have the child choose a game to play.

LESSON 46: STORY PROBLEMS WITH ROUNDING

OBJECTIVES:

1. To solve story problems using rounding

MATERIALS:

1. Worksheet 30, Story Problems with Rounding

ACTIVITIES FOR TEACHING:	EXPLANATIONS:

ACTIVITIES FOR TEACHING:

Warm-up. Give the child the worksheet. Tell her to do just the warm-up section. Remind her to check her work when she is done. Solution is shown on the right.

6	5	1	12
7	**5**	**5**	17
6	**4**	3	**13**
19	14	9	42

Ask: What is 7888 rounded to the nearest 10? [7890] What is 7888 rounded to the nearest 100? [7900] What is 7888 rounded to the nearest 1000? [8000]

Worksheet 30. These problems are to be solved during the lesson.

Problem 1. Tell the child to read the first problem twice:

Cave Creek is a town in Arizona with a population of 5,015. Nearby is the town of Youngtown with 6,156 people. What is their combined population to the nearest thousand? [11,000]

Tell her to solve the problem herself and then discuss it. Ask: Did you need to add both populations together? [no] Why not? [Cave Creek's population is close to 5 thousand and Youngtown's population is close to 6 thousand, so the total is 11 thousand.]

Ask: If Cave Creek's population increased to 5,615, what would the population of the two towns be to the nearest thousand? [12,000]

Problem 2. Tell her to read the second problem twice:

Harper is adding these numbers: 267, 98, 319, and 728. Which sum is more likely correct, 1412 or 2294? [1412]

Tell her to solve the problem. Ask: Was it necessary to add the numbers together? [no] What could you do? [Add the rounded numbers]

$$300 + 100 + 300 + 700 = 1400$$

Ask: How does that help solve the problem? [1412 is much closer to 1400 than 2294 is.]

RightStart™ Mathematics Level D Second Edition

© Activities for Learning, Inc. 2015

ACTIVITIES FOR TEACHING:	EXPLANATIONS:

Problems 3–5. Tell the child to do the remaining three problems.

3. The Lange family traveled 217 miles on Saturday, 179 miles on Sunday, 230 miles on Monday, and 90 miles on Tuesday. Did they travel about 500 miles or 700 miles?

$$200 + 200 + 200 + 100 = 700$$
They traveled about 700 miles.

4. The Picker orchard planted apple trees: 275 Honeycrisp, 345 Red Delicious, and 178 Cortland. Do you think they planted a thousand trees?

$$300 + 300 + 200 = 800$$
No, they did not plant 1000 trees.

5. Morgan wants to read about 500 pages. One book has 165 pages, two other books have 188 pages each. Will Morgan reach the goal after reading the three books?

$$200 + 200 + 200 = 600$$
Yes, Morgan reached the goal.

In conclusion. Ask: How can rounding help you solve problems? [It's faster if you do not need an exact answer.]

If there is additional time following this lesson, have the child choose a game to play.

© Activities for Learning, Inc. 2015

LESSON 47: REVIEW AND GAMES 2

OBJECTIVES:

1. To review recent topics
2. To develop skills through playing math card games

MATERIALS:

1. Worksheet 31-A or 31-B, Review 2
2. *Math Card Games* book, P32

ACTIVITIES FOR TEACHING:

Worksheet 31-A. Give the child the worksheet. Tell her to listen to the problems and write the answers. Read each problem twice.

$109 - 10$ $\qquad$ 9×6 $\qquad$ $42 \div 6$

Tell her to complete the worksheet. Solutions are below.

EXPLANATIONS:

The Review worksheets each have two versions. The second version can be used in various ways: as a quiz, as a test, as a check after tutoring, and so forth.

Write only the answers.

99

54

7

Write the answers.

$760 + 58 = $ 818

$27 \div 9 = $ 3

$10 \times 4 + 10 \times 6 = $ 100

Subtract.

$4728 - 2736$

1992

Fill in the table.

	Round to nearest 10.	Round to nearest 100.	Round to nearest 1000.
5737	5740	5700	6000
2481	2480	2500	2000
705	710	700	1000
8237	8240	8200	8000

Write >, <, or = on the lines.

$67 + 249 \underline{\ =\ } 249 + 67$

$53 + 94 \underline{\ <\ } 54 + 96$

$259 + 77 \underline{\ =\ } 260 + 76$

$736 - 45 \underline{\ >\ } 736 - 46$

$8 \times 8 \underline{\ >\ } 7 \times 9$

$2 \times 5 + 4 \underline{\ <\ } 2 \times (5 + 4)$

$11 \times 8 + 11 \times 9 \underline{\ =\ } 11 \times (8 + 9)$

$174 + 287 \underline{\ <\ } 500$

$10,000 \underline{\ >\ } 5375 + 1845$

$6821 - 1338 \underline{\ >\ } 3000$

Solve the equations.

$8 \times 2 + 8 \times n = 64$

$n = $ 6

$(25 + 75) \times m = 700$

$m = $ 7

$1 + p \times 9 = 64$

$p = $ 7

Solve the problem.

Matilda read two books that had 79 pages each. She also read a third book with 183 pages. Did she read 500 pages?

$100 \times 2 + 200 = 400$

She did not read 500 p.

ACTIVITIES FOR TEACHING:

EXPLANATIONS:

Ring around the Products game. Play the Ring around the Products game found in the *Math Card Games* book, P32.

Worksheet 31-B. Give the child the worksheet. Tell her to listen to the problems and write the answers. Read each problem twice.

$107 - 10$ $\qquad$ 9×8 $\qquad$ $45 \div 9$

Tell her to complete the worksheet. Solutions are below.

Write only the answers.

97

72

5

Write the answers.

$484 + 70 = \underline{554}$

$40 \div 8 = \underline{5}$

$9 \times 2 + 9 \times 8 = \underline{90}$

Subtract.

$6349 - 2357$

3992

Fill in the table.

	Round to nearest 10.	Round to nearest 100.	Round to nearest 1000.
8565	8570	8600	9000
1948	1950	1900	2000
807	810	800	1000
4618	4620	4600	5000

Write >, <, or = on the lines.

$891 + 28 \underline{=} 28 + 891$

$47 + 86 \underline{>} 46 + 85$

$453 + 62 \underline{=} 454 + 61$

$570 - 38 \underline{>} 570 - 39$

$7 \times 7 \underline{>} 8 \times 6$

$7 \times 2 + 1 \underline{<} 7 \times (2 + 1)$

$12 \times 7 + 12 \times 9 \underline{=} 12 \times (7 + 9)$

$589 + 137 \underline{<} 900$

$10,000 \underline{>} 3525 + 2974$

$4127 - 2338 \underline{<} 6000$

Solve the equations.

$9 \times 7 + 9 \times n = 90$

$n = \underline{3}$

$(45 + 55) \times m = 600$

$m = \underline{6}$

$1 + p \times 8 = 57$

$p = \underline{7}$

Solve the problem.

184 children are at a game. There are also 79 men and 98 women. Were there at least 600 people attending the game?

$200 + 100 + 100 = 400$

No, there were not 600

© Activities for Learning, Inc. 2015

LESSON 48: COMPOSING 6-DIGIT NUMBERS

OBJECTIVES:
1. To learn to compose 6-digit numbers
2. To read 6-digit numbers

MATERIALS:
1. Worksheet 32, Composing 6-Digit Numbers
2. Dry erase board
3. Place-value cards

ACTIVITIES FOR TEACHING:

Warm-up. Give the child the worksheet. Tell her to do just the warm-up section. Solution is shown on the right.

3	4	9	16
9	7	11	27
13	8	12	33
25	19	32	76

Ask: How many digits do you need after the 5 to write 5000? [3] How many digits do you need after the 5 to write 500? [2] How many digits do you need after the 5 to write 50? [1] How many digits do you need after the 5 to write 5? [0]

Composing large numbers using 1000. Give the child the dry erase board and the place-value cards. Tell her she needs all the ones, tens, and hundreds cards, but only the 1000-card of the thousands.

Tell her to find two place-value cards: 2 and 1000. Say: Use your 2-card to change the 1000-card into 2000. Slide your 2-card a little ways to the left to give more space before the zeros to see the groups. See the figures below.

Composing 2000 with the 2-card and the 1000-card.

Tell her to compose 13 with her place-value cards and then change the 2 thousand into 13 thousand. See below.

Composing 13 thousand.

Repeat for 87 thousand and 50 thousand.

87 thousand.   50 thousand.

Say: Let's go even higher. Compose 648 thousand.

648 thousand.

EXPLANATIONS:

Thinking of digits in columns hampers a full understanding of place value. Large numbers need to be understood in groups of three digits. Avoid teaching the child to read a number by starting at the ones and proceeding to the left, that is, reading a number backward.

ACTIVITIES FOR TEACHING:	EXPLANATIONS:

Writing large numbers. Tell the child to write 648 thousand. Say: After the thousands, we usually write a comma if the number is greater than 10 thousand. See below.

In addition to using a comma to indicate thousands, a period or a space is sometimes used. Some calculators show a mark similar to an apostrophe.

648,000

Tell her: Add 222 to 648,000 with place-value cards and then write the sum.

| 6 | 4 | 8 | 0 | 0 | 0 | + | 2 | 2 | 2 | = | 6 | 4 | 8 | 2 | 2 | 2 |

648 thousand + 222.

648,222

Tell her to read the new number. [six hundred forty-eight thousand two hundred twenty-two]

Repeat for 257,000 + 14. [257,014]

| 2 | 5 | 7 | 0 | 0 | 0 | + | 1 | 4 | = | 2 | 5 | 7 | 0 | 1 | 4 |

257 thousand + 14.

257,014

Ask: What would happen if we did not write the zero in the number? [The number would be 25,714.]

Tell the child to write any number with six digits and then to read it.

Worksheet 32. Tell the child to complete the worksheet. The solutions are:

10 thousand **10,000**   72 thousand **72,000**
102 thousand **102,000**   245 thousand **245,000**

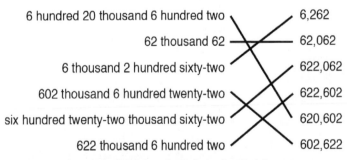

41,632 **forty-one thousand six hundred thirty-two**
519,803 **five hundred nineteen thousand eight hundred three**

In conclusion. Ask: What is the fewest number of digits a number can have to be in the thousands? [four] What symbol do we usually write after a group of thousands? [comma]

If there is additional time following this lesson, play the Rows and Columns game, found in *Math Card Games* book, A53.

LESSON 49: COMPOSING LARGER NUMBERS

OBJECTIVES:
1. To introduce the *millions*
2. To read up to 9-digit numbers

MATERIALS:
1. Worksheet 33, Composing Larger Numbers
2. Dry erase board
3. Place-value cards

ACTIVITIES FOR TEACHING:

Warm-up. Give the child the worksheet. Tell her to do just the warm-up section. Solution is shown on the right.

11	6	8	25
14	7	9	30
9	12	7	28
34	25	24	83

Ask: What is the fewest number of digits a number can have to be in the thousands? [four] What symbol do we usually write after a group of thousands? [comma]

Adding 1. Give the child the dry erase board and the place-value cards.

Write: 999 + 1

and tell her to write the number that comes after 999. [1000]

Write: 99,999 + 1

and tell her to write the number that comes after 99,999. [100,000]

Write: 999,999 + 1

and tell her to write the number that comes after 999,999. [1,000,000] Say: It needs a comma after the 1. It is a thousand thousands. We call it *one million*.

Composing larger numbers. Tell her to use only the ones, tens, and hundreds from her place-value cards for the next activities.

Show the child how to compose 2 million, 333 thousand, 444 with place-value cards as shown below.

$$\boxed{2}\ \boxed{3|3|3}\ \boxed{4|4|4}$$
2 million 333 thousand 444.

Tell her to write the number using commas.

2,333,444

EXPLANATIONS:

Introducing the child to the millions gives her a deeper sense of place value and a deeper sense of numbers themselves.

ACTIVITIES FOR TEACHING:	EXPLANATIONS:

Next tell her to compose and write 55 million 666 thousand 777.

|5|5| |6|6|6| |7|7|7|
55 million 666 thousand 777.

55,666,777

Tell the child to change the number by subtracting 700. Show her how to get a zero by turning an unused hundred card upside as shown. Tell her to read it.

|5|5| |6|6|6| |0|7|7| |5|5| |6|6|6| |0|7|7|
Subtracting 700.   **55 million 666 thousand 77.**

Tell her to change the number again, this time by subtracting 600 thousand.

|5|5| |0|6|6| |0|7|7|
55 million 66 thousand 77.

Tell the child to write a number with eight or nine digits and then read it aloud.

Worksheet 33. Tell the child to complete the worksheet. The solutions are:

950 thousand **950,000**   1 million **1,000,000**
37 million **37,000,000**   408 million **408,000,000**

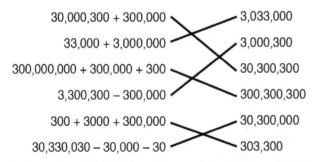

60,002,840 **sixty million two thousand eight hundred forty**
320,080,903 **three hundred twenty million eighty thousand nine hundred three**

In conclusion. Ask: What number comes after 99? [100] What number comes after 99,999? [100 thousand] What number comes after 999? [1 thousand] What number comes after 999,999? [1 million] What number comes after 9,999,999? [10 million]

If there is additional time following this lesson, play the Rows and Columns game, found in *Math Card Games* book, A53.

LESSON 50: COMPARING LARGER NUMBERS

OBJECTIVES:
1. To visualize large numbers
2. To compare large numbers

MATERIALS:
1. Worksheet 34, Comparing Larger Numbers
2. Centimeter cubes
3. Cubes made from geometry panels *

ACTIVITIES FOR TEACHING:

Warm-up. Ask: What are symbols that group numbers called? [parentheses] If an equation has addition and multiplication without parentheses, what do you do first? [multiplication]

Give the child the worksheet. Tell her to do just the warm-up section. Solutions are:

$(48 \div 6) + 9 = \mathbf{17}$ $8 \times 3 \times 3 = \mathbf{72}$ $8 - (64 \div 8) = \mathbf{0}$

$(3 \times 7) + (7 \times 7) = \mathbf{70}$ $6 + 3 \times 5 = \mathbf{21}$ $(6 + 3) \times 2 = \mathbf{18}$

Ask: What number comes after 99? [100] What number comes after 99,999? [100 thousand] What number comes after 999? [1 thousand] What number comes after 999,999? [1 million] What number comes after 9,999,999? [10 million]

Constructing a thousand. Give the child the centimeter cubes and geometry panel cubes.

Ask: About how many centimeter cubes do you think will fit in the large cube? Tell her to use her centimeter cubes and find out. [1000]

Ask the child to explain how she found her answer. [Ten cubes fit in a row making 10; put nine more rows next to the first row, making a square of 100; and on that square stack nine more squares, making 1000 little centimeter cubes in the large cube.]

Visualizing the larger numbers. Ask: How many little cubes fit in the large yellow cube? [1000] Suppose you put ten of those yellow cubes in a row, how many little centimeter cubes will you have in the row? [10,000] Now if you place nine more rows next to the first row, how many little centimeter cubes will you have in the square? [100,000] Next if you stack nine more squares on top of the first square, how many little centimeter cubes will you have in the cube? [1,000,000]

EXPLANATIONS:

* If the panels have not been used yet, the edges need to be creased. Bend the edges along the perforated lines toward the colored side. Place the panel on a hard surface and bend gently. Bending two panels at a time works well.

Leave the rubber bands off most of the edges of the top and front faces to gain access inside.

It is ideal to use show large hand motions to show building the imaginary rows, squares, and cubes. Invite the child to do the same.

RightStart™ Mathematics Level D Second Edition

© Activities for Learning, Inc. 2015

101

ACTIVITIES FOR TEACHING:	EXPLANATIONS:

Comparing large numbers. Write the following numbers:

23,487,000

233,890,500

23,490,000

and tell the child to read them. Point out that when she sees a comma, she says a special word like thousand or million.

Ask: Which number is the largest? [233,890,500] How do you know? [233 million is greater than 23 million] Which number is next greatest? [23,490,000] How can you tell it is greater than 23,487,000? [They are both 23 million, but 490 thousand is greater than 487 thousand.]

Avoid suggesting counting the number of digits to determine the greatest number. It will not work when decimals are involved.

Worksheet 34. Tell the child to complete the worksheet. The solutions are:

United States
Brazil
Russia
South Africa
Canada
Australia
Sweden
Iceland

Fargo
Montreal
Toronto
Philadelphia
Houston
Chicago
Los Angeles
New York
Mexico City

In conclusion. Ask: What is one thousand multiplied by 10? [10,000] What is ten thousand multiplied by 10? [100,000] What is a hundred thousand multiplied by 10? [million] What is one thousand thousands? [million]

If there is additional time following this lesson, play the On the Next Decade game, found in Math Card Games book, A56.

© Activities for Learning, Inc. 2015

ENRICHMENT LESSON 51: THE BILLIONS

OBJECTIVES:
1. To introduce the *billions*
2. To read up to 12-digit numbers

MATERIALS:
1. Dry erase board
2. Place-value cards
3. Worksheet 35, The Billions

ACTIVITIES FOR TEACHING:

Warm-up. Ask: What number comes after 99? [100] What number comes after 99,999? [100 thousand] What number comes after 999? [1 thousand] What number comes after 999,999? [1 million] What number comes after 9,999,999? [10 million]

Ask: What is one thousand multiplied by 10? [10,000] What is ten thousand multiplied by 10? [100,000] What is a hundred thousand multiplied by 10? [million] What is one thousand thousands? [million]

Number of digits. Write:

91568203

and ask: How could you make this number easier to read? [use commas]

Add the incorrect commas as shown:

915,682,03

and ask: Is this correct? [no, commas in wrong places] Ask the child to correct it.

91,568,203

Ask: Is this the right way to read it: 91 thousand 568 thousand 203? [no] Is this the right way to read it: 91 thousand 568 million 203? [no] Tell the child to read it. [91 million 568 thousand 203]

The billions. Give the child the dry erase board and the place-value cards. Write:

1,000

10,000

100,000

1,000,000

and ask: How many thousands in each number? [1, 10, 100, 1000] What is another name for a thousand thousands? [million]

EXPLANATIONS:

This the first of several enrichment lessons designed to bring the world of math into everyday life. If necessary because of time restraints, the lesson may be omitted without loss of continuity.

RightStart™ Mathematics Level D Second Edition

© Activities for Learning, Inc. 2015

ACTIVITIES FOR TEACHING:	EXPLANATIONS:

ACTIVITIES FOR TEACHING:

Say: Would you like to know what we call a thousand millions? We call it one *billion*. We write it like this:

1,000,000,000

Tell her: About 7 billion people live on the earth. Write:
7,000,000,000

Ask: How many digits come after the billion's comma? [9] How many digits come after the million's comma? [6]

Write: 7,283,472,658

and tell her that this number is closer to the actual number of the number of people living on earth. Tell her to compose the number with her place-value cards and to read it. See below.

7 283 472 658
Composing 7,283,472,658.

Write: 1,355,692,576

and tell her that is the population of China. Tell her to compose the number with her place-value cards and to read it. See below.

1 355 692 576
Composing 1,355,692,576.

Repeat for the population of India, 1,236,344,622.

1 236 344 622
Composing 1,236,344,622.

Ask: Which country, China or India, has more people? [China] How do you know? [They both have more than 1 billion, but China has 355 million and India has 236 million.]

Worksheet 35. Give the child the worksheet. Tell her to solve the first problem, then discuss it. The solutions are:

397,152	152,397
898,765,430	430,765,898
997,586,421,200	
299,792,458	

In conclusion. Ask: What is ten tens? [hundred] What is ten hundreds? [thousand] What is a thousand thousands? [million] What is a thousand millions? [billion]

EXPLANATIONS:

Learning about billions helps child develop the concept that numbers continue indefinitely.

If there is additional time following this lesson, play the On the Next Decade game, found in *Math Card Games* book, A56.

© Activities for Learning, Inc. 2015

104

LESSON 52: INTRODUCING REMAINDERS

OBJECTIVES:

1. To learn the term *remainder*
2. To solve some division problems with remainders

MATERIALS:

1. Worksheet 36, Introducing Remainders
2. Short Multiplication Table, Appendix p. 1

ACTIVITIES FOR TEACHING:	EXPLANATIONS:

Warm-up. Ask: Which operation calls the answer a sum? [addition] Which operation calls the answer a difference? [subtraction] Which operation calls the answer a product? [multiplication] Which operation calls the answer a quotient? [division]

Give the child the worksheet and short multiplication table. Tell her to do just the warm-up section. Solutions are:

$3 + 7 \times 5 = \mathbf{38}$ $(3 + 7) \times 2 = \mathbf{20}$ $6 \times 6 + 8 \times 8 = \mathbf{100}$

$28 \div 7 - 3 = \mathbf{1}$ $28 - (4 \times 3) = \mathbf{16}$ $(63 \div 9) - (24 \div 8) = \mathbf{4}$

Worksheet 36. Tell the child to read the first problem:

1. The prize for winners at a fair is a bag with five bouncing balls. Davis is preparing the prizes. He has 35 balls. How many bags can he fill?

Tell the child to write the equation for finding the number of bags.

$$b = 35 \div 5$$
$$b = 7 \text{ bags}$$

Tell her to solve it any way she likes, then to discuss it.

Say: Let's change the problem so Davis has 37 balls to put into bags. Ask: Can Davis still fill 7 bags? [yes] Can he fill eight bags? [no] How many balls does he have left over? [2] Tell her the amount left over is called the *remainder*. Show her how to write the equation.

$$b = 7 \text{ bags r2}$$

Say: To find the quotient of 37 divided by 5 on the short multiplication table, first find the 5-row. Then go across the 5-row and down the column until you find the largest number that is not more than 37. See the figure on the next page. Ask: What is it? [35] What is the quotient? [7] Say: To get the remainder, find the difference between 37 and 35. [2]

RightStart™ Mathematics Level D Second Edition

© Activities for Learning, Inc. 2015

ACTIVITIES FOR TEACHING:	EXPLANATIONS:

1									
2	4								
3	6	9							
4	8	12	16						
5	10	15	20	25					
6	12	18	24	30	36				
7	14	21	28	35	42	49			
8	16	24	32	40	48	56	64		
9	18	27	36	45	54	63	72	81	
10	20	30	40	50	60	70	80	90	100

37 ÷ 5

Tell her the problem is changing again. Say: Davis has a friend helping. Jamie has 18 balls. How many bags of five bouncing balls can Jamie make? [3 bags r3]

Ask: How many bags can the two children make together? [11 bags]

One way to write the solution is as follows:

7 bags r2 + 3 bags r3 = 10 bags r5 = 11 bags

Problems 2–4. Tell the child to solve the remaining problems. Tell her to discuss them.

2. Angie has 21 goodies and is putting them into cups. Each cup must have 6 goodies. How many cups can she fill? How many goodies are left over? [c = 3 cups r3]

3. Jared has three trays, each tray with 21 goodies to put into cups. Each cup must have 6 goodies. How many goodies are left over? [3]

This problem can be solved two ways. For the first method, each tray is considered separately:

$$c = 21 \div 6 = 3 \text{ r}3$$

for 3 trays, r = 3 × 3 = 9, but 6 makes another cup, so r = 3.

For the second method, the total number of goodies is 63.

$$c = 63 \div 6 = 10 \text{ r}3$$

4. Maddie is making tables with four legs. How many tables can she make with 38 legs? How many legs will not be used? [t = 38 ÷ 4 = 9 tables r2, 2 legs not used]

Worksheet 36. Tell the child to complete the worksheet. The solutions are:

18 ÷ 7 = **2 r4**   19 ÷ 2 = **9 r1**   73 ÷ 8 = **9 r1**   73 ÷ 9 = **8 r1**
64 ÷ 8 = **8**   46 ÷ 10 = **4 r6** 54 ÷ 10 = **5 r4** 99 ÷ 10 = **9 r9**

In conclusion. Ask: What will the remainder be when you divide an even number by 2? [zero] What will the remainder be when you divide an odd number by 2? [1]

If there is additional time following this lesson, play the Twenties game, found in *Math Card Games* book, A59.

© Activities for Learning, Inc. 2015

LESSON 53: REMAINDERS AFTER DIVIDING BY NINE

OBJECTIVES:
1. To find remainders after dividing by nine by using the sum of the digits
2. To discover some patterns

MATERIALS:
1. Worksheet 37, Remainders after Dividing by Nine
2. *Math Card Games* book, A63

ACTIVITIES FOR TEACHING:

Warm-up. Give the child the worksheet. Tell her to do just the warm-up section. Solutions are:

$9 \times 1 = 9$ $9 \times 2 = 18$ $9 \times 3 = 27$ $9 \times 4 = 36$ $9 \times 5 = 45$

$9 \times 6 = 54$ $9 \times 7 = 63$ $9 \times 8 = 72$ $9 \times 9 = 81$ $9 \times 10 = 90$

Tell her to look at the multiples of nine in the warm-up. Ask: What happens when you add the digits for each product? [They total 9.]

Worksheet 37. Tell her to read the instructions and to fill in the two tables. The solutions are shown below.

Number	Divide by 9	Sum of digits
11	1 r 2	2
13	1 r 4	4
14	1 r 5	5
20	2 r 2	2
30	3 r 3	3
40	4 r 4	4
42	4 r 6	6
18	2 r 0	9
45	5 r 0	9

Number	Divide by 9	Sum of digits
49	5 r 4	13
94	10 r 4	13
59	6 r 5	14
95	10 r 5	14
69	7 r 6	15
96	10 r 6	15
64	7 r 1	10
73	8 r 1	10
99	11 r 0	18

Tell her to discuss and to make corrections where necessary.

Say: In the first table, compare the remainders to the sum of the digits. Ask: Do you see a pattern? [the same, except for 9, which is 0]

Say: Now look at the second table. Ask: Do you see any interesting patterns? How could the sum of the digits in the last column help you find the remainders? Give the child a few minutes to study it by herself before discussing her ideas.

She might notice interchanging the digits, as in 49 and 94, gives the same remainder. Also, in 49, think of 9 as a 0, so the remainder is 4.

EXPLANATIONS:

See page iii, number 23 of "Some General Thoughts on Teaching Mathematics," for additional information.

Why using the sum of the digits works to find a remainder after dividing by 9 can be demonstrated as follows:

Write the number 5671 in expanded form:

$$5000 = 999 \times 5 + 5$$
$$600 = 99 \times 6 + 6$$
$$70 = 9 \times 7 + 7$$
$$1 = + 1$$

$5671 = $ a multiple of 9, $+ 5 + 6 + 7 + 1$.

Therefore, $5671 \div 9$ has a remainder of $5 + 6 + 7 + 1$, which is the sum of its digits.

Adapted from *The Teaching of Arithmetic* by David Eugene Smith, 1913.

The child's answers for the remainders and the sum of the digits need to be correct for the following activities.

RightStart™ Mathematics Level D Second Edition   © Activities for Learning, Inc. 2015

ACTIVITIES FOR TEACHING:	EXPLANATIONS:

Adding the sum of the digits then the sum of those digits gives the remainder. For 49, 4 + 9 = 13 and 1 + 3 = 4.

Practice. Tell her this method can be used to find the remainders for larger numbers when dividing by nine.

Write: 29 [2]

            59 [5]

and ask: How could you easily find the remainders? [Think of the 9s as 0 and see the other numbers.]

Write: 333 [0]

and ask: How could you easily find the remainders? [The three 3s equals 9, which is 0.]

Repeat for: 817 [7]

[The 8 and 1 makes 9, which is 0; only 7 remains.]

Write: 2588 [5]

Tell her this number has no simple ways to find nines, so add the digits in order, 2 + 5 + 8 + 8 = 23. Then add 2 + 3 to get 5.

Repeat for: 35875 [1]

Here the remainder is 3 + 5 + 8 + 7 + 5 = 28; 2 + 8 = 10; 1 + 0 = 1.

Worksheet 37. Tell the child to complete the worksheet. The solutions are:

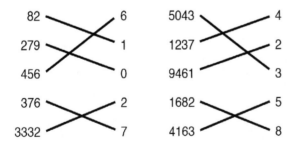

Check Numbers game. Play the Check Numbers game found in the *Math Card Games* book, A63.

In conclusion. Ask: Think of three numbers added together will give you 9? [3 + 3 + 3, 2 + 3 + 4, and so forth]

Check numbers are remainders after dividing by 9. The name of this game will make sense after the next lesson. Ignore the Background section in the description for game A63.

108

LESSON 54: CHECK NUMBERS

OBJECTIVES:

1. To introduce *check numbers*
2. To use check numbers to find errors

MATERIALS:

1. Worksheet 38, Check Numbers
2. *Math Card Games* book, A38

ACTIVITIES FOR TEACHING:	EXPLANATIONS:

ACTIVITIES FOR TEACHING:

Warm-up. Give the child the worksheet. Tell her to do just the warm-up section. Solutions are:

```
266       7      9821       1
385   ✕   4      7214   ✕   2
427       5      4681       5

845       3      3653       6
921   ✕   8      5424   ✕   8
```

Ask the child to say the multiples of 3s to 30. [3, 6, 9, ..., 30]

Check numbers. Say: Those remainders that you have been working with can be used to check answers when adding, subtracting, multiplying, or dividing. We will call the remainder after dividing by 9 its *check number*.

Write:

$$
\begin{array}{r}
2702 \\
+\ 3817 \\
\hline
6519
\end{array}
$$

and ask the child what the check numbers are for each number. Write the check numbers in parentheses after the number as shown below.

$$
\begin{array}{r}
2702\ (2) \\
+\ 3817\ \underline{(1)} \\
6519\ (3)\ \checkmark
\end{array}
$$

Ask: Are the check numbers of the two addends, 2 and 1, equal to the check number of the sum? [yes, 2 + 1 = 3] Write a check mark to show that it checks.

Finding errors using check numbers. Write the problem 29 + 29 with two different answers as shown.

$$
\begin{array}{rr}
29\ (2) & 29\ (2) \\
+\ 29\ \underline{(2)} & +\ 29\ \underline{(2)} \\
59\ (5) & 58\ (4)\ \checkmark
\end{array}
$$

Tell her to find the wrong answer using check numbers.

Ask: Which check numbers add up correctly? [the problem on the right] Place a check mark near the answer as shown. Ask: Is 58 is the correct answer? [yes]

EXPLANATIONS:

Check numbers have several other names with the most common being *casting out nines*. Other names include *digital roots* and *check digits*.

When the check numbers do not match, there is an error. However, check number agreement does not guarantee a correct answer: digits may be transposed or a 0 substituted for a 9. It is similar to using a spell-checker, which catches most, but not all misspellings.

RightStart™ Mathematics Level D Second Edition

© Activities for Learning, Inc. 2015

ACTIVITIES FOR TEACHING:	EXPLANATIONS:

Repeat for 59 + 27, using incorrect sums of 76 and 87.

$$59\ (5)\qquad 59\ (5)$$
$$\underline{+\ 27\ (0)}\qquad \underline{+\ 27\ (0)}$$
$$76\ (4)\qquad 87\ (6)$$
$$86\ (5)\ \checkmark$$

This time neither answer checks. Cross out the wrong answers and write the correct answer [86] and its check number. [5] Ask: Do the check numbers add up now? [yes] See above.

Worksheet 38. Tell the child to complete the worksheet. The solutions are shown to the right.

$$39\ (3)\qquad 28\ (1)$$
$$\underline{+\ 21\ (3)}\qquad \underline{+\ 57\ (3)}$$
$$60\ (6)\checkmark\qquad 75\ (3)$$
$$\mathbf{85\ (4)}\checkmark$$

$$75\ (3)\qquad 85\ (4)$$
$$\underline{+\ 29\ (2)}\qquad \underline{+\ 62\ (8)}$$
$$105\ (6)\qquad 147\ (3)\checkmark$$
$$\mathbf{104\ (5)}\checkmark$$

$$53\ (8)\qquad 81\ (0)$$
$$\underline{+\ 223\ (7)}\qquad \underline{+\ 54\ (0)}$$
$$276\ (5)\qquad 135\ (0)\checkmark$$
$$276\ (\mathbf{6})\checkmark$$

$$462\ (3)\qquad 397\ (1)$$
$$\underline{+\ 86\ (5)}\qquad \underline{+\ 483\ (6)}$$
$$448\ (7)\qquad 870\ (7)$$
$$\mathbf{548\ (8)}\checkmark\qquad \mathbf{880\ (7)}\checkmark$$

Preparation for Corners™ Three game. Write:

$$82\ (1)\qquad 48\ (3)$$
$$36\ (0)\qquad 26\ (8)$$
$$45\ (0)\qquad 74\ (2)$$
$$\underline{+\ 19\ (1)}\qquad \underline{+\ 93\ (3)}$$
$$172\ (2)\qquad 241\ (7)\checkmark$$
$$\mathbf{182\ (2)}\checkmark$$

3 =   6 =   9 =
12 =   15 =   18 =

and ask the child to think of two addends that are 10 or less to complete the equations. See below.

3 = 1 + 2	6 = 1 + 5	9 = 1 + 8
	6 = 2 + 4	9 = 2 + 7
12 = 2 + 10	6 = 3 + 3	9 = 3 + 6
12 = 3 + 9		9 = 4 + 5
12 = 4 + 8	15 = 5 + 10	
12 = 5 + 7	15 = 6 + 9	18 = 9 + 9
12 = 6 + 6	15 = 7 + 8	18 = 10 + 8

Corners™ Three game. Play the Corner™ Three game found in the Math Card Games book, A38. Tell her instead of using sums equal to 5, 10, 15, or 20, she will be using sums equal to 3, 6, 9, 12, 15, and 18. Tell her to score on her worksheet and to use check numbers. Start with a score of 150.

In conclusion. While looking at the game scores, ask: What happens when you add a multiple of three to another multiple of three? [sum is a multiple of three] What are the possible check numbers for multiples of three? [0, 3, 6]

© Activities for Learning, Inc. 2015

110

LESSON 55: IDENTIFYING MULTIPLES

OBJECTIVES:
1. To practice multiples using a calculator
2. To realize that the sum of two multiples will also be a multiple

MATERIALS:
1. Worksheet 39, Identifying Multiples
2. Short Multiplication Table, Appendix p. 1
3. Casio SL-450S calculator

ACTIVITIES FOR TEACHING:

Warm-up. Give the child the worksheet, short multiplication table, and calculator. Tell her to do just the warm-up section. Solutions are:

2394 **(0)**	6892 **(7)**	5733 **(0)**
+ 4782 **(3)**	+ 2147 **(5)**	+ 3088 **(1)**
7176 (3)	**9039** (3)	**8821** (1)

Multiples practice. Ask: What are the first three multiples of five? [5, 10, 15] Say: The calculator can also show multiples. To get the multiples of 5, press ⑤ ⊕ ⊕. A little *K* will appear on the left side of the calculator. Then press ⊜ ⊜ ⊜, which will give 5, 10, 15, 20. Continue to 100.

Tell the child to practice by saying the next multiple before pressing the ⊜ key and checking to see that they are correct.

Tell her to practice the 6s, 7s, and 9s in the same way.

Detecting multiples. Tell her to look at the fives on her short multiplication table. See below. Ask: How could you tell if a number is a multiple of five? [It ends in either a 5 or a 0.]

Multiples of 5.

Multiples of 6.

How can you tell if a number is a multiple of 10? [ends in zero] How can you tell if a number is a multiple of 9? [check number is zero] If necessary, tell her to look at the check numbers. Ask: How can you tell if a number

EXPLANATIONS:

See page ii, number 8 of "Some General Thoughts on Teaching Mathematics," for additional information.

Use the short multiplication table for each of the following questions to discover patterns between multiples and their check numbers.

RightStart™ Mathematics Level D Second Edition

© Activities for Learning, Inc. 2015

| | **ACTIVITIES FOR TEACHING:** | **EXPLANATIONS:** |

ACTIVITIES FOR TEACHING:

is a multiple of 2? [even number] How can you tell if a number is a multiple of 3? [check number is 0, 3, or 6]

Tell her the next one is harder. Say: Look at the multiples of 6 on your short multiplication table. Ask: How could you tell if a number is a multiple of 6? [even number and check number is 0, 3, or 6] If necessary, tell her to look at check numbers. See the previous page.

Write the following numbers:

10   5   9   3   90   15

Ask: Which of these numbers are multiples of 10? [10 and 90] Which are multiples of 5? [10, 5, 90, and 15] Which are multiples of 9? [9 and 90]

Sums of multiples. Write:

$$30 + 45 = 75$$

and ask: 30 and 45 are both multiples of what number? [5] Is the sum also a multiple of 5? [yes] Tell her to think of any two numbers that are multiples of 5, to add them, and to see if her sum is a multiple of 5. [yes]

Repeat for: $12 + 15 =$

Ask: 12 and 15 are multiples of what number? [3] What is the sum? [27] Is the sum a multiple of 3? [yes]

Worksheet 39. Tell the child to complete the worksheet. The solutions are shown below.

Number	Multiple of					
	5	10	9	2	3	6
4				y		
18			y	y	y	y
22				y		
24				y	y	y
22 + 24				y		
45	y		y		y	
54			y	y	y	y
45 + 54			y		y	
15	y				y	
30	y	y		y	y	y
15 + 30	y		y		y	
36			y	y	y	y
42				y	y	y
36 + 42				y	y	y
90	y	y	y	y	y	y

If a number is a multiple of 2 and 3, will it be a multiple of 6? **yes**

The number 234 is a multiple of 9 and 2. The number 711 is a multiple of 9, but not 2. Will their sum be a multiple of 9? **yes** Will their sum be a multiple of 2? **no**

In conclusion. Ask: What do you know about the sum of two numbers that are both multiples of seven? [It will be a multiple of seven.]

EXPLANATIONS:

If there is additional time following this lesson, play the Multiplying Three One-Digit Numbers game, found in *Math Card Games* book, A55.

© Activities for Learning, Inc. 2015

LESSON 56: REVIEW AND GAMES 3

OBJECTIVES:

1. To review recent topics
2. To develop skills through playing math card games

MATERIALS:

1. Worksheet 40-A or 40-B, Review 3
2. *Math Card Games* book, P36

ACTIVITIES FOR TEACHING:

Worksheet 40-A. Give the child the worksheet. Tell her to listen to the problems and write the answers. Read each problem twice.

$$1000 \times 10 \qquad 7 \times 8 \qquad 63 \div 9$$

Tell her to complete the worksheet. Solutions are below.

EXPLANATIONS:

The Review worksheets each have two versions. The second version can be used in various ways: as a quiz, as a test, as a check after tutoring, and so forth.

Write only the answers.

10,000

56

7

Write the answers.

$760 + 58 = $ 818

$27 \div 9 = $ 3

$10 \times 4 + 10 \times 6 = $ 100

Write the check numbers for the following numbers.

297 (0)   1801 (1)   41,872 (4)   5208 (6)

Add. Show check numbers
10,728 + 9736.

$$10{,}728 \ (0)$$
$$+ \ 9736 \ (7)$$
$$20{,}464 \ (7)$$

Write the numbers.

45 thousand ___45,000___

two hundred eight thousand ___208,000___

6 hundred thousand seventy-seven ___600,077___

17 million 17 thousand 17 ___17,017,017___

Write >, <, or = on the lines.

1 thousand ___<___ 1 million

10 thousand ___=___ 1000 × 10

8 × 8 ___>___ 7 × 9

174 + 287 ___<___ 500

10,000 ___>___ 5375 + 1845

	Round to nearest 10.	Round to nearest 100.
9280	9280	9300
7851	7850	7900
937	940	900
48,573	48,570	48,600

Solve the equations.

$9 \times 2 + 9 \times 8 = a$ $36 - b = 32$ $c + 1 \times 9 = 16$

$a = $ 90 $b = $ 4 $c = $ 7

Solve the problem.

Anna's goal is to walk 15 miles in a week. From Monday to Friday, she walks a mile to school and another mile home. How many more miles does she need to walk to reach her goal? Write an equation and find the solution.

$2 \times 5 + m = 15$

$m = 5$ miles

RightStart™ Mathematics Level D Second Edition

© Activities for Learning, Inc. 2015

113

ACTIVITIES FOR TEACHING:

Multiplying Three One-Digit Numbers game. Play the Multiplying Three One-Digit Numbers game found in *Math Card Games* book, P36.

Worksheet 40-B. Give the child the worksheet. Tell her to listen to the problems and write the answers. Read each problem twice.

$10,000 \times 10$ $\qquad$ 8×9 $\qquad$ $40 \div 8$

Tell her to complete the worksheet. Solutions are below.

EXPLANATIONS:

See page ii, number 11 of "Some General Thoughts on Teaching Mathematics," for additional information.

Write only the answers.

100,000

72

5

Write the answers.

$484 + 70 =$ 554

$56 \div 8 =$ 7

$9 \times 2 + 9 \times 8 =$ 90

Write the check numbers for the following numbers.

567 (0)   4691 (2)   45,861 (6)   3958 (7)

Add. Show check numbers

26,735 + 8409

26,735 (5)
+ 8409 (3)
35,144 (8)

Write the numbers.

23 thousand   23,000

four hundred six thousand   406,000

3 hundred thousand eighty-nine   300,089

56 million 56 thousand 56   56,056,056

Write >, <, or = on the lines.

1 hundred thousand < 1 million

$10 \times 10 \times 10$ = 1000

7×7 > 6×8

$589 + 137$ < 900

$10,000$ > $3525 + 2974$

	Round to nearest 10.	Round to nearest 100.
5720	5720	5700
8362	8360	8400
816	820	800
34,359	34,360	34,400

Solve the equations.

$8 \times 2 + 8 \times 8 = a$

$a =$ 80

$48 - b = 43$

$b =$ 5

$c + 11 \times 1 = 19$

$c =$ 8

Solve the problem.

Aaron plans to practice the piano 130 minutes in a week. He practices 20 minutes every day from Monday to Friday. How many more minutes does Aaron need to practice to reach his goal? Write an equation and find the solution.

$20 \times 5 + m = 130$

$m = 30$ minutes

© Activities for Learning, Inc. 2015

Enrichment Lesson 57: Building Pascal's Triangle

OBJECTIVES:
1. To build Pascal's triangle

MATERIALS:
1. One set of Pascal's Triangle Parts 1–4, Appendix pp. 2–5
2. **Scissors and glue or tape**
3. Worksheet 41, Building Pascal's Triangle
4. Pascal's Triangle Patterns, Appendix p. 6

ACTIVITIES FOR TEACHING:

Preparation for the large Pascal's triangle. This large triangle is made from four appendix pages. Part 1 is kept intact. Parts 2 and 3 need the top and a side cut off. Part 4 needs to be cut out on the dotted lines. See below.

Four individual parts of Pascal's triangle.

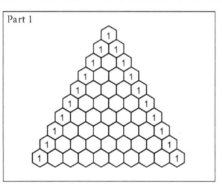
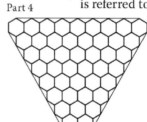
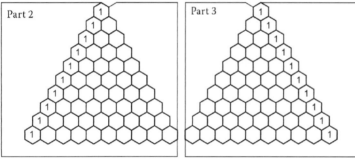

Large Pascal's triangle assembled.

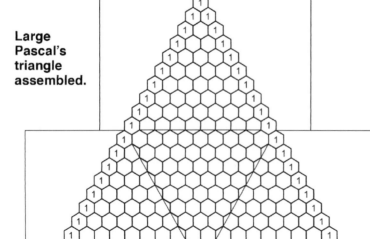

EXPLANATIONS:

This year's Math Project consists of building Pascal's triangle and finding multiples patterns.

There are three phases to this project:

a) Build a 14-row Pascal's triangle individually on a worksheet. The top hexagon is referred to as row 0.

b) On a wall, build a 19-row Pascal's triangle.

c) Find and color multiples on copies of the Pascal's triangle, revealing interesting patterns. These can be displayed on the wall around the Pascal's triangle.

The first two phases are done in this lesson and the third phase is done in the next lesson.

The fourth part is glued over the "hole."

ACTIVITIES FOR TEACHING:

Pascal's triangle. Explain to the child that today and the next day she will be working on a math project called Pascal's triangle. Say: It is a special arrangement of numbers that makes interesting patterns. People knew about the basic idea over 2000 years ago. We call it Pascal's triangle because Blaise Pascal in the 1600s discovered many more patterns.

Worksheet 41. Have the child complete the worksheet. Tell the child to look at the grayed 2. See the left figure below. Say: The 2 is found by adding the numbers in the two hexagons directly above it, 1 + 1.

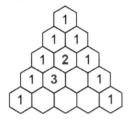 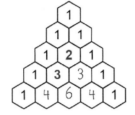

Tell her to look at the grayed 3; it is the sum of 1 + 2 above it. Ask: What number goes in the hexagon next to the 3? [another 3 because 2 + 1]

Tell her to look at the next row. Ask: What do you write in first empty hexagon? [4 because 1 + 3] What do you write in next hexagon? [6] What do you write in last hexagon? [4] See the right figure above.

Tell her to complete her triangle. Say: Add carefully and check your answers using check numbers. You will need to write small in the bottom rows.

The solutions are on Appendix page 6 and in the next lesson.

Filling in the large Pascal's triangle. Have the child fill in the hexagons on the large Pascal's triangle with the correct numbers. The solutions for the last five rows are as follows:

```
        1   15  105  455  1365 3003 5005 6435 6435 5005 3003 1365 455  105  15  1
      1   16  120  560  1820 4368 8008 11440 12870 11440 8008 4368 1820 560  120  16  1
    1   17  136  680  2380 6188 12376 19448 24310 24310 19448 12376 6188 2380 680  136  17  1
  1   18  153  816  3060 8568 18564 31824 43758 48620 43758 31824 18564 8568 3060 816  153  18  1
1   19  171  969  3876 11628 27132 50388 75582 92378 92378 75582 50388 27132 11628 3876 969  171  19  1
```

In conclusion. Ask: What is Pascal's triangle? [numbers in the shape of a triangle with 1s on the sides and the other numbers found by adding the two numbers above it]

EXPLANATIONS:

The child may want to spend several days completing the large Pascal's triangle.

If there is additional time following this lesson, play the Corners™ Three game, found in *Math Card Games* book, A38.

Enrichment Lesson 58: Pascal's Triangle Patterns

OBJECTIVES:
1. To find multiples in the Pascal's triangle
2. To learn to use a calculator to determine whether or not a number is a multiple

MATERIALS:
1. 3 to 8 copies of Pascal's Triangle Patterns, Appendix p. 6
2. **Colored pencils or markers**
3. Casio SL-450S calculator

ACTIVITIES FOR TEACHING:

Appendix 6. Give the child the appendix pages, shown below.

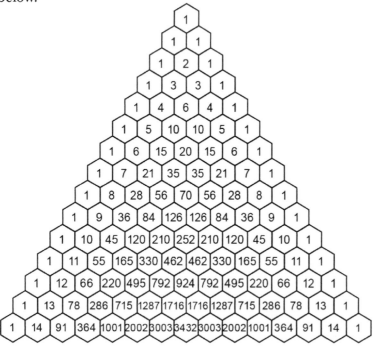

Ask: Are any of the numbers in the triangle a multiple of 5? [yes] Tell her to use a colored pencil or marker and color all the hexagons with numbers that are multiples of 5. The results are shown in the first figure on the next page.

Multiples on a calculator. Tell her there is a way to use a calculator to see if a number is a multiple. To check for multiples of 5:

press ⑤ ÷ ÷. The *K* will appear on the left side.

Then press 10 ⊜, which will show 2.

Then press 45 ⊜, which will show 9.

Then press 46 ⊜, which will show 9.2.

Say: When quotient has a number after the dot, it means that number has a remainder; therefore, it is not a multiple. So, 46 is not a multiple of 5.

Tell her to try other numbers.

EXPLANATIONS:

This experience gives the child a sense of multiples in an enjoyable activity.

RightStart™ Mathematics Level D Second Edition © Activities for Learning, Inc. 2015

ACTIVITIES FOR TEACHING:

More multiples. Give the child more copies of the appendix page. Tell her to do other multiples. Write and say: The easiest to hardest multiples to do are these:

   5   10   9   2   3   6   7   4

The results are shown below. Display the child's work near the large Pascal's triangle.

EXPLANATIONS:

Some other multiples that will also work, but are increasingly more challenging are 13, 12, 11, 14, 15, and 8.

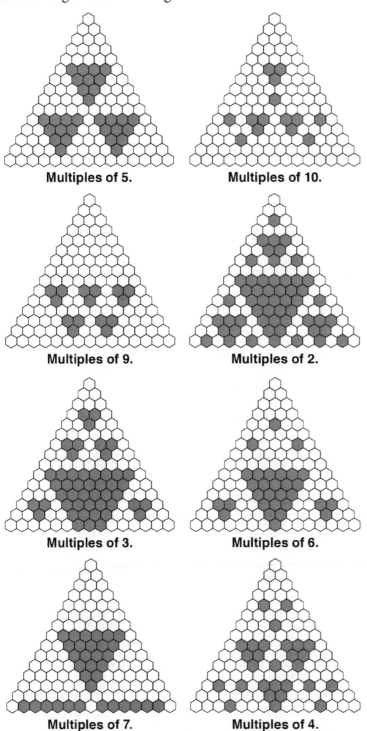

Multiples of 5. Multiples of 10. Multiples of 9. Multiples of 2. Multiples of 3. Multiples of 6. Multiples of 7. Multiples of 4.

In conclusion. Ask: Which patterns do you like best?

© Activities for Learning, Inc. 2015

Lesson 59: Checking Subtraction by Adding Up

OBJECTIVES:
1. To check subtraction by adding up
2. To find errors by adding up

MATERIALS:
1. Worksheet 42, Checking Subtraction by Adding Up
2. *Math Card Games* book, A70 (as reference)

ACTIVITIES FOR TEACHING:

Warm-up. Give the child the worksheet. Tell her to do just the warm-up section. Solutions are:

4 + 5 × 5 = **29**	(4 + 5) × 5 = **45**	(7 × 4) + (8 × 8) = **92**
(56 ÷ 7) − 5 = **3**	42 − (6 × 4) = **18**	(72 ÷ 8) − (32 ÷ 8) = **5**

Ask: What number comes after 99? [100] What number comes after 99,999? [100 thousand] What number comes after 999? [1 thousand] What number comes after 999,999? [1 million]

Comparing subtraction and addition. Present the following problem:

Lonnie has 20 cards and gives 7 cards to a friend. How many cards does Lonnie have now? [13]

Draw a part-whole circle set and tell the child to write the numbers in the circles as shown on the right.

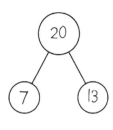

Write the problem both vertically and horizontally:

$$20 - 7 = 13 \qquad \begin{array}{r} 20 \\ -7 \\ \hline 13 \end{array}$$

Ask: How many cards do Lonnie and the friend have together? [20] How do you know? [add the 7 and 13]

Checking multi-digit subtraction. Say: Could we use this addition idea to see if we subtracted correctly? Write:

$$\begin{array}{r} 428 \\ -157 \\ \hline 331 \end{array}$$

Say: Suppose I think the answer is 331. Let's see if I'm right. I'll cover the top number, the 428, and add the other two numbers.

$$\begin{array}{r} \boxed{428} \\ -157 \\ +331 \\ \hline 488 \end{array}$$

EXPLANATIONS:

The part-whole circles are a link between addition and subtraction.

ACTIVITIES FOR TEACHING:	EXPLANATIONS:

Uncover the top number. Ask: Is the difference right? [no] Tell the child to correct the subtraction and then do the addition.

$$
\begin{array}{r}
428 \\
- 157 \\
\hline
+ 271 \\
\hline
428
\end{array}
$$

Ask: Is the subtraction correct this time? [yes]

Practice. Write:

$$
\begin{array}{r}
4620 \\
- 3906 \\
\hline
\end{array}
$$

1714   1326   714

Tell the child one of the three answers is correct. Tell her to find it by adding up. [714]

Worksheet 42. Tell the child to complete the subtraction problems on the worksheet. The solutions are:

8272	8272	8272		7505	7505	7505
− 3446	− 3446	− 3446		− 1371	− 1371	− 1371
5826	5836	(4826)		6174	(6134)	6274
9272	**9282**	**8272**		**7545**	**7505**	**7645**

2642	2642	2642		7129	7129	7129
− 1295	− 1295	− 1295		− 2736	− 2736	− 2736
1447	1357	(1347)		(4393)	4493	4383
2742	**2652**	**2642**		**7129**	**7229**	**7119**

9513	9513	9513
− 7885	− 7885	− 7885
1728	(1628)	1638
9613	**9513**	**9523**

Building Differences game. Play the Building Differences game, the subtraction version of the Sum Building game found in *Math Card Games* book, A70.

Playing the game Building Differences provides the child an opportunity to play with subtraction like a puzzle.

Write the following digits: 1 2 5 5 6 6 7 8 9 0. Say: Use six or more digits to make a subtraction problem, including the difference. No number may start with zero.

Some possibilities are:

89	785	105	791
− 28	− 120	− 26	− 586
61	665	79	205

Worksheet 42. Play the same game with the digits on her worksheet. Some possibilities are:

74	987	474	791
− 64	− 347	− 96	− 387
10	640	378	404

In conclusion. Ask: When you subtract a part from the whole, what is the difference? [the other part] When you add the two parts together, what do you get? [the whole]

© Activities for Learning, Inc. 2015

120

LESSON 60: CHECKING SUBTRACTION WITH CHECK NUMBERS

OBJECTIVES:
1. To check subtraction by adding up
2. To check subtraction with check numbers

MATERIALS:
1. Worksheet 43, Checking Subtraction with Check Numbers

ACTIVITIES FOR TEACHING:

Warm-up. Give the child the worksheet. Tell her to do just the warm-up section. Solutions are:

49 ÷ 7 = 7	24 ÷ **6** = 4	42 ÷ 6 = **7**	8 × **4** = 32
50 ÷ 5 = **10**	7 × **5** = 35	(9 × **1**) + (9 × 3) = 36	

Ask: When you subtract a part from the whole, what is the difference? [the other part] When you add the two parts together, what do you get? [the whole]

Checking subtraction with check numbers. Write the following subtraction problem with two different answers as shown:

$$
\begin{array}{r} 62\,(\ ) \\ -\,49\,(\ ) \\ \hline 27\,(\ ) \end{array}
\qquad
\begin{array}{r} 62\,(\ ) \\ -\,49\,(\ ) \\ \hline 13\,(\ ) \end{array}
$$

Tell the child to write the check numbers.

$$
\begin{array}{r} 62\,(8) \\ -\,49\,(4) \\ \hline 27\,(0) \end{array}
\qquad
\begin{array}{r} 62\,(8) \\ -\,49\,(4) \\ \hline 13\,(4)\;\checkmark \end{array}
$$

Ask: How do you check subtraction problems? [by adding up] Say: Adding up also is the easiest way to use check numbers for subtraction.

Ask: In the first example, does 0 + 4 = 8? [no] Say: So that answer must be wrong. Ask: In the second example, does 4 + 4 = 8? [yes] Say: So that answer might be right. Ask: Does 13 and 49 equal 62? [yes]

Repeat for the following example:

$$
\begin{array}{r} 3574\,(\ ) \\ -\,1958\,(\ ) \\ \hline 1626\,(\ ) \end{array}
\qquad
\begin{array}{r} 3574\,(\ ) \\ -\,1958\,(\ ) \\ \hline 1616\,(\ ) \end{array}
$$

Tell the child to write the check numbers.

$$
\begin{array}{r} 3574\,(1) \\ -\,1958\,(5) \\ \hline 1626\,(6) \end{array}
\qquad
\begin{array}{r} 3574\,(1) \\ -\,1958\,(5) \\ \hline 1616\,(5)\;\checkmark \end{array}
$$

EXPLANATIONS:

Some advanced children might realize that there is another way to check this example with check numbers. Instead of adding up: 5 + 5 = 10 and 1 + 0 = 1, add 9 (which is the same as zero) to the 1. Nine plus the check number, 1, makes 10; then 10 − 5 = 5, which checks.

RightStart™ Mathematics Level D Second Edition

© Activities for Learning, Inc. 2015

ACTIVITIES FOR TEACHING:

Say: Add the check numbers for the left subtraction. Ask: Does it work? [no, 6 + 5 = 11, 1 + 1 = 2, not 1] Say: Add the check numbers for the subtraction on the right. Ask: Does it work? [yes, 5 + 5 = 10, which is 1]

Worksheet 43. Tell the child to complete the worksheet. Explain to her that she will subtract the same number repeatedly. Tell her to do the worksheet and to look for patterns. The solutions are:

```
  3790 (1)        5620 (4)        4580 (8)
- 379 (1)       - 562 (4)       - 458 (8)
  3411 (0)        5058 (0)        4122 (0)
- 379 (1)       - 562 (4)       - 458 (8)
  3032 (8)        4496 (5)        3664 (1)
- 379 (1)       - 562 (4)       - 458 (8)
  2653 (7)        3934 (1)        3206 (2)
- 379 (1)       - 562 (4)       - 458 (8)
  2274 (6)        3372 (6)        2748 (3)
- 379 (1)       - 562 (4)       - 458 (8)
  1895 (5)        2810 (2)        2290 (4)
- 379 (1)       - 562 (4)       - 458 (8)
  1516 (4)        2248 (7)        1832 (5)
- 379 (1)       - 562 (4)       - 458 (8)
  1137 (3)        1686 (3)        1374 (6)
- 379 (1)       - 562 (4)       - 458 (8)
   758 (2)        1124 (8)         916 (7)
- 379 (1)       - 562 (4)       - 458 (8)
   379 (1)         562 (4)         458 (8)
- 379 (1)       - 562 (4)       - 458 (8)
     0 (0)           0 (0)           0 (0)
```

In conclusion. Ask: How do you use check numbers to check differences? [add up the check numbers]

EXPLANATIONS:

All three columns of subtraction end with zero, forming a pattern. The check numbers in the first and third columns also form patterns; in the first column, they decrease by 1 and in the third column, they increase by 1.

If there is additional time following this lesson, play the Sum Building game, found in *Math Card Games* book, A70.

© Activities for Learning, Inc. 2015

Lesson 61: Multiplying with Multiples of Tens

OBJECTIVES:
1. To multiply a whole number by multiples of ten on the abacus

MATERIALS:
1. Worksheet 44, Multiplying with Multiples of Tens
2. AL Abacus

ACTIVITIES FOR TEACHING:

Warm-up. Give the child the worksheet. Tell her to do just the warm-up section. Solutions are:

    4123 (**1**)   6724 (**1**)   9118 (**1**)
 − 2808 (**0**)   − 4182 (**6**)   − 2407 (**4**)
    1315 (**1**)   2542 (**4**)   6711 (**6**)

Ask: What is 2 × 3? [6] What is 4 × 3? [12] What is 3 × 2? [6] What is 3 × 4? [12]

Multiplying with 10s. Give the child the abacus.
Write:

$$40 \times 3 =$$

Tell the child to use side 2 of the abacus to find the product. [120] Enter 40 three times and trade, getting the answer of 120. See below.

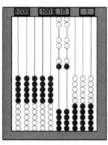 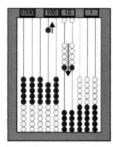 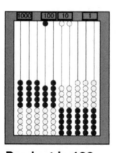

40 three times.   **Trading.**   **Product is 120.**

Repeat for:

$$400 \times 3 =$$

Tell her to find the product the same way. [1200] See below.

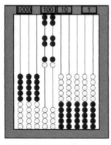 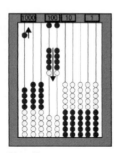 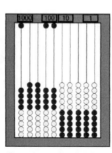

400 three times.   **Trading.**   **Product is 1200.**

EXPLANATIONS:

This lesson works at the concrete level while the next lesson works with equations.

ACTIVITIES FOR TEACHING:	EXPLANATIONS:

Write: 4000 × 3 =

Ask: What do you think the product is? [12,000] Tell her to show on her abacus. See below.

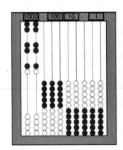 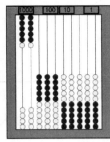

4000 three times.   4000 × 3 is 12,000.

Next write: 20 × 10 =

Say: Find the product on your abacus. [200] See below.

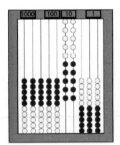 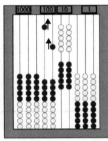 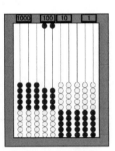

20 ten times.   Trading.   Product is 200.

Continue with: 200 × 10 =

Tell her to find the product. [2000]

Write: 12 × 10 =

and ask her to find the product. [120]

Worksheet 44. Tell the child to complete the worksheet. The solutions are as follows:

4 × 3 = **12**   2 × 10 = **20**
40 × 3 = **120**   20 × 10 = **200**
400 × 3 = **1200**   200 × 10 = **2000**
4000 × 3 = **12,000** 2000 × 10 = **20,000**
12 × 10 = **120**   6 × 5 = **30**
120 × 10 = **1200**   60 × 5 = **300**
1200 × 10 = **12,000** 600 × 5 = **3000**
10 × 8 = **80**   7 × 1 = **7**
10 × 80 = **800**   7 × 10 = **70**
10 × 800 = **8000**   7 × 100 = **700**
10 × 8000 = **80,000** 7 × 1000 = **7000**
30 × 2 = 3 × 20   50 × 10 < 100 × 50
40 × 4 = 8 × 20   32 × 10 > 10 × 23

In conclusion. Ask: What is 90 multiplied by 10? [900] What is 50 multiplied by 3? [150] What is 80 multiplied by 6? [480]

If there is additional time following this lesson, play the Sum Building game, found in *Math Card Games* book, A70.

© Activities for Learning, Inc. 2015

LESSON 62: MORE MULTIPLYING WITH MULTIPLES OF TENS

OBJECTIVES:

1. To multiply a whole number by multiples of ten using the distributive property
2. To learn the term *annex*

MATERIALS:

1. Worksheet 45, More Multiplying with Multiples of Ten
2. *Math Card Games* book, N43
3. Place-value cards

ACTIVITIES FOR TEACHING:	EXPLANATIONS:

Warm-up. Give the child the worksheet. Tell her to do just the warm-up section. Solutions are:

$$6280 \ (7)$$
$$- \ 4915 \ (1)$$
$$\overline{1365} \ (6)$$

$$4703 \ (5)$$
$$- \ 3642 \ (6)$$
$$\overline{1061} \ (8)$$

$$5814 \ (0)$$
$$- \ 2782 \ (1)$$
$$\overline{3032} \ (8)$$

Multiplying by 10. Write: $16 \times 10 =$
and ask: What is the product? [160] Explain that we can also find the product by using the distributive property and equations. Write as follows:

$$16 \times 10 = (10 + 6) \times 10$$
$$= (10 \times 10) + (6 \times 10)$$
$$= 100 + 60$$
$$= 160$$

Say: This means that 16 is 10 and 6. Ten tens is 100 and 6 tens is 60, which is $100 + 60 = 160$.

Worksheet 45. Tell the child to write the equations on her worksheet for explaining 13×10. See the solution below.

$$13 \times 10 \ = (10 + 3) \times 10$$
$$= (10 \times 10) + (3 \times 10)$$
$$= 100 + 30$$
$$= 130$$

Multiplying 50 × 4. Tell the child to think of several ways to find the product of 50×4. One way is to think that 50 times 2 is 100, so 50 times 4 must be 200. A second way is as follows:

$$50 \times 4 \ = (5 \times 10) \times 4$$
$$= 5 \times 10 \times 4$$
$$= 5 \times 4 \times 10$$
$$= 20 \times 10$$
$$= 200$$

Multiplying 20 × 9. Tell the child to write the equations on her worksheet for explaining 20×9. See the next page.

See page ii, number 3 of "Some General Thoughts on Teaching Mathematics," for additional information.

RightStart™ Mathematics Level D Second Edition

© Activities for Learning, Inc. 2015

ACTIVITIES FOR TEACHING:

$$20 \times 9 = (10 \times 2) \times 9$$
$$= 10 \times (2 \times 9)$$
$$= 10 \times 18$$
$$= 180$$

Tell the child to do 6×60 on her own then discuss it.

Annexing zeros. Write: $18 \times 10 =$

and ask: What is the product? [180] Say: You know the product is the 18 with a 0 after it. Putting a zero after a number is called *annexing* a zero. Ask: What do you do to multiply 78×10? [annex a zero] What do you do to multiply 78×100? [annex two zeros]

Can You Find Times game. This game is a variation of the Can You Find from the *Math Card Games* book, N43. Use all the place-value cards.

Say the expressions below. Eight cards will be left at the end of the game: 2, 3, 6, 9, 1000, 4000, 5000, and 8000.

1. Can you find 68?   [60 & 8]
2. Can you find 68 tens?   [600 & 80]
3. Can you find 68 hundreds?   [6000 & 800]
4. Can you find 7?   [7]
5. Can you find 7×10?   [70]
6. Can you find 7×100?   [700]
7. Can you find 7×1000?   [7000]
8. Can you find 1×25?   [20 & 5]
9. Can you find 10×25?   [200 & 50]
10. Can you find 100×25?   [2000 & 500]
11. Can you find 91?   [90 & 1]
12. Can you find 91×10?   [900 & 10]
13. Can you find 91×100?   [9000 & 100]
14. Can you find 2×17?   [30 & 4]
15. Can you find 20×17?   [300 & 40]
16. Can you find 200×17?   [3000 & 400]

Worksheet 45. Tell the child to complete the worksheet. Solutions are:

$40 \times 8 = \mathbf{320}$	$60 \times 7 = \mathbf{420}$	$90 \times 6 = \mathbf{540}$
$50 \times 7 = \mathbf{350}$	$8 \times 80 = \mathbf{640}$	$3 \times 70 = \mathbf{210}$
$90 \times 5 = \mathbf{450}$	$8 \times 70 = \mathbf{560}$	$300 \times 6 = \mathbf{1800}$
$6 \times 80 = \mathbf{480}$	$90 \times 9 = \mathbf{810}$	$400 \times 4 = \mathbf{1600}$

2
1
3

In conclusion. Ask: What do we call placing zeros at the end of a number to multiply by 100? [annexing]

EXPLANATIONS:

To multiply by 10, we do not *add* a zero, rather we *annex* a zero. Adding zero to a number does not change the number; for example, adding 0 to 18 is still 18.

We need to keep in mind that annexing only works for whole numbers. While it is valid for 54×10, it is not valid for 0.54×10.

Some children may need the numbers written where they can see them.

© Activities for Learning, Inc. 2015

LESSON 63: MULTIPLYING MULTI-DIGIT NUMBERS HORIZONTALLY

OBJECTIVES:
1. To review adding on side 2 of the abacus
2. To multiply a two-digit number by a single-digit number on the abacus

MATERIALS:
1. Worksheet 46, Multiplying Multi-Digit Numbers Horizontally
2. AL Abacus
3. Dry erase board

ACTIVITIES FOR TEACHING:

Warm-up. Give the child the worksheet. Tell her to do just the warm-up section. Solutions are:

4685 (**5**)	9882 (**0**)	3641 (**5**)
− 3249 (**0**)	− 1906 (**7**)	− 2837 (**2**)
1436 (**5**)	7976 (**2**)	804 (**3**)

Multiplying 24 × 3. Give the child the abacus and dry erase board.

Write: 24 × 3 =

and ask: How can you find the product in more than one way? Give her time to think about, then discuss it. [72]

One way is to add 24 three times: 24 + 24 = 48 and 48 + 24 = 72.

Another way is to partition 24 into 20 and 4 as follows:

$$24 \times 3 = (20 + 4) \times 3$$
$$= (20 \times 3) + (4 \times 3)$$
$$= 60 + 12$$
$$= 72$$

A shortened version is:

$$24 \times 3 = 60 + 12 = 72$$

Repeated addition on side 2 of the abacus. Ask: How could you use the abacus to find the product? One way is to think of multiplication as adding the same number. Write: 24 × 3 = 24 + 24 + 24

See below. Trading is not necessary to see the answer.

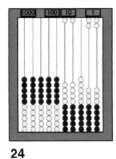
24

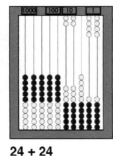
24 + 24

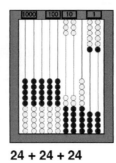
24 + 24 + 24

EXPLANATIONS:

Doing simple multiplication horizontally aligns with algebraic operations. It also makes mental multiplication easier. The traditional multiplication algorithm will be thoroughly taught in the next grade.

ACTIVITIES FOR TEACHING:	EXPLANATIONS:

Multiplying on side 2 of the abacus. Tell the child there is another way to use side 2 to multiply 24 × 3. Demonstrate as follows:

Prepare the abacus by moving the beads away from the bottom as shown in the left figure below. Then enter 24 at the bottom as shown in the second figure.

Only the multiplicand, the quantity that is multiplied by another, is entered; the multiplier is not.

Next multiply 20 by 3. Remove the 20 immediately before entering the 60 as shown in the third figure.

If the multiplicand is not removed, there may not be enough beads.

Lastly multiply 4 × 3 and enter 12 as shown in the fourth figure. The final result, the product, is shown in the fifth figure.

In the future short division will be taught using the inverse of this multiplication procedure.

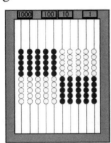 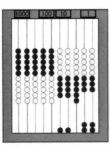 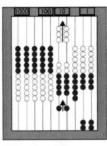 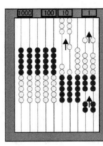 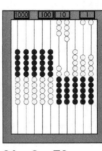

Abacus prepared.   **24 entered.**   **20 × 3 = 60**   **4 × 3 = 12**   **24 × 3 = 72**

Worksheet 46. Tell the child to do the same multiplication, 24 × 3, and write down the steps on the worksheet.

Next ask her to complete the second multiplication, 32 × 4. The solution is shown below.

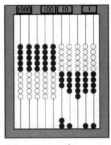 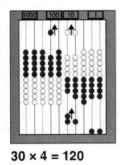 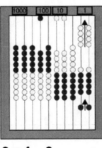 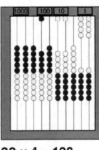

32 entered.   **30 × 4 = 120**   **2 × 4 = 8**   **32 × 4 = 128**

Tell her to complete the worksheet. The remaining solutions are:

   19 × 4 = **76**   18 × 5 = **90**
   37 × 6 = **222**   58 × 7 = **406**
   87 × 6 = **522**   52 × 5 = **260**
   25 × 4 = **100**   45 × 5 = **225**

In conclusion. Ask: When you multiply 55 by 3, which two numbers do you need to multiply by 3? [50 and 5]

If there is additional time following this lesson, play the Building Race game, found in *Math Card Games* book, A71.

© Activities for Learning, Inc. 2015

Lesson 64: Multi-Digit Multiplication

OBJECTIVES:
1. To learn the term *partial product*
2. To multiply numbers in a vertical format

MATERIALS:
1. Worksheet 47, Multi-Digit Multiplication
2. AL Abacus

ACTIVITIES FOR TEACHING:

Warm-up. Give the child the worksheet. Tell her to do just the warm-up section. Solutions are:

4263 (**6**)	8441 (**8**)	6422 (**5**)
− 2357 (**8**)	− 5289 (**6**)	− 1397 (**2**)
1906 (**7**)	**3152** (**2**)	**5025** (**3**)

Birthday problem. Give the child the abacus. Ask: How many days old is a person on their ninth birthday? What do you need to do to find out? Lead her to think about the number the days in a year. Ask the child to write the equation needed to solve the problem. [$365 \times 9 = d$]

Tell the child that you will show her how to do this multiplication on side 2 of the abacus. Say: First write the equation vertically: 365
                                                                                                                                                                                     × 9

Say: Move the beads halfway up on your abacus. Enter 365 at the bottom. See the left figure below. Say: Now multiply 5×9 and write the *partial product* of 45. See the right figure below for the multiplying and the written partial product.

EXPLANATIONS:

Having the child write out all the steps for multi-digit multiplication helps her understand the process in preparation for the traditional algorithm, which will be taught next year.

This process shows the partial products being combined vertically, unlike "lattice multiplication" or Montessori's "checkerboard" multiplication that combine the partial products diagonally.

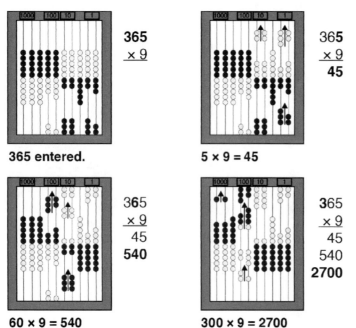

ACTIVITIES FOR TEACHING:	EXPLANATIONS:

Say: Now multiply 60 × 9. Ask: What is the partial product? [540] Write it below the other partial product 45. See the left figure at the bottom of the previous page.

Ask: What do we multiply next? [300 × 9] What is the partial product? [2700] Say: Write it below the other partial product. See the bottom right figure on the previous page.

Ask: What do you do to get the final product? [add the partial products] See the figures below. The left figure shows the trading and the right figure shows the solution.

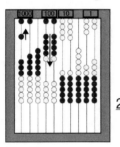

```
        365           365
        × 9           × 9
         45            45
        540           540
       2700          2700
                     3285
```

Trading.   **The final product.**

Ask: What does the answer mean? [the number of days a person has lived when they turn 9 years old] For the equation, $d = 3285$ days. Ask: What is that number rounded to the nearest thousand? [3000]

If desired, discuss that leap years will actually add 2 (or 3) days to the total.

Worksheet 47. Tell the child to complete the worksheet. The solutions are:

```
   49        268        691
  × 6        × 3        × 7
   54         24          7
  240        180        630
  294        600       4200
             804       4837

  789        475       1879
  × 4        × 8        × 2
   36         40         18
  320        560        140
 2800       3200       1600
 3156       3800       2000
                       3758
```

The products on this worksheet will be checked in the next lesson with check numbers. Therefore, do not correct any errors at this time.

In conclusion. Ask: When you multiply large numbers, what do you call each part of the product? [partial product]

If there is additional time following this lesson, play the Building Race game, found in *Math Card Games* book, A71.

LESSON 65: USING CHECK NUMBERS WITH MULTIPLICATION

OBJECTIVES:
1. To provide more practice in multiplying numbers in a vertical format
2. To apply check numbers to multiplying

MATERIALS:
1. Worksheet 48, Using Check Numbers with Multiplication
2. Dry erase board
3. AL Abacus
4. Worksheet 47, Multi-Digit Multiplication (from the previous lesson)

ACTIVITIES FOR TEACHING:	EXPLANATIONS:

Warm-up. Give the child the worksheet. Tell her to do just the warm-up section. Solutions are:

$$4217 \ (5)$$
$$\underline{- 3909 \ (3)}$$
$$308 \ (2)$$

$$9907 \ (7)$$
$$\underline{- 8888 \ (5)}$$
$$1019 \ (2)$$

$$6352 \ (7)$$
$$\underline{- 3739 \ (4)}$$
$$2613 \ (3)$$

Ask: When you multiply large numbers, what do you call each part of the product? [partial product] When you multiply 44 by 5, which two numbers do you need to multiply by 5? [40 and 4]

Check numbers. Give the child the dry erase board and abacus. Tell the child to write four 29s vertically and to add them up. Ask: What is the check number for each 29? [2] Tell the child to write the check numbers. See below.

$$29 \ (2)$$
$$29 \ (2)$$
$$29 \ (2)$$
$$\underline{+ \ 29 \ (2)}$$
$$116 \ (8) \ \checkmark$$

Ask: Is the check number for 116 equal to the check numbers for the 29s? [yes] Say: Now write this addition problem as a multiplication problem. See below.

$$29 \ (2)$$
$$\underline{\times 4 \ (4)}$$
$$116 \ (8) \ \checkmark$$

Ask: What happened to the check numbers? [They need to be multiplied, $2 \times 4 = 8$.]

Repeat for $645 + 645 + 645$, both adding and multiplying, using check numbers. See below.

$$645 \ (6)$$
$$645 \ (6)$$
$$\underline{+ \ 645 \ (6)}$$
$$1935 \ (0) \ \checkmark$$

$$645 \ (6)$$
$$\underline{\times 3 \ (3)}$$
$$1935 \ (0) \ \checkmark$$

RightStart™ Mathematics Level D Second Edition

© Activities for Learning, Inc. 2015

ACTIVITIES FOR TEACHING:	EXPLANATIONS:

Worksheet 47. Tell the child to take her worksheet from the last lesson and check her work using check numbers. Tell her to correct any errors. The results are as follows below.

49 (**4**)	268 (**7**)	691 (**7**)
× 6 (**6**)	× 3 (**3**)	× 7 (**7**)
294 (**6**)	804 (**3**)	4837 (**4**)
789 (**6**)	475 (**7**)	1879 (**7**)
× 4 (**4**)	× 8 (**8**)	× 2 (**2**)
3156 (**6**)	3800 (**2**)	3758 (**5**)

Tell her to share her results and discuss. Ask: Did the check numbers help you find any errors?

Worksheet 48. Tell the child to complete Worksheet 48. The solutions are:

36 (**0**)	75 (**3**)	84 (**3**)
× 3 (**3**)	× 3 (**3**)	× 7 (**7**)
18	15	28
90	210	560
108 (0)	225 (0)	588 (3)
219 (**3**)	409 (**4**)	450 (**0**)
× 4 (**4**)	× 8 (**8**)	× 2 (**2**)
36	72	0
40	0	100
800	3200	800
876 (3)	3272 (5)	900 (0)
1234 (**1**)	2089 (**1**)	1298 (**2**)
× 3 (**3**)	× 4 (**4**)	× 9 (**0**)
12	36	72
90	320	810
600	0	1800
3000	8000	9000
3702 (3)	8356 (4)	11,682 (0)

In conclusion. Ask: How can check numbers help with multiplication? [checking the products]

If there is additional time following this lesson, play the Slower Multiplication Card Speed game, found in *Math Card Games* book, P30.

© Activities for Learning, Inc. 2015

LESSON 66: REVIEW AND GAMES 4

OBJECTIVES:
1. To review recent topics
2. To develop skills through playing math card games

MATERIALS:
1. Worksheet 49-A or 49-B, Review 4
2. *Math Card Games* book, P37
3. Math journal

ACTIVITIES FOR TEACHING:	EXPLANATIONS:

Worksheet 49-A. Give the child the worksheet. Tell her to listen to the problems and write the answers. Read each problem twice.

2000×10 $\qquad$ 20×8 $\qquad$ $32 \div 8$

Tell her to complete the worksheet. Solutions are below.

Write only the answers.

20,000

160

4

Write the answers.

$238 + 509 = \underline{747}$

$64 \div 8 = \underline{8}$

$30 \times 6 = \underline{180}$

Subtract. Show check numbers.

$10,489 - 512$

$10,489$ (4)
$- 512$ (8)
$9,977$ (5)

Multiply. Show check numbers.

428×3

428 (5)
$\times 3$ (3)
24
60
1200
1284 (6)

Which answer is correct? How do you know?

3318 (6) $\qquad$ 3318 (6) $\quad$ The second one is correct. Adding
$- 1592$ (8) $\qquad$ $- 1592$ (8) $\quad$ up check numbers 7 and 8 gives 6.
1826 (8) $\qquad$ 1726 (7)

The correct answer can also be found by adding up the lower two numbers.

Write the numbers in words.

100,011 $\quad$ one hundred thousand and eleven

3,062,000 $\quad$ three million sixty-two thousand

One hundred thousand eleven is also correct.

Write = or ≠ (unequal) on the lines.

$60 \times 9 \underline{=} 54 \times 10$

$30 \times 30 \underline{=} 900$

$100 \times 20 \underline{\neq} 200$

$8 \times 70 \underline{=} 560$

	Round to nearest 100.	Round to nearest 1000.
5720	5700	6000
67,562	67,600	68,000
945	900	1000

Solve the problem.

In December and January, Alex's puppy slept 10 hours a day. How many hours was that altogether? Write an equation and find the solution.

$h = (31 + 31) \times 10$
$h = 62 \times 10$
$h = 620$ hours

ACTIVITIES FOR TEACHING:

EXPLANATIONS:

Distribution Corners game. Play the Distribution Corners game found in *Math Card Games* book, P37. Tell her to do the scoring in her math journal.

Worksheet 49-B. Give the child the worksheet. Tell her to listen to the problems and write the answers. Read each problem twice.

$$3000 \times 10 \qquad 30 \times 7 \qquad 56 \div 7$$

Tell her to complete the worksheet. Solutions are below.

Write only the answers.

$$\underline{30,000}$$
$$\underline{210}$$
$$\underline{8}$$

Write the answers.

$678 + 263 = \underline{941}$

$72 \div 8 = \underline{\ 9\ }$

$40 \times 7 = \underline{280}$

Subtract. Show check numbers.
10,729 – 827

$$\begin{array}{r} 10,729 \ (1) \\ -\ 827 \ (8) \\ \hline 9,902 \ (2) \end{array}$$

Multiply. Show check numbers.
734 × 3

$$\begin{array}{r} 734 \ (5) \\ \times\ 3 \ (3) \\ \hline 12 \\ 90 \\ 2100 \\ \hline 2202 \ (6) \end{array}$$

Which answer is correct? How do you know?

$$\begin{array}{r} 5483 \ (2) \\ -\ 2679 \ (6) \\ \hline 2804 \ (5) \checkmark \end{array} \quad \begin{array}{r} 5483 \ (2) \\ -\ 2679 \ (6) \\ \hline 2814 \ (6) \end{array}$$

The first one is correct. Adding up check numbers 5 and 6 gives 2.

The correct answer can also be found by adding up the lower two numbers.

Write the numbers in words.

200,013 ___two hundred thousand and thirteen___

6,108,000 ___six million one hundred and eight thousand___

Two hundred thousand thirteen is also correct.

Write = or ≠ (unequal) on the lines.

$40 \times 8 \ \underline{=}\ 32 \times 10$

$20 \times 50 \ \underline{\neq}\ 100$

$100 \times 30 \ \underline{=}\ 3000$

$7 \times 80 \ \underline{=}\ 560$

	Round to nearest 100	Round to nearest 1000
8093	8100	8000
75,873	75,900	76,000
1165	1200	1000

Solve the problem.

In September and October, Regan played outside every day for two hours. How many hours was that altogether? Write an equation and find the solution.

$h = (30 + 31) \times 2$
$h = 61 \times 2$
$h = 122$ hours

© Activities for Learning, Inc. 2015

LESSON 67: UNIT FRACTIONS

OBJECTIVES:
1. To understand unit fractions as dividing 1 into equal parts
2. To compare unit fractions

MATERIALS:
1. Worksheet 50, Unit Fractions
2. Fraction chart pieces

ACTIVITIES FOR TEACHING:

Warm-up. Give the child the worksheet. Tell her to do just the warm-up section. Solutions are:

$60 \times 7 = $ **420** $\quad 9 \times 90 = 810$

$(8 \times $ **5**$) + (8 \times 3) = 64 \quad 56 \div 8 = 7$

```
  62  (8)
×  8  (8)
  16
 480
 496  (1)
```

Have the child say the ordinal numbers from 1–10. [first, second, third, . . . , tenth]

Working with halves. Give the child the fraction chart pieces and tell her to spread them out face down.

Say: Find the longest piece. Now find a piece that is half as long. [the half piece] Set it below the longest piece. See the figure shown below.

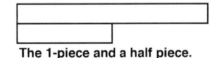

The 1-piece and a half piece.

Ask: How many one-half pieces do you need to make a whole? [2] Tell her to find the other one-half piece and set it under the 1-piece as shown below.

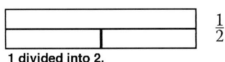

$\frac{1}{2}$

1 divided into 2.

Ask: How many pieces is the 1 divided into? [2] Tell her to turn over one of the smaller pieces and see the symbol, $\frac{1}{2}$. Say: It means 1 divided, or partitioned, into 2 equal parts.

Working with thirds. Now tell her to find three fraction pieces that divide the 1-piece into 3 equal parts. Tell her to set it under the 1 as shown below.

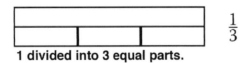

$\frac{1}{3}$

1 divided into 3 equal parts.

Ask: How do you think we write one third? Tell her to turn over one of the pieces and check. Ask: What does it mean? [1 divided into 3 equal parts.]

EXPLANATIONS:

A unit fraction is a fraction with 1 in the numerator.

There are several ways to approach fractions:
- One or more equal parts of a whole.
- One or more equal parts of a set.
- Division of two whole numbers.
- Location on a number line.
- Ratio of two numbers.

Mathematically, fractions are understood as the division of two whole numbers. This broader view of fractions will give the child a better basic understanding of the nature of fractions.

ACTIVITIES FOR TEACHING:

Working with fourths. Repeat with fourths. See figure below. Ask: What is each smaller piece labeled? [one fourth] What does it mean? [1 divided into 4 equal parts.]

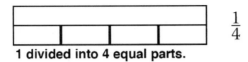
1 divided into 4 equal parts.

The whole fraction chart. Ask the child to turn the pieces over and build the fraction chart as shown below. Tell her she will need it for the worksheet.

Worksheet 50. Tell the child to complete the worksheet. Discuss her answers. Questions and solutions are:

How many fourths equal a whole? **4**
How many eighths are in a whole? **8**
How many tenths are in 1? **10**
Which is more, $\frac{1}{3}$ or $\frac{1}{4}$? $\frac{1}{3}$
Which is more, $\frac{1}{6}$ or $\frac{1}{4}$? $\frac{1}{4}$
Which is less, $\frac{1}{10}$ or $\frac{1}{9}$? $\frac{1}{10}$
How many thirds are in a whole? **3**
How many fourths are in a half? **2**
Missing fractions are: $\frac{1}{2}$ $\frac{1}{3}$ $\frac{1}{4}$ $\frac{1}{4}$ $\frac{1}{5}$ $\frac{1}{8}$

Fraction stairs. Tell the child to take one of each fraction piece and make fraction stairs or some other kind of order. Some examples are shown below. Ask: Are these stairs like the usual stairs? [no]

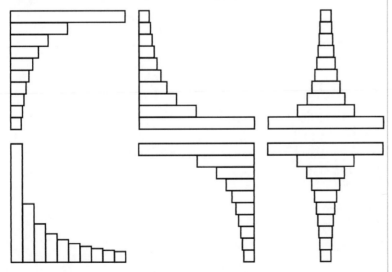

In conclusion. Ask: What do you call 1 divided by 2? [one half] What do you call 1 divided by 4? [one fourth] What do we call 1 divided by 12? [one twelfth]

EXPLANATIONS:

The fraction chart should never be assembled on top of the completed chart.

If there is additional time following this lesson, play the Distribution Corners game, found in *Math Card Games* book, P37.

© Activities for Learning, Inc. 2015

Lesson 68: Fractions as Division

OBJECTIVES:
1. To help the child discover that *a* units divided into *b* parts equals *a* times the fraction $\frac{1}{b}$

MATERIALS:
1. Worksheet 51, Fractions as Division
2. Fraction chart pieces
3. Three 1-strips, Appendix p. 7 *
4. **Scissors**, optional *
5. **Tape**
6. Dry erase board

ACTIVITIES FOR TEACHING:

Warm-up. Give the child the worksheet. Tell her to do just the warm-up section. Solutions are:

$4 + 7 \times 5 = \mathbf{39}$ $67 - (20 \times 3) = \mathbf{7}$ 457 **(7)**
$(72 \div 9) - (36 \div 6) = \mathbf{2}$ $63 \div 9 - 5 = \mathbf{2}$ $\underline{\times 6}$ **(6)**
                                                                          42
                                                                          300
                                                                          <u>2400</u>
                                                                          2742 (6)

Ask: What do you call 1 divided by 2? [one half] What do you call 1 divided by 3? [one third] What do you call 1 divided by 4? [one fourth] What do we call 1 divided by 8? [one eighth] What do you call 1 divided by 10? [one tenth]

Dividing 1 by 4. Give the child the fraction chart pieces and the three 1-strips. If the strips have not been separated, tell the child to cut them apart.

Tell her divide a 1-strip into fourths by folding it twice. See below. Ask: How does the folded part compare to the fourths from your fraction chart pieces? [same as one fourth]

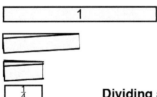
Dividing a 1-strip into four equal parts.

Dividing 2 by 4. Tell her to tape two 1-strips together to get 2. Then tell her to fold it into four equal parts. See the figures below. Ask: How does it compare to the fourths from your fraction chart pieces? [same as two fourths] Say: So 2 divided by 4 is equal to how many fourths? [two fourths]

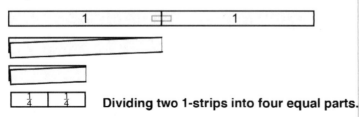
Dividing two 1-strips into four equal parts.

EXPLANATIONS:

* Either cut the 1-strips apart before the lesson or give the child a set of three to cut apart.

ACTIVITIES FOR TEACHING:	EXPLANATIONS:

Dividing 3 by 4. Tell her to tape the third 1-strip to the other two 1-strips. See the figure below. Tell her to fold it into four equal parts. Ask: How does the folded part compare to the fourths from your fraction chart pieces? [three fourths]

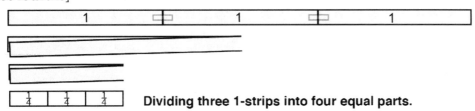
Dividing three 1-strips into four equal parts.

Writing the results. Write:

$$1 \div 4 = \tfrac{1}{4} \quad 2 \div 4 = \tfrac{2}{4} \quad 3 \div 4 = \tfrac{3}{4}$$

Tell the child to write the fractions for the following on her dry erase board:

two divided by three [$\tfrac{2}{3}$]

three divided by three [$\tfrac{3}{3}$]

four divided by five [$\tfrac{4}{5}$]

These 1-strips will also be used in the next lesson. Separate the individual strips by removing or cutting the tape.

Worksheet 51. Tell the child to complete the worksheet. The solutions are below.

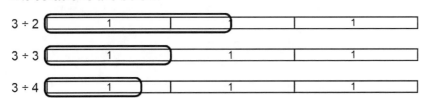

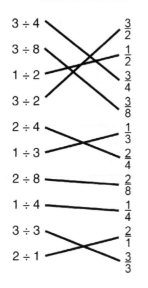

Problem: Ask the child to share her solutions. One solution is to divide the bars into fourths and give each friend three pieces. The other solution is to remove one-fourth from each bar. Three friends get the shortened bar and the fourth friend gets the 3 pieces. All get $\tfrac{3}{4}$ of the bar. See the figures below.

Dividing all the bars into four equal parts.

Lopping a fourth from each bar.

In conclusion. Ask: What is 3 divided by 4? [three fourths] What is 4 divided by 5? [four fifths]

If there is additional time following this lesson, play the Unit Fraction War game, found in *Math Card Games* book, F2.1.

Lesson 69: Non-Unit Fractions

OBJECTIVES:
1. To learn that $\frac{a}{b}$ is *a* times the fraction $\frac{1}{b}$

MATERIALS:
1. Worksheet 52, Non-Unit Fractions
2. Fraction chart pieces
3. Three 1-strips, Appendix p. 7 *

ACTIVITIES FOR TEACHING:

Warm-up. Give the child the worksheet. Tell her to do just the warm-up section. Solutions are:

8 × 60 = **480**	(6 × 60) + (6 × 30) = 540	379 **(1)**
42 ÷ 7 = **6**	32 ÷ 4 = **8** 360 ÷ 90 = **4**	× 6 **(6)**
		54
		420
		1800
		2274 **(6)**

Ask: What do you call 1 divided by 3? [one third] What do you call 2 divided by 3? [two thirds] What do you call 3 divided by 3? [three thirds or one]

Dividing the 1-strips. Give the child the fraction chart pieces and three 1-strips. Say: As you did in the last lesson, divide 2 strips into 4 parts. Compare to the fourths from your fraction chart pieces. Ask: Two divided by 4 is how many one-fourths? [two] See below.

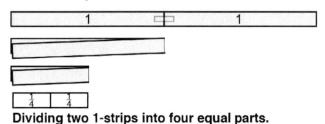

Dividing two 1-strips into four equal parts.

Write as follows:

$$2 \div 4 = \frac{2}{4} = \text{two } \tfrac{1}{4}\text{s}$$

Ask: How could you divide the same two strips into 8 parts? [fold it once more] Tell her to compare it to the eighths from the fraction chart pieces. Ask: Two divided by 8 is how many one-eighths? [two] See the figure on the left.

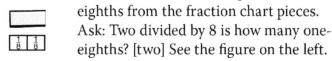

Write as follows:

$$2 \div 8 = \frac{2}{8} = \text{two } \tfrac{1}{8}\text{s}$$

Finding the fraction with the strips. Tell the child to lay out three eighths from the fraction chart pieces. Then tell her to fold the three 1-strips to be equal to the three eighths. [folded three times (into eighths)] See figure on the next page.

EXPLANATIONS:

* These are the same 1-strips used in the previous lesson.

ACTIVITIES FOR TEACHING: | EXPLANATIONS:

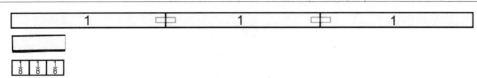

Dividing three 1-strips to match the three $\frac{1}{8}$s.

Ask: What did you divide the 3 strips into? [eighths] Say and write: three $\frac{1}{8}$ s = 3 ÷ 8 = $\frac{3}{8}$

Can You Find Fraction game. In preparation for playing the Can You Find Fraction game, tell the child to build the fraction stairs with the 1 on top and the pieces along the left edge. See figure on the right. Tell her to spread out the remaining fraction pieces face up.

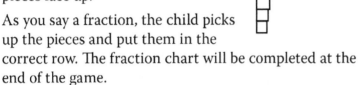

As you say a fraction, the child picks up the pieces and put them in the correct row. The fraction chart will be completed at the end of the game.

3 fourths	3 sevenths	3 tenths
5 eighths	3 ninths	2 tenths
3 ninths	2 fifths	2 thirds
2 eighths	1 half	4 tenths
2 sevenths	2 ninths	4 sixths
1 sixth	2 fifths	1 seventh

Worksheet 52. Tell the child to complete the worksheet. The solutions are below.

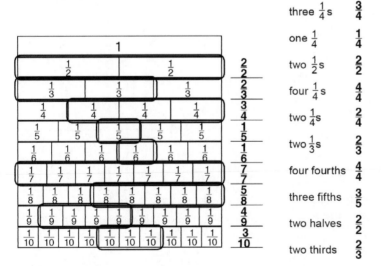

1. **five, six, five**
2. **six-sevenths**

In conclusion. Ask: What is 3 divided by 4? [three fourths] What do we call three one-fourths? [three fourths] What is 4 divided by 5? [four fifths] What do we call four one-fifths? [four fifths]

If there is additional time following this lesson, play the Unit Fraction War game, found in *Math Card Games* book, F2.1.

Lesson 70: Fraction Pairs That Total One

OBJECTIVES:
1. To find pairs of fractions that add to one

MATERIALS:
1. Worksheet 53, Fraction Pairs That Total One
2. Fraction chart pieces
3. Fraction cards (without the percent cards)
4. *Math Card Games* book, F3

ACTIVITIES FOR TEACHING:

Warm-up. Give the child the worksheet. Tell her to do just the warm-up section. Solutions are:

two $\frac{1}{3}$s	$\frac{2}{3}$	two fourths	$\frac{2}{4}$
two $\frac{1}{2}$s	$\frac{2}{2}$	four fifths	$\frac{4}{5}$
three $\frac{1}{5}$s	$\frac{3}{5}$	three thirds	$\frac{3}{3}$
one $\frac{1}{4}$	$\frac{1}{4}$	one half	$\frac{1}{2}$

Ask: What is 2 divided by 3? [two thirds] What do we call two one-thirds? [two thirds] What is 3 divided by 8? [three eighths] What do we call three one-eighths? [three eighths]

Fraction chart. Give the child the fraction chart pieces. Tell the child to assemble the fraction chart with the fraction pieces.

Fractions equaling 1. Ask the child to find the 1 and to set it aside. Draw a part-whole circle set; write 1 in the whole and $\frac{3}{5}$ in a part-circle. See the left figure below.

Ask the child to find the fraction pieces to show three fifths and to lay them under the 1. See the right figure below. Ask: How much is needed to make 1? [$\frac{2}{5}$] Write or tell the child to write it in the other part-circle.

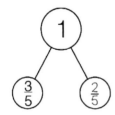 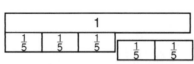

Three fifths and two fifths = 1.

Repeat for other fractions, such as one sixth, [five sixths] seven tenths, [three tenths] and one half. [one half]

EXPLANATIONS:

To focus the child's attention on fractions, not arithmetic, do not teach the algorithm that the sum of the two numerators equals the denominator.

ACTIVITIES FOR TEACHING:

Finding pairs of cards that equal one. Give the child the fraction cards. Tell her to spread her cards out face up. Next she is to pick up a card and find the match so that the pair equals one. Tell her to find ten different pairs, which will be used in the following game.

Concentrating on One game. Play the Concentrating on One game, found in the *Math Card Games* book, F3, using the pairs of cards she found.

Worksheet 53. Tell the child to complete the worksheet. The solutions are shown below.

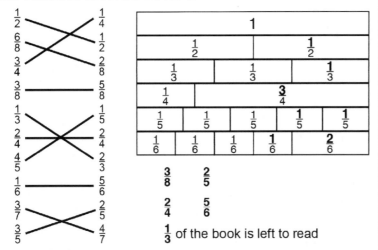

$\frac{3}{8}$ $\frac{2}{5}$

$\frac{2}{4}$ $\frac{5}{6}$

$\frac{1}{3}$ of the book is left to read

In conclusion. Ask: Why does it take 10 tenths to make 1, but only 3 thirds to equal 1? [tenths are smaller] How many twelfths do you need to equal a whole? [twelve]

EXPLANATIONS:

LESSON 71: THE RULER CHART

OBJECTIVES:

1. To compare fractions involving the 1s, halves, fourths, and eighths
2. To provide the foundation for reading a ruler to eighths

MATERIALS:

1. Worksheet 54, The Ruler Chart
2. Fraction chart pieces
3. *Math Card Games* book, F7
4. Ruler, optional

ACTIVITIES FOR TEACHING:

Warm-up. Give the child the worksheet and fraction chart pieces. Tell him to do just the warm-up section. Solutions are:

$$\frac{1}{6} > \frac{1}{8} \qquad \frac{2}{5} < \frac{2}{3} \qquad \frac{2}{4} = \frac{3}{6} \qquad \frac{1}{2} > \frac{3}{8}$$

$$\frac{1}{2} = \frac{4}{8} \qquad \frac{3}{4} > \frac{5}{8} \qquad \frac{1}{3} > \frac{1}{4} \qquad \frac{2}{6} < \frac{2}{3}$$

Ask: What is 1 divided by 4? [one fourth] What is 2 divided by 4? [two fourths] What do we call two one-fourths? [two fourths] What is 3 divided by 4? [three fourths] What do we call three one-fourths? [three fourths] What is 4 divided by 4? [four fourths or one] What do we call four one-fourths? [four fourths or one]

Fractions on a ruler. Ask the child to build the fraction chart, using only the one, halves, fourths, and eighths pieces. See below.

1							
$\frac{1}{2}$				$\frac{1}{2}$			
$\frac{1}{4}$		$\frac{1}{4}$		$\frac{1}{4}$		$\frac{1}{4}$	
$\frac{1}{8}$	$\frac{1}{8}$	$\frac{1}{8}$	$\frac{1}{8}$	$\frac{1}{8}$	$\frac{1}{8}$	$\frac{1}{8}$	$\frac{1}{8}$

Partial fraction chart.

Ask the following questions to be answered by referring to his partial fraction chart:

1. How many fourths in 1? [4]
2. How many eighths in a whole? [8]
3. How many fourths in one-half? [2]
4. How many eighths in one-half? [4]
5. Which is more, $\frac{2}{8}$ or $\frac{1}{4}$? [same]
6. Which is more, $\frac{5}{8}$ or $\frac{1}{2}$? [$\frac{5}{8}$]
7. What fraction is the same as $\frac{6}{8}$? [$\frac{3}{4}$]
8. What fraction is the same as $\frac{4}{8}$? [$\frac{1}{2}$ or $\frac{2}{4}$]
9. Which is more, 1 or $\frac{7}{8}$? [1]

EXPLANATIONS:

The first half of these RightStart™ Mathematics lessons referred to the child as a female and the second half refers to the child as a male.

RightStart™ Mathematics Level D Second Edition

© Activities for Learning, Inc. 2015

ACTIVITIES FOR TEACHING:	EXPLANATIONS:

Fraction War game. Play the Fraction War game, found in the *Math Card Games* book, F7. Give the child the fraction cards. Tell him to find the ones, halves, fourths, and eighths. Then tell him to pick the cards up in random order and play the game using the cards he found.

Some of the cards will be needed for the worksheet.

Worksheet preparation. After he has completed the game, tell him to collect the seven different fraction cards from the game. Then tell him to put them in order from least to greatest. See below.

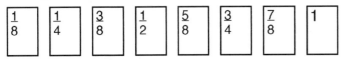

Explain that these fractions will be needed for the first activity on the worksheet.

Worksheet 54. Tell the child to complete the worksheet. The solutions are shown below.

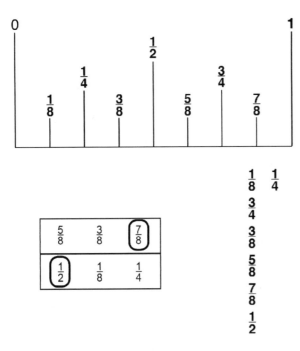

After he has completed the worksheet, ask: Does the partial chart remind you of anything? [a ruler] If appropriate, show him a ruler.

In conclusion. Ask: Which is greater, seven eighths or one half? [seven eighths] Which is greater, three fourths or one half? [three fourths] Which is greater, three fourths or five eighths? [three fourths]

© Activities for Learning, Inc. 2015

Lesson 72: Adding Halves and Fourths

OBJECTIVES:
1. To divide rectangles into fourths three different ways
2. To informally add simple mixed numbers with halves and fourths

MATERIALS:
1. 4 rectangles, Appendix p. 8 *
2. Ruler
3. Math journal or dry erase board
4. Worksheet 55, Adding Halves and Fourths

ACTIVITIES FOR TEACHING:

Warm-up. Ask: What is 1 divided by 4? [one fourth] What is 2 divided by 4? [two fourths] What do we call two one-fourths? [two fourths or one half] What is 3 divided by 4? [three fourths] What do we call three one-fourths? [three fourths] What is 4 divided by 4? [four fourths or one] What do we call four one-fourths? [four fourths or one]

Rectangles into halves. Give the child the four rectangles, ruler, and either math journal or dry erase board. Tell him to keep one rectangle whole and to fold the other three rectangles into congruent halves, each a different way. See below.

Dividing the rectangle into halves in different ways.

Perimeters of the rectangle and halves. Ask: Do you think the halves all have the same perimeter? Remind the child that perimeter is the distance around the edges of a closed figure. Tell him to measure the sides of the whole rectangle using the inches on his ruler. Then tell him to draw the rectangle in his math journal or on his dry erase board and write the measurements. [4" by 3"] Tell him to find the perimeter. See below.

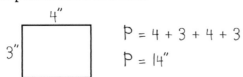

Tell him: Draw the rectangles that are divided into halves. Calculate the measurements from the original rectangle. You can check your calculations with your ruler. Then find the perimeters. The drawings and equations are on the next page.

EXPLANATIONS:

* Either cut out the rectangles before the lesson or give the child a page of rectangles to cut apart.

These are not to be cut apart, only folded. The wholes will be needed again.

Congruent is defined as fitting exactly on top.

See page iii, number 20 of "Some General Thoughts on Teaching Mathematics," for additional information.

Some children may prefer to write the measurements on all four sides of the rectangle. Eventually he will discover it is not necessary.

ACTIVITIES FOR TEACHING:

EXPLANATIONS:

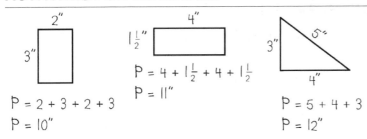

$P = 2 + 3 + 2 + 3$
$P = 10"$

$P = 4 + 1\frac{1}{2} + 4 + 1\frac{1}{2}$
$P = 11"$

$P = 5 + 4 + 3$
$P = 12"$

Ask the child to explain how he added the numbers with fractions. [add the whole numbers and then add the fractions]

Remind the child that area is the amount of space something takes up. Ask: Is the area of each half rectangle the same? [yes, each is half of the same rectangle] Are the perimeters the same? [no] Discuss the differences in perimeter.

Rectangles into fourths. Now ask the child to divide each of the four paper rectangles into congruent fourths in different ways. See below.

Dividing the rectangle into fourths in different ways.

Worksheet 55. Give the child the worksheet and tell him to complete it. Tell him to refer to his folded rectangles for drawing the fourths.

Ask the child to explain how he found the size of the fourths and calculated the perimeters. The measurements and solutions are shown below.

$\frac{3}{4}"$ × 4"
$P = 4 + \frac{3}{4} + 4 + \frac{3}{4}$
$P = 9\frac{1}{2}"$ or $P = 9\frac{2}{4}"$

1" × 3"
$P = 1 + 3 + 1 + 3$
$P = 8"$

2" × $1\frac{1}{2}"$
$P = 1\frac{1}{2} + 2 + 1\frac{1}{2} + 2$
$P = 7"$

Triangle with sides $2\frac{1}{2}"$, $2\frac{1}{2}"$, $1\frac{1}{2}"$, base 3"
$P = 2\frac{1}{2} + 2\frac{1}{2} + 3$
$P = 8"$

or

Triangle base 4", sides $2\frac{1}{2}"$, $2\frac{1}{2}"$
$P = 2\frac{1}{2} + 2\frac{1}{2} + 4$
$P = 9"$

In conclusion. Ask: What do we call the distance around a closed figure? [perimeter] What do we call the amount of space a closed figure takes up? [area]

If there is additional time following this lesson, play the Fraction War game, found in *Math Card Games* book, F7.

© Activities for Learning, Inc. 2015

146

LESSON 73: QUARTERS OF AN HOUR

OBJECTIVES:

1. To review the term *quarter*
2. To work with quarters of an hour
3. To review the abbreviations for minute (min) and hour (hr)

MATERIALS:

1. Geared clock
2. Worksheet 56, Quarters of an Hour
3. Minute clock cards, both sets

ACTIVITIES FOR TEACHING:	EXPLANATIONS:
Warm-up. Ask: What do we call the distance around a figure? [perimeter] What is the perimeter of a square that has one side 8 inches long? [32 inches; 8 + 8 + 8 + 8 or 8 × 4] What do we call the amount of space a figure takes up? [area] What is the area the square that has 8 inches on one side? [8 × 8 = 64 square inches]	
Reviewing half hours. Set the clock with the minute hand at 12. Steadily move the minute hand forward and say: Let me know when the clock has moved 1 hour. Ask: Where is the minute hand? [at 12] Continuing moving the minute hand and say: Let me know when a half hour has gone by. Ask: Where is the minute hand now? [at 6] Say: Let me know when another half hour has gone by. Ask: Where is the minute hand? [at 12]	
Quarter hours. Tell him that *quarter* is another name for *one fourth*. With the minute hand at 12, ask: If I go a quarter of a hour, what number will I stop at? [3] Where will I stop if I go another quarter hour? [6] Where is the next quarter? [9] Where is the next quarter hour? [12]	
Worksheet 56. Give the child the worksheet and tell him to do the first chart. It is shown below. Discuss his answers.	The abbreviations for hour (hr) and minute (min) are given on the worksheet. Encourage the child to read the information on the worksheet himself.

1 hr			
$\frac{1}{2}$ hr		$\frac{1}{2}$ hr	
$\frac{1}{4}$ hr	$\frac{1}{4}$ hr	$\frac{1}{4}$ hr	$\frac{1}{4}$ hr

Minutes in an hour. Ask: How many minutes does the minute hand move during an hour? [60 min] Move the hour hand halfway around and ask: How many minutes in a half hour? [30 min] Repeat for a quarter hour. [15 min]

Worksheet 56. Tell him to do the second chart on his worksheet. It is shown on the next page. Discuss his answers.

RightStart™ Mathematics Level D Second Edition   © Activities for Learning, Inc. 2015

ACTIVITIES FOR TEACHING:

60 min			
30 min		30 min	
15 min	15 min	15 min	15 min

Tell the child to answer the following questions by referring to his worksheet:

1. How many half hours make a whole hour? [2]
2. How many minutes are in a half hour? [30 min]
3. How long is 2 half hours? [60 min, 1 hr]
4. How long is a quarter of an hour? [15 min]
5. How long is 2 quarters of an hour? [30 min, half hour]
6. How long is 3 quarters of an hour? [45 min]
7. Which is longer, 1 hour or 3 quarters of a hour? [1 hr]
8. How long is 4 quarters of an hour? [60 min, or 1 hr]
9. How long is 3 halves of an hour? [90 min, or 1 hr and 30 min]

Quarter Hour Later Memory game. Give the child the two sets of minute cards. Tell him to lay each set of cards face down.

The first player turns over a card from the first color and says aloud what time it would be a quarter of an hour later, ignoring the hours. He then chooses a card from the other color. If he finds the correct card, he collects both cards and takes another turn. If they do not match, both cards are returned face down. The second player then takes her turn. Turns continue until all the cards are collected.

Worksheet 56. Tell the child to complete the worksheet. See below for the solutions:

$\frac{1}{2}$ hr, 30 min $\frac{1}{4}$ hr, 15 min $\frac{1}{4}$ hr, 15 min $\frac{1}{2}$ hr, 30 min

1:05, 1:20, 1:35, 1:50, 2:05, 2:20, 2:35, 2:50, 3:05

For the school bus problem, tell the child to solve it himself, then discuss it.

Most assume there are 10 trips, to and from school for 5 days, giving answers of $2\frac{1}{2}$ **hr**, and **150 min**. However, some might say a week has 7 days, giving an answer of $3\frac{1}{2}$ **hr**. Others might say the two children are bussed only one way giving an answer of $1\frac{1}{4}$ **hr**.

In conclusion. Tell him: Start at 8:00 and count by quarter hours to 10:00. [8:00, 8:15, 8:30, 8:45, 9:00, 9:15, 9:30, 9:45, 10:00]

EXPLANATIONS:

If there is additional time following this lesson, play the Fraction War game, found in *Math Card Games* book, F7.

© Activities for Learning, Inc. 2015

148

Lesson 74: Fractions of a Dollar

OBJECTIVES:
1. To review the parts of a dollar
2. To relate the value of coins to fractions

MATERIALS:
1. Plastic coins
2. Worksheet 57, Fractions of a Dollar

ACTIVITIES FOR TEACHING:	EXPLANATIONS:
Warm-up. Tell the child to start at 3:15 and count by quarter hours to 5:30. [3:15, 3:30, 3:45, 4:00, 4:15, 4:30, 4:45, 5:00, 5:15, 5:30]	
Ask: How many quarter hours make a whole hour? [4] How many minutes are in a quarter hour? [15 min] How long is 2 quarter hours? [30 min, half hour] How long is a quarter of an hour? [15 min] How long is 4 quarters of an hour? [60 min, one hour] How long is 3 quarters of an hour? [45 min]	
Reviewing parts of a dollar. Give the child the coins. Tell him a dollar is 100 cents; the word *cent* means *hundred.* Ask: Can you think of any other words that start like *cent* and mean hundred? [century and centennial]	Another possibility is *centipede*, which doesn't actually have 100 legs; it just looks like it. *Centimeter* might also come to mind. There are 100 centimeters in a meter.
Tell the child to lay out the five coins of different sizes. Find the largest coin, the half-dollar. Ask: What is the value of a half-dollar? [50¢] Explain they are hardly ever used any more.	
Tell him to find the next largest coin, the quarter. Ask: How much is a quarter of a dollar worth? [25¢]	
Say: You have three coins left. Ask: Which one is smallest, but worth the most? [dime] How much is a dime worth? [10¢] How many dimes does it take to make a dollar? [10] A dime is what fraction of a dollar? [one tenth]	
Ask: What coin is worth half of a dime? [nickel] How much it is worth? [5¢] Tell the child that the dime used to be made from silver, which is very expensive so a smaller size was chosen.	
Ask: Of these coins, which is worth the least? [penny] How much is a penny worth? [1¢] How many pennies does it take to equal a dollar? [100] How can you easily tell a penny from a dime? [color] Tell him that some countries no longer use a coin for one cent.	

RightStart™ Mathematics Level D Second Edition

© Activities for Learning, Inc. 2015

ACTIVITIES FOR TEACHING:

EXPLANATIONS:

Worksheet 57. Give the child the worksheet and tell him to do the charts. Explain that the nickel and penny are too small for the charts. The completed charts are shown below. Discuss the child's answers.

1 Dollar									
Half-dollar				Half-dollar					
Quarter		Quarter		Quarter		Quarter			
Dime	Dime	Dime	Dime	Dime	Dime	Dime	Dime	Dime	Dime

100¢									
50¢				50¢					
25¢		25¢		25¢		25¢			
10¢	10¢	10¢	10¢	10¢	10¢	10¢	10¢	10¢	10¢

Then tell him to answer the questions by referring to his worksheet. Solutions are below.

1. How many quarters equal a dollar? **4**
2. How many quarters are equal to 2 dollars? **8**
3. How many dimes are equal to a dollar? **10**
4. How many pennies in a dollar and a half? **150**
5. Which is greater, 3 quarters or 1 dollar? **$1**
6. How much does 2 quarters equal? **50¢**
7. How many quarters are in a dollar and a half? **6**
8. How many dimes are equal to half a dollar? **5**
9. Which is greater, 6 quarters or 3 half dollars? **same**
10. Which coin is one-tenth of a dollar? **dime**
11. If half a small pizza costs a dollar and a half, what does a whole pizza cost? **$3**

$2.00, $2.25, $2.50, $2.75, $3.00, $3.25, $3.50, $3.75, $4.00

In conclusion. Tell him: Start at $3.50 and count by quarters to $5.50. [$3.50, $3.75, $4.00, $4.25, $4.50, $4.75, $5.00, $5.25, $5.50]

If there is additional time following this lesson, play the Fraction of Twelve game, found in *Math Card Games* book, F14.

Note: The next lesson will need a variety of empty containers.

© Activities for Learning, Inc. 2015

Lesson 75: Gallons and Quarts

OBJECTIVES:
1. To become familiar with gallons and quarts, relating them to fractions

MATERIALS:
1. **1 gallon container, filled with water**
2. **2 half-gallon containers**
3. **At least 2 quart containers**
4. **Funnel**, optional
5. Worksheet 58, Gallons and Quarts

ACTIVITIES FOR TEACHING:	**EXPLANATIONS:**

Warm-up. Tell the child to start at 10:45 and count by quarter hours to 12:30. [10:45, 11:00, 11:15, 11:30, 11:45, 12:00, 12:15, 12:30]

Tell him to start at $1.75 and count by quarters to $3.50. [$1.75, $2.00, $2.25, $2.50, $2.75, $3.00, $3.25, $3.50]

Ask: How many quarters equal a dollar? [4] How many quarters are equal to a half dollar? [2] How many pennies in a quarter? [25] Which is greater, 1 dollar or 3 quarters? [$1] How many quarters are in a dollar and a half? [6]

Gallons and quarts. Show the child the gallon container and tell him it is a container that holds one *gallon*. Ask: How much water does it hold? [1 gallon] How much milk would fit? [1 gallon] How much juice would it have when it was full? [1 gallon]

This lesson could be done outdoors.

Next show him the half-gallon container. Tell him it is a *half-gallon* container. Ask: How much water will it hold? [half of a gallon] What fraction of the water from the gallon will fit in the half-gallon container? [one half] Fill the half-gallon container and show the level of the water remaining in the gallon jug. Ask: How many half-gallon containers are needed to hold the water in the gallon container? [2] Pour it into the second half-gallon container.

Ask the child to participate in the pouring activities.

RightStart™ Mathematics Level D Second Edition © Activities for Learning, Inc. 2015

ACTIVITIES FOR TEACHING:	EXPLANATIONS:

Now show him the quart containers. Tell him that a quarter of a gallon, a fourth, is called a *quart*. Ask: How many quarts will be needed to empty the half-gallon? [2] What do we call half of a half-gallon? [quart] How many quart containers are needed to hold the water in the half-gallon? [2] How many quarts equal a gallon? [4]

Worksheet 58. Give the child the worksheet and tell him to fill in the charts. They are shown below.

1			
$\frac{1}{2}$		$\frac{1}{2}$	
$\frac{1}{4}$	$\frac{1}{4}$	$\frac{1}{4}$	$\frac{1}{4}$

1 gallon			
half-gallon		half-gallon	
quart	quart	quart	quart

Summarizing. Tell the child to answer the following questions by referring to his worksheet:

How many half-gallons in a gallon? [2]

How many quarts in a gallon? [4]

What is one fourth of a gallon? [quart]

What is one half of a half-gallon? [quart]

Worksheet 58. Tell the child to complete the worksheet. Discuss the answers. The solutions are as follows:

a. 4 quarts = 1 gallon

b. 1 half-gallon > 1 quart

c. 1 gallon > 3 quarts

d. 2 quarts < 2 half-gallons

e. $\frac{1}{4}$ gallon = 1 quart

f. 6 quarts < 2 gallons

g. 1 half-gallon = 2 quarts

h. $\frac{1}{2}$ gallon > 1 quart

i. 10 quarts < 10 gallons

j. 3 gallons = 12 quarts

k. **64 oz**

l. **64 oz**

m. **128 oz**

n. **128 oz**

o. **96 oz**

In conclusion. Ask: Do we measure time in gallons? [no] Do we measure perimeter in gallons? [no] Do we measure height in gallons? [no] What do we measure in gallons? [how much a container will hold]

If there is additional time following this lesson, have the child choose a game to play.

© Activities for Learning, Inc. 2015

Enrichment Lesson 76: Musical Notes

OBJECTIVES:
1. To understand the value of musical notes as related to fractions

MATERIALS:
1. Dry erase board
2. Worksheet 59, Musical Notes

ACTIVITIES FOR TEACHING:	EXPLANATIONS:
Ways to write time. Introduce the topic of written music by relating it to time. Ask: What is time? [how long it takes for something to happen] What words do we use to talk about time? [hours, minutes, days, weeks, months, years] How do we show time on paper? [clock circles, numbers, hour hand, minute hand, calendars]	
Tell the child there is another kind of time we talk and write about — in music. Ask: What are some words we use to talk about musical time? [beat, rhythm, claps] Tell him to sing and clap to the beat of "Twinkle, Twinkle, Little Star." Do it a second time, but ask: How many beats do you think the words "How" and "I" get? [1] Tell him that a beat is the same as a clap. Sing it a third time, asking him to find two words with one syllable that each get two beats. [star, are]	Twinkle, Twinkle, Little Star *Twinkle, Twinkle, Little Star* *How I wonder what you are.* *Up above the sky so high,* *Like a diamond in the sky.* *Twinkle, Twinkle, Little Star* *How I wonder what you are.*
Ask: What kinds of things do we need to write down on paper when we write music? [number of beats, pitch, and so on] Explain that today we are going to talk about writing beats, or musical time.	
Musical notes. Draw the whole note and tell him it is called a *whole note*. Write the name below. See below. Tell him to draw it on his dry erase board and write the name. Next draw a half note and say it is called a *half note*. Continue with quarter notes and eighth notes.	
	If you refer to the shape of a note, call it by its mathematical name, *ellipse*, not oval.
Worksheet 59. Give the child the worksheet and tell him to look at the top part of the worksheet. Tell him that often the whole note gets 4 beats and that is what we will use today. Ask: How many beats does the half note get? [2] How many beats does the quarter note get? [1] How many beats does the eighth note get? [one half]	
Tell him to fill in the charts, using his notes from his dry erase board. See the figures on the next page.	

ACTIVITIES FOR TEACHING:	EXPLANATIONS:

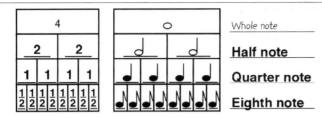

Beats per measure. Explain that music is organized in measures. Remind him that each measure will have four beats. Draw a rectangle and say: This is a measure. See the left figure below.

Empty measure. **A measure with a whole note.**

Draw a second measure and add a whole note. See the figure above on the right. Ask: How many beats does the note get? [4] How many beats does the measure need? [4] Can any more notes fit in the measure? [no]

Draw another measure with a half note and a quarter note. See the left figure below. Ask: How many beats does the measure have? [3] Is that enough? [no] How much more does it need? [1 more beat] Tell the child to draw it. See the right figure below.

Incomplete measure. **Complete measure.**

Repeat for a measure with 3 quarter notes and an eighth note. [1 more eighth note is needed] See the figures below.

Incomplete measure. **Complete measure.**

Worksheet 59. Ask the child to complete the worksheet. The solutions are shown below.

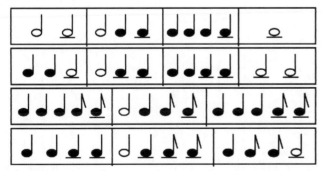

In conclusion. Ask: How does written music show how many beats a word or syllable get? [the shape of the notes] A whole note is twice as long as what note? [half note] An eighth note is half as long as what note? [quarter note]

If there is additional time following this lesson, play the Fraction of Twelve game, found in *Math Card Games* book, F14.

© Activities for Learning, Inc. 2015

LESSON 77: ASSESSMENT REVIEW 2

OBJECTIVES:
1. To review concepts learned in previous lessons

MATERIALS:
1. Worksheet 60, Assessment Review 2
2. AL Abacus, if needed

ACTIVITIES FOR TEACHING:

Worksheet 60. Give the child the worksheet. Tell him that today will be a review for the upcoming assessment. He will complete the two-page worksheet, then discuss the solutions.

Tell the child to listen to the problems and write the answers. Read each problem twice.

300×20 30×7 $48 \div 8$

Tell him to complete the worksheet. Solutions are below and on the next page.

EXPLANATIONS:

This lesson is a review of concepts learned so far. It is designed to prepare the child for the upcoming assessment lesson.

The child may use the abacus where needed.

1-3. Write only the answers.

6,000
210
6

4-9. Write the answers.

$47 + 65 = \underline{112}$ $80 - 19 = \underline{61}$
$72 \div 8 = \underline{9}$ $63 - 25 = \underline{38}$
$60 \times 3 = \underline{180}$ $100 - \underline{28} = 72$

10. Multiply 586×7.

$$
\begin{array}{r}
586 \ (1) \\
\times 7 \ (7) \\
\hline
42 \\
560 \\
3500 \\
\hline
4102 \ (7) \checkmark
\end{array}
$$

11. Multiply 6209×8.

$$
\begin{array}{r}
6209 \ (8) \\
\times 8 \ (8) \\
\hline
72 \\
1600 \\
48000 \\
\hline
49,672 \ (1) \checkmark
\end{array}
$$

12. Multiply 4536×9.

$$
\begin{array}{r}
4536 \ (0) \\
\times 9 \ (0) \\
\hline
54 \\
270 \\
4500 \\
36000 \\
\hline
40,824 \ (0) \checkmark
\end{array}
$$

13-22. Subtract the same number.

$$
\begin{array}{r}
4780 \ (1) \\
- 478 \ (1) \\
\hline
4302 \ (0) \\
- 478 \ (1) \\
\hline
3824 \ (8) \\
- 478 \ (1) \\
\hline
3346 \ (7) \\
- 478 \ (1) \\
\hline
2868 \ (6) \\
- 478 \ (1) \\
\hline
2390 \ (5) \\
- 478 \ (1) \\
\hline
1912 \ (4) \\
- 478 \ (1) \\
\hline
1434 \ (3) \\
- 478 \ (1) \\
\hline
956 \ (2) \\
- 478 \ (1) \\
\hline
478 \ (1) \\
- 478 \ (1) \\
\hline
0 \ (0)
\end{array}
$$

23-25. Write these mixed-up numbers correctly using digits.

7 hundreds 4 tens 3 thousands   3740

3 thousands 2 tens 4 ones 3 hundreds   3324

4 hundreds 8 ones 9 thousands   9408

26-37. Fill in the table.

	Round to nearest 10.	Round to nearest 100.	Round to nearest 1000.
3784	3780	3800	4000
6219	6220	6200	6000
607	610	600	1000
18,535	18,540	18,500	19,000

RightStart™ Mathematics Level D Second Edition

© Activities for Learning, Inc. 2015

155

ACTIVITIES FOR TEACHING:

EXPLANATIONS:

38-43. Match expressions with fractions.

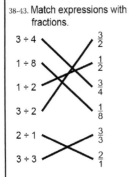

44-47. Fill in the blanks.

$1 = \frac{1}{2} + \frac{1}{2}$

$1 = \frac{3}{4} + \frac{1}{4}$

$\frac{3}{5} + \frac{2}{5} = 1$

$\frac{1}{8} + \frac{2}{8} + \frac{5}{8} = 1$

48-49. Circle the greatest fraction in each row.

| $\frac{5}{6}$ | $\frac{3}{6}$ | $(\frac{7}{6})$ |
| $\frac{1}{4}$ | $(\frac{4}{4})$ | $\frac{3}{4}$ |

50-57. Fill in the blanks.

$4 \times 3 = \underline{12}$ $\quad 10 \times 8 = \underline{80}$

$40 \times 3 = \underline{120}$ $\quad 10 \times 80 = \underline{800}$

$400 \times 3 = \underline{1200}$ $\quad 10 \times 800 = \underline{8,000}$

$4000 \times 3 = \underline{12,000}$ $\quad 10 \times 8000 = \underline{80,000}$

58-60. Solve the problems.

A coach has two hours for coaching. He has three teams. What fraction of an hour can he spend with each team?

$2 \div 3 = \frac{2}{3}$ hr

A side of a square mat is $17\frac{1}{2}$ feet long. What is the perimeter of the mat? Write an equation and find the solution.

$P = 17\frac{1}{2} \times 4 = 68 + 2$

$P = 70$ feet

There were 36 pairs of geese nesting on Otter Lake. Two hundred and nine goslings hatched from their eggs. What is the total number of geese?

$G = 36 \times 2 + 209$

$G = 72 + 209 = 281$ geese

Worksheet solutions. Check the answers to the review worksheet with the child. Discuss the various methods for the solutions.

The next day will be a day of games. Games review and practice the facts and skills in an enjoyable environment.

© Activities for Learning, Inc. 2015

LESSON 78: REVIEW GAMES

OBJECTIVES:

1. To review recent topics by playing math card games

MATERIALS:

1. *Math Card Games* book, N46, P32, P36, and F3
2. AL Abacus, optional
3. Short Multiplication Table, Appendix p. 1, optional
4. Fraction chart

ACTIVITIES FOR TEACHING:	EXPLANATIONS:
Warm-Up. Ask: Does 67 + 29 = 29 + 67? [yes] Say: The commutative property works for addition. Ask: Does 7 × 9 = 9 × 7? [yes] Does the commutative property work for multiplication? [yes] Does 9 − 7 = 7 − 9? [no] Does the commutative property work for subtraction? [no]	This lesson is a review of concepts learned so far by playing games. It is designed to prepare the child for the assessment in the next lesson.
Write: $\qquad 2 \times 4 \times 5 = \underline{\quad}$	Although it is helpful for the child to know these names of the properties, it is not necessary. The concepts are essential to understand.
and ask: Does the order of multiplication matter? [no] How many different ways could you find the product? One way is 2 × 4 is 8 and 8 × 5 = 40. Another way is 5 × 4 is 20 and 20 × 2 = 40. Still another way is 2 × 5 = 10 and 10 × 4 = 40. Say: This is the associative property. Ask: Which way do you think is easiest?	See page ii, numbers 1 and 11 of "Some General Thoughts on Teaching Mathematics," for additional information.
Write: $\qquad (4 + 2) \times 5 = (4 \times 5) + (2 \times 5)$	
and ask: Is this true? [yes] Say: This is the distributive property. We can add two numbers and then multiply, or we can multiply each number and then add.	
Write: $\qquad (4 − 2) \times 5 = (4 \times 5) − (2 \times 5)$	
and ask: Does the distributive property work for subtraction and multiplication? [yes] Say: The distributive property works for numbers being added or subtracted and then multiplied.	
Rounding War game. Give the child the abacus and play the Rounding War game found in the *Math Card Games* book, N46.	Use the Background section in the description for game N46 if additional review is necessary, otherwise it may be ignored.
Play a second game using the hundreds. Use side 2 of the abacus when necessary.	
Ring around the Products game. Ask: What is 6 × 6? [36] What is 7 × 5? [35] 5 × 7? [35] Ask: What is 7 × 7? [49] What is 8 × 6? [48] 6 × 8? [48] Ask: What is 8 × 8? [64] What is 7 × 9? [63] 9 × 7? [63] Ask: What is 9 × 9? [81] What is 8 × 10? [80] 10 × 8? [80]	Choose one or both of the multiplication games provided, P32 and P36.
Play the Ring around the Products game found in the *Math Card Games* book, P32. Use the short multiplication table or the abacus as needed.	

RightStart™ Mathematics Level D Second Edition

© Activities for Learning, Inc. 2015

ACTIVITIES FOR TEACHING:	EXPLANATIONS:

Multiplying Three One-Digit Numbers game. Play the Multiplying Three One-Digit Numbers game found in the *Math Card Games* book, P36.

Concentrating on One game. Give the child the fraction chart. Ask: What is 1 divided by 4? [one fourth] What is 2 divided by 4? [two fourths] What do we call two one-fourths? [two fourths or one half] What is 3 divided by 4? [three fourths] What do we call three one-fourths? [three fourths] What is 4 divided by 4? [four fourths or one] What do we call four one-fourths? [four fourths or one]

Ask: What does one fourth need to make 1? [three fourths] What does one third need to make 1? [two thirds] What does two fifths need to make 1? [three fifths] What does three eighths need to make 1? [five eighths]

Play the Concentrating on One game found in the *Math Card Games* book, F3.

In conclusion. Ask: What is opposite of addition? [subtraction] What is opposite of subtraction? [addition] What is opposite of multiplication? [division] What is opposite of division? [multiplication]

© Activities for Learning, Inc. 2015

158

LESSON 79: ASSESSMENT 2

OBJECTIVES:
1. To assess concepts learned in previous lessons

MATERIALS:
1. Worksheet 61, Assessment 2
2. AL Abacus, if needed

ACTIVITIES FOR TEACHING:	EXPLANATIONS:
Worksheet 61. Give the child the worksheet.	

Tell him to listen to the problems and write the answers. Read each problem twice.

4000×10 $\qquad$ 60×7 $\qquad$ $56 \div 8$

Tell him to complete the worksheet. Solutions are below and on the next page.

The child may use the abacus where needed.

1-3. Write only the answers.

40,000
420
7

4-9. Write the answers.

$58 + 63 = 121$ $90 - 73 = 17$
$72 \div 9 = 8$ $52 - 15 = 37$
$70 \times 4 = 280$ $100 - 31 = 69$

10. Multiply 495 × 8.

```
 495 (0)
 × 8 (8)
  40
 720
3200
3960 (0) ✓
```

11. Multiply 5083 × 7.

```
 5083 (7)
  × 7 (7)
    21
   560
 35000
35,581 (4) ✓
```

12. Multiply 7594 × 9.

```
 7594 (7)
  × 9 (0)
    36
   810
  4500
 63000
68,346 (0) ✓
```

13-22. Subtract the same number.

```
  6950 (2)
 - 695 (2)
  6255 (0)
 - 695 (2)
  5560 (7)
 - 695 (2)
  4865 (5)
 - 695 (2)
  4170 (3)
 - 695 (2)
  3475 (1)
 - 695 (2)
  2780 (8)
 - 695 (2)
  2085 (6)
 - 695 (2)
  1390 (4)
 - 695 (2)
   695 (2)
 - 695 (2)
     0 (0)
```

23-25. Write these mixed-up numbers correctly using digits.

1 hundred 4 thousands 2 tens $\underline{4120}$

8 thousands 1 one 6 tens 4 hundreds $\underline{8461}$

6 hundreds 7 ones 2 thousands $\underline{2607}$

26-37. Fill in the table.

	Round to nearest 10.	Round to nearest 100.	Round to nearest 1000.
1388	1390	1400	1000
5875	5880	5900	6000
864	860	900	1000
12,580	12,580	12,600	13,000

RightStart™ Mathematics Level D Second Edition

© Activities for Learning, Inc. 2015

ACTIVITIES FOR TEACHING:

EXPLANATIONS:

38-43. Match expressions with fractions.

$3 \div 2$ —————— $\frac{3}{2}$

$1 \div 6$ $\frac{3}{1}$

$1 \div 2$ $\frac{1}{6}$

$4 \div 3$ $\frac{4}{4}$

$3 \div 1$ $\frac{1}{2}$

$4 \div 4$ $\frac{4}{3}$

44-47. Fill in the blanks.

$1 = \frac{2}{3} + \frac{1}{3}$

$1 = \frac{1}{2} + \frac{1}{2}$

$\frac{3}{4} + \frac{1}{4} = 1$

$\frac{1}{10} + \frac{6}{10} + \frac{3}{10} = 1$

48-49. Circle the greatest fraction in each row.

$\frac{1}{8}$	$\frac{7}{8}$	$\frac{3}{8}$
$\frac{3}{3}$	$\frac{2}{3}$	$\frac{1}{3}$

50-57. Fill in the blanks.

$6 \times 7 = \underline{42}$

$60 \times 7 = \underline{420}$

$600 \times 7 = \underline{4200}$

$6000 \times 7 = \underline{42,000}$

$10 \times 5 = \underline{50}$

$10 \times 50 = \underline{500}$

$10 \times 500 = \underline{5,000}$

$10 \times 5000 = \underline{50,000}$

58-60. Solve the problems.

A music teacher has three hours for giving lessons. He has four students. What fraction of an hour can he spend with each student?

$3 \div 4 = \frac{3}{4}$ hr

One side of a square dog pen is $23\frac{1}{2}$ feet. What is the perimeter of the pen? Write an equation and find the solution.

$P = 23\frac{1}{2} \times 4 = 92 + 2$

$P = 94$ feet

How many trees are still growing in North Park? They planted 54 walnut trees, 638 oak trees and 89 maple trees, but storms knocked down 10 trees.

$G = 54 + 638 + 89 - 10$

$G = 771$ trees

© Activities for Learning, Inc. 2015

LESSON 80: MAKING ONE WITH FRACTIONS

OBJECTIVES:
1. To learn the term *denominator*
2. To learn the term *equivalent*
3. To learn that two or more fractions can be equivalent

MATERIALS:
1. Fraction chart pieces
2. *Math Card Games* book, F6

ACTIVITIES FOR TEACHING:	EXPLANATIONS:
Warm-up. Ask: How many quarter hours make a whole hour? [4] How many minutes are in a quarter hour? [15 min] How long is 4 quarters of an hour? [60 min, one hour] How long is 2 quarter hours? [30 min, half hour] How long is 3 quarters of an hour? [45 min] How long is 8 quarters of an hour? [2 hours] How long is 6 quarters of an hour? [90 min, $1\frac{1}{2}$ hr] Ask: How many quarters equal a dollar? [4] How many pennies in a quarter? [25] How many quarters are equal to a half dollar? [2] Which is greater, 3 quarters or 1 dollar? [$1] How many quarters are in two dollars? [8] How many quarters are in a dollar and a half? [6] **Denominator.** Give the child the fraction chart pieces. Write: $\frac{1}{2}$ and tell the child that the bottom number in a fraction is called the *denominator*. Write the word for him: de nom in a tor Tell him the word "denominator" means "naming"; it is related to "nominate." Say: The denominator names the size of the fraction. Ask: What is the denominator in the fraction one half? [2] What is the denominator in one tenth? [10] What is the denominator in nine tenths? [10] **Fractions with even denominators.** Tell the child to assemble the fraction chart in a special way. Tell him to use the 1-piece and the fractions with even denominators. See the figure below.	For some children, learning terms like *numerator* and *denominator* are easier if they are learned one at a time.

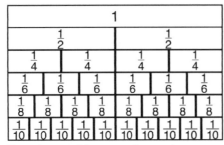

Fractions with even denominators.

ACTIVITIES FOR TEACHING:	EXPLANATIONS:

Ask: Do you see several ways to make one half? How many fourths are equal to one half? [2] How many sixths are equal to one half? [3] How many eighths are equal to one half? [4] How many tenths are equal to one half? [5] Tell him to name the fractions that are equal to one half. [$\frac{2}{4}$, $\frac{3}{6}$, $\frac{4}{8}$, $\frac{5}{10}$] Tell him that fractions that are equal are called *equivalent*.

Denominators with multiples of three. Tell him to make the chart with the 1-piece and the denominators with multiples of three: the thirds, sixths, and ninths. See the figure below.

1								
$\frac{1}{3}$			$\frac{1}{3}$			$\frac{1}{3}$		
$\frac{1}{6}$		$\frac{1}{6}$		$\frac{1}{6}$		$\frac{1}{6}$		$\frac{1}{6}$
$\frac{1}{9}$	$\frac{1}{9}$	$\frac{1}{9}$	$\frac{1}{9}$	$\frac{1}{9}$	$\frac{1}{9}$	$\frac{1}{9}$	$\frac{1}{9}$	$\frac{1}{9}$

Denominators with multiples of three.

Ask: How many sixths are equal to one third? [2] How many ninths are equal to one third? [3] Tell him to name the fractions that are equivalent to two thirds. [$\frac{4}{6}$, $\frac{6}{9}$] Tell him to name the fractions that are equivalent to three thirds. [$\frac{6}{6}$, $\frac{9}{9}$]

Denominators with multiples of five. Tell him to make the chart with the 1-piece and the denominators with multiples of five. See the figure below.

1									
$\frac{1}{5}$		$\frac{1}{5}$		$\frac{1}{5}$		$\frac{1}{5}$		$\frac{1}{5}$	
$\frac{1}{10}$	$\frac{1}{10}$	$\frac{1}{10}$	$\frac{1}{10}$	$\frac{1}{10}$	$\frac{1}{10}$	$\frac{1}{10}$	$\frac{1}{10}$	$\frac{1}{10}$	$\frac{1}{10}$

Denominators with multiples of five.

Ask: How many tenths to you need to equal one fifth? [2] How many tenths equal two fifths? [4] How many tenths equal three fifths? [6] How many tenths are equivalent to five fifths? [10] Tell him to name a fraction from the chart that is equivalent to two fifths. [$\frac{4}{10}$] Tell him to name a fraction that is equal to five fifths. [$\frac{10}{10}$]

The game of One. Play the One game found in *Math Card Games* book, F6.

In conclusion. Ask: What is the denominator in the fraction three fourths? [4] In the fraction three fourths, what is three divided by? [4] Are one half and two fourths equivalent fractions? [yes] How many fourths are equivalent to five fifths? [4]

© Activities for Learning, Inc. 2015

162

LESSON 81: COMPARING FRACTIONS

OBJECTIVES:
1. To learn the term *numerator*
2. To compare fractions

MATERIALS:
1. Worksheet 62, Comparing Fractions
2. Whole fraction chart and 1-pieces *
3. *Math Card Games* book, F9

ACTIVITIES FOR TEACHING:	EXPLANATIONS:
Warm-up. Give the child the worksheet. Tell him to do just the warm-up section. Solutions are:	* The 1-piece will be used for comparing fractions on the whole fraction chart. See the picture to the right. A 30-60 triangle or a ruler would also work.

$800 \times 6 = \textbf{4800}$ $(7 \times 6) + (7 \times \textbf{0}) = 42$

$32 \div 8 = \textbf{4}$ $490 \div 7 = \textbf{70}$ $\textbf{36} \div 9 = 4$

$$
\begin{array}{r}
8756 \ \textbf{(8)} \\
\times\,9 \ \textbf{(0)} \\
\hline
54 \\
450 \\
6300 \\
72000 \\
\hline
78804 \ \textbf{(0)}
\end{array}
$$

Ask: What do you call the bottom number in a fraction? [denominator] What is the denominator in the fraction two fifths? [5] In the fraction two fifths, what is two divided by? [5] How many more fifths are needed to make a whole? [3]

Introducing numerator. Give the child the whole fraction chart and the 1-piece for comparing.

Write: $\frac{3}{4}$ $\frac{1}{4}$ $\frac{2}{4}$

and ask the child: What is the same about these fractions? [same denominators]

Tell him the top number in a fraction is called the *numerator*. The word "numerator" is related to the word "number." Say: It tells the *number* of parts.

Write the word for him:

num er a tor

Ask: Which of the three written fractions is the greatest? [$\frac{3}{4}$] How do you know? Discuss his answers. Summarize by saying: If the denominators are the same, the fraction with the greatest numerator will be the greatest.

Preparation for Harder Fraction War game. Write and ask which is more: $\frac{1}{3}$ —— $\frac{3}{10}$

Show the child how to use the whole fraction chart and the 1-piece to compare the two fractions. See the figure on the next page.

RightStart™ Mathematics Level D Second Edition

© Activities for Learning, Inc. 2015

ACTIVITIES FOR TEACHING:	EXPLANATIONS:

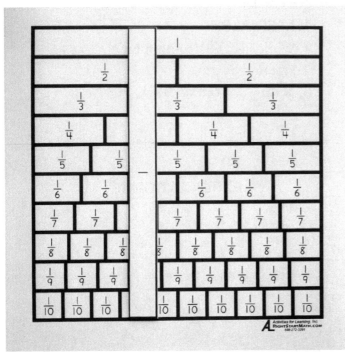

Using the left edge of the 1-piece to compare $\frac{1}{3}$ and $\frac{3}{10}$.

Harder Fraction War game. Play the Harder Fraction War game found in *Math Card Games* book, F9.

Worksheet 62. Tell him to complete the worksheet. Solutions are shown below.

$\frac{1}{6} > \frac{1}{7}$ $\frac{1}{6}$ ⓵$\frac{1}{3}$ $\frac{1}{4}$
$\frac{2}{8} < \frac{3}{8}$ $\frac{2}{8}$ $\frac{3}{8}$ ⓵$\frac{4}{8}$
$\frac{5}{10} = \frac{1}{2}$ ⓵$\frac{4}{10}$ $\frac{8}{9}$ $\frac{2}{2}$
$\frac{3}{8} > \frac{3}{9}$ $\frac{3}{8}$ $\frac{3}{7}$ ⓵$\frac{3}{6}$
$\frac{2}{4} = \frac{3}{6}$
$\frac{1}{2} > \frac{2}{5}$
$\frac{6}{6} = \frac{3}{3}$ ⓵$\frac{1}{6}$ $\frac{1}{7}$ $\frac{1}{8}$
$\frac{5}{8} < \frac{3}{4}$ $\frac{2}{8}$ $\frac{2}{5}$ ⓵$\frac{2}{2}$
$\frac{2}{9} < \frac{1}{3}$ ⓵$\frac{9}{10}$ $\frac{8}{9}$ $\frac{7}{8}$
$\frac{7}{8} > \frac{6}{7}$ $\frac{3}{8}$ $\frac{4}{9}$ ⓵$\frac{1}{2}$

numerator
denominator

In conclusion. Ask: What is the top number in a fraction called? [numerator] What does a fraction equal when the numerator and denominator are the same? [1]

LESSON 82: FRACTION LINE

OBJECTIVES:
1. To learn to write whole numbers as fractions
2. To write fractions at their appropriate places on a number line

MATERIALS:
1. Worksheet 63, Fraction Line
2. Fraction chart
3. *Math Card Games* book, F18

ACTIVITIES FOR TEACHING:	EXPLANATIONS:

Warm-up. Give the child the worksheet. Tell him to do just the warm-up section. Solutions are:

$(6 \times 6) + (\mathbf{0} \times 6) = 36$ $(48 \div 8) - 3 = \mathbf{3}$

$990 - (90 \times 9) = \mathbf{180}$ $(990 - 90) \times 9 = \mathbf{8100}$

$$
\begin{array}{r}
9276 \ (\mathbf{6}) \\
\times 8 \ (\mathbf{8}) \\
\hline
48 \\
560 \\
1600 \\
72000 \\
\hline
74208 \ (\mathbf{3})
\end{array}
$$

Ask: What do you call the bottom number in a fraction? [denominator] What do you call the top number in a fraction? [numerator] What is the denominator in the fraction two thirds? [3] What is the numerator in the fraction two thirds? [2] How many more thirds are needed to make a whole? [1]

Whole numbers as fractions. Give the child the whole fraction chart.

Write: $3 \div 4$

Ask: How can we write this as a fraction? $[\frac{3}{4}]$

$$3 \div 4 = \frac{3}{4}$$

Write: $4 \div 1$

Ask: How can we write this as a fraction? $[\frac{4}{1}]$

$$4 \div 1 = \frac{4}{1}$$

Ask: What is it equal to? [4]

Repeat for $3 \div 1$. $[\frac{3}{1}]$ Ask: What is it equal to? [3]

Summarize by asking: When the denominator is 1, what is the fraction equal to? [the numerator]

This exercise makes whole numbers look like fractions. It will be helpful when reciprocals and certain fraction algorithms are studied.

There is no good way to read $\frac{4}{1}$ as a fraction. Saying 4 "over" 1 is not mathematically correct, but it is the best we can do.

RightStart™ Mathematics Level D Second Edition

© Activities for Learning, Inc. 2015

ACTIVITIES FOR TEACHING:	EXPLANATIONS:

Worksheet 63. Tell him to complete the worksheet. Solutions are below.

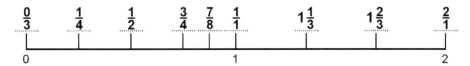

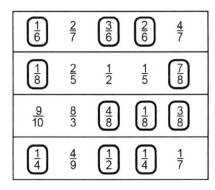 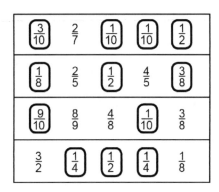

$\frac{5}{6}$

$\frac{5}{1}$

One or Two game variation. Play the One or Two game variation found in *Math Card Games* book, F18. This simpler variation includes the following modifications:

   No need to remove the four fraction cards listed.
   The cards taken must total only 1 (not 2).
   Only one set of cards totaling 1 may be taken per turn.

In conclusion. Ask: How does dividing a number by 1 change the number? [It does not change.] How do you write a whole number as a fraction? [Write 1 as the denominator.]

These modifications will speed up the game.

LESSON 83: MULTIPLES PATTERNS

OBJECTIVES:
1. To review the multiples
2. To discover patterns in the multiples

MATERIALS:
1. Worksheet 64, Multiples Patterns
2. AL Abacus or Short Multiplication Table
3. *Math Card Games* book, P2

ACTIVITIES FOR TEACHING:

Warm-up. Ask: How many digits do you need after the 7 to write 70? [1] How many digits do you need after the 7 to write 700? [2] How many digits do you need after the 7 to write 7000? [3]

Remind the child that a digit is a number from 0 to 9 that we use to make all our numbers. Ask: What are the digits in the number 81? [8 and 1] What are the digits in 365? [3, 6, and 5] What are the digits in 1000? [1 and three 0s]

Worksheet 64. Give the child the worksheet and abacus. Tell him to fill in the blanks in the rectangles on the worksheet, using an abacus or the short multiplication table. If necessary, remind him that the 3s and 7s have only three numbers in a row. Solutions are as follows:

2	4	6	8	10
12	14	16	18	20

4	8	12	16	20
24	28	32	36	40

6	12	18	24	30
36	42	48	54	60

8	16	24	32	40
48	56	64	72	80

3	6	9
12	15	18
21	24	27
30		

7	14	21
28	35	42
49	56	63
70		

5	10
15	20
25	30
35	40
45	50

9	18	27	36	45
90	81	72	63	54

Multiples patterns in general. Ask: How many multiples are in each pattern? [10] What is the relationship between the first and last numbers in each pattern? [last number 10 times greater than first number]

EXPLANATIONS:

Math has been called the "science of patterns." Patterns make learning easier, sometimes produce a source of insight, and often provide a basis for beauty.

See page ii, numbers 1 and 10 of "Some General Thoughts on Teaching Mathematics," for additional information.

The worksheet will be completed in the next lesson.

RightStart™ Mathematics Level D Second Edition

© Activities for Learning, Inc. 2015

ACTIVITIES FOR TEACHING:	EXPLANATIONS:

Twos. Tell him to look at the 2s multiples. Ask: What is special about the numbers? [even numbers] How much more is each number in the second row compared to the number above it? [10 more] What do you notice about the digits in the ones place in the two rows? [same]

Fours. Tell him to look at the 4s multiples. Ask: Do you see any odd numbers? [no] How much greater is each number in the second row compared to the first row? [20 more] What do you notice about the digits in the ones place in the two rows? [same]

Look at the 2s patterns and the first row of the 4s. Ask: Where do you see the 2s multiples in the 4s? [every other one]

Sixes. Tell him to look at the 6s multiples. Ask: Are the numbers even or odd? [even] How does the second row compare to the first row? [30 more] Do the digits in the ones place in the first row repeat in the second row? [yes]

Tell the child to look at the 3s multiples. Ask: How do the even 3s compare to the 6s? [same as the first row of the 6s]

Eights. Tell him to look at the 8s multiples. Ask: How are the 8s pattern like the 2s, 4s, and 6s? [The ones repeat in the second row.] How much more is the second row compared to the first row? [40] What do you notice about the digits in the ones place in each row? [the even numbers backward]

The threes, fives, sevens, and nine patterns will be discussed in the next lesson.

Multiples Memory game. Play the Multiples Memory found in *Math Card Games* book, P2.

In conclusion. Ask: What is the mathematical word for skip counting? [multiples] Why do the 2s, 4s, 6s, and 8s have only even numbers? [They are always adding even numbers to even numbers.]

© Activities for Learning, Inc. 2015

168

LESSON 84: MORE MULTIPLES PATTERNS

OBJECTIVES:
1. To review the multiples
2. To discover patterns in the multiples

MATERIALS:
1. AL Abacus
2. Math journal
3. Worksheet 64, Multiples Patterns (used in the previous lesson)
4. *Math Card Games* book, P2

ACTIVITIES FOR TEACHING:

EXPLANATIONS:

Warm-up. Ask: How many digits do you need after the 8 to write 80? [1] How many digits do you need after the 8 to write 800? [2] How many digits do you need after the 8 to write 8000? [3]

Remind the child that a digit is a number from 0 to 9 that we use to make all our numbers. Ask: What are the digits in the product of 6 × 8? [4 and 8] What are the digits in the product of 60 × 7? [4, 2, and 0] What are the digits in the product of 7 × 800? [5, 6, and two 0s]

Writing the multiples and Worksheet 64. Give the child the abacus. Tell the child to use his math journal and write the multiples in patterns, using an abacus or the short multiplication table.

When he has finished ask him to compare his answers to the worksheet from the previous lesson. Solutions are as follows:

2	4	6	8	10
12	14	16	18	20

4	8	12	16	20
24	28	32	36	40

6	12	18	24	30
36	42	48	54	60

8	16	24	32	40
48	56	64	72	80

3	6	9
12	15	18
21	24	27
30		

7	14	21
28	35	42
49	56	63
70		

5	10
15	20
25	30
35	40
45	50

9	18	27	36	45
90	81	72	63	54

Threes. Tell him to look at the 3s multiples. Ask: Are the numbers even or odd? [both] What is the pattern? [alternating evens and odds] Look at the ones digits starting at the 0 in 30. Ask: Where is the 1? [in 21] Where are the other digits from 3 to 9? [They continue up the column and over to the bottom of the next column.]

RightStart™ Mathematics Level D Second Edition

© Activities for Learning, Inc. 2015

ACTIVITIES FOR TEACHING:	EXPLANATIONS:

Ask: Is there anything special about the digits in the tens place? [first row, 0; second row, 1; third row, 2]

Tell him to look at the first column. Ask: What is the sum of adding the digits in each number? [3] What is the sum of the digits in the second column? [6] What is the sum of the digits in the third column? [9]

Tell him to add the opposite corners, 3 + 27. [30] Ask: What other numbers sum to 30? [21 + 9, 12 + 18, 6 + 24]

Sevens. Tell him to look at the 7s multiples. Ask: Do the 7s multiples have an interesting pattern for the ones digits? [The digits 1 to 9 start at the upper right, 21, and continue down the column and over to the next left column.] Do the tens digits have an interesting pattern? [first row, 0, 1, 2; second row, 2, 3, 4; third row, 4, 5, 6] Are the multiples even or odd? [both] How many are even and how many are odd? [5 of each]

Tell him to add the opposite corners, 7 + 63. [70] Ask: What other numbers add to 70? [49 + 21, 28 + 42, 14 + 56]

Fives. Tell him to look at the 5s multiples. Ask: What patterns do you see with the 5s multiples? [The ones are 5 in first column and 0 in the second column. Also the tens increase by 1 in both columns.]

Nines. Tell him to look at the 9s multiples. Ask: What is the sum of the digits for each number? [9] What do you notice when the second row is written from right to left? [digits are reversed] What is the pattern of the digits in the ones place? [decrease by 1] What is the pattern of the digits in the tens place? [increase by 1] Are the multiples even or odd? [alternate]

Another interesting pattern: Using two numbers that total 10, add the multiples corresponding to the same position. The sums will always equal multiples of 10. For example, using the 3s and 7s patterns, add 3 + 7, [10] 6 + 14, [20] 9 + 21, [30] and so forth.

Multiples Memory game. Play the Multiples Memory found in *Math Card Games* book, P2. Tell him to choose a multiple that is hard for him.

Worksheet 64. Tell the child to complete the questions on the bottom of the worksheet. The solutions are below.

   2, 4, 6, 8
   none
   8
   6
   7
   3, 7, 9
   9

In conclusion. Ask: What is your favorite pattern?

© Activities for Learning, Inc. 2015

Lesson 85: Growing Geometric Patterns

OBJECTIVES:
1. To grow geometric patterns
2. To analyze geometric patterns
3. To explore *terms* through patterns

MATERIALS:
1. Worksheet 65, Growing Geometric Patterns
2. Tiles, about 20 each of four colors

ACTIVITIES FOR TEACHING:

Warm-up. Give the child the worksheet. Tell him to do just the warm-up section. Solutions are:

(70 × 6) + (7 × 60) = **840**   9 + 8 × 6 = **57**   6283 **(1)**
(560 ÷ 8) − 60 = **10**   100 − (6 × 9) = **46**   × 7 **(7)**
                                                       21
Growing geometric patterns. Give   560
the child the tiles.   1400
                                                       42000
Pattern 1. Lay out the following tile   43981 **(7)**
pattern and tell him to copy the pattern
with his tiles. Ask: What do you do to
make the next term? [add 2 to the previous term]

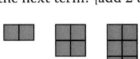

Beginning the pattern.

Tell him to continue the pattern for two more terms. Ask: How many tiles are in each term? [2, 4, 6, 8, 10]

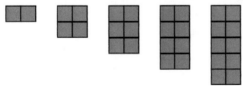

Continuing the pattern.

Pattern 2. Lay out the pattern shown in the left figure below. Tell the child to copy it. Ask: How do you continue it? [Each row has 2 tiles less than the previous row.] See the right figure below. Ask: How many tiles are in each row? [9, 7, 5, 3, 1]

   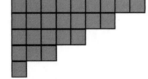

Beginning the pattern.   **Continuing the pattern.**

EXPLANATIONS:

A *term* is a unit in a series. The child will learn the meaning through hearing the word in context.

RightStart™ Mathematics Level D Second Edition   © Activities for Learning, Inc. 2015

ACTIVITIES FOR TEACHING:	EXPLANATIONS:

Pattern 3. Next lay out the squares pattern for him to copy as shown below. Notice the color pattern.

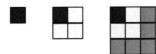

Beginning the pattern.

Ask: What is this pattern? [squares] How does this pattern continue? [row and column added each term] Tell him to continue the pattern for two more terms. See the figure below.

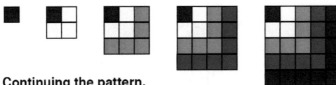

Continuing the pattern.

Ask: How many tiles are in each term? [1, 4, 9, 16, 25] Tell him to say the multiplication equation for each term. [$1 \times 1 = 1, 2 \times 2 = 4, 3 \times 3 = 9, 4 \times 4 = 16, 5 \times 5 = 25$]

Ask: How many tiles did you add going from the first term to the second? [3] How many tiles did you add going from the second term to the third? [5] How many tiles did you add going to the next term? [7] What is the pattern? [consecutive odd numbers]

Worksheet 65. Tell the child to complete the worksheet. Solutions are shown below.

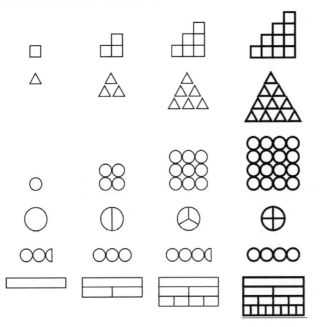

In conclusion. Tell the child to name some patterns he see around him.

If there is additional time following this lesson, play the What's on Top game, found in *Math Card Games* book, P12.

© Activities for Learning, Inc. 2015

172

LESSON 86: NUMERIC PATTERNS

OBJECTIVES:

1. To discover a numeric pattern and to continue it

MATERIALS:

1. Tiles
2. Worksheet 66, Numeric Patterns

ACTIVITIES FOR TEACHING:	EXPLANATIONS:
Warm-up. Ask: What is the mathematical word for skip counting? [multiples] Do the 2s, 4s, 6s, and 8s have even or odd multiples? [only even] Why are they only even? [They are always adding even numbers to even numbers.] Do the 3s, 5s, 7s, and 9s have even or odd multiples? [both] What is the pattern of even and odd? [they alternate]	
Tell the child to say the multiples of 3 to 30, [3, 6, 9, 12, 15, 18, 21, 24, 27, 30] the multiples of 6 to 60, [6, 12, 18, 24, 30, 36, 42, 48, 54, 60] and the multiples of 7 to 70. [7, 14, 21, 28, 35, 42, 49, 56, 63, 70]	As he says the multiples, encourage him to visualize either his abacus or the multiples patterns.

Pattern 1. Write the following pattern:

    4   6   8   ___   ___

and say: We want to find what two terms come next. Ask: How can you get from 4 to 6? [add 2] To show this, write a "+ 2" in the space between the 4 and 6 as shown below. Ask: Does the "+ 2" also work for going from 6 to 8? [yes] What do you need to do to continue this pattern? [add 2] What are the next two terms? [10, 12]

    4^{+2} 6   8   ___   ___

    4^{+2} 6^{+2} 8   <u>10</u>   <u>12</u>

Pattern 2. Write the next pattern:

    90   80   70   ___   ___

Ask: How can you get from 90 to 80? [subtract 10] Write or ask the child to write a "– 10" in the space between the 90 and 80 as shown below. Ask: Does the "– 10" also work for going from 80 to 70? [yes] How do you continue this pattern? [subtract 10] What are the next two terms? [60, 50]

    90^{-10} 80   70   ___   ___

    90^{-10} 80^{-10} 70   <u>60</u>   <u>50</u>

RightStart™ Mathematics Level D Second Edition

© Activities for Learning, Inc. 2015

ACTIVITIES FOR TEACHING:			**EXPLANATIONS:**	

ACTIVITIES FOR TEACHING:

Pattern 3. For the third example, write:

  2   4   8   ___   ___

Ask: What operation do we do to get from 2 to 4? [+ 2 or × 2] Does adding 2 work for going from 4 to 8? [no]

  2^{+2} 4   8   ___   ___

Ask: What other operation could we try? [multiply by 2, or double] Does that work from 4 to 8? [yes] What are the next two terms? [16 and 32] See below.

  $2^{×2}$ 4   8   ___   ___

  $2^{×2}$ $4^{×2}$ 8   <u>16</u>   <u>32</u>

Summarize by saying: When discovering a pattern, you need to guess and then check to see if it works for the next number. If it doesn't work, try something else.

Worksheet 66. Give the child the worksheet and tell him to complete the first five problems on his worksheet. Remind him that the fifth problem is like the squares they did in the last lesson.

Tell him to discuss the solutions before completing the worksheet. Solutions are given below.

35	37	39	**41**	**43**
102	101	100	**99**	**98**
9	18	27	**36**	**45**
16	24	32	**40**	**48**
1	4	9	**16**	**25**
35	30	25	**20**	**15**
18	24	30	**36**	**42**
3	6	9	**12**	**15**
3	6	12	**24**	**48**
4	40	400	**4000**	**40,000**
80	40	20	**10**	**5**
0¢	25¢	50¢	**75¢**	**$1.00**
$0.05	$0.10	$0.15	**$0.20**	**$0.25**
$0.01	$0.10	$1.00	**$10.00**	**$100.00**
$1.00	$1.50	$2.00	**$2.50**	**$3.00**
1	$1\frac{1}{2}$	2	**$2\frac{1}{2}$**	**3**
0	$\frac{1}{4}$	$\frac{1}{2}$	**$\frac{3}{4}$**	**1**
5	$4\frac{1}{2}$	4	**$3\frac{1}{2}$**	**3**
$\frac{1}{2}$	$\frac{1}{3}$	$\frac{1}{4}$	**$\frac{1}{5}$**	**$\frac{1}{6}$**

In conclusion. Ask: Did this lesson seem like you were doing puzzles?

EXPLANATIONS:

See page ii number 2 and page iii number 15 of "Some General Thoughts on Teaching Mathematics" for additional information.

The child should not be required to write the little numbers showing the operation.

If there is additional time following this lesson, play the What's on Top game, found in *Math Card Games* book, P12.

© Activities for Learning, Inc. 2015

174

LESSON 87: CHINESE CHECKERBOARD REVISITED

OBJECTIVES:
1. To practice finding patterns

MATERIALS:
1. Worksheet 67, Chinese Checkerboard
2. **A Chinese checkers game board, if available**
3. *Math Card Games* book, P19

ACTIVITIES FOR TEACHING:	EXPLANATIONS:
Warm-up. Ask: What are the next three terms in the pattern 3, 6, 9? [12, 15, 18] What are the next three terms in the pattern 9, 18, 27? [36, 45, 54] What are the next three terms in the pattern 7, 14, 21? [28, 35, 42] What are the next three terms in the pattern 8, 16, 24? [32, 40, 48]	
Worksheet 67. Give the child the worksheet and remind him of the Chinese checkerboard game from earlier in the year. Show the child a Chinese checkerboard, if available. Tell him to read the instructions:	The Chinese checkerboard problem was briefly discussed in Lesson 12.
Find the number of dots on these Chinese checkerboards. Circle your groups. Solve it two different ways.	
Have the child explain his solution. [121] Four solutions are shown on the next page.	There is an amazing number of solutions.
Multiples Solitaire game. Play the Multiples Solitaire game found in *Math Card Games* book, P19.	
In conclusion. Tell the child to name two shapes that he frequently saw on the Chinese checkerboard. [equilateral triangles, hexagons, parallelograms, rhombuses, and quadrilaterals]	

RightStart™ Mathematics Level D Second Edition

© Activities for Learning, Inc. 2015

ACTIVITIES FOR TEACHING:

EXPLANATIONS:

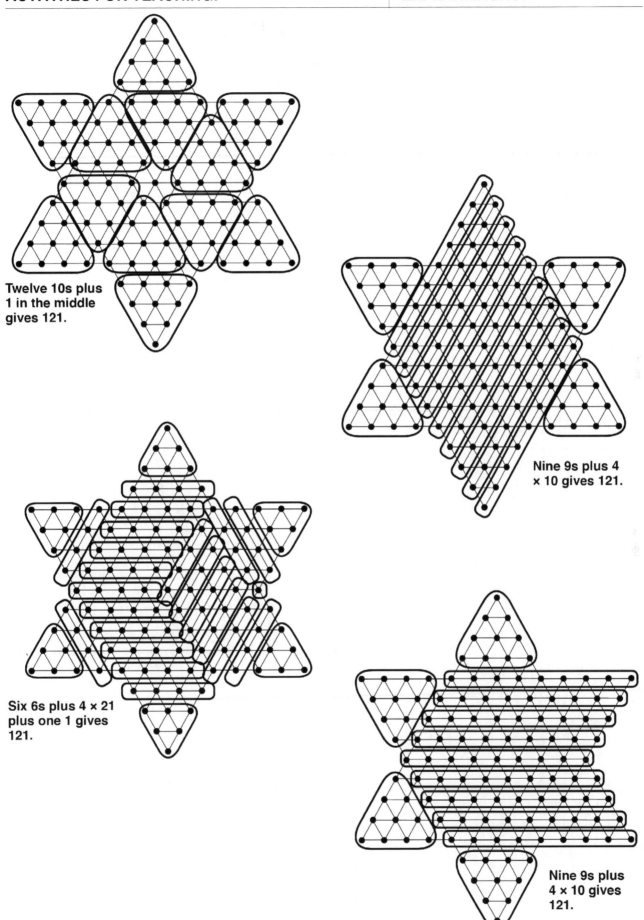

Twelve 10s plus 1 in the middle gives 121.

Nine 9s plus 4 × 10 gives 121.

Six 6s plus 4 × 21 plus one 1 gives 121.

Nine 9s plus 4 × 10 gives 121.

LESSON 88: REVIEW AND GAMES 5

OBJECTIVES:
1. To review recent topics
2. To develop skills through playing math card games

MATERIALS:
1. Worksheet 68-A or 68-B, Review 5
2. *Math Card Games* book, P27

ACTIVITIES FOR TEACHING:

Worksheet 68-A. Give the child the worksheet. Tell him to listen to the problems and write the answers. Read each problem twice.

500×20 $\qquad$ 40×4 $\qquad$ $49 \div 7$

Tell him to complete the worksheet. Solutions are below.

Write only the answers.

10,000

160

7

Write the answers.

$574 + 86 =$ _660_

$63 \div 7 =$ _9_

$70 \times 4 =$ _280_

Find 2638 × 8.

$$\begin{array}{r} 2638 \ (1) \\ \times 8 \ (8) \\ \hline 64 \\ 240 \\ 4800 \\ 16000 \\ \hline 21\,104 \ (8) \checkmark \end{array}$$

Find 4638 − 2876.

$$\begin{array}{r} 4638 \ (3) \\ - 2876 \ (5) \\ \hline 1\,762 \ (7) \checkmark \end{array}$$

Put these fractions in order from least to greatest.

$\frac{1}{2}$	$\frac{1}{3}$	$\frac{1}{4}$
$\frac{1}{3}$	$1\frac{1}{3}$	$\frac{3}{3}$
$\frac{1}{2}$	$\frac{5}{8}$	$\frac{1}{4}$
$\frac{3}{1}$	$\frac{3}{4}$	$\frac{3}{8}$
$\frac{4}{1}$	$\frac{1}{1}$	$\frac{5}{1}$

$\frac{1}{4}$	$\frac{1}{3}$	$\frac{1}{2}$
$\frac{3}{3}$	$\frac{3}{3}$	$1\frac{1}{3}$
$\frac{1}{4}$	$\frac{1}{2}$	$\frac{5}{8}$
$\frac{3}{8}$	$\frac{3}{4}$	$\frac{3}{1}$
$\frac{1}{1}$	$\frac{4}{1}$	$\frac{5}{1}$

Continue each pattern with one more term.

Write the next two terms for each pattern.

14	24	34	44	54
14	21	28	35	42
14	12	10	8	6

Solve the problem.

Nathan bought three items for $21 each. Sales tax was four dollars. What was the total cost?

$T = 21 \times 3 + 4$

$T = \$67$

EXPLANATIONS:

ACTIVITIES FOR TEACHING:

EXPLANATIONS:

Card Exchange game. Play the Card Exchange game found in *Math Card Games* book, P27.

Worksheet 68-B. Give the child the worksheet. Tell him to listen to the problems and write the answers. Read each problem twice.

600×20 70×8 $81 \div 9$

Tell him to complete the worksheet. Solutions are below.

Write only the answers.

12,000

560

9

Write the answers.

$658 + 91 = 749$

$56 \div 7 = 8$

$80 \times 4 = 320$

Find 3649×7.

3649 (4)
$\times 7$ (7)
63
280
4200
21000
$25,543$ (1) ✓

Find $7345 - 4318$.

7345 (1)
$- 4318$ (7)
3027 (3) ✓

Put these fractions in order from least to greatest.

| $\frac{1}{3}$ | $\frac{1}{6}$ | $\frac{1}{4}$ | $\frac{1}{6}$ | $\frac{1}{4}$ | $\frac{1}{3}$ |

| $\frac{1}{4}$ | $1\frac{1}{4}$ | $\frac{4}{4}$ | $\frac{1}{4}$ | $\frac{4}{4}$ | $1\frac{1}{4}$ |

| $\frac{7}{8}$ | $\frac{5}{8}$ | $\frac{3}{4}$ | $\frac{5}{8}$ | $\frac{3}{4}$ | $\frac{7}{8}$ |

| $\frac{2}{5}$ | $\frac{2}{1}$ | $\frac{2}{3}$ | $\frac{2}{5}$ | $\frac{2}{3}$ | $\frac{2}{1}$ |

| $\frac{5}{1}$ | $\frac{2}{1}$ | $\frac{3}{1}$ | $\frac{2}{1}$ | $\frac{3}{1}$ | $\frac{5}{1}$ |

Continue each pattern with one more term.

Write the next two terms for each pattern.

12	22	32	42	52
12	15	18	21	24
12	10	8	6	4

Solve the problem.

Natalie bought three books for $13 each. Sales tax was two dollars. What was the total cost?

$T = 13 \times 3 + 2$

$T = \$41$

© Activities for Learning, Inc. 2015

LESSON 89: MONTHS OF THE YEAR

OBJECTIVES:

1. To work with the months of the year as a measure of time

MATERIALS:

1. Worksheet 69, Months of the Year
2. Dry erase board

ACTIVITIES FOR TEACHING:

Warm-up. Give the child the worksheet. Tell him to do just the warm-up section. Solutions are:

4638 **(3)**	4638 **(3)**	4638 **(3)**
× 7 **(7)**	− 2876 **(5)**	+ 2876 **(5)**
56	1762 **(7)**	7514 **(8)**
210		
4200		
28000		
32466 **(3)**		

Ask the child to say the "Thirty Days Has September" rhyme with you. Repeat a few times.

The months. Ask: How much time does it take the earth to travel around the sun? [a year] That is a long time, so what do we divide the year into? [months] Tell the child to say the months of the year and to raise his fingers to show the number of syllables in each month's name. Ask: What do the months measure? [time]

Tell him a month is approximately the time between full moons, which is about 29 days. Tell him that the words *month* and *Monday* are related to the word *moon*.

Tell the child to think about the first two lines in "Thirty Days Has September." Ask: How many months have 30 days? [4] What are they? [September, April, June, and November] How many months have 31 days? [7] What are they? [January, March, May, July, August, October, and December] What month is missing? [February] How many days does it have? [28 days until leap year when it has 29 days]

Worksheet 69. Tell him to complete the chart and questions 1 through 7 on the worksheet. Say: Spell the months correctly; they are spelled very much the way we pronounce them. The completed chart and answers are shown on the next page.

EXPLANATIONS:

Thirty Days Has September

Thirty days has September,
April, June, and November.
The rest have 31 to carry,
But only 28 for February,
Except in leap year, that's the time
When February has 29.

The pronunciation of *February* is changing. The first *r* is rapidly being replaced by the *yoo* sound.

RightStart™ Mathematics Level D Second Edition

© Activities for Learning, Inc. 2015

ACTIVITIES FOR TEACHING:

1	January	31
2	February	28
3	March	31
4	April	30
5	May	31
6	June	30
7	July	31
8	August	31
9	September	30
10	October	31
11	November	30
12	December	31

1. Name the month with two *u*'s. **August**
2. Name the month with two *r*'s. **February**
3. Name the month with four syllables. **January and February**
4. Name the month with the most letters. **September**
5. How many months in a year? **12**
6. How many months have 30 days? **4**
7. How many months have 31 days? **7**

Writing dates. Tell the child that there are several ways to write the date. Write the following:

August 19, 2015   Aug. 19, 2015   8-19-15   8/19/15

Explain: One way to write the date is to write the month, the day, a comma, and the year. See the first example above. Another way is to abbreviate the month by using the first three letters of the month. See the second example.

Another way to write the date is to use the number of the month and the last two digits of the year with dashes between the numbers. See the third example. One more way is to use slashes rather than dashes between the numbers. See the last example.

For practice in writing dates, tell the child to write the following dates four ways on his dry erase board:

The date for the first day of the next month

The date for one week from today

The date of his last birthday

The date for the next New Year's Day

Tell the child to complete questions 8 through 10 on his worksheet.

British dates. Explain that in other countries, including the United Kingdom and Europe, people write the day of the month before the month as shown below.

19 August 2015   19 Aug. 2015   19-8-15   19/8/15

Say: In this format, units are written in order from the smallest to the largest: day, month, and year.

In conclusion. Ask: What do we call the time that the earth takes to go around the sun? [year] How is the year divided? [months] Tell the child to name the months that have 30 days. [September, April, June, and November]

EXPLANATIONS:

Questions 1 – 4 are included to help the child become more aware of the spelling of the names of the months.

If there is additional time following this lesson, play the What's on Top game, found in *Math Card Games* book, P12.

© Activities for Learning, Inc. 2015

180

LESSON 90: CALENDAR FOR ONE YEAR

OBJECTIVES:
1. To use a calendar for information
2. To solve calendar problems

MATERIALS:
1. Worksheet 70, Calendar for One Year
2. Calendar of the current year, Appendix p. 9

ACTIVITIES FOR TEACHING:

Warm-up. Give the child the worksheet. Tell him to do just the warm-up section. Solutions are:

```
  4182 (6)        4182 (6)         4182 (6)
  × 6 (6)       − 2814 (6)       + 2814 (6)
    12          1368 (0)         6996 (3)
   480
   600
 24000
 25092 (0)
```

Ask the child to say the "Thirty Days Has September" rhyme with you.

Calendar for a year. Give the child the calendars for the current year. Give the child time to study it. Ask: What does "S M T W T F S" mean? [the days of the week]

Tell him to find the current month and to circle today's date. Also tell him to find other important dates, such as birthdays and holidays.

Ask: Are any months the same? [non-leap years: January & October; leap years: January & July] Which months start on the same day? [non-leap years: January & October, February & March & November, April & July, and September & December; leap years: January & July, February & August, March & November, and September & December]

Ask: What day of the week is New Year's Day of the next year? How do you know? [day after December 31st]

Tell him that Thanksgiving in the United States is the fourth Thursday in November. Ask: What is the date? Then tell him that in Canada, Thanksgiving is the second Monday in October. Ask: What is the date?

Tell him the scouts (or other club) meet on the first Monday of the month. Ask: How many times will they meet in the year? [12]

Next tell him that another club decided to meet on the fifth Wednesday of the month. Ask: How many times will the club meet in the year?

EXPLANATIONS:

Thirty Days Has September

Thirty days has September,
April, June, and November.
The rest have 31 to carry,
But only 28 for February,
Except in leap year, that's the time
When February has 29.

In some countries, calendars begin on Monday, not Sunday.

See page iii, number 26 of "Some General Thoughts on Teaching Mathematics," for additional information.

RightStart™ Mathematics Level D Second Edition

© Activities for Learning, Inc. 2015

ACTIVITIES FOR TEACHING:

Ask: What is the date one week after July 4th? [July 11th] What is the date two weeks after July 4th? [July 18th] How could you tell without looking at the calendar? [add 7 or 14]

Tell the child that Memorial Day is the last Monday in May and Labor Day is the first Monday in September. You might tell him that many people think of Memorial Day as the beginning of summer and Labor Day as the end of summer. Ask: How many days are between Memorial Day and Labor Day? [98 days unless Memorial Day is May 25 when it is 105 days] This can be calculated by adding the number of days in June, July, and August and then adding the extra days in May and September.

Golden birthdays. Explain that some people celebrate golden birthdays. A golden birthday occurs when a person's age is the same as the day of the month of their birthday. For example, a child who's birthday is October 9 has a golden birthday on their 9th birthday.

Ask: At what age will a baby born on July 2 have a golden birthday? [age 2] If the baby was born July 2, of this year, when will the baby have their golden birthday? [in 2 years] What year will a person born February 22, 2002, have a golden birthday? [2002 + 22 = 2024]

Worksheet 70. Tell him to look at the list of the days of the week on the worksheet. Explain that in English, the names of the days and the names of the months always start with a capital letter, which is not true in all languages.

Ask: In which day does the first vowel sound the same as the vowel in the word *month*? [Monday] In which days is the "er" sound spelled with "ur"? [Thursday and Saturday] What silent letters does Wednesday have? [first *d* and second *e*]

Tell him to complete the worksheet. Solutions are below.
  2. Name the two days that start with the letter s̲.
     Sunday Saturday
  3. Name the two days that start with the letter t̲.
     Tuesday Thursday
  4. Which day is named after the sun? **Sunday**
  5. Which day is named after the moon? **Monday**
  6. Name the day with three syllables. **Saturday**
  7. Name the day with the most letters. **Wednesday**
  8. How many days have the letter u̲ in their names? **4**

In conclusion. Ask: How many days are in a week? [7] How many months are in a year? [12] How many weeks are in a year? [52] How many days are in a year? [365 or 366]

EXPLANATIONS:

This calendar will be used in the next lesson.

Pronouncing the last syllable as *day*, rather than *dee* helps in spelling. Questions 2 – 8 are included to help the child become more aware of the spelling of the names of the days.

If there is additional time following this lesson, play the Mixed Up Products game, found in *Math Card Games* book, P13.1.

© Activities for Learning, Inc. 2015

182

LESSON 91: CALENDARS FOR TWO YEARS

OBJECTIVES:

1. To become aware of similarities and differences of calendars for two consecutive years
2. To construct a bar graph with birthdays

MATERIALS:

1. Worksheet 71, Calendars for Two Years
2. Calendars of the current year and the following year, Appendix p. 9
3. **A colored pencil or marker**

ACTIVITIES FOR TEACHING:	EXPLANATIONS:

Warm-up. Give the child the worksheet. Tell him to do just the warm-up section. Solutions are:

```
 7293 (3)        7293 (3)        7293 (3)
 × 8 (8)        − 4623 (6)      + 4623 (6)
   24           2670 (6)        11916 (0)
  720
 1600
56000
58344 (6)
```

Ask the child to say the "Thirty Days Has September" rhyme with you.

The following year's calendar. Give the child the next year's calendar. The child also will need the calendar for the current year from the previous lesson.

Leap years. Ask: What do we call the time it takes the earth to go around the sun? [a year] Explain that it is the earth going around the sun that gives us the seasons. Tell him that a year is closer to $365\frac{1}{4}$ days. Hundreds of years ago, the calendar year was too short, which over time made spring on the calendar come in February.

Explain that today our calendars adjust with an extra day every four years called a *leap day*. That day is February 29th. When the last two digits of a year is a multiple of four, the year will be a *leap year*. Ask: What are next five leap years following the year 2000? [2004, 2008, 2012, 2016, 2020]

Two years. Tell the child to compare the calendars for the two years. Ask: Do the corresponding months have the same number of days? [yes, except possibly February] Does March start on the same day in each year? [no] Ask him the following or similar questions:

1. Is either year a leap year?

2. Can two consecutive years be leap years? [No, leap years occur only every four years.]

3. What day of the week is New Year's Day in both years?

4. What day of the week is July 4th in both years?

Thirty Days Has September

Thirty days has September,
April, June, and November.
The rest have 31 to carry,
But only 28 for February,
Except in leap year, that's the time
When February has 29.

Leap years were added to the calendar about 500 years ago.

In the U.S., a president is elected in the leap years.

RightStart™ Mathematics Level D Second Edition

© Activities for Learning, Inc. 2015

ACTIVITIES FOR TEACHING:	EXPLANATIONS:

5. What day of the week is today's date in the next year?
6. What day is your birthday in each year?
7. What day of the week is Thanksgiving this year? [Thursday] Next year? [Thursday] What is the date for Thanksgiving this year? Next year? How does it change? What are the possible dates for Thanksgiving? [November 22 – 28]

Thanksgiving in the United States is the fourth Thursday in November. In Canada, Thanksgiving is the second Monday in October.

Worksheet 71. Tell the child to read and answer the first question:

How many days are there from your birthday this year to your birthday next year? [365 or 366]

Many children are surprised at the answer to this question.

Birthday bar graph. Explain to the child that he is going to find out which months are the most popular for having a birthday. Draw the following 12 × 5 grid:

See page ii, number 5 of "Some General Thoughts on Teaching Mathematics," for additional information.

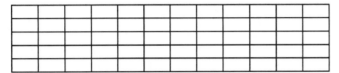

The worksheet has 10 rows, rather than the five shown here.

Tell him each column represents a month. Ask him to name the first letter of each month as you write it below the column. [J F M A M J J A S O N D] See below.

Explain that the months are the categories; we are sorting birthdays by months. Ask: What is a good title for the categories? [Months] Write it below the months. Tell him to write the months and a title on his worksheet.

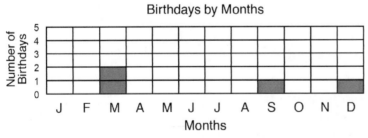

The child could write "x's" rather than color the rectangles.

Tell him that each rectangle in the columns represents one birthday. Write the scale numbers vertically along the left side. Ask: What is a good title for the scale? [Number of Birthdays] Tell him to write the scale numbers and a title on his worksheet. See the figure above.

Some families make a large graph and attach it to a wall.

Ask: What is a good title for the whole graph? [Birthdays by Month]

Have each person on the family say the month of their birthday. Tell the child to color or mark the appropriate rectangle on his worksheet.

In conclusion. Ask: Which month has the most birthdays? Which month has the fewest birthdays? Tell him to find out the birthdays of extended family and friends to add to his graph.

If there is additional time following this lesson, play the Multiplication Old Main game, found in *Math Card Games* book, P14.

© Activities for Learning, Inc. 2015

Lesson 92: Measuring and Graphing Lengths

OBJECTIVES:
1. To review the concept of measurement
2. To practice reading a ruler
3. To construct a bar graph with perimeter data

MATERIALS:
1. Fraction chart pieces
2. *Math Card Games* book, F7
3. Worksheet 72, Measuring and Graphing Lengths
4. A set of tangrams

ACTIVITIES FOR TEACHING:

Warm-up. Ask: What do we call the time that the earth takes to go around the sun? [year] How is the year divided? [months] How are the months divided? [into weeks] How are the weeks divided? [into days]

Ask: How many days are in a week? [7] How many months are in a year? [12] How many weeks are in a year? [52] How many days are in a year? [365 or 366]

Fraction War game. Give the child the fraction chart pieces. Ask him to build the fraction chart with the one, halves, fourths, and eighths turned face down. See below.

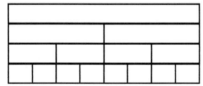

Partial fraction chart without the fraction numerals showing.

Give the child the fraction cards. Tell him to find the ones, halves, fourths, and eighths. Then tell him to pick the cards up in random order.

Play the Fraction War game, found in the *Math Card Games* book, F7, using the blank fraction pieces for reference.

Worksheet 72. Give the child the worksheet and a set of tangrams. Tell him to look at the ruler on his worksheet. See below.

Ask: What is the ruler divided into? [eighths] Where is 3 and a half on the ruler? [halfway between 3 and 4] Where is 1 and three-fourths? [three-fourths the way between 1 and 2]

Tell him to read the instructions on the worksheet. Ask the child to explain what he is to do. [Measure the sides

EXPLANATIONS:

Play this game for about 10 minutes.

185

ACTIVITIES FOR TEACHING:

of all the tangram pieces and show the measurements on the graph.] Tell him to write the categories, scales, and titles on his graph before he begin measuring.

Say: Find a small triangle. Measure its longest side. [2 in.] See below. Ask: Where do you put the "x"? [in the column for 2 in.] See below.

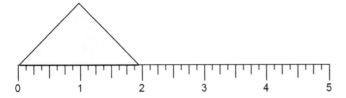

Tell him to measure a shorter side of the same small triangle. Ask: What does this side measure? [$1\frac{3}{8}$ in.] Where do you put the "x"? [between $1\frac{1}{4}$ and $1\frac{1}{2}$]

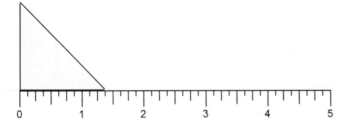

Tell him to complete the worksheet. Solutions are below.

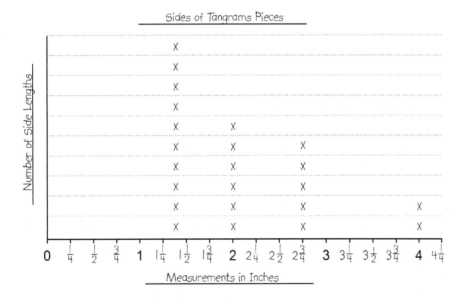

1. How many sides are there altogether? **23**
2. How many different lengths are there? **4**
3. Which is the most common length? **$1\frac{3}{8}$ inches**

In conclusion. Ask: Did you have to measure all the sides of the tangram pieces or did you know some of them? [many sides are equal]

EXPLANATIONS:

Titles may vary.

Some children will measure every side, while others will realize the equality of many of the sides.

© Activities for Learning, Inc. 2015

Lesson 93: Scoring Corners™ with a Bar Graph

OBJECTIVES:
1. To construct a bar graph
2. To use information from a bar graph

MATERIALS:
1. Worksheet 73, Scoring Corners™ with a Bar Graph
2. *Math Card Games* book, A9
3. **Colored marker**
4. Casio SL-450S calculator

ACTIVITIES FOR TEACHING:

Warm-up. Give the child the worksheet. Tell him to do just the warm-up section. Solutions are:

```
    8362 (1)         8362 (1)         8362 (1)
  ×    6 (6)       − 2638 (1)       + 2638 (1)
  ─────────        ─────────        ─────────
       12           5724 (0)         11000 (2)
      360
     1800
    48000
    ─────
    50172 (6)
```

Corners™ game. Give the child the Corners™ cards. Explain that he will play the Corners™ game, found in *Math Card Games* book, A9, using a different way to find his final score.

Worksheet 73. Tell him to look at the numbers on the left side of the graph on the worksheet. See the graph below. Explain that in this graph, the categories are written on the left side. Ask: Since you are going to play the Corners™ game, what do you think the categories represent? [scores]

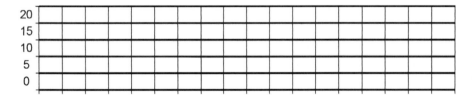

Ask: If you played 1 to a 9, what would you color? [the rectangle next to the 10 category] If you played 4 to a 6, what would you color? [next rectangle] If you played a 1 to a 1, what would you color? [rectangle next to the 0] What is the scale below the graph? [number of times for each score] See the figure on the next page.

EXPLANATIONS:

The child could write "x's" rather than color the rectangles.

ACTIVITIES FOR TEACHING:

EXPLANATIONS:

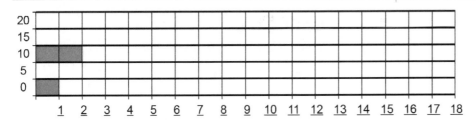

Tell him to read the instructions on the worksheet. Give him time to write the scale numbers, titles, and a guess.

Play the Corners™ game and have each player record their scores on a graph.

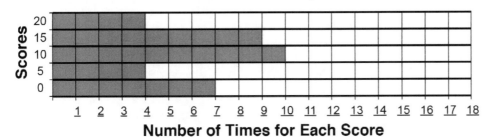

Titles and scores will vary.

Calculating the score. After the game is over, tell him calculate the scores. Ask him to share how he found the results. One organized solution is shown below.

$$20 \times 4 = 80$$
$$15 \times 9 = 135$$
$$10 \times 10 = 100$$
$$5 \times 4 = 20$$
$$0 \times 7 = \underline{0}$$
$$335$$

Checking scores with a calculator. Give the child the calculator. Tell him to use the memory feature on his calculator to check his score and the other players' scores.

See Lesson 42 for more details about using calculator memory.

In conclusion. Ask: Did you guess correctly which score was the most common? What are the advantages of scoring the Corners™ game like this? [no arithmetic until the game is over] What are the disadvantages of this scoring? [You don't know who is winning while playing.]

© Activities for Learning, Inc. 2015

Lesson 94: Reading a Bar Graph

OBJECTIVES:
1. To learn the term *population*
2. To interpret scales
3. To read a bar graph and obtain information

MATERIALS:
1. Worksheet 74, Reading a Bar Graph
2. Dry erase board

ACTIVITIES FOR TEACHING:

Warm-up. Give the child the worksheet. Tell him to do just the warm-up section. Solutions are:

```
  3698 (8)        3698 (8)        3698 (8)
  × 7 (7)        − 3179 (2)      + 3179 (2)
    56            519 (6)         6877 (1)
   630
  4200
 21000
 25886 (2)
```

Reading number lines. Give the child the dry erase board.

Explain that the number of people who live in a place, such as a village, a town, or a country is called the *population*. Discuss the population of your area.

Draw the following number line:

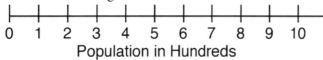
Population in Hundreds

Ask: If a village has a population of 600, where would that population be shown on the graph? [at the 6] If 50 more people moved into the village, where would that be on the graph? [halfway between 6 and 7]

Add the following arrows as shown in the figure below and tell the child to write down the populations. [50, 350, 720, 990] Ask: Can you get an exact answer? [no]

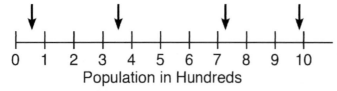
Population in Hundreds

Change the word "Hundreds" to "Thousands" as shown below.

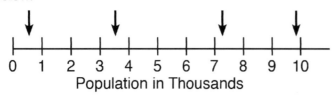
Population in Thousands

EXPLANATIONS:

ACTIVITIES FOR TEACHING:	EXPLANATIONS:

Tell him that now we are showing the population of towns, which usually are larger than villages. Ask: What does a 4 mean now? [4 thousand] What is the value halfway between 6 and 7? [6500] Tell him to write down the value of the arrows. [500, 3500, 7200, 9900]

Change the word "Thousands" to "Millions." See below.

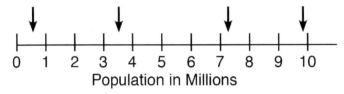

Ask: Can you think of large cities that have millions of people? [New York, San Diego, Chicago, Los Angeles, Houston]

Worksheet 74. Tell him to look at the worksheet. Ask: What does the graph tell us? [population of some states] Why do you think abbreviations were used on the graph? [not enough space for the whole name]

The data for the states' populations are from 2012.

Ask the following questions and discuss the answers:

1. What are the categories? [states]

2. What is the scale? [millions]

3. Does the graph show the exact number of people living in those states? [no]

4. Do we know the exact population of a state? [No, it is constantly changing because of babies being born, people dying, and people moving in and out of a state.]

5. What is special about the states listed on the chart? [All start with the letter *M*.]

6. Are they in any particular order? [alphabetical]

7. Which state has 6 million 600 thousand people? [Massachusetts]

8. Which state has 5 million 400 thousand people? [Minnesota]

Tell him to complete the worksheet. Solutions are below.

This worksheet will be needed in the next lesson.

1. Which state has a population of 6,000,000? **Missouri**
2. Which state has a population of 6,600,000? **Massachusetts**
3. Which state has a population of 1 million? **Montana**
4. What state has the greatest number of people? **Michigan**
5. What is the population of Maine? **1,300,000**
6. What state has twice the population of Mississippi? **Missouri**
7. Which state has a population closest to Minnesota's? **Maryland**
8. What is the difference in population between Minnesota and Missouri? **600,000**

Answers to questions 5 and 8 may vary.

In conclusion. Ask: What do you call the number of people living in a certain place? [population] Do you think it is easier to compare populations with a list of numbers or a bar graph?

If there is additional time following this lesson, have the child choose a game to play.

© Activities for Learning, Inc. 2015

190

LESSON 95: CONSTRUCTING A BAR GRAPH

OBJECTIVES:
1. To review the concept of area
2. To construct a bar graph with area data

MATERIALS:
1. Worksheet 75, Constructing a Bar Graph
2. **Map of the U.S. showing the states**
3. Worksheet 74, Reading a Bar Graph, from the previous lesson
4. A tile, cubic centimeter, ruler, and meter stick

ACTIVITIES FOR TEACHING:	EXPLANATIONS:

Warm-up. Give the child the worksheet. Tell him to do just the warm-up section. Solutions are:

$$9876 \ (3)$$
$$\underline{\times 4 \ (4)}$$
$$24$$
$$280$$
$$3200$$
$$\underline{36000}$$
$$39504 \ (3)$$

$$9876 \ (3)$$
$$\underline{- 678 \ (3)}$$
$$9198 \ (0)$$

$$9876 \ (3)$$
$$\underline{+ 678 \ (3)}$$
$$10554 \ (6)$$

Reviewing area and Worksheet 74. Refer to the U.S. map and tell the child to find the states of Montana, Minnesota, and Maine. Ask: Which of the three states is the largest? [Montana] Which state is the smallest? [Maine] What word describes how much space a flat figure takes up? [area] Does Minnesota or Montana have greater area? [Montana] Looking at the previous worksheet, which state has greater population? [Minnesota]

Units of area. Tell the child to gather these items: a tile, cubic centimeter, ruler, and meter stick.

Ask: Can we measure area with inches? [no] Can we measure area with centimeters? [no] Can we measure area with hours? [no] Show a tile and ask: Can we measure area with this square inch? [yes] Why is it called a square inch? [an inch on each side]

Show one face of the cubic centimeter and ask: Can we measure area with this square centimeter? [yes] Why is it called a square centimeter? [a centimeter on each side] Would a square centimeter be a good unit to measure the area of this room? [no] Why not? [too small]

Give him the ruler and tell him: The ruler is 12 inches long and is called 1 foot. Ask: How could you make a square foot with the ruler? [If you had four rulers, you could layout a square foot.] If four rulers are available, create a square foot. See the figure on the next page. Ask: Would a square foot be a good unit to measure the area of this room? [yes]

RightStart™ Mathematics Level D Second Edition   © Activities for Learning, Inc. 2015

ACTIVITIES FOR TEACHING:	EXPLANATIONS:

Give him the meter stick and ask: Would a square meter be large enough to measure the area of a state? [no]

Square miles. Tell him that in the United States, we usually measure these areas in square miles. Help him relate the length of a mile with a familiar distance. Ask: Can you imagine how large a square mile is? [a square whose sides are a mile long]

For a child familiar with acres, tell him that 640 acres fit in a square mile.

Worksheet 75. Tell the child the worksheet has a table giving the areas of eight states. He is to make a bar graph to show these areas. Discuss the categories, scales, and titles.

Tell him to complete the worksheet. Solutions are below.

Worksheet 74 will be needed for reference.

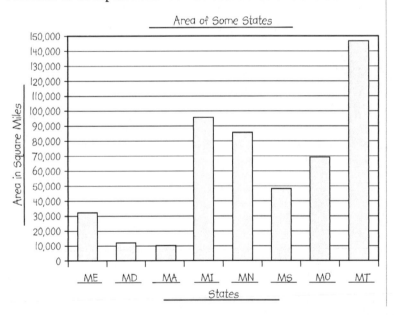

Titles and scales may vary.

1. Which state has the largest area? **Montana** Does it have the largest population? **no**
2. Which state is 3 times larger than Massachusetts? **Maine**
3. Which state is about half the size of Michigan? **Mississippi**
4. The population graphs keep changing. Do the area graphs also change? **no**
5. Would Missouri and Mississippi fit in Montana at the same time? **yes**
6. How many of the smaller states could fit inside Montana at the same time? **4**

In conclusion. Ask: What is area? [amount of space a flat figure takes up] Would you measure how deep a small lake is in miles or square miles? [miles] Would you measure how large a small lake is in miles or square miles? [square miles]

If there is additional time following this lesson, play the Constructing a Bar Graph game, found in *Math Card Games* book, A53.

© Activities for Learning, Inc. 2015

LESSON 96: REVIEW AND GAMES 6

OBJECTIVES:
1. To review recent topics
2. To develop skills through playing math card games

MATERIALS:
1. Worksheet 76-A or 76-B, Review 6
2. *Math Card Games* book, P32

ACTIVITIES FOR TEACHING:

Worksheet 76-A. Give the child the worksheet. Tell him to listen to the problems and write the answers. Read each problem twice.

$400 \times 30 \qquad 60 \times 4 \qquad 81 \div 9$

Tell him to complete the worksheet. Solutions are below.

EXPLANATIONS:

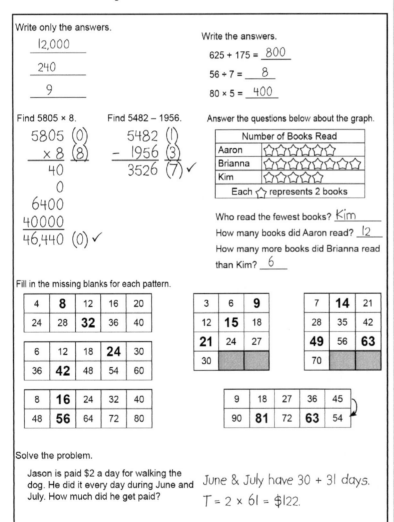

RightStart™ Mathematics Level D Second Edition © Activities for Learning, Inc. 2015

ACTIVITIES FOR TEACHING:

Ring around the Products game. Play the Ring around the Products game found in *Math Card Games* book, P32.

Worksheet 76-B. Give the child the worksheet. Tell him to listen to the problems and write the answers. Read each problem twice.

300×50 $\qquad$ 50×6 $\qquad$ $72 \div 9$

Tell him to complete the worksheet. Solutions are below.

Write only the answers.

15,000

300

8

Write the answers.

$451 + 249 = $ 700

$56 \div 8 = $ 7

$50 \times 8 = $ 400

Find 4709×7.

$$
\begin{array}{r}
4709 \;(2) \\
\times 7 \;(7) \\
\hline
63 \\
0 \\
4900 \\
28000 \\
\hline
32,963 \;(5) \checkmark
\end{array}
$$

Find $7345 - 4318$.

$$
\begin{array}{r}
7345 \;(1) \\
- 4318 \;(7) \\
\hline
3027 \;(3) \checkmark
\end{array}
$$

Answer the questions below about the graph.

Number of Pages Read	
William	☆☆☆☆☆☆
George	☆☆☆☆☆
Charlotte	☆☆☆
Each ☆ represents 5 pages	

Who read the most pages? William

How many pages did Charlotte read? 15

How many pages did William and George read together? 55

Fill in the missing blanks for each pattern.

4	8	12	**16**	20
24	28	32	**36**	40

6	**12**	18	24	30
36	42	48	**54**	60

8	16	24	**32**	40
48	56	64	**72**	80

3	6	**9**
12	15	**18**
21	24	**27**
30		

7	14	**21**
28	35	42
49	**56**	63
70		

9	18	**27**	36	45
90	81	**72**	63	54

Solve the problem.

Jocelyn gets $3 a day for caring for some animals. She did it every day during July and August. How much money did she make?

July & August each have 31 days.

$T = 3 \times 62 = \$186$.

© Activities for Learning, Inc. 2015

194

LESSON 97: TIME TO THE MINUTE

OBJECTIVES:
1. To review time to five-minute intervals
2. To read time to the minute

MATERIALS:
1. Geared clock
2. Set of hour cards and minute cards
3. Clock, Appendix p. 10
4. *Math Card Games* book, C27
5. Worksheet 77, Time to the Minute

ACTIVITIES FOR TEACHING:	EXPLANATIONS:
Warm-up. Tell the child to say the time you set on the geared clock. Start with 2:00, 6:00, 11:00, 5:00 then add in half hours, such as 3:30, 8:30, 10:30, and so forth.	

Next set the clock to various five minute increments and tell the child to say the times. Possibilities include:

> 2:00
> 2:15
> 2:30
> 2:45
> 3:05
> 3:20
> 3:35
> 3:50

Telling time on the clock. Give the child the hour cards and minute cards. Set the geared clock for 7:20. Ask the child to find the matching hour card and minute card and set them aside. See the figure on the right. Continue setting the clock with times listed below. All the cards will be used at the end.

9:15	10:40
4:00	5:10
6:35	8:05
11:50	12:55
2:30	3:45
1:25	

7 :20

Composing the time.

Telling time to the minute. Ask: Which hand on a clock is the hour hand? [the shorter hand] How long does it take for the minute hand to go all the way around the clock? [1 hour] How far does the hour hand travel in an hour? [from one number to the next number]

RightStart™ Mathematics Level D Second Edition

© Activities for Learning, Inc. 2015

ACTIVITIES FOR TEACHING:

Ask: How many minutes are in an hour? [60] How long does it take the minute hand to travel from the 1 to the 2 on the clock? [5 minutes] How many little spaces are there between the 1 and 2 on the clock? [five]

Set the geared clock with times listed below and the ask the child to say them or write them.

9:10	9:12
9:20	9:24
9:30	9:33
9:35	9:38
9:45	9:49
9:55	9:56
10:00	10:03

Name That Time. Give the child the paper clock from the appendix. Play the Name That Time game, found in *Math Card Games* book, C27.

Worksheet 77. Give the child the worksheet. Explain that analog clocks use hands while digital clocks use digits. Tell him he is to match the digital clock that is in the middle to an analog clock on either side. Solutions are below.

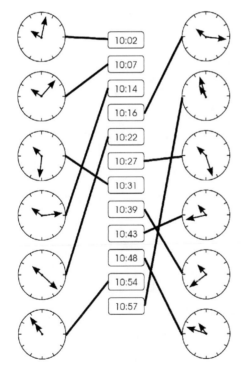

In conclusion. Ask: How many minutes are in an hour? [60] How many minutes are between two numbers on a clock? [5] If the time is 9:28, how long until 9:30? [2 min]

EXPLANATIONS:

196

LESSON 98: ADDING MINUTES

OBJECTIVES:

1. To add minutes on a clock

MATERIALS:

1. Clock, Appendix p. 10
2. *Math Card Games* book, C25
3. Worksheet 78, Adding Minutes

ACTIVITIES FOR TEACHING:	EXPLANATIONS:
Warm-up. Give the child the paper clock from the appendix. Ask: Which hand on a clock is the hour hand? [the shorter hand] Which hand on a clock is the minute hand? [the longer hand] How long does it take for the minute hand to go all the way around the clock? [1 hour] How many minutes are in an hour? [60]	
Ask: How many minutes are between two numbers on a clock? [5] If the time is 3:42, how long until 3:45? [3 min] If the time is 12:14, what time is it 6 minutes later? [12:20]	
Around the Clock game. Play the Around the Clock game, found in *Math Card Games* book, C25. The players start at the the top, at 12, and add minutes until one of the players reaches 12 or more.	If the child is having difficulties with game C25, games C23 and C24 in the *Math Card Games* book may be beneficial.
Worksheet 78. Give the child the worksheet. Explain: This worksheet is like connecting the dots, but now you are connecting the clocks. Start at the clock by the arrow at the top. Then read what it says below the clock and follow the directions.	
The first instruction says: Find 10 min later. Draw a line from that clock to the clock that is 10 minutes later. The first line is drawn lightly for you.	
Then read what is below the second clock and draw a line to the next clock. Some clocks will not be used. The solution is shown on the next page.	

RightStart™ Mathematics Level D Second Edition

© Activities for Learning, Inc. 2015

| **ACTIVITIES FOR TEACHING:** | **EXPLANATIONS:** |

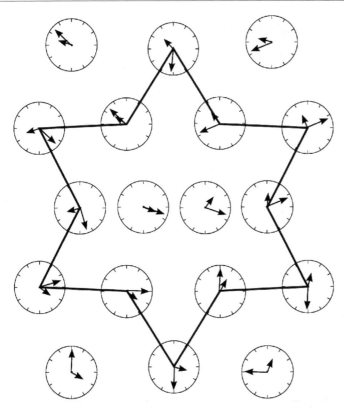

In conclusion. Ask: If the time is 2:00, what time will it be in 33 minutes? [2:33] If the time is 2:00, what time was it 20 minutes ago? [1:40] If the time is 2:10, what time will it be in 37 minutes? [2:47]

Lesson 99: Time Problems

OBJECTIVES:
1. To estimate the location of the hour hand
2. To solve problems involving time

MATERIALS:
1. Worksheet 79, Time Problems
2. Geared clock

ACTIVITIES FOR TEACHING:

Warm-up. Give the child the worksheet. Tell him to do just the warm-up section. Solutions are:

(6 × 80) + (3 × 80) = **720**   8 + 7 × 6 = **50**   68 **(5)**
(540 ÷ 9) – 15 = **45**   61 – (8 × 7) = **5**   × 7 **(7)**
                                                                        56
                                                                        420
                                                                        476 **(8)**

Observing the hour hand. Set the geared clock to 3:00. Ask: What happens to the hour hand when the minute hand goes all the way around and back to 12? [It moves to 4.] Where do you think the hour hand will be when the time is set for 4:30? [halfway between 4 and 5] Repeat for 4:47 [three-fourths of the distance between 4 and 5] and 5:13. [one-fourth the distance between 5 and 6]

Worksheet 79. Tell the child to read the directions for the clocks and to complete that part of the worksheet. The solutions are below.

12:35   5:02   9:28   10:44

Ask him to discuss his answers.

Problem 1. These problems are to be solved during the lesson and can be done mentally. Remind him to check if his answer make sense. Give him several minutes of quiet time to solve each problem. Then tell him to explain his solution.

Tell the child to read and solve the first problem:

  1. Isabel needs to be ready for lessons at 4:30. She needs 5 minutes for a snack, 10 minutes to change her clothes, and 15 minutes to walk there. When should she start getting ready?

Adding the times, 5, 10, and 15 minutes gives 30 minutes. So she needs to start at 4:00.

EXPLANATIONS:

ACTIVITIES FOR TEACHING:

Problem 2. Tell the child to read and answer the second problem:

> 2. Isaac needs to practice his trombone for 35 minutes. He takes a 10-minute break during practice. If he starts at 7:30, when will his practice be over?

His total time is 35 + 10 = 45 minutes. It takes 30 minutes to get to 8:00 and the remaining 15 minutes gives 8:15 for the end of his practice time.

Problem 3. Tell the child to solve the third problem:

> 3. Ryan and his family are leaving at 10:40 to go to his cousins' home. Driving time is 2 hours and 36 minutes. They make two stops, each 12 minutes long. What time will they arrive?

The two stops are 24 minutes. Adding that to the 36 minutes gives 1 hour. So the total time is 3 hours. They will arrive at 10:40 + 3 hours which is 1:40.

Problem 4. Tell the child to solve the fourth problem:

> 4. Abby leaves at 7:45 to go fishing. She arrives home at 2:00. How long was she gone?

It takes 15 minutes to get to 8:00 and 4 hours from 8:00 to 12:00 and 2 more hours from 12:00 to 2:00. So the total time is 6 hours and 15 minutes.

In conclusion. Ask: If the time is 11:00, what time will it be in 63 minutes? [12:03] If the time is 11:00, what time was it 90 minutes ago? [9:30] If the time is 11:00, what time will it be in 2 hours and 2 minutes? [1:02]

EXPLANATIONS:

If there is additional time following this lesson, play the Fifteen Minutes Later game and Thirty Minutes Later game, found in *Math Card Games* book, C23 and C24.

© Activities for Learning, Inc. 2015

Lesson 100: Finding Perimeter in Feet and Inches

OBJECTIVES:
1. To review that 1 foot equals 12 inches
2. To measure in feet and inches
3. To find perimeter in feet and inches

MATERIALS:
1. Worksheet 80, Finding Perimeter in Feet and Inches
2. 4-in-1 ruler
3. **2 sheets of construction paper (9 inches by 12 inches)**

ACTIVITIES FOR TEACHING:

Warm-up. Give the child the worksheet. Tell him to do just the warm-up section. Solutions are:

```
   3649 (4)         3649 (4)         3649 (4)
   × 7 (7)         − 2772 (0)       + 2772 (0)
     63              877 (4)         6421 (4)
    280
   4200
  21000
  25543 (1)
```

Reviewing a foot. Give the child the ruler. Ask: What units does your ruler have for measuring? [inches and centimeters] What is the highest number on the centimeter side? [30] What is the highest number on the inch side? [12]

Say: There is a special name for 12 inches – a foot. A *foot* received its name because it was about the length of a man's foot. Ask: How many inches are in one foot? [12 in.] How many inches are in two feet? [24 in.] How many inches are in a half of a foot? [6 in.] Tell him *ft* is the abbreviation for foot and for feet. It does not have a period after the *t*.

Perimeter in feet and inches. Tell him that today he will use feet and inches to find perimeter. Explain that when using feet and inches, the number of inches cannot be greater than 11 just as the number of hundreds, tens, or ones cannot be more than 9.

Show the child two sheets of construction paper joined the long way and two sheets joined the short way. See below.

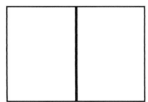 

9 by 12 in. construction paper.

Ask: Which do you think has the greater perimeter?

EXPLANATIONS:

The child will find the answer by solving Problem 1 on the worksheet.

ACTIVITIES FOR TEACHING:

Worksheet 80. Give the child the construction paper and tell him to read the instructions on the worksheet.

Problem 1. Tell him to lay the two papers side by side. Finding the perimeter is the first problem on his worksheet.

Show him how he can use two rulers for measuring. Discuss where to place the second ruler: not at the edge of the ruler, but at the marking for 12 inches. See the figure below.

One way using rulers to measure lengths over 1 foot.

Tell him to measure the papers and find the perimeters. Then discuss it.

1 ft 6 in.

P = 1 ft 6 in. + 1 ft + 1 ft 6 in. + 1 ft
P = 5 ft

2 ft

P = 2 ft + 9 in. + 2 ft + 9 in.
P = 5 ft 6 in.

Ask him: Did you guess correctly the greater perimeter?

Problem 2. Ask the child to measure a sibling or friend's height.

Problems 3–4. Tell the child to do the last two problems then discuss. Solutions are below.

$6\frac{1}{4}$ in.

$2\frac{1}{4}$ in.

$P = 6\frac{1}{4}$ in. $+ 2\frac{1}{4}$ in. $+ 6\frac{1}{4}$ in. $+ 2\frac{1}{4}$ in.
$P = 17$ in. $= 1$ ft 5 in.

$4\frac{1}{2}$ in.

$P = 4\frac{1}{2}$ in. $\times 6$
$P = 24$ in. $+ 3$ in. $= 2$ ft 3 in.

In conclusion. Tell him: Show how much an inch is with your fingers. Show how much a foot is with your hands. Ask: How many inches are in a foot? [12]

EXPLANATIONS:

If there is additional time following this lesson, play the Short Chain Solitaire game, found in *Math Card Games* book, C23.

© Activities for Learning, Inc. 2015

202

LESSON 101: SQUARE MILES

OBJECTIVES:
1. To read for information
2. To solve problems with information obtained by reading
3. To work with square miles

MATERIALS:
1. Worksheet 81, Square Miles
2. Geared clock
3. *Math Card Games book*, P29

ACTIVITIES FOR TEACHING:	EXPLANATIONS:

Warm-up. Give the child the worksheet. Tell him to do just the warm-up section. Solutions are:

4792 **(4)**	4792 **(4)**	4792 **(4)**
× 8 **(8)**	− 2974 **(4)**	+ 2974 **(4)**
16	1818 **(0)**	7766 **(8)**
720		
5600		
32000		
38336 **(5)**		

Tell the child to say the time set on the geared clock. Include time to the minute, such as 4:32, 8:56, 5:22, and 11:06.

Square miles. Tell the child: Think how long a mile is. Relate the distance to something familiar to the child. Ask: How large is a square mile? [a square that is a mile on each side]

Worksheet 81, Problems 1–7. Tell the child to read the first paragraph and answer the questions. See below.

> Minnesota is the twelfth largest state among the 50 states in the United States. The state is 408 miles long and 348 miles wide. It covers 86,943 square miles. Of this total, seven thousand three hundred twenty-nine square miles is covered by water. The highest point in Minnesota is Eagle Mountain at 2301 feet. The mountain is 15 miles from the shore of Lake Superior, which is the lowest point at 602 feet above sea level.

1. How many states are larger than Minnesota? **11**

2. How many states are smaller than Minnesota? **38**

3. Write the state's area in words. **eighty-six thousand nine hundred forty-three square miles**

4. Round the state's area to the nearest thousand. **87,000 square miles**

5. Seven thousand three hundred twenty-nine square miles is water, how much is land? **79,614 square miles**

6. How much longer is the state than it is wide? **60 miles**

7. What is the difference between the highest and lowest points? **1699 feet**

See page iii, number 14 of "Some General Thoughts on Teaching Mathematics," for additional information.

RightStart™ Mathematics Level D Second Edition

© Activities for Learning, Inc. 2015

ACTIVITIES FOR TEACHING:	EXPLANATIONS:

Tell him to discuss his answers. Tell the child to correct any misspellings.

Problems 8–10. Tell the child to read the second paragraph and answer the questions. See below for the paragraph and solutions.

Minnesota is divided into 87 counties; counties are divided into townships. Townships are square-shaped pieces of land with each side 6 miles long. The maps on the right show two counties in southern Minnesota and their townships.

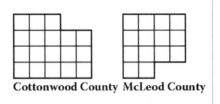
Cottonwood County   McLeod County

8. How many townships are in Cottonwood County? **18** In McLeod County? **14**

9. Find the perimeter of each county. **108 and 96 miles**

10. Find the area of each county. **648 and 504 square miles**

Tell the child to discuss his methods on Problem 10. One way to find the area of Cottonwood County is to see it as 20 – 2 townships. Each township is 6 square miles, so the area is:

$$A = 36 \times 20 - 36 \times 2 = 720 - 72$$
$$A = 648 \text{ square miles}$$

One way to find the area of McLeod County is to notice it has four fewer townships, which is 36 × 4 less:

$$A = 648 - 36 \times 4 = 648 - 144$$
$$A = 504 \text{ square miles}$$

Find the Two Factors game. If time permits, play the Find the Two Factors game, found in *Math Card Games* book, P29.

In conclusion. Ask: What do you call an area that is a square whose sides are 12 inches long? [a square foot] What do you call an area that is a large square whose sides are 1 mile long? [a square mile] Which is greater, 1 mile or 1 square mile? [They cannot be compared.]

Many real-life problems depend upon factors beyond the immediate problem.

Problems 9 and 10 can be solved several different ways.

LESSON 102: MEASURING AREAS

OBJECTIVES:

1. To compare areas using square inches and square centimeters

MATERIALS:

1. Worksheet 82, Measuring Areas
2. Geared clock
3. Tiles
4. Centimeter cubes

ACTIVITIES FOR TEACHING:	**EXPLANATIONS:**

Warm-up. Give the child the worksheet. Tell him to do just the warm-up section. Solutions are:

6735 **(3)**	6735 **(3)**	6735 **(3)**
× 8 **(8)**	− 5376 **(3)**	+ 5376 **(3)**
40	**1359 (0)**	**12111 (6)**
240		
5600		
48000		
53880 (6)		

Tell the child to say the time set on the geared clock. Include time to the minute, such as 8:23, 7:58, 1:42, and 10:35.

Reviewing square inches. Give the child the tiles and centimeter cubes.

Show a tile and ask: How long is a side of a tile? [1 in.] What do we call the space that the tile covers? [area] What is the area of a tile? [1 square inch] Show him how to write it:

$$A = 1 \text{ in}^2$$

Explain that we read it as "1 square inch." The little 2 means we have inches in two directions.

Reviewing square centimeters. Tell the child to look at one of the centimeter cubes. Ask: What is the length of a edge? [1 cm] What is the area of one of the faces? [1 square centimeter] Show him how to write it:

$$A = 1 \text{ cm}^2$$

Explain: There is no period after the "cm" abbreviation. There is a period after the "in." for inches so it is not confused with the word "in". It is not needed in "in^2".

Ask: What does the little 2 mean after "cm"? [a centimeter in two directions]

Worksheet 82. Tell him to do the Problems 1–4 on the worksheet. Ask him to share his solution. Some children will need to fill in the entire rectangle as shown on the next page on the left. Others will see the area as the

Explanations: Be sure to read "2 in^2" as "two square inches." Avoid saying "two inches squared," which may have a different interpretation.

RightStart™ Mathematics Level D Second Edition

© Activities for Learning, Inc. 2015

ACTIVITIES FOR TEACHING:	EXPLANATIONS:

number of rows multiplied by the number of columns as shown below on the right.

The solutions to Problems 1–4 are below.

1. How long is a side of a tile? **1 in.**
2. What is the area of one tile? **1 in²**

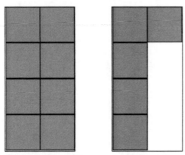

Measuring the area with tiles.

3. How many tiles does it take to cover the area inside the rectangle? **2 × 4 = 8**
4. What is the area of the rectangle in in²? **8 in²**

Discuss his solutions, then tell the child to complete the worksheet. Solutions are below.

5. How long is an edge of a centimeter cube? **1 cm**
6. What is the area of a face of a cube? **1 cm²**

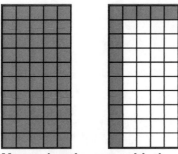

Measuring the area with the face of centimeter cube.

7. How many centimeter cubes does it take to cover the area inside the rectangle? **5 × 10 = 50**
8. What is the area of the rectangle in cm²? **50 cm²**
9. Why are the area answers different for the same rectangle?

In conclusion. Ask: What do you call the amount of space a figure covers? [area] Can we measure the area in square centimeters? [yes] Can we measure the area in centimeters? [no] Can we measure the area in feet? [no] Can we measure the area in square feet? [yes]

If there is additional time following this lesson, play the Multiples Solitaire game, found in *Math Card Games* book, C23.

© Activities for Learning, Inc. 2015

LESSON 103: FINDING AREAS

OBJECTIVES:
1. To find areas of non-rectangular shapes

MATERIALS:
1. Worksheet 83, Finding Areas
2. Geared clock

ACTIVITIES FOR TEACHING:

Warm-up. Give the child the worksheet. Tell him to do just the warm-up section. Solutions are:

```
  8573 (5)        8573 (5)        8573 (5)
  × 6 (6)        − 3758 (5)      + 3758 (5)
    18           4815 (0)        12331 (1)
   420
  3000
 48000
 51438 (3)
```

Tell the child to say the time set on the geared clock. Include time to the minute, such as 9:13, 4:57, 3:13, and 12:04.

Worksheet 83. Tell the child to read the instructions on the worksheet. Ask: Are the squares in the figures square inches? [no] Are the squares square centimeters? [no] Tell him: The little squares have no special name so they are called *square units*.

Tell him to work alone to find the area of the first problem two different ways. After a few minutes, tell him to discuss and see if he can think of a different method to solve the problem. Discuss as many different solutions as possible. Some are shown below and on the next page.

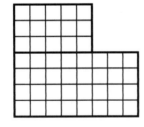

$A = 5 \times 3 + 8 \times 4$
$A = 15 + 32 = 47$ units^2

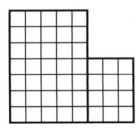

$A = 5 \times 7 + 3 \times 4$
$A = 35 + 12 = 47$ units^2

EXPLANATIONS:

Be sure to read "47 units^2" as "forty-seven square units." Avoid saying "forty-seven units squared" which may have a different interpretation.

ACTIVITIES FOR TEACHING:

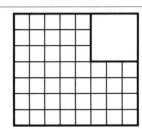

$A = 8 \times 7 - 3 \times 3$
$A = 56 - 9 = 47 \text{ units}^2$

Tell the child to complete the worksheet. Several solutions are shown below.

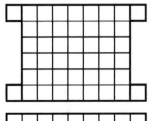

$A = 7 \times 6 + 4$
$A = 42 + 4 = 46 \text{ units}^2$

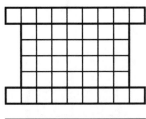

$A = 9 \times 2 + 7 \times 4$
$A = 18 + 28 = 46 \text{ units}^2$

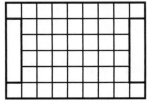

$A = 9 \times 6 - 2 \times 4$
$A = 54 - 8 = 46 \text{ units}^2$

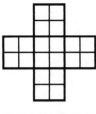

$A = 5 \times 2 \times 2$ or $A = 5 \times 4$
$A = 20 \text{ units}^2$

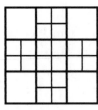

$A = 6 \times 6 - 4 \times 4$
$A = 36 - 16 = 20 \text{ units}^2$

In conclusion. Ask: When you calculate areas using different methods for the same figure, does it matter if your answers do not agree? [yes, something is wrong]

EXPLANATIONS:

If there is additional time following this lesson, play the Multiples Solitaire game, found in *Math Card Games* book, C23.

Lesson 104: Area of Tangram Pieces

OBJECTIVES:
1. To find the total area by adding the areas of its parts

MATERIALS:
1. Worksheet 84, Area of Tangram Pieces
2. Geared clock
3. A set of tangrams
4. Ruler (for drawing straight lines), optional

ACTIVITIES FOR TEACHING:

Warm-up. Give the child the worksheet. Tell him to do just the warm-up section. Solutions are:

```
  6834 (3)      6834 (3)      6834 (3)
  × 7 (7)     − 4386 (3)    + 4386 (3)
    28         2448 (0)      11220 (6)
   210
  5600
 42000
 47838 (3)
```

Tell the child to say the time set on the geared clock. Include time to the minute, such as 6:03, 2:54, 8:29, and 10:41.

The tangram pieces. Give the child a set of tangrams.

Tell him: Find the smallest triangle. We will call its area 1 unit^2. Ask: What is the area of the other small triangle? [1 unit^2] What is the area of the square? [2 unit^2] How do you know? [Two small triangles fill the square.]

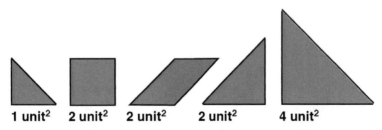

1 unit^2 2 unit^2 2 unit^2 2 unit^2 4 unit^2

Ask: What is the area of the parallelogram? [2 unit^2] What is the area of the medium triangle? [2 unit^2] What is the area of the large triangle? [4 unit^2] See below.

Ask: What is the total area of all seven pieces? [16 unit^2]

Worksheet 84. Tell him to write the area of the tangram pieces on the worksheet.

Tell him to look at the 10 outlines. Ask: Which ones do you think have the largest area? Tell him: Put a little x near the ones that you think are the largest. You will see how close your guess was when you finish the worksheet.

EXPLANATIONS:

Remember to read "1 unit^2" as "one square unit."

Although area is referred to as "square" units, it is not necessary that it be in the shape of a square. Any two-dimensional shape will work.

Actually, the area of the smallest triangle in the tangram set is very close to 1 in^2 – it is 0.97 in^2.

See page iii, number 15 of "Some General Thoughts on Teaching Mathematics," for additional information.

ACTIVITIES FOR TEACHING:

Tell him: You are to make the shape shown on the worksheet with the tangram pieces. The first three, A, B, and C, have the same shape, but can be made three different ways. Make the shapes and draw them on your worksheet. Notice the position of the small triangle in each figure. You may use a ruler if you want.

Tell the child to discuss his answers. Ask: What is the area of each figure? [4 unit^2] How did you figure it out? [The two small triangles each has 1 unit^2 and the other piece has 2 unit^2 giving a total of 4 unit^2.]

Tell him to complete the worksheet. Remind him to make each shape with his tangram pieces before copying to the worksheet. Solutions are shown below.

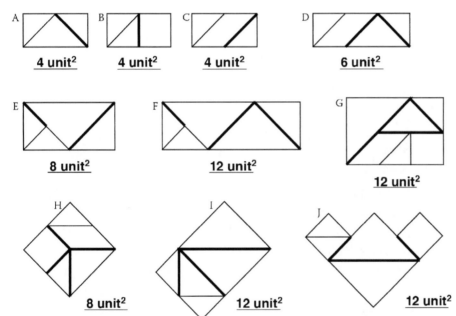

After he has completed the worksheet, ask: Did you guess correctly which shapes had the largest areas?

In conclusion. Ask: Did you notice that the areas of all the figures on the worksheet are even numbers? What would you have to do to make a tangram shape with an odd number of square units? [Use only one of the small triangles.]

EXPLANATIONS:

Many of these outlines have more than one solution.

If there is additional time following this lesson, have the child choose a game to play.

© Activities for Learning, Inc. 2015

Lesson 105: Area and Perimeter Comparisons

OBJECTIVES:
1. To review measuring with a ruler
2. To compare area and perimeter

MATERIALS:
1. Worksheet 85, Area and Perimeter Comparisons
2. Geared clock
3. 4-in-1 ruler
4. Centimeter cubes
5. Math journal

ACTIVITIES FOR TEACHING:

Warm-up. Give the child the worksheet. Tell him to do just the warm-up section. Solutions are:

```
  7296 (6)       7296 (6)        7296 (6)
  × 6 (6)       − 6927 (6)      + 6927 (6)
    36           369 (0)         14223 (3)
   540
  1200
 42000
 43776 (0)
```

Tell the child to say the various times set on the geared clock.

Measuring centimeters. Give the child the 4-in-1 ruler, centimeter cubes, and math journal.

Tell him: Find the side of the ruler with centimeters. Make a row of eight centimeter cubes. Measure it with your ruler. You may use either centimeter scale on the ruler. What does the row measure with the ruler? [8 cm] See the figure below.

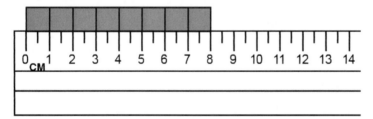

Drawing a rectangle. Tell the child: In your math journal, draw a rectangle that is 12 cm wide and 8 cm high. Be sure to write the width and height on your figure. Then calculate the area of the rectangle and the perimeter.

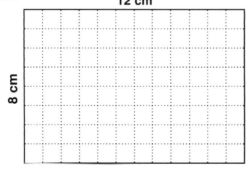

EXPLANATIONS:

The 4-in-1 ruler has a centimeter scale divided into halves and a second centimeter scale divided into tenths.

The rectangles in the math journal are 1 cm^2.

ACTIVITIES FOR TEACHING:	**EXPLANATIONS:**

After he has found the solution, tell him to discuss it.

Finding the area is straightforward:

$$A = 12 \times 8 = 96 \text{ cm}^2$$

Many children will find the perimeter by adding the individual sides:

$$P = 12 + 8 + 12 + 8 = 40 \text{ cm}$$

Some children will notice they can multiply by 2:

$$P = (12 + 8) \times 2 = 40 \text{ cm}$$

Worksheet 85. Tell the child to complete the worksheet. Solutions are below.

1. Draw a line 6 cm long.

2. Draw a line $4\frac{1}{2}$ cm long.

3. Draw 1 square centimeter.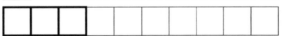

4. Draw 3 square centimeters.

$A = 17 \times 6 = 102 \text{ cm}^2$ $P = 17 + 17 + 6 + 6 = 46 \text{ cm}$

5. $A = 27 \times 6 = 162 \text{ cm}^2$ $A = 24 \times 7 = 168 \text{ cm}^2$

   $P = 2 \times (27 + 6) = 66 \text{ cm}$ $P = (24 + 7) \times 2 = 62 \text{ cm}$

6. **Rectangle B has greater area.**

7. **Rectangle A has greater perimeter.**

Ask: Are you surprised at the answers to the last two problems?

In conclusion. Ask: Which is more, 7 centimeters or $6\frac{1}{2}$ centimeters? [7 centimeters] Which is more, 2 centimeters or 2 square centimeters? [They cannot be compared.]

If there is additional time following this lesson, play the Corners™ game, found in *Math Card Games* book, A9.

Lesson 106: Finding Perimeter and Area of Squares

OBJECTIVES:
1. To find perimeter and area of squares
2. To find patterns in the perimeters and areas perimeters

MATERIALS:
1. Worksheet 86, Finding Perimeter and Area of Squares
2. Geared clock
3. Short Multiplication Tables, Appendix p. 1

ACTIVITIES FOR TEACHING:

Warm-up. Give the child the worksheet. Tell him to do just the warm-up section. Solutions are:

```
   6285 (3)        6285 (3)        6285 (3)
   × 8 (8)        − 5826 (3)      + 5826 (3)
     40            459 (0)         12111 (6)
    640
   1600
  48000
  50280 (6)
```

Tell the child to say the various times set on the geared clock.

Worksheet 82. Tell the child to look at the worksheet. Explain: You are to draw squares and find the perimeter and area and write them in the table. Ask: What is the perimeter of the smallest square? [1 cm + 1 cm + 1 cm + 1 cm = 4 cm] What is the area [1 cm²]

Ask: What will the size of the next square? [2 cm × 2 cm] Tell him to draw it, starting at the upper left corner. See the left figure below.

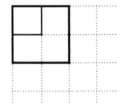

n	P	A
1	4	1
2	8	4
3		

The second square drawn and the perimeter and area recorded.

Ask: What is the perimeter? [2 cm + 2 cm + 2 cm + 2 cm = 8 cm or 2 cm × 4 = 8 cm] What is the area? [2 cm × 2 cm = 4 cm²] Tell the child to write his answers in the table. See the right figure above.

Tell him to continue with the remaining squares. The solutions are shown on top of the next page.

Ask the child to explain how he found the area for the 11 × 11 square. One way is to start with 100 and add: 10 for the additional row, 10 for the additional column, and 1 for the corner, giving 121.

EXPLANATIONS:

Many children will discover that to find the perimeter they can multiply one side by 4 rather that add four times. It should not be memorized as a "formula" for the perimeter of a square.

213

ACTIVITIES FOR TEACHING:

EXPLANATIONS:

n	P	A
1	4	1
2	8	4
3	12	9
4	16	16
5	20	25
6	24	36
7	28	49
8	32	64
9	36	81
10	40	100
11	44	121
12	48	144

Repeat for the 12 × 12 square. One way is to start with the 11 × 11 square, then add the two 11s and the last 1, giving 121 + 22 + 1 = 144. A second way is to start with 100 and add two 20s and 4, giving 100 + 40 + 4 = 144.

Patterns. Ask: What pattern do you see with the perimeters? [multiples of 4] What is the difference between any two adjacent perimeters? [4] What is the difference between the first two areas? [3] What is the difference between the next two areas? [5] What is the difference between the next two areas? [7] What is the pattern? [odd numbers, difference between the areas increase by two]

Tell the child to look at his short multiplication table. Ask: Where on the short multiplication table can you find the numbers that are in the area column? [at the end of the rows]

This worksheet will be needed for the next lesson.

In conclusion. Ask: Can you measure perimeter in centimeters? [yes] Can you measure perimeter in inches? [yes] Can you measure area in inches? [no] Can you measure area in square inches? [yes] Can you measure area in square feet? [yes]

If there is additional time following this lesson, play the Zero Corners™ game, found in *Math Card Games* book, S9.

© Activities for Learning, Inc. 2015

Enrichment Lesson 107: Graphing Area and Perimeter

OBJECTIVES:
1. To graph perimeters of squares
2. To graph areas of squares
3. To compare the graphs

MATERIALS:
1. Worksheet 86, Finding Perimeter and Area of Squares, from the previous lesson
2. Worksheet 87, Graphing Area and Perimeter
3. Ruler or straight edges
4. *Math Card Games* book, P23

ACTIVITIES FOR TEACHING:

Worksheets 86 and 87. Give the child the worksheet and the ruler. Tell the child he will need the worksheet and data from the last lesson in order to do today's worksheet.

The first chart, the bar graph outline for the perimeter, only needs the bars drawn. The second graph needs titles, as well as the bars. The completed graphs are shown below.

EXPLANATIONS:

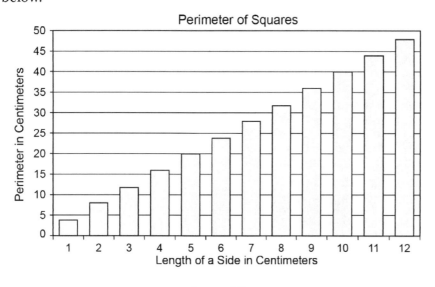

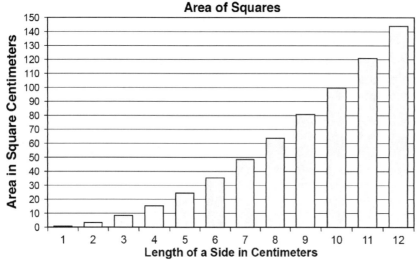

RightStart™ Mathematics Level D Second Edition © Activities for Learning, Inc. 2015

ACTIVITIES FOR TEACHING:	EXPLANATIONS:

Comparing the graphs. When the child has completed the graphs, tell him to use a ruler or straight edge to observe the relationship between the perimeters in the first graph. Tell him to do it for the second graph. See the figures below.

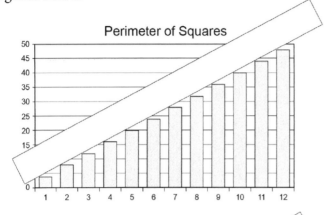

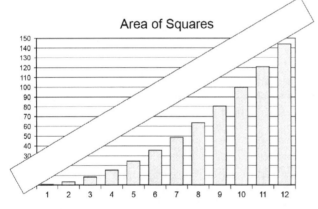

Ask: Which graph shows the data as a straight line? [perimeter] Why is that? [difference between each square is always 4] Which graph shows a slower start and then a steeper climb? [area] Why is that? [difference between each square increases]

Ask: What would happen if you added squares up to 20 to your perimeter graph? [The bars would gradually increase.] What would happen if you added squares up to 20 to your area graph? [The bars would get really tall.]

Crazy Squares game. Play the Crazy Squares game found in *Math Card Games* book, P23.

In conclusion. Ask: How are these two graphs different from the other graphs you have made this year? [These graphs show relationships.]

© Activities for Learning, Inc. 2015

LESSON 108: REVIEW AND GAMES 7

OBJECTIVES:
1. To review recent topics
2. To develop skills through playing math card games

MATERIALS:
1. Worksheet 88-A or 88-B, Review 7
2. *Math Card Games* book, D6

ACTIVITIES FOR TEACHING:

Worksheet 88-A. Give the child the worksheet. Tell him to listen to the problems and write the answers. Read each problem twice.

700×9 $\frac{1}{2}$ of 42 $49 \div 7$

Tell him to complete the worksheet. Solutions are below.

Write only the answers.
6300
21
7

Write the answers.
$52 - 15 = 37$
$72 \div 8 = 9$
$42 \times 10 = 420$

Write the time.
1:04

Find 5678×7.

This is 1 cm: ——
This is 1 inch: ————
Draw 1 cm² below.   Draw 1 in² below.

Find the perimeter and area for the figure below.
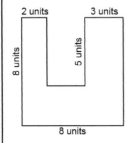

$P = 2 + 5 + 3 + 5 + 3 + 8 + 8 + 8$
$P = 42$ units
$A = 8 \times 8 - 5 \times 3 = 64 - 15$
$A = 49$ units²

Solve the problems.

It takes Jill 12 minutes to unicyle around the block. If she leaves at 6:50 p.m. and goes around the block twice, what time will she be back?

6:50 p.m. + 12 × 2 =
7:14 p.m.

Jack knows that 16 × 3 = 48. He has 48 cards to give to each of his three friends. How many cards does each friend get?

$c = 48 \div 3$
$c = 16$ cards

EXPLANATIONS:

The square centimeter and square inch are drawn to actual size.

There are several other ways the area could be found.

ACTIVITIES FOR TEACHING:

Equal Quotients game. Play the Equal Quotients game found in *Math Card Games* book, D6.

Worksheet 88-B. Give the child the worksheet. Tell him to listen to the problems and write the answers. Read each problem twice.

800×8 $\qquad \frac{1}{2}$ of 48 $\qquad 54 \div 6$

Tell him to complete the worksheet. Solutions are below.

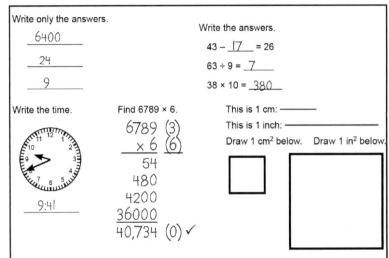

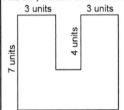

EXPLANATIONS:

The square centimeter and square inch are drawn to actual size.

There are several other ways the area could be found.

© Activities for Learning, Inc. 2015

Lesson 109: Finding Factors

OBJECTIVES:
1. To find several rectangles with the same area using factors
2. To calculate the perimeters of rectangles with the same area

MATERIALS:
1. Worksheet 89, Finding Factors
2. Centimeter cubes
3. Math journal
4. *Math Card Games* book, P29

ACTIVITIES FOR TEACHING:

Warm-up. Give the child the worksheet. Tell him to do just the warm-up section. Solutions are:

```
  5864 (5)          5864 (5)          5864 (5)
   ×7 (7)          − 4685 (5)        + 4685 (5)
    28              1179 (0)          10549 (1)
   420
  5600
 35000
 41048 (8)
```

Finding factors. Give the child the centimeter cubes and math journal.

Tell him to take 12 centimeter cubes and make arrays using all 12 cubes.

Ask him to draw his arrays in his math journal. See below.

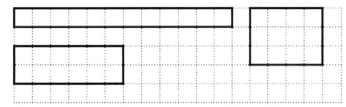

Three rectangles having an area of 12 unit².

Tell him to find the perimeters of the three rectangles he drew. See below.

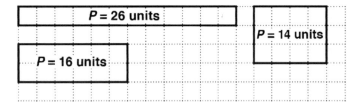

Next, tell him to draw three rectangles each with an area of 20 square units in his math journal. See the figure on the next page.

Ask: What happens to the perimeter as the dimensions of the rectangles change? [The perimeter of the rectangle decreases the closer the rectangle is to a square.]

EXPLANATIONS:

Factors were discussed in Lesson 18. Factors are the numbers that make the product. A factor is to multiplication as an addend is to adding.

ACTIVITIES FOR TEACHING:

EXPLANATIONS:

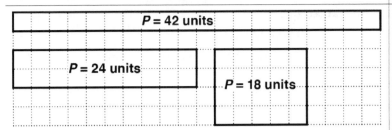

Worksheet 89. Tell him to complete the worksheet. See below.

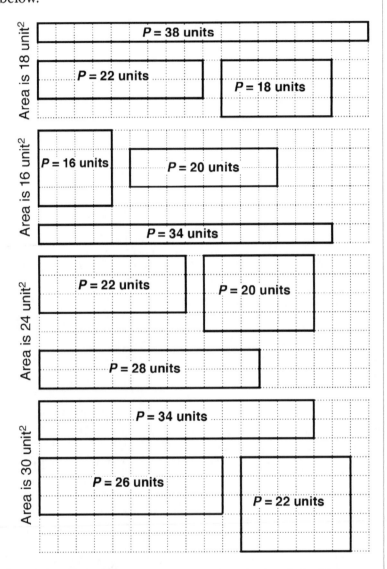

Find the Two Factors game. Play the Find the Two Factors game found in *Math Card Games* book, P29.

In conclusion. Ask: If two rectangles have the same area, must their perimeters be equal? [no] What two numbers multiplied together equal 36? [2 and 18; 3 and 12; 4 and 9; or 6 and 6] What two numbers multiplied equal 48? [2 and 24; 3 and 16; 4 and 12; or 6 and 8]

220

LESSON 110: AREA AND PERIMETER PROBLEMS

OBJECTIVES:
1. To solve multi-step problems involving area and perimeter

MATERIALS:
1. Worksheet 90, Area and Perimeter Problems

ACTIVITIES FOR TEACHING:

EXPLANATIONS:

Warm-up. Give the child the worksheet. Tell him to do just the warm-up section. Solutions are:

7295 **(5)**	7295 **(5)**	7295 **(5)**
$\times$ 6 **(6)**	$-$ 5927 **(5)**	$+$ 5927 **(5)**
30	**1368 (0)**	**13222 (1)**
540		
1200		
42000		
43770 **(3)**		

Worksheet 90. These problems are to be solved during the lesson. Give him several minutes of quiet time to solve each problem before discussing. Remind the child to check if his answers make sense. Then tell him to explain his solution.

Explaining to another person how one solves a problem helps clarify the thought process.

Problem 1. Ask the child to read the first problem:

The Lee family is laying a patio with patio stones that are 1 square foot each. How many patio stones do they need? See the figure at the right.

8 feet / 16 feet

To solve this problem, the child must realize that find the area will give the number of square feet, which is the number of patio stones. $A = 8 \times 16 = 128 \text{ ft}^2$. They need 128 patio stones. The arithmetic could be done mentally as follows:

$$A = 8 \times 16 = 8 \times (8 \times 2) = 64 \times 2 = 128 \text{ ft}^2$$

Sometimes math programs lay out detailed steps for children to follow when solving problems. Often, a simple intuitive approach combined with seeing how peers solved the problem is more instructive.

Parentheses are optional.

Problem 2. Ask the child to read and solve the next problem:

The Lees are paying six dollars for each patio stone. What will the patio stones cost?

$$C = 128 \times 6 = \$768$$

Problem 3. Ask the child to read and solve the third problem:

Next the Lee family decides to build a fence around the patio. What is the cost if fencing is $9 a foot?

Building a fence around a rectangular shape should

RightStart™ Mathematics Level D Second Edition

© Activities for Learning, Inc. 2015

ACTIVITIES FOR TEACHING:	EXPLANATIONS:

trigger a perimeter calculation. Once perimeter is known, the cost can be calculated.

$$P = 8 + 16 + 8 + 16 = 48 \text{ feet}$$
or
$$P = (8 + 16) \times 2 = 48 \text{ feet}$$
$$C = 48 \times 9 = \$432$$

This set of problems may be extended by asking: Can you think of something else you could find out about the Lee's patio? One possibility is: How much do the patio stones and fencing cost together? [$C = 768 + 432 = \$1200$]

Extending problems is a good way to become a good problem solver. It requires deeper thinking.

Problem 4. Ask the child to read and solve the fourth problem:

> One case of canned pet food is shown below. Mr. Berg is buying three cases. What is the total cost if each can is $2?

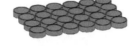

The first thing needed to find out is how many cans are in a case. The figure shows $6 \times 4 = 24$ cans. Then the cost of three cases at $2 a can is:

$$C = 24 \times 3 \times 2 = \$144$$

Another way is to find the cost of one case:

$$C_1 = 24 \times 2 = \$48$$

And then find the cost of 3 cases:

$$C = \$48 \times 3 = \$144$$

Or, find the total number of cans

$$N = 24 \times 3 = 72$$

And then the total cost is:

$$C = 72 \times 2 = \$144$$

Problem 5. Ask the child to solve the fifth problem:

The perimeter of a gym is 340 feet. The longer side is 110 feet. What is the length of the shorter side?

First, it is helpful to label the figure. See the figure at the right. Then one way is to write the perimeter equation: $340 = 110 \times 2 + L \times 2$

$$2L = 120$$
$$L = 60 \text{ ft}$$

There are other ways to solve this problem.

In conclusion. Ask: What operation do you use to find the distance around something? [addition] What operation do you use to find half of something? [division] What operation do you use to find the difference between two things? [subtraction]

If there is additional time following this lesson, play the Crazy Squares game, found in *Math Card Games* book, P23.

© Activities for Learning, Inc. 2015

Lesson 111: Measuring in Grams

OBJECTIVES:
1. To learn how much a *gram* is in weight
2. To weigh small objects

MATERIALS:
1. Worksheet 91, Measuring in Grams
2. **Two 9-ounce clear plastic cups,*** and two pieces of string 8" (20 cm) long
3. Math balance
4. Centimeter cubes, tiles, geometric solids, tangrams, 3 multiplication cards
5. **Small objects to weigh ****

ACTIVITIES FOR TEACHING:

Warm-up. Give the child the worksheet. Tell him to do just the warm-up section. Solutions are:

2448 **(0)**	2448 **(0)**	2448 **(0)**
× 7 **(7)**	− 967 **(4)**	+ 967 **(4)**
56	1481 **(5)**	3415 **(4)**
280		
2800		
14000		
17136 **(0)**		

Preparation. To prepare the math balance to be used as a scale, punch two holes in the plastic cups near the top on opposite sides. See the figure below. Tie each end of the string at the holes as shown. On each math balance, place a cup on both 10-pegs. Be sure the balance is level.

Weighing with centimeter cubes. Give the child the math balance with cups, centimeter cubes, tiles, geometric solids, tangrams, and cards. Tell him we will now use the math balance as a scale and will not use the numbers.

Tell him to pick up one cube. Ask: Is it heavy? [no] What do you think will happen if you put a cube into each cup? Tell him to put a cube in each cup. [balances] See below.

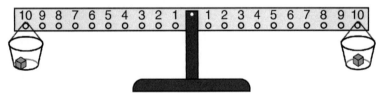

The math balance used as a scale.

Tell him that each cube weighs *1 gram*. Explain that we can use the cubes to weigh other things. Tell to measure the weight of a tile. [3 g] See below.

One tile weighs 3 g.

EXPLANATIONS:

* Paper cups would work, but clear plastic cups allow the child to see the contents of the cups more easily, but use only cups with plastic code 1. The code is found in the recycling triangle on the bottom. A cup with plastic code 6 is brittle and often breaks when making the hole, leaving sharp edges.

** Some suggestions for objects for weighing include: coins, erasers, toys, teaspoon of sugar, piece of folded paper, and paper clips.

ACTIVITIES FOR TEACHING:	EXPLANATIONS:

Next, tell him to weigh a math balance weight. [10 g]

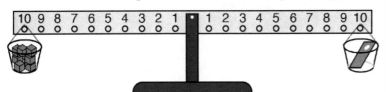

Verifying the 10-g weight weighs 10 g, the weight of 10 cubes.

Ask: What is written on the weight? [10 g] Explain that the abbreviation for gram or grams is a lower case *g* without a period.

Weighing the large tangram triangle. Tell him to find the weight of the large tangram triangle. Ask: What happened? [Six was not enough, but 7 was too much.] Tell him: We can say the weight is *between* 6 and 7 grams. Now weigh two large triangles. [between 13 and 14 g]

Weighing the cone. Tell the child to find and weigh the cone, thinking about how he does it. Have him discuss it. A good way is to start with a 10-gram weight and add more 10-gram weights until it is too much. Then remove one 10-gram weight and add centimeter cubes the same way.

Plastic cups will be used in the next lesson.

Worksheet 91. Tell him to complete the worksheet. The solutions are below.

1 centimeter cube	1 g
2 centimeter cubes	2 g
20 centimeter cubes	20 g
1 tile	3 g
math balance weight	10 g
3 tiles & 1 centimeter cube	10 g

3 multiplication cards	4 g
1 large tangram triangle	between 6 and 7 g

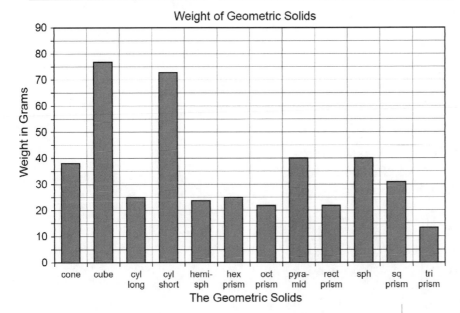

The recorded weights will vary.

In conclusion. Ask: Can you weigh a sphere? [yes] Can you weigh a circle? [no] Can you weigh a line? [no]

If there is additional time following this lesson, play the Equal Quotients game, found in *Math Card Games* book, D6.

© Activities for Learning, Inc. 2015

Lesson 112: Liters and Kilograms

OBJECTIVES:
1. To learn how much a *liter* is
2. To weigh a liter of water
3. To learn that a liter of water weighs 1 kg
4. To compare objects weighing a kilogram

MATERIALS:
1. Geometry panel squares
2. Centimeter cubes and ruler
3. **1-quart (4 cups or 1 liter) clear measuring cup**
4. **Water and empty container** *
5. A math balance & cups from the previous lesson

ACTIVITIES FOR TEACHING:

Warm-up. Ask: What operation do you use to find the distance around something? [addition] What operation do you use to find the area of something? [multiplication] What operation do you use to find half of something? [division] What operation do you use to find the difference between two things? [subtraction]

Building a cube. Demonstrate how to make a cube with the geometry panels. Take two square panels and align two edges with the white sides together. Hold them together and ask the child to place a rubber band around the edges. Explain that the notches at the vertices keeps the rubber bands in place. Repeat for the remaining edges. See the figure below.

Cube made with geometry panels.

Tell the child that the amount of space inside the cube is called a *liter*. Write it so he can see how it is spelled.

Liter problem. Give the child the square geometry panels, centimeter cubes and ruler. Tell the child to make a cube. Then find out how many cubic centimeters will fit in the cube. [1000] You might want to remove some rubber bands in order to see inside. Have the child explain his work.

One way is to find out how many cubes will fit in a row [10] and how many rows will fit. [10] Then find out how many of these 10 × 10 squares will fill up the cube. [10] The cube holds 1000 cubic centimeters.

EXPLANATIONS:

*An empty half-gallon (two liter) container from milk or juice is ideal.

Even though this activity seems to be similar to Lesson 50, that lesson was focused on quantity; whereas, this lesson focuses on volume, or capacity.

Having the child place the rubber band is modeling how two people can work together.

Outside the U.S., "liter" is usually spelled "litre."

RightStart™ Mathematics Level D Second Edition © Activities for Learning, Inc. 2015

ACTIVITIES FOR TEACHING:	EXPLANATIONS:

Another way is to use the ruler to measure how many centimeters will fit. [10 × 10 × 10 = 1000] Ask: How many cubic centimeters fit in a liter? [1000]

Weighing a liter of water. Tell the child to gather the measuring cup, water, second container, centimeter cubes, and math balance with cups. He will also need something to write on.

Point out the 1-liter mark on the measuring cup and fill it with water to that level. Explain that you want to weigh the liter of water. Ask: Will the whole liter of water fit into a math balance cup at one time? [no] What should we do? [weigh a bit at a time]

Remove one of the cups on the math balance and pour some of the water into it until it is about half full. Replace the cup on the scale and hold the beam of the scale while the child adds weights to make it balance. If all the 10 g weights do not fit into the cup, hang some on the 10-peg, either in front or back. See the figure below.

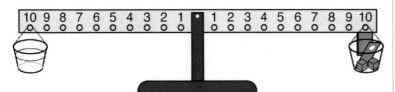

Weighing a liter a water, a small amount at a time.

Tell the child to record the weight. Pour this recorded water into the second container. Continue weighing the liter of water; pour more of the water into the cup on the scale. When all the water is weighed, tell the child to find the total weight by adding the recorded amounts. [1000 g]

The total weight of the water will probably vary from the expected weight of 1000 g. You might ask the child why he thinks this happened. [spilled some water, didn't empty the cup completely, didn't weigh exactly]

Tell him: One thousand grams has a special name, a *kilogram*; the prefix "kilo" means "thousand." Lift up the container that now has the 1 liter of water and ask: What does the water in this container weigh? [1 kg or 1000 g] Let the child feel the weight. Ask: Does the amount of water look like it would fill up the yellow cube you made earlier in the lesson? [yes]

A kilogram is equal to 2.2 pounds.

Tell the child to find things in the room that weigh about one kilogram. It may be useful for him to hold out his arms like the math balance with the liter of water in one hand and an object in the other to compare the weights.

In conclusion. Ask: How many grams are in a kilogram? [1000] What does a liter of water weigh? [1 kg] Does a cup of water weigh more or less than a kilogram? [less]

If there is additional time following this lesson, play the Find the Two Factors game, found in *Math Card Games* book, P29.

© Activities for Learning, Inc. 2015

226

LESSON 113: MEASUREMENT PROBLEMS

OBJECTIVES:
1. To solve problems involving weight and volume

MATERIALS:
1. Worksheet 92, Measurement Problems
2. *Math Card Games* book, D6

ACTIVITIES FOR TEACHING:	EXPLANATIONS:

Warm-up. Give the child the worksheet. Tell him to do just the warm-up section. Solutions are:

$$
\begin{array}{ll}
6585\ (\mathbf{6}) & \\
\underline{\times\ 7\ (\mathbf{7})} & \\
\mathbf{35} & \\
\mathbf{560} & \\
\mathbf{3500} & \\
\underline{\mathbf{42000}} & \\
\mathbf{46095}\ (\mathbf{6}) &
\end{array}
\qquad
\begin{array}{l}
6585\ (\mathbf{6}) \\
\underline{-\ 5856\ (\mathbf{6})} \\
\mathbf{729}\ (\mathbf{0})
\end{array}
\qquad
\begin{array}{l}
6585\ (\mathbf{6}) \\
\underline{+\ 5856\ (\mathbf{6})} \\
\mathbf{12441}\ (\mathbf{3})
\end{array}
$$

Worksheet 92. These problems are to be solved during the lesson. Give him several minutes of quiet time to solve each problem. Remind the child to check if his answers make sense. Then tell him to explain his solution.

Explaining to another person how one solves a problem helps clarify the thought process and may lead to deeper understanding.

Problem 1. Ask the child to read the first problem:

Each person needs about 4 liters of water a day. How much water will a family of five need for a week?

This problem can be solved by thinking about how much water one person needs for a week and then multiplying that by the number of family members:

$$W = 4 \times 7 = 28 \text{ and } 28 \times 5 = 140 \text{ liters}$$

Or, find out how much water the family needs for a day and multiplying that by 7:

$$W = 4 \times 5 = 20 \text{ and } 20 \times 7 = 140 \text{ liters}$$

Or, solve it with one equation:

$$W = 4 \times 5 \times 7 = 140 \text{ liters}$$

Problem 2. Ask the child to read and solve the next problem:

Four children are sharing 1 liter of water. How many grams of water does each child get?

To solve this, he needs to remember that:

$$1 \text{ liter weighs } 1000 \text{ g}$$

Then:
$$W = \tfrac{1}{4} \text{ of } 1000 = 250 \text{ g}$$

There are other various ways to solve these problems.

RightStart™ Mathematics Level D Second Edition

© Activities for Learning, Inc. 2015

ACTIVITIES FOR TEACHING:	EXPLANATIONS:

Problem 3. Ask the child to read and solve the third problem:

> The perimeter of a regular hexagonal flower garden is 54 meters. What is the distance along one side?

Since all the sides of a regular hexagon are congruent, the perimeter is six times that of one side.

$$P = 6 \times s$$

$$54 = 6 \times s$$

$$s = 9 \text{ meters}$$

Problem 4. Ask the child to read and solve the fourth problem:

> Keegan needs 400 g of flour. First he measured 237 g, then he added 149 g. How much more flour does he need?

The equation can be written as:

$$237 + 149 + f = 400$$

Which simplifies to:

$$386 + f = 400$$

$$f = 14 \text{ g}$$

Problem 5. Ask the child to solve the fifth problem:

> The average adult weighs about 70 kg. (The abbreviation for kilograms is kg.) A weight of about 23 kg is average for 8-year-old children. How much more will children weigh when they are adults?

The equations can be written as:

$$23 + W = 70$$

$$W = 47 \text{ kg}$$

Equal Quotients game. Play Equal Quotients found in the *Math Card Games* book, D6.

In conclusion. Ask: What operation do you use to find the distance around something? [addition] What operation do you use to find half of something? [division] What operation do you use to find the difference between two things? [subtraction]

If there is additional time following this lesson, have the child choose a game to play.

© Activities for Learning, Inc. 2015

Lesson 114: Naming Angles

OBJECTIVES:
1. To review or learn the terms *parallel*, *perpendicular*, and *right angle*
2. To introduce the concept of rotation
3. To learn the meaning of 90°, 180°, 270°, and 360°

MATERIALS:
1. **Two rulers or pencils for showing angles**
2. **Cards with the words, North, East, South, and West, attached to the appropriate walls in the room**
3. Worksheet 93, Naming Angles

ACTIVITIES FOR TEACHING:

Warm-up. Draw the following sets of lines:

Say: *Parallel* lines do not meet even when they are extended; they always have the same distance between them. Ask: Which sets of lines are parallel? [first and fourth]

Say: Two lines that meet like the corner in a square are *perpendicular* lines. Ask: Which lines are perpendicular? [second and third] Ask: What about the fifth set of lines? [neither parallel nor perpendicular]

Right angles. Tell the child: The corner angle formed by perpendicular lines has another name, *right angle*. It is called right angle because when one line is horizontal, the other line seems to stand upright. It does not mean the opposite of left nor the opposite of wrong.

Making turns. Tell the child: Stand and face straight ahead. Turn all the way around. That was one revolution. Now turn a half revolution. Ask: What happened? [facing the back] Say: Turn half way again. Ask: What happened? [facing the front]

Tell him: Turn to the right a quarter of a revolution. Turn another quarter, and another quarter, and one more quarter. Ask: How many quarters did you need to make a whole turn? [4] How many quarters made a half turn? [2]

Measuring angles. Hold two rulers or pencils horizontally. Slowly move one vertically as shown below. Ask him to tell you when you reach a right angle.

Rotating a ruler through various degrees to 90°.

EXPLANATIONS:

ACTIVITIES FOR TEACHING:	EXPLANATIONS:

Tell him: We measure how far something turns in degrees. A quarter turn is 90°. These degrees are different from degrees for measuring temperature.

Move one ruler through 180° as shown below and ask him how many degrees that is. [twice 90, or 180] Move it to three quarters and ask how many degrees. [270] Continue with a full circle and ask how many degrees. [360] Write the numbers and ask: What pattern are the numbers 90, 180, 270, and 360? [multiples of 90]

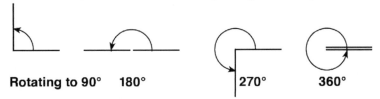

Rotating to 90°   180°   270°   360°

In mathematics, angles are measured starting at the 3 o'clock position and proceed counterclockwise.

In geography, angles start at the north, or top, and proceed clockwise.

Tell the child to repeat the rotation with his arms.

Relating directions and degrees. Tell the child to point to the posted North sign. Then tell him to face north and to do the following:

Turn 90° right and tell the direction? [east]
Turn 180° left and tell the direction? [west]
Turn 90° left and tell the direction? [south]
Turn 180° left and tell the direction? [north]

Worksheet 93. Give the child the worksheet and tell him to complete it. The solutions are as follows:

= **parallel**, + **perpendicular**, right angle **90°**

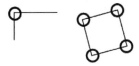

Capital letters with right angles: **E, F, H, L, T**

180°	180°
_90°_ | _90°_	_90°_ | _90°_

Start	Turn	End
North	left 90°	**West**
East	right 90°	**South**
West	right 90°	**North**
North	left 180°	**South**
South	right 270°	**East**
East	right 360°	**East**

In conclusion. Ask: Which capital letters of the alphabet have right angles? [E, F, H, L, T] Which letter has only one right angle? [L] Which letter has two right angles? [T] How many right angles does "E" have? [4] How many does "H" have? [4]

Answers may vary depending on how the child has learned their letters.

If there is additional time following this lesson, have the child choose a game to play.

Lesson 115: Measuring Sides in Triangles

OBJECTIVES:
1. To measure centimeters in tenths
2. To find perimeters of triangles

MATERIALS:
1. 4-in-1 ruler
2. A fraction chart
3. Worksheet 94, Measuring Sides in Triangles

ACTIVITIES FOR TEACHING:

EXPLANATIONS:

Warm-up. Tell the child to stand and face straight ahead. Tell him to turn left 180°. Ask: What happened? [facing the back] Say: Turn right 90°. Turn right 90° again. Now turn right 180°. Ask: What happened? [facing the back again] Say: Turn left 270°. Turn right 90°. Ask: What happened? [facing the front]

Ask: What is one fourth plus three fourths? [1] What is two thirds plus one third? [1] What is three fifths plus one fifth? [four fifths] What is one tenth plus two tenths? [three tenths]

Centimeters on a ruler. Give the child the ruler. Tell the child to look at the centimeter side of the ruler. See below.

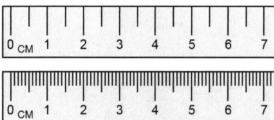

The two centimeter scales on the 4-in-1 ruler.

Ask: What are the centimeters divided into on the ruler? [halves and tenths]

Show him the fraction chart shown on the right and ask: Which rows on the fraction chart are like the space between any two numbers on the ruler? [halves and tenths]

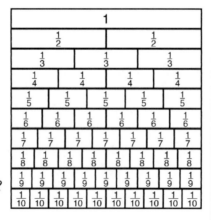

Worksheet 94. Give the child the worksheet. Tell the child to complete the first three questions. Then tell him to share his solution.

RightStart™ Mathematics Level D Second Edition © Activities for Learning, Inc. 2015

ACTIVITIES FOR TEACHING:	EXPLANATIONS:

Question 1. When measuring the line, the ruler divided into halves will give the answer of $2\frac{1}{2}$ cm. The ruler divided into tenths will give the answer of $2\frac{5}{10}$ cm.

Question 2. The second line measures $3\frac{7}{10}$ cm.

Question 3. The lines are shown below (to scale).

Tenths of a centimeter will be written in fraction form for now, rather than the usual decimal notation.

———————————|————————————————

Tell the child to write the equation:

$$L = 6\frac{6}{10} + 7\frac{7}{10} = 13\frac{13}{10}$$

Ask: Why does the ruler say the two lines are $14\frac{3}{10}$ cm?
[Because $\frac{13}{10} = 1\frac{3}{10}$, $13\frac{13}{10} = 14\frac{3}{10}$]

Another look at the fraction chart may benefit some children.

At this point, we are adding mixed numbers intuitively. The algorithms will be taught next year.

Worksheet 94. Tell the child to complete the worksheet. The solutions are below.

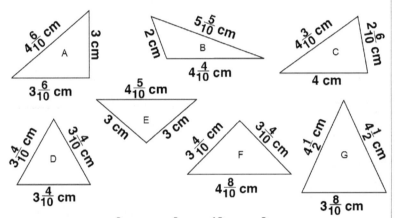

Triangle A: $P = 4\frac{6}{10} + 3 + 3\frac{6}{10} = 10\frac{12}{10} = 11\frac{2}{10}$ cm

Triangle B: $P = 5\frac{5}{10} + 4\frac{4}{10} + 2 = 11\frac{9}{10}$ cm

Triangle C: $P = 4\frac{3}{10} + 2\frac{6}{10} + 4 = 10\frac{9}{10}$ cm

Triangle D: $P = 3\frac{4}{10} + 3\frac{4}{10} + 3\frac{4}{10} = 9\frac{12}{10} = 10\frac{2}{10}$ cm

Triangle E: $P = 4\frac{5}{10} + 3 + 3 = 10\frac{5}{10}$ cm

Triangle F: $P = 3\frac{4}{10} + 3\frac{4}{10} + 4\frac{8}{10} = 10\frac{16}{10} = 11\frac{6}{10}$ cm

Triangle G: $P = 4\frac{1}{2} + 4\frac{1}{2} + 3\frac{8}{10} = 12\frac{8}{10}$ cm

Measurements may vary by a tenth of a centimeter.

In conclusion. Ask: Does adding with tenths remind you of other kinds of adding? [possibly adding ones and tens]

This worksheet will be needed for reference in the next lesson.

If there is additional time following this lesson, play the Corners™ with Tenths game, found in *Math Card Games* book, F22.2.

© Activities for Learning, Inc. 2015

Lesson 116: Measuring Angles in Triangles

OBJECTIVES:
1. To review the term *angle*
2. To use a goniometer to measure angles
3. To introduce *acute* and *obtuse* angles

MATERIALS:
1. Goniometer
2. 30-60 triangles and 45 triangles
3. Worksheet 95, Measuring Angles in Triangles
4. Worksheet 94, Measuring Sides in Triangles from the previous lesson

ACTIVITIES FOR TEACHING:

Warm-up. Ask: What is five tenths plus four tenths? [nine tenths] What is seven tenths plus six tenths? [thirteen tenths or one and three tenths]

Tell the child to show the rotation of the angles with his arms. See below.

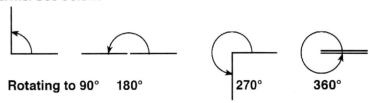

Rotating to 90°   180°   270°   360°

The goniometer. Give the child the goniometer and triangles. Tell him that a goniometer (GON-ee-OM-i-ter) measures the *angles*. An angle is the space between two lines at their vertex.

Lay the goniometer flat on a surface and demonstrate how to open it by holding the bottom part with your right hand and gently opening the top part with your left hand. See the left figure below.

The goniometer.

Tell him to open his goniometer so the inside edges are perpendicular. See the right figure above. Tell him to look at the number inside the little magnifying bubble and ask: What number do you see? [90]

Measuring angles. Tell him to measure the angles in the triangles with his goniometer. See the figures below.

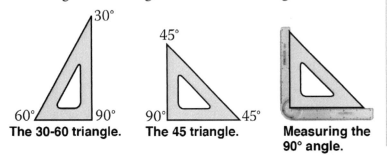

The 30-60 triangle.   **The 45 triangle.**   **Measuring the 90° angle.**

EXPLANATIONS:

If the two parts of the goniometer come apart, they can be snapped back together. Align the part with the bump on top of the other part and press down.

RightStart™ Mathematics Level D Second Edition   © Activities for Learning, Inc. 2015

ACTIVITIES FOR TEACHING:

Acute and obtuse angles. Tell him: Move your goniometer from 0° to 90°. Angles between 0° to 90° are called *acute* angles. Now move your goniometer from 90° to 180°. Angles between 90° to 180° are called *obtuse* angles. Ask: What do you call angles that are 90°? [right angles]

Write the words, "acute," "right," and "obtuse" in a column as shown on the left. Ask the child to help complete the chart as shown on the right.

Acute	Acute	< 90°	∠
Right	Right	= 90°	∟
Obtuse	Obtuse	> 90° & <180°	∠

Starting the chart.   **The completed chart.**

Worksheet 95. Give the child the worksheet and tell him to complete it. He will need Worksheet 94 from the previous lesson for the last three questions. The solutions are below.

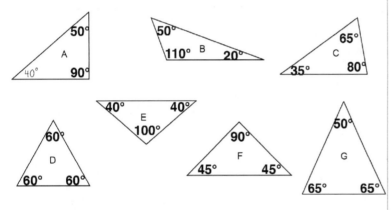

1. Name the acute triangles. **C, D, G**
2. Name the right triangles. **A, F**
3. Name the obtuse triangles. **B, E**
4. What pattern do you see when two angles in a triangle are equal? **The opposite sides are congruent.**
5. What is the relationship in a triangle between the largest angle and the largest side? **The largest side is opposite the largest angle.**
6. What is the sum of the angles in a triangle? **180°**

In conclusion. Ask: What is an acute angle? [an angle less than 90°] What is a right angle? [an angle equal to 90°] What is an obtuse angle? [an angle greater than 90°] Which triangle relationship did you think was the most surprising?

EXPLANATIONS:

This chart is also on the worksheet for reference.

Some children may prefer to remove the worksheet from the workbook.

The triangles in this lesson are the same as those in the previous lesson.

The answers to Questions 4, 5, and 6 are truly amazing. Encourage the child to make these discoveries.

The angles can be added mentally.

If there is additional time following this lesson, play the Make Sixteen Cents game, found in *Math Card Games* book, M6.

© Activities for Learning, Inc. 2015

234

LESSON 117: DOLLARS AND CENTS

OBJECTIVES:

1. To practice finding coins to make a certain amount
2. To introduce the *decimal point*
3. To practice adding money mentally using the dollar and cent notation

MATERIALS:

1. Penny, nickel, dime, and quarter
2. *Math Card Games* book, M7 and A9
3. Math journal

ACTIVITIES FOR TEACHING:	EXPLANATIONS:
Warm-up. Show the child the penny, nickel, dime, and quarter. Tell him to find the largest coin, the quarter. Ask: How much is a quarter of a dollar worth? [25¢] How many quarters equal a dollar? [4] A quarter is what fraction of a dollar? [one fourth]	

Ask: Which coin is smallest? [dime] How much is a dime worth? [10¢] How many dimes does it take to make a dollar? [10] A dime is what fraction of a dollar? [one tenth]

Ask: What coin is worth half of a dime? [nickel] How much it is worth? [5¢] Which coin is worth the least? [penny] How much is a penny worth? [1¢] How many pennies does it take to equal a dollar? [100] How can you easily tell a penny from a dime? [color]

Make Twenty-Seven Cents game. Play the Make Twenty-Seven Cents game, found in *Math Card Games* book, M7.

Writing dollars and cents. Say: When we write an amount with both dollars and cents, we use a *decimal point* between the dollars and the cents. Write:

$2.35

Say: We read this as two dollars and thirty-five cents. The decimal point looks like a period. When we come to the decimal point, we say "and."

Emphasize: We cannot use both a dollar sign and a cent sign for the same amount.

Write and have the child read the amounts for $5.75, $7.39, and $32.57.

Now ask him to write the cost of a plant that sells for three dollars and 98 cents in his math journal. [$3.98] Continue with:

18 dollars and 64 cents [$18.64]

13 dollars and 98 cents [$13.98]

65 dollars and 50 cents [$65.50]

RightStart™ Mathematics Level D Second Edition

© Activities for Learning, Inc. 2015

ACTIVITIES FOR TEACHING:	EXPLANATIONS:

Say: Write the time for 2 minutes after 3 o'clock. [3:02]
Ask: Did you remember to write the zero before the 2?

Write: $3.02

Say: When we write 3 dollars and 2 cents, we need to write a zero before the 2, just like the minutes.

Tell him to write the price of a notebook costing 2 dollars and 5 cents. [$2.05]

Ask him to write the following:

   31 dollars and 1 cent [$31.01]

   15 dollars and 9 cents [$15.09]

   17 dollars and 14 cents [$17.14]

Reading dollar amounts. Write:

                   $24.98

Ask him to read it aloud. [24 dollars and 98 cents] Write and ask him to read the following:

   $36.51 [36 dollars and 51 cents]

   $25.03 [25 dollars and 3 cents]

   $301.07 [301 dollars and 7 cents]

   $0.40 [40 cents]

Say: If there is no dollar amount, we write a zero before the decimal point.

Corners™ with Dimes game. Play the Corners™ with Dimes game, a variation of the Corners™ game found in the *Math Card Games* book, A9.

Say: In this game, the numbers on the Corners™ cards represent dimes. If a 4 is played to a 1, the score is 5 dimes, or 50¢. So we write:

                 $0.50

$0.50
1.50
3.00
5.00
6.50

It is not necessary to write the dollar sign after the first line.

Ask: If you play a 3 on a 7 on your next turn, how many points do you get? [10 dimes, which is 1 dollar] What is your total score now? [$1.50] So we write:

                 $1.50

Ask: If you play a 6 on a 9 on your next turn, how many points do you get? [1 dollar and fifty cents] What is your total score now? [$3.00] Write:

                 $3.00

Tell the child to write his scores in his math journal. The accumulative scoring will look like the sample above.

In conclusion. Ask: What is a dollar and fifty cents plus fifty cents? [2 dollars] What is a dollar fifty plus 4 dollars? [5 dollars and fifty cents]

© Activities for Learning, Inc. 2015

236

LESSON 118: MORE DOLLARS AND CENTS

OBJECTIVES:

1. To practice finding coins to make a certain amount
2. To understand dollar and cent notation
3. To practice adding money mentally using the dollar and cent notation

MATERIALS:

1. *Math Card Games* book, M10 and A9
2. Math journal

ACTIVITIES FOR TEACHING:	EXPLANATIONS:
Warm-up. Ask: What is two dollars and twenty five cents plus twenty five cents? [2 dollars and fifty cents] What is a dollar and seventy five cents plus 3 dollars? [4 dollars and seventy five cents] What is 6 dollars and twenty five cents plus 2 dollars and seventy five cents? [9 dollars]	
Make the Amount game. Play the Make the Amount game, found in *Math Card Games* book, M10.	If the multiplication cards are in their envelopes, have the child use the cards from two envelopes, from 6–9.
Tenths. Write:	
$1000.00	
Ask: What is one-tenth of one thousand dollars? [$100.00] Tell the child to write it:	
$100.00	
Ask: What is one-tenth of one hundred dollars? [$10.00] Tell the child to write it:	Some children will find it helpful to visualize the abacus when finding one-tenth of 100.
$10.00	
Ask: What is one-tenth of ten dollars? [$1.00] Tell the child to write it:	
$1.00	
Ask: What is one-tenth of one dollar? [a dime, $0.10] Tell the child to write it:	
$0.10	
Ask: What is one-tenth of one dime? [a penny, $0.01] Tell the child to write it:	
$0.01	
What pattern do you see? [The 1s move to the right.]	
Say: The decimal point goes after the ones place. Remind him, if the amount is less than 1 dollar, we write a zero before the decimal point.	

RightStart™ Mathematics Level D Second Edition

© Activities for Learning, Inc. 2015

ACTIVITIES FOR TEACHING:	EXPLANATIONS:

Corners™ with Pennies game. Play the Corners™ with Pennies game, a variation of the Corners™ game found in the *Math Card Games* book, A9.

Say: In this game, the numbers on the Corners™ cards will represent pennies. Ask: If a 2 is played to an 8, the score is 10 pennies, which is 10¢. So we write:

$0.10

Ask: If you play a 2 on a 3 on your next turn, how many points do you get? [5 cents] What is your total score now? [$0.15] So we write:

$0.15

Ask: If you play a 7 on an 8 on your next turn, how many points do you get? [15 cents] What is your total score now? [$0.30] Write:

$0.30

The accumulative scoring will look like the sample on the right.

Ask: Do you think your scores will get as high as they did in Corners™ with Dimes game? [no] Tell the child to play the game and write his scores in his math journal. Remind him to write a zero if the amount is less than a dollar.

$0.10
0.15
0.30
0.45
0.65

In conclusion. Tell him to name the dollars and cents for the following coins: 9 dimes and 5 pennies, [95 cents] 200 pennies, [two dollars] 5 quarters, [$1.25] 14 dimes, [$1.40] and 11 nickels. [55 cents]

© Activities for Learning, Inc. 2015

238

LESSON 119: MONEY PROBLEMS

OBJECTIVES:

1. To solve story problems involving dollars and cents

MATERIALS:

1. Worksheet 96, Money Problems

ACTIVITIES FOR TEACHING:	EXPLANATIONS:

ACTIVITIES FOR TEACHING:

Warm-up. Give the child the worksheet. Tell him to do just the warm-up section. Solutions are:

3238 (7)	3238 (7)	3238 (7)
× 6 **(6)**	− 947 **(2)**	+ 947 **(2)**
48	**2291 (5)**	**4185 (0)**
180		
1200		
18000		
19428 (6)		

Ask: What is one half of $6.60? [$3.30] What is one half of $24.00? [$12.00] What is one fourth of $4.00? [$1.00]

Worksheet 92. Give the child several minutes of quiet time to read and solve each problem. Then tell him to explain his solutions.

Problem 1. Tell the child to read and solve the first problem.

> 1. Sophia shoveled sidewalks at the rate of $4.50 an hour. She worked 9 hours. How much money did Sophia make?

Some children might think of solving $4.50 × 9 by breaking it into dollars and cents; that is, $4 × 9 + 50¢ × 9 = $36 + $4.50 = $40.50.

Another way is to multiply $4.50 by 10 and subtract $4.50, 4.50 × 10 − 4.50 = $45 − $4.50 = $40.50.

Others might use multiplication; let them discovery where to put the decimal point by using common sense.

Problem 2. Tell the child to read and solve the second problem.

> 2. Mr. McPherson wants to buy tile for a floor that is 10 ft long and 8 ft wide. Each tile is 1 sq ft and costs $9.50. What will all the tile cost?

The area of the floor is 10 × 8 = 80 sq ft. The cost is $9.50 × 80 = $760. This can be calculated by finding 9 × 80 and 50¢ × 80 = 720 + 40 = $760.

RightStart™ Mathematics Level D Second Edition

© Activities for Learning, Inc. 2015

ACTIVITIES FOR TEACHING:	EXPLANATIONS:

Problem 3. Tell the child to solve the third problem.

  3. Phil is buying pizza. One eighth of the pizza is $2.50. What does the whole pizza cost?

The child needs to know that a whole pizza contains eight eighths, then $2.50 × 8 = $20.00.

Problem 4. Tell the child to solve the fourth problem.

  4. Daphne bought 4 cans of cat food for $1.20 each and 3 cans of dog food for $1.20 each? What was the total cost?

He could find the answer by finding the cost of the cat food and the dog food separately: $1.20 × 4 + $1.20 × 3 = $8.40. Or, because the cost per can is the same, he could multiply $1.20 × 7 to get $8.40.

Problem 5. Tell the child to solve the fifth problem.

  5. Phoebe needs fifteen dollars to buy a gift. She earned $4.48 on Monday, $4.86 on Tuesday, and $3.76 on Wednesday. How much more money does Phoebe need?

First find out how much Phoebe earned: 4.48 + 4.86 + 3.76 = $13.10. Then $15.00 − $13.10 = $1.90, or better yet, $13.10 + m = $15.00, m = $1.90.

For the last way, m is 90¢ to get to $14 and $1 to get to $15 giving a total of $1.90.

In conclusion. Ask: What is a dollar and fifty cents multiplied by 2? [3 dollars] What is fifty cents multiplied by 5? [2 dollars and 50 cents] What is half of 5 dollars? [2 dollars and fifty cents]

If there is additional time following this lesson, play the Change from Fifty Cents game, found in *Math Card Games* book, M12.

© Activities for Learning, Inc. 2015

Lesson 120: Review and Games 8

OBJECTIVES:
1. To review recent topics
2. To develop skills through playing math card games

MATERIALS:
1. Worksheet 97-A or 97-B, Review 8
2. *Math Card Games* book, D6

ACTIVITIES FOR TEACHING:

Worksheet 97-A. Give the child the worksheet. Tell him to listen to the problems and write the answers. Read each problem twice.

80¢ × 2   ½ of $4.40   63 ÷ 9

Tell him to complete the worksheet. Solutions are below.

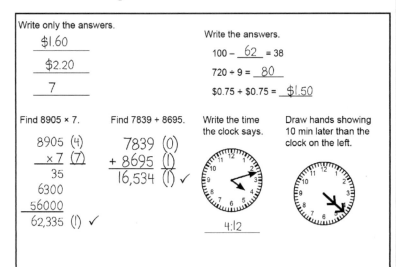

EXPLANATIONS:

There are several other ways the angles can be drawn.

ACTIVITIES FOR TEACHING:

Equal Quotients game. Play the Equal Quotients game found in *Math Card Games* book, D6.

Worksheet 97-B. Give the child the worksheet. Tell him to listen to the problems and write the answers. Read each problem twice.

$50¢ \times 5$ $\frac{1}{2}$ of $2.20 $64 \div 8$

Tell him to complete the worksheet. Solutions are below.

Write only the answers.

$2.50

$1.10

8

Write the answers.

$100 - \underline{33} = 67$

$720 \div 8 = \underline{90}$

$0.85 + 0.65 = \underline{\$1.50}$

Find 9816 × 8.

$$\begin{array}{r} 9816 \,(6) \\ \times\ 8 \,(8) \\ \hline 48 \\ 80 \\ 6400 \\ 72000 \\ \hline 78,528 \,(3)\checkmark \end{array}$$

Find 4813 + 7549.

$$\begin{array}{r} 4813 \,(7) \\ +\ 7549 \,(7) \\ \hline 12,362 \,(5)\checkmark \end{array}$$

Write the time the clock says.

9:52

Draw hands showing 10 min later than the clock on the left.

Draw the following lines freehand.

Draw a parallel to the line below.	Draw a right angle.	Draw a 45° angle.	Draw an angle greater than 90°.

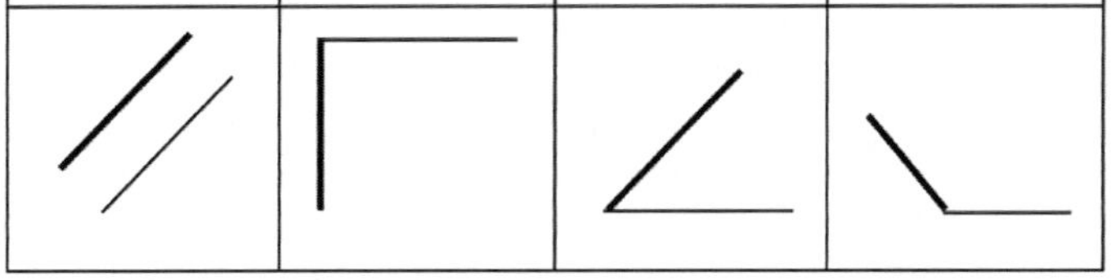

Solve the problems.

Lucy has little cups that hold 100 g each. She has 600 g of chocolate milk. How many children can have a little cup of milk?

$c \times 100 = 600$
$c = 6$ children

Gil bought three regular cups of lemonade for 25¢ each and one large cup for 35¢. What is the total cost?

$C = 3 \times 25¢ + 35¢$
$C = \$1.10$

EXPLANATIONS:

There are several other ways the angles can be drawn.

© Activities for Learning, Inc. 2015

Review Lesson 121: Drawing Horizontal Lines

OBJECTIVES:
1. To learn to use the T-square
2. To learn to draw horizontal lines with a T-square
3. To review horizontal and diagonal
4. To review polygons

MATERIALS:
1. Worksheet 98, Drawing Horizontal Lines
2. T-square
3. **Tape** *
4. Drawing board with worksheet taped on **
5. **Sharp pencil (preferably mechanical) and eraser**

ACTIVITIES FOR TEACHING:

Warm-up. Ask: What is one half of $8.80? [$4.40] What is one half of $13.00? [$6.50] What is one half of $4.82? [$2.41]

Ask: What is a two dollars and fifty cents multiplied by 2? [5 dollars] What is twenty five cents multiplied by 5? [one dollars and 25 cents] What is eighty cents multiplied by 10? [8 dollars]

Preparation. Tape the worksheet to the drawing board before giving them to the child. To do this, place the T-square along a side of the board. Then position a horizontal line on the paper so it is aligns with the top edge of the T-square, then tape the top two corners. See the figure below.

T-square.

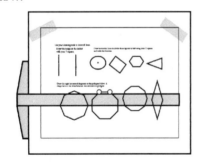

Aligning and taping the worksheet to the drawing board.

Introducing the drawing tools. Show the child a dry erase board with a worksheet attached and tell him the dry erase board is now a drawing board. Next show him the T-square and tell him it is called a T-square. Ask: Why do you think it is called a T-square? [looks like the letter T] Is this the same reason a certain shirt is called a T-shirt? [yes]

Worksheet 98 and tools. Give the child the T-square and the drawing board with the attached worksheet. For a right-handed user, the T-square is placed along the left side of the board. For a left-handed user, the T-square is placed along the right side. See the figures on the next page.

EXPLANATIONS:

This review lesson is designed for children with no experience using the drawing tools.

* The best tape is "removable" tape, which can be reused several times and doesn't tear the corners of the paper.

** The dry erase board is also the drawing board. See **preparation instructions** for preparing the worksheet in advance.

Teaching geometry with a drawing board, T-square, and triangles helps the child learn the informal, practical side of geometry. It also helps develop coordination, which improves with practice.

Tape is not used at the bottom corners because it interferes with moving the T-square.

The little white dots indicate where to align the T-square.

RightStart™ Mathematics Level D Second Edition © Activities for Learning, Inc. 2015

ACTIVITIES FOR TEACHING:

EXPLANATIONS:

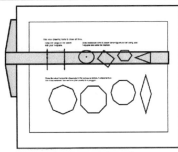 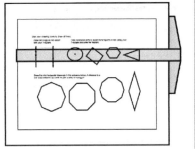

T-square position for right-handed user.

T-square position for left-handed user.

Drawing horizontal lines. Say: Use the T-square to draw horizontal lines. It slides up and down the side of the board. Hold it tight against the board with one hand while you draw the line with your writing hand along the top of the T-square.

Tell the child to check every time to be sure the T-square is hugging the board before drawing a line.

For the first figure on the worksheet, tell the child: Draw horizontal lines to make the rungs on a ladder. The little white dots tell you where to align your T-square. All lines must be drawn with the T-square.

Polygons and diagonals. After he has drawn the rungs on the ladder, say: There are eight figures on your worksheet; seven of them are *polygons*. A polygon is a flat closed figure made with straight lines. Ask: Which figure is not a polygon? [the first figure, an ellipse] Do you notice anything special about the first two polygons in the second row? [same figure, but oriented differently]

Tell him to read and follow the instructions on the worksheet. Stress that he must use his T-square to draw all the lines, which will be horizontal.

Solutions are shown below.

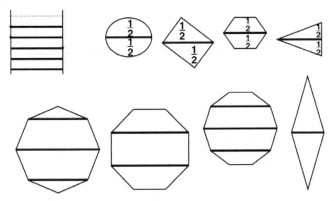

In conclusion. Ask: What is a polygon? [a closed figure with straight lines] What direction is a horizontal line? [a straight line from side to side] What is a diagonal line? [a line between any two vertices in a polygon]

During this geometry section, be certain to continue playing games. Games reinforce the concepts taught throughout the year. Choose games that address the topics needing additional review.

If there is additional time following this lesson, play the Change from a Dollar game, found in *Math Card Games* book, M14.

© Activities for Learning, Inc. 2015

244

REVIEW LESSON 122: DRAWING LINES WITH A 30-60 TRIANGLE

OBJECTIVES:
1. To learn to use the 30-60 triangle with the T-square
2. To review vertical
3. To draw the diagonals in a hexagon

MATERIALS:
1. Worksheet 99, Drawing Lines with a 30-60 Triangle
2. Drawing board with worksheet taped on
3. T-square and 30-60 triangle

ACTIVITIES FOR TEACHING:

Warm-up. Ask: What is twenty five cents multiplied by 5? [one dollars and 25 cents] What is eighty cents multiplied by 10? [8 dollars]

Ask: What is a polygon? [a closed figure with straight lines] What direction is a horizontal line? [a straight line from side to side] What is a diagonal line? [a line between any two vertices in a polygon]

Drawing vertical lines. Give the child the drawing board with worksheet attached, T-square, and 30-60 triangle. Tell the child that today he will draw vertical lines using both his T-square and 30-60 triangle. To draw vertical lines, the triangle needs to touch the T-square while the T-square hugs the board. The T-square needs to be at least a centimeter or quarter inch below the lower starting point to allow for visibility of the work area and accuracy.

To hold the tools in place, demonstrate the following procedure for right-handers:

1. The left hand moves the T-square below the starting point and holds it in place. See the left figure below.

2. The right hand moves the triangle toward the correct place on the T-square. See right figure below.

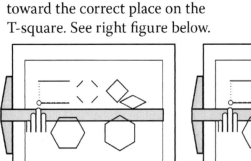
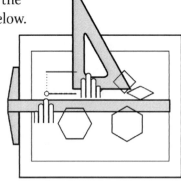

Holding the T-square.   **Moving the triangle.**

3. Both hands hold the tools momentarily. See the left figure on the next page.

4. The left hand takes over holding both tools, see the right figure on the next page.

EXPLANATIONS:

This review lesson is designed for children who have had no previous experience using the drawing tools.

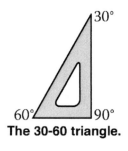
The 30-60 triangle.

The T-square must be below the starting point in order to draw a precise line.

The little white dot indicates where to align the triangle.

If appropriate, also demonstrate this procedure for the child who is left-handed.

RightStart™ Mathematics Level D Second Edition © Activities for Learning, Inc. 2015

ACTIVITIES FOR TEACHING:	EXPLANATIONS:

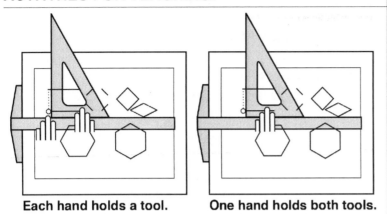

Each hand holds a tool.   One hand holds both tools.

Worksheet 99. For the first problem on the worksheet, tell the child to draw vertical lines to make the slats for the fence. Lines are generally drawn from bottom to top. Tell him to do the horizontal and vertical lines on the worksheet. Remind him that all lines must be made with his T-square and the 90° of his 30-60 triangle. Solutions are shown on the bottom right.

Drawing the 60° lines. Now point to the 60° on the triangle and tell him to look at the bottom half of his worksheet. Ask: Do you see any diagonals that you could draw with this angle? [yes] Show him how to draw it. See the left figure below.

Ask: Do you see the another diagonal at that angle to draw in the first hexagon? [yes] Show him how to flip the triangle over and draw it. See the second figure below.

Some children find it helpful to place their triangle on the small figure to determine its correct orientation.

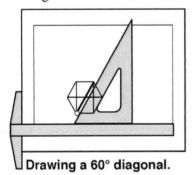
Drawing a 60° diagonal.

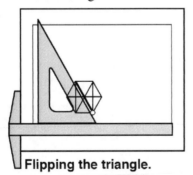
Flipping the triangle.

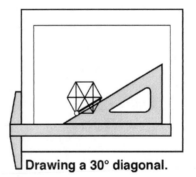
Drawing a 30° diagonal.

Drawing the 30° lines. Point to the 30° on the triangle. Ask: Do you see any diagonals that you could draw with this edge? [yes] Show him how to draw it. See the right figure above.

Worksheet 99. Tell him to complete the worksheet. Remind him that he will need to flip his triangle to draw some of the lines. Solutions are shown at the right.

In conclusion. Ask: How many sides does a hexagon have? [six] What direction is a vertical line? [a straight line from top to bottom] What is a diagonal line? [a line between any two vertices in a polygon]

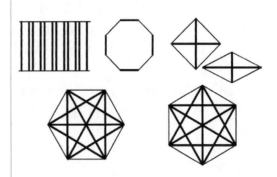

© Activities for Learning, Inc. 2015

Lesson 123: Drawing Shapes in a Hexagon

OBJECTIVES:
1. To plan ahead to draw shapes within a hexagon
2. To review the names of some shapes

MATERIALS:
1. Worksheet 100, Drawing Shapes in a Hexagon
2. Drawing board with worksheet taped on
3. T-square and 30-60 triangle

ACTIVITIES FOR TEACHING:

Warm-up. Ask: What direction is a horizontal line? [a straight line from side to side] What direction is a vertical line? [a straight line from top to bottom] What is a diagonal line? [a line between any two vertices in a polygon]

Ask: What is a polygon? [a closed figure with straight lines] How many sides does a hexagon have? [six] Is a hexagon a polygon? [yes] How many sides does a quadrilateral have? [four] Is a quadrilateral a polygon? [yes] How many sides does a triangle have? [three] Is a triangle a polygon? [yes]

Worksheet 100. Give the child the drawing board with worksheet attached, T-square, and 30-60 triangle. Tell the child: Today you will draw shapes using your drawing tools. Before starting you will plan how to do each one. The shapes are shown below.

Shape 1. Tell him to think about how he would draw the first shape then discuss it. It can be done by drawing the horizontal line with a T-square. The left line is drawn with the 60° angle of the 30-60 triangle. The triangle is flipped over to draw the last line.

Shape 2. Repeat the instructions by telling him to think about how you would draw the second shape. Then have him share his idea. The large equilateral triangle is drawn in the same way as the first shape. The smaller triangles

EXPLANATIONS:

Encourage the child to ask questions when he does not understand.

See page iii, number 15 of "Some General Thoughts on Teaching Mathematics," for additional information.

ACTIVITIES FOR TEACHING:

are drawn by aligning at a vertex, but only drawing within the equilateral triangle. See the figure at the right.

Ask: Do you see the seven triangles? [three obtuse triangles, three small triangles, and one large triangle] What shape is in the middle of the figure? [hexagon]

Shape 3. For the third shape, the child will need the 30° angle to draw the missing lines of the hexagon. He will need the 60° angle to draw the longer sides of the rectangle.

Shape 4. This shape is a little tricky. There is no way to know how long to draw the lines because the lines do not start or stop at the starting points. One way is to first draw the vertical line a little longer than you think. See the first figure below.

Next draw the horizontal lines as shown in the second figure. Lastly, erase the extra parts of the vertical line.

Shape 5. If the child suggests drawing the horizontal lines first, ask if there is another way. [draw the 60° lines first] See the figure on the right.

Ask: Why is the figure called a *rhombus*? [all four sides are equal]

Shape 6. The child might see this construction as similar to that of the equilateral triangle with one vertex removed. See the figure on the right.

Ask: Why is the figure called a *trapezoid*? [It has four sides and only one set of parallel lines.]

Worksheet 100. Tell him to look at all the little hexagons on his worksheet and ask: How many triangles do you see? [14: shape 1 has 4, shape 2 has 7, shape 3 has 2, shapes 4 and 5 have none, and shape 6 has 1] Tell him that a quadrilateral is polygon with four sides. Ask: How many quadrilaterals do you see? [4]

Tell him to do the worksheet with his drawing tools.

In conclusion. Ask: Does it help to plan how to solve a problem before actually solving it? [yes] What do you do if you didn't draw a line long enough? [use the tools to draw it longer] What do you do when a line is too long? [erase]

EXPLANATIONS:

An obtuse angle is an angle greater than 90°. An obtuse triangle has an obtuse angle.

Erasing is a natural part of drawing. A child who is a perfectionist may initially have a problem with this.

Remind the child that the T-square must be below the starting point in order to draw a precise line with the triangle.

If there is additional time following this lesson, play the Short Chain Solitaire game, found in *Math Card Games* book, A47.

© Activities for Learning, Inc. 2015

Lesson 124: Drawing 30° and 60° Lines in a Circle

OBJECTIVES:
1. To learn the term *diameter*
2. To learn to create and use *tick marks*
3. To make figures using the T-square and 30-60 triangle

MATERIALS:
1. Worksheet 101, Drawing 30° and 60° Lines in a Circle
2. Drawing board with worksheet taped on
3. T-square and 30-60 triangle
4. **Colored pencils or markers**

ACTIVITIES FOR TEACHING:	EXPLANATIONS:
Warm-up. Ask: What direction is a horizontal line? [a straight line from side to side] What direction is a vertical line? [a straight line from top to bottom] What is a diagonal line? [a line between any two vertices in a polygon] Ask: Does it help to plan how to solve a problem before actually solving it? [yes] What do you do when a line is too long? [erase] What do you do if you didn't draw a line long enough? [use the tools to draw it longer] *Worksheet 101.* Give the child the drawing board with worksheet attached, T-square, and 30-60 triangle. Tell the child: Today you will draw shapes using your drawing tools. Before starting you will plan how to do each one. The figures are shown below. *Diameter.* Tell him to look at the first figure. Ask: What is special about the lines? [They all go through the center of the circle.] Tell him: A line that goes through the center of a circle and touches both edges is called a *diameter*. The "dia" part of the words "diameter" and "diagonal" means "across." Ask: How many diameters are in the second figure? [3 in the circle] How many diagonals are in that figure? [3 in the hexagon] Tell him that in this figure, the diameters and diagonals are the same. *Figure 3.* The third figure requires *tick marks*. Explain: We need the starting points at the end of the diameter, but we do not want to draw the diameter. So, we pretend	Diameters exist only in circles; diagonals exist only in polygons and polyhedrons.

RightStart™ Mathematics Level D Second Edition

ACTIVITIES FOR TEACHING:	EXPLANATIONS:

to draw the diameter and draw a little mark for a starting point. It is called a *tick mark*. See the figures below.

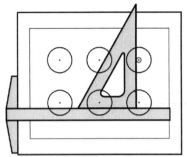 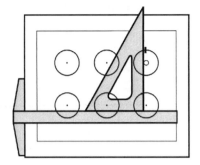

Tick marks should not be erased. They show how a construction is done.

Drawing a tick mark.

Then the two lines starting at the top can be drawn from the tick mark to the edges of the circle. Another tick mark will be needed at the bottom of the circle.

Figure 4. Tell him to think about how he would draw the fourth figure, then discuss it. This is the same as Figure 3 with extra diagonals drawn in.

Figures 5–6. Tick marks will be needed for these figures.

Tell him to complete the worksheet using his drawing tools. The solutions are below.

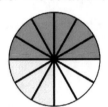

Make $\frac{1}{2}$ of the circle one color and $\frac{1}{4}$ another color. What fraction of the circle is not colored? $\frac{1}{4}$

The hexagon is the whole. What fraction is 1 triangle? $\frac{1}{6}$ What fraction is 1 parallelogram? $\frac{1}{3}$ What fraction is 1 trapezoid? $\frac{1}{2}$

How many:
Sets of parallel lines? **3**
Trapezoids? **6**

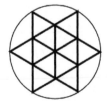

Count the number of triangles.
Small: **12** Medium: **6**
Large: **2**

The hexagon is what fraction of the hexagonal star? $\frac{1}{2}$

Count the number of figures.
Equilateral triangles: **22**
Hexagons: **2** Small rhombuses: **6** Large rhombuses: **3**

Have the child discuss his answers to the questions on the worksheet.

In conclusion. Ask: What do we call a line that goes across a circle? [diameter] What do we call a line between two vertices in a polygon? [diagonal] What do we call a little mark that sometimes helps to draw a figure? [tick mark]

Triangles often overlooked.   **Rhombus often overlooked.**

© Activities for Learning, Inc. 2015

Lesson 125: Drawing 45° Lines in a Square

OBJECTIVES:
1. To introduce the 45 triangle
2. To see figures within other figures

MATERIALS:
1. Worksheet 102, Drawing 45° Lines in a Square
2. Drawing board with worksheet taped on
3. T-square and 45 triangle
4. Ruler

ACTIVITIES FOR TEACHING:

Warm-up. Ask: What direction is a horizontal line? [a straight line from side to side] What direction is a vertical line? [a straight line from top to bottom] What do we call a line that goes across a circle? [diameter] What do we call a line between two vertices in a polygon? [diagonal]

Ask: Does it help to plan how to solve a problem before actually solving it? [yes] What do we call a little mark that sometimes helps to draw a figure? [tick mark]

Worksheet 102. Give the child the drawing board with worksheet attached, T-square, 45 triangle, and ruler. Tell the child: Today you will use a different triangle to draw shapes. As you did in the last lesson, you will plan how to do each figure before starting.

The figures to be constructed are shown below.

Figure 1. Tell him to look at the first square and the 45 triangle. Ask: How would you draw the diagonals? [Use the 45° angle on the triangle, then flip it over and draw the other diagonal.]

Figure 2. Ask: In the second figure, how will you know where to draw the vertical and horizontal lines? [align the triangle with the intersection of the diagonals]

Figure 3. Tell him to think about how he would draw the third figure, then discuss it. A tick mark is needed to draw the medium square. See the figures on the next page.

EXPLANATIONS:

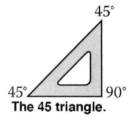
The 45 triangle.

ACTIVITIES FOR TEACHING:

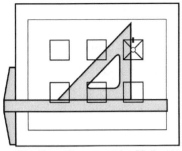
Finding the center of the top.

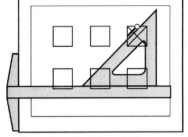
Drawing a side of the medium square.

Figure 4. Ask: How is the fourth figure different from the third figure? [It is the same as the third figure except the diagonals inside the small square are not needed.]

Figure 5. Ask: How is the fifth figure different from the fourth figure? [no diagonals shown and more squares]

Figure 6. This figure requires many tick marks.

Tell him to complete the worksheet using his drawing tools. The solutions are below.

What fraction of the square is:
A small right triangle? $\frac{1}{4}$
A large right triangle? $\frac{1}{2}$

How many right triangles:
Small? **8** Medium? **4**
Large? **4**

The medium square is what fraction of the largest square? $\frac{1}{2}$
The small square is what fraction of the medium square? $\frac{1}{2}$

Find the perimeter of the large and small squares: **16 cm 8 cm**
What is the area? **16 cm² 4 cm²**

How many squares are there?
6 How many right triangles? **20**

How many different sizes of squares are there? **4**

In conclusion. Ask: What angle does the diagonal of a square make with a side? [45°] What fraction of a square does a diagonal divide the square into? [one-half] What fraction of the whole square is one of the little 16 squares? [one-sixteenth]

EXPLANATIONS:

Tick marks should not be erased. They show how a construction is done.

If there is additional time following this lesson, play the Multiples Solitaire game, found in *Math Card Games* book, A47.

Lesson 126: Drawing 45° Lines in a Circle

OBJECTIVES:
1. To find fractions of geometric figures
2. To construct an octagon

MATERIALS:
1. Worksheet 103, Drawing 45° Lines in a Circle
2. Drawing board with worksheet taped on
3. T-square and 45 triangle
4. **Colored pencils or markers**

ACTIVITIES FOR TEACHING:	EXPLANATIONS:

Warm-up. Ask: What do we call a line that goes across a circle? [diameter] What do we call a line between two vertices in a polygon? [diagonal]

Ask: What do we do before starting to draw? [plan the solution] What do we call a little mark that sometimes helps to draw a figure? [tick mark] What do you do if you didn't draw a line long enough? [use the tools to draw it longer] What do you do when a line is too long? [erase]

Worksheet 103. Give the child the drawing board with worksheet attached, T-square, and 45 triangle. As you have been doing, you will plan how to do each figure before starting.

The figures are shown below.

Figures 1–2. Tell him to look at the first little figure. Ask: What is special about the lines? [diameters] How many diameters are in the figure? [4 in the circle] How many diagonals are in the second figure? [2 in the square] Why aren't the horizontal and vertical diameters also diagonals? [Those lines did not go from vertex to vertex.]

As a reminder, diameters exist only in circles; diagonals exist only in polygons and polyhedrons.

Figure 3. Ask: In the third figure, how will you know where to start without drawing a diameter? [tick mark] See the figures on the next page.

ACTIVITIES FOR TEACHING:	EXPLANATIONS:

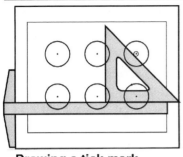 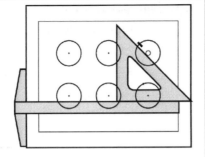

Drawing a tick mark.

Figure 4. Tell him to think about how he would draw the fourth figure, then discuss it. One square is identical to the square in the previous figure. The other square also needs a tick mark as a starting point.

Figures 5–6. Tell him to look at the last two figures and ask: Why do you think you are given a tick mark? [It is not possible to make that tick mark with a 45 triangle.]

Tell him: The shape in Figure 5 is an *octagon*. It is a special octagon, a *regular* octagon, because its eight sides are equal and its eight angles are equal.

Tell him to complete the worksheet using his drawing tools. The solutions are below.

  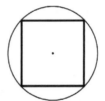

Make $\frac{3}{8}$ of the circle one color and $\frac{1}{4}$ another color. What fraction of the circle is not colored? $\frac{3}{8}$

Count the number of triangles.
Small: **8** Medium: **4**
Large: **4**

Measure the diameter of the circle: **5** cm. Measure the diagonal of the square: **5** cm

  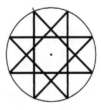

How many right triangles do you see? **8** Color them. Color the octagon another color.

How many sides does an octagon have? **8** Write the word to make the figure a traffic sign.

Count: Sets of parallel lines: **4**
Octagons: **1** Squares: **2**

In conclusion. Ask: How many sides does an octagon have? [8] How many sets of parallel lines are in a regular octagon? [4] How many sides does a hexagon have? [6] How many sets of parallel lines are in a regular hexagon? [3]

If there is additional time following this lesson, play the Ring Around the Products game, found in *Math Card Games* book, P32.

Lesson 127: Drawing Congruent Figures

OBJECTIVES:
1. To review meaning of *congruent*
2. To draw congruent figures

MATERIALS:
1. Tangrams
2. Worksheet 104, Drawing Congruent Figures
3. Drawing board with worksheet taped on
4. T-square, 45 triangle, and 30-60 triangle

ACTIVITIES FOR TEACHING:	EXPLANATIONS:

Warm-up. Ask: How many sides does a rectangle have? [4] How many sets of parallel lines are in a rectangle? [2] How many sets of perpendicular lines? [4]

Ask: How many sides does a hexagon have? [6] How many sets of parallel lines are in a regular hexagon? [3] How many sets of perpendicular lines? [none]

How many sides does an octagon have? [8] How many sets of parallel lines are in a regular octagon? [4]

Congruent tangrams. Give the child the tangrams. Tell him to lay them out in no particular order. See below.

The seven tangram pieces.

The child might notice that the tangram triangles are smaller versions of the 45 triangle.

Say: Two figures are *congruent* if they fit exactly on top of the other. Find the congruent shapes. [the two small triangles and the two large triangles] See below.

The congruent pairs.

Ask: Must the two figures face the same direction? [no] Show the medium triangle. Say: This triangle looks like the other triangles. Ask: Why isn't it congruent? [It is not exactly the same size.]

Tell him to take the two little triangles and combine to make them congruent with the parallelogram. See the left figures below. Repeat for the square. See the right figures.

The tangrams will not be needed for the remainder of the lesson.

ACTIVITIES FOR TEACHING:

Worksheet 104. Give the child the drawing board with worksheet attached, T-square, and both triangles. Tell the child: Today you will draw congruent figures without any measuring or tracing. You will need to decide whether to use the 30-60 triangle or the 45 triangle.

Figure 1. Tell the child to read the directions at the top and for the first problem. Ask: What does it ask you to do? [Draw the figure on the dotted line exactly as the one above it.]

Ask him to think about how to do it, using only the tools, then discuss it. He will need to draw two tick marks. The simplest way is to draw the edges of the triangle as shown in the left figure below.

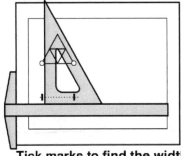
Tick marks to find the width of the triangle.

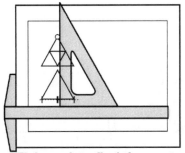
Tick mark to find the center of the triangle.

He will also need to find the center of the baseline. See the right figure above.

Tell him to complete the worksheet. The solutions are below.

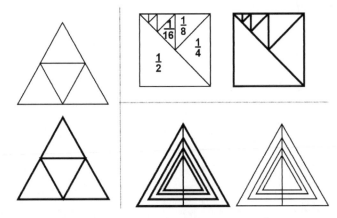

In Problem 2, the diagonal of the square determines the length of the baseline.

In Problem 3, use tick marks to show the tops and bases for each triangle.

In conclusion. Ask: Is your 45 triangle congruent with your 30-60 triangle? [no] Are there any congruent windows in your room?

EXPLANATIONS:

For clarity, only the figures on the worksheet being discussed are shown.

Figures 1 and 3 need the 30-60 triangle. Figure 2 needs the 45 triangle.

Some children might like to continue writing the fractions: 1/32, 1/64, 1/128, and another 1/128.

If there is additional time following this lesson, play the Multiplication Card Speed game, found in *Math Card Games* book, P31.

© Activities for Learning, Inc. 2015

LESSON 128: COMPLETING THE WHOLE

OBJECTIVES:
1. To construct the whole when a fraction is given

MATERIALS:
1. A few tiles
2. Tangrams
3. Worksheet 105, Completing the Whole
4. Drawing board with worksheet taped on
5. T-square, 30-60 triangle, and 45 triangle

ACTIVITIES FOR TEACHING:

Warm-up. Ask: How many minutes are in a quarter hour? [15 min] How many quarter hours make a whole hour? [4] How long is 2 quarter hours? [30 min, half hour] How long is 3 quarters of an hour? [45 min] How long is 8 quarters of an hour? [2 hours]

Ask: How many pennies in a quarter? [25] How many quarters equal a dollar? [4] Which is greater, 3 quarters or 1 dollar? [$1] How many quarters are in two dollars? [8] How many quarters are in a dollar and a half? [6]

Completing the whole with tiles. Give the child the tiles.

Tell him to place two tiles together. Say: Those two tiles are half of a figure. Add the tiles you need to make the whole. See below.

One half.

Figures showing the whole.

Ask the child to explain his solution. One way is:

If you have four, then two would be half.

Next tell him to lay out three tiles in a row. Tell him it represents three fifths of a whole. Ask him to make the whole. See below.

Three fifths.

Figure showing the whole.

Ask the child to explain the solution. One way is:

When you have three tiles and it is three fifths, then one tile is one fifth. So five tiles are five fifths, which makes the whole.

EXPLANATIONS:

RightStart™ Mathematics Level D Second Edition © Activities for Learning, Inc. 2015

ACTIVITIES FOR TEACHING:	EXPLANATIONS:

Completing the whole with tangrams. Give the child the tangrams.

Tell him to find one of the smaller triangles. Say: We will call it half a figure. Build the whole figure, including that piece. Several possibilities are shown below.

One half.   Figures showing the whole.

Next tell him to find the square. Say: The square represents two thirds of a whole. Add what you need to make the whole. See below.

Two thirds.   Figure showing the whole.

Ask the child to explain the solution. One way is:

Think of dividing the square by a diagonal. Then each piece is one third. Three thirds are needed so adding the small triangle will make three thirds.

Worksheet 105. Give the child the drawing board with worksheet attached, T-square, and both triangles. When he has completed the worksheet, ask him to explain how he did it. The solutions are shown below.

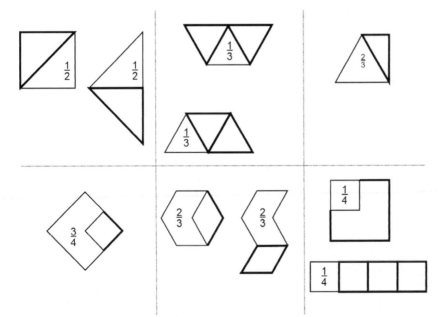

There are other solutions in addition to those shown.

In conclusion. Ask: If you have one fourth of something, how many more fourths do you need to make a whole? [3] If you divide a square into two equal parts, what fraction is one part? [one half] If you divide that half again into two equal parts, what fraction is one part? [one fourth]

If there is additional time following this lesson, play the Multiplication Card Speed game, found in *Math Card Games* book, P31.

© Activities for Learning, Inc. 2015

Lesson 129: Finding a Fraction of a Figure

OBJECTIVES:
1. To construct the whole when a fraction is given

MATERIALS:
1. Tangrams
2. Worksheet 106, Finding a Fraction of a Figure
3. Drawing board with attached worksheet
4. T-square, 30-60 triangle, and 45 triangle
5. **Colored pencils or markers**

ACTIVITIES FOR TEACHING:

Warm-up. Ask: If you have one fourth of something, how many more fourths do you need to make a whole? [3] If you divide a circle into two equal parts, what fraction is one part? [one half] If you divide that half again into two equal parts, what fraction is one part? [one fourth] If you divide that fourth again into two equal parts, what fraction is one part? [one eighth]

Finding a fraction of a tangram arrangement. Give the child the tangrams. Ask him to make the following fractions with his pieces.

1. Tell him to make a rectangle using two small triangles and the square. Write: $\frac{3}{4}$

and ask: Which fraction pieces show this fraction of your rectangle? [the square and one small triangle] See below.

The whole.   The fraction $\frac{3}{4}$.

2. Next write: $\frac{2}{4}$

and ask: In the same rectangle, which fraction pieces shows this fraction? [either the two triangles or the square] See the left figure below.

The fraction $\frac{2}{4}$.   The fraction $\frac{1}{2}$.

3. Repeat for $\frac{1}{2}$. [same answer] See the right figure above.

4. Next tell him to lay out the large triangle. Write:

$\frac{2}{2}$

and tell him to show that fraction of the large triangle. [no change, the fraction two halves equal 1] See below.

The whole.   The fraction $\frac{2}{2}$.

EXPLANATIONS:

RightStart™ Mathematics Level D Second Edition © Activities for Learning, Inc. 2015

ACTIVITIES FOR TEACHING:	EXPLANATIONS:

Ask: What are some ways to think about what the fraction means? [two halves or 2 divided by 2]

5. Write: $\frac{3}{2}$

and tell him to start with the large triangle and to show that fraction. See the figures below.

The whole.   **The fraction $\frac{3}{2}$.**

6. Write: $\frac{2}{1}$

and tell him to start with the large triangle and to show that fraction, using only triangles. See the figures below.

The whole.   **The fraction $\frac{2}{1}$.**

We do not have a good way to read the fraction $\frac{2}{1}$ in English. The only possibility is *two over one*, which obscures its meaning.

Ask: What is the fraction equal to? [2 because 2 divided by 1 is 2]

Worksheet 106. Give the child the drawing board with worksheet attached, T-square, and both triangles. Tell him to complete the worksheet. The solutions are shown below.

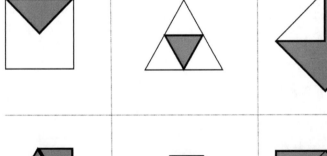
  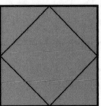

When the worksheet is completed, ask the child to explain how he found the solutions, especially the last one.

In conclusion. Ask: What is two halves equal to? [1] What is three thirds equal to? [1] How many tenths are needed to equal one? [10]

If there is additional time following this lesson, play the Concentrating on Sixths game, found in *Math Card Games* book, F19.

LESSON 130: ORGANIZING QUADRILATERALS

OBJECTIVES:
1. To review definitions of quadrilaterals
2. To view quadrilaterals in categories
3. To introduce the figure *kite*

MATERIALS:
1. Worksheet 107, Organizing Quadrilaterals
2. Drawing board with worksheet attached
3. T-square, 30-60 triangle, and 45 triangle

ACTIVITIES FOR TEACHING:	**EXPLANATIONS:**

Warm-up. Ask: What is two halves equal to? [1] What is four fourths equal to? [1] How many tenths are needed to equal one? [10] Is three halves more or less than one? [more] What is three halves plus three halves? [3]

Ask: What do we call a line that goes across a circle through the center? [diameter] What do we call a line that goes between two vertices in a polygon? [diagonal]

Reviewing terms. Draw the following figures and the chart, but without the "x's".

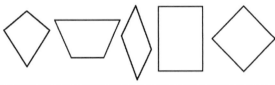

Draw the first figure as a *kite*: the upper sides are congruent and the lower sides are congruent. *Kite* is the geometrical term for this figure.

Quadrilateral	×	×	×	×	×
Parallelogram			×	×	×
Rectangle				×	×
Square					×

Quadrilateral. Tell the child: A quadrilateral is a closed figure with four lines. The prefix *quad* means four. Point to each figure in turn and ask: Is this a quadrilateral? Ask the child to mark an "x" in the appropriate box if the figure is a quadrilateral. See the chart above showing all the figures to be quadrilaterals.

Parallelogram. Tell him: A parallelogram is a quadrilateral with opposite sides parallel. Ask the child to mark the parallelograms with an "x." See the second row in the chart above. Ask: Do you agree? Why isn't the second figure a parallelogram? [only 1 set of parallel lines]

The word parallel can be heard in parallelogram.

Strictly speaking, we only need to specify that a rectangle has *one* right angle and two sets of parallel lines. Having one right angle in a parallelogram inevitably means the other angles will be right angles. However, it is simpler to think of a rectangle as having four right angles.

Rectangle. Tell him: A rectangle is a parallelogram with right angles. Ask the child to mark the rectangles with an "x." See the third row in the chart above.

Square. Tell him: A square is a rectangle with equal sides. Ask the child to mark the squares with an "x." See the last row in the chart above.

Occasionally, a rectangle is considered to be a figure having unequal adjacent sides, thus excluding a square. Mathematically, a square is a special rectangle.

RightStart™ Mathematics Level D Second Edition © Activities for Learning, Inc. 2015

ACTIVITIES FOR TEACHING:	EXPLANATIONS:

Kite. Point to the first figure on the left page and ask: What does this figure look like? [a kite] Does this kite have any parallel sides? [no] Does a kite have any congruent sides? [yes, two sets]

Worksheet 107. Give the child the drawing board with worksheet attached, T-square, 30-60 triangle, and 45 triangle.

Tell the child to look at the worksheet and ask: In the first column, how many parallel lines do the figures have? [none] How many sets of parallel lines does the figure have in the second column? [1] How many sets of parallel lines do the figures have in the third column? [2]

Explain that the little matching slash marks on the kite show sides that are equal. Ask: If you take a kite and push up on the tail so all the sides are the same, what figure would you have? [rhombus] Say: That is why there is a line on the chart from the kite to the rhombus.

Tell him to draw sample figures in the boxes and answer the questions. Solutions are shown below.

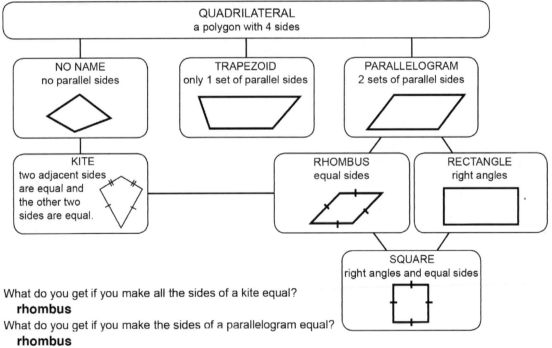

What do you get if you make all the sides of a kite equal?
   rhombus
What do you get if you make the sides of a parallelogram equal?
   rhombus
What do you get if you make one set of parallel sides in a square longer?
   rectangle
What do you get if you make the angles in a parallelogram into right angles?
   rectangle, square

In conclusion. Ask: What special parallelogram has congruent sides? [rhombus] What special parallelogram has congruent angles? [rectangle] What special parallelogram has congruent sides and angles? [square]

If there is additional time following this lesson, play the Concentrating on Eighths game, found in *Math Card Games* book, F20.

© Activities for Learning, Inc. 2015

Lesson 131: Drawing Symmetrical Figures

OBJECTIVES:
1. To review the terms *symmetry*, *line of symmetry*, and *reflection*
2. To draw geometric reflections

MATERIALS:
1. Tangrams
2. Geometry reflector
3. Worksheet 108, Drawing Symmetrical Figures
4. Drawing board with worksheet attached
5. T-square, 30-60 triangle, and 45 triangle

ACTIVITIES FOR TEACHING:

Warm-up. Ask: What is one half of $6.00? [$3.00] What is one half of $8.30? [$4.15] What is one half of an hour? [half hour or 30 minutes] What is one half of a half hour? [quarter hour or 15 minutes] What is one half of a whole? [one half] What is one half of one half? [one fourth] What is one half of one fourth? [one eighth] What is one half of 11? [5 and one half]

Reflections with tangrams. Give the child the tangrams and geometry reflector. Give him a few minutes to discover reflections with the tangrams.

Tell him to place the reflector along the longer side of a large triangle. Ask: What do you see in the reflector? [triangle reflected] Tell him to do it again with a shorter side. See the figures below.

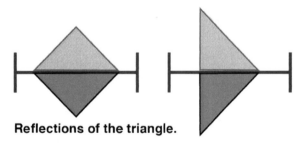

Reflections of the triangle.

Tell him to place the reflector on the line of symmetry on the large triangle. Ask: Do you see the actual triangle and the reflected triangle? See the figure below.

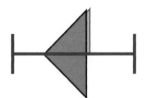

Triangle and its reflection.

Worksheet 108. Give the child the drawing board with worksheet attached, T-square, and both triangles. Tell him to read the directions.

EXPLANATIONS:

Reflections are easier to see if the background surface is light-colored, especially when red tangram pieces are used.

A line of symmetry is a line of reflection, the line that acts as a mirror.

RightStart™ Mathematics Level D Second Edition © Activities for Learning, Inc. 2015

ACTIVITIES FOR TEACHING:	EXPLANATIONS:

Ask: How can you use the reflector to see the whole figure? [place it on the dotted lines]

Remind him that all lines drawn with the T-square must be drawn on *top* of, never underneath, the T-square. A good technique for drawing some of these lines is to first match the correct angle and then flip the triangle to draw the new line. See below.

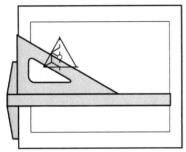
Matching the angle.

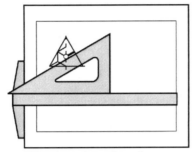
Flipping the triangle.

Tell him to complete the worksheet with his drawing tools. Have him check his figures with the reflector. Ask him to explain how he did some of them.

The solutions are shown below.

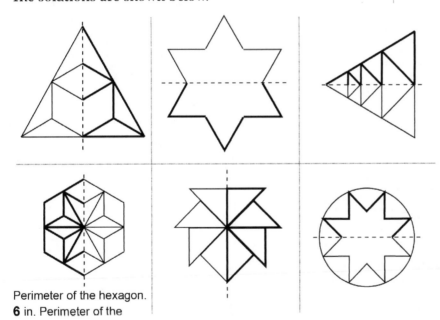

Perimeter of the hexagon. **6** in. Perimeter of the star. **6** in.

In conclusion. Ask: What fraction of each completed figure on the worksheet did you draw? [one half] When you look at yourself in the mirror, is your reflection the way you actually look? [no] Where is your right hand in the mirror? [on the left]

If there is additional time following this lesson, play the Concentrating on Eighths game, found in *Math Card Games* book, F20.

© Activities for Learning, Inc. 2015

Lesson 132: Congruent Shapes

OBJECTIVES:
1. To practice recognizing congruent shapes through visualizing

MATERIALS:
1. Tangrams
2. Four tiles
3. Worksheet 109, Congruent Shapes
4. **Colored pencils or markers**

ACTIVITIES FOR TEACHING:

Warm-up. Show the two large triangles from the tangrams in the position shown on the top left below. Ask: Are these triangles congruent? [yes] Then flip one triangle over as shown below on the top right. Ask: Are these triangles congruent? [yes] Stress that even if a figure needs to be flipped over to fit exactly, it is still congruent.

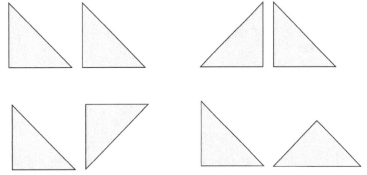

These sets of triangles are congruent. A flip or turn may be necessary before matching.

Continue with the second row, asking if these are also congruent. [yes] Ask: What does congruent mean? [exactly the same when you put one on top of the other]

Shapes with four tiles. Give the child the tiles. Tell him to find all the different ways to combine four tiles with at least one edge touching another tile. Tell the child to draw a solution. Ask if he can find another solution. Continue until all five are found. See the solutions below.

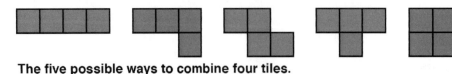

The five possible ways to combine four tiles.

EXPLANATIONS:

ACTIVITIES FOR TEACHING:

Worksheet 109. Give the child the worksheet. Tell him to read the directions. Ask the child to explain them. The solutions are below.

EXPLANATIONS:

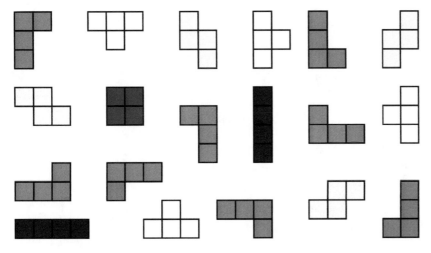

The child might recognize these shapes as the pieces used in the computer game Tetris.

How many shapes of each color are there?

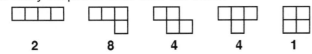

2   8   4   4   1

What is the area of each shape in square centimeters? **4 cm²**
What is the area of all the shapes? **76 cm²**
What are the perimeters of each shape in centimeters? **Square is 8 cm; others, 10 cm**

In conclusion. Ask: What do we mean when we say two figures are congruent? [exactly the same] Are your hands congruent? [yes] If two figures look the same, but one is turned sideways, can they still be congruent? [yes]

If there is additional time following this lesson, have the child choose a game to play.

© Activities for Learning, Inc. 2015

LESSON 133: ARITHMETIC REVIEW

OBJECTIVES:
1. To review concepts learned during the year

MATERIALS:
1. Worksheet 110, Arithmetic Review

ACTIVITIES FOR TEACHING:

Worksheet 110. Give the child the worksheet. Tell him that today will be a review for the upcoming final assessment. He will complete the two-page worksheet, then discuss the solutions.

Tell him to listen to the problems and write the answers. Read each problem twice.

60¢ × 2 $\frac{1}{2}$ of $10.50   56 ÷ 8

Tell him to complete the worksheet. Solutions are below and on the next page.

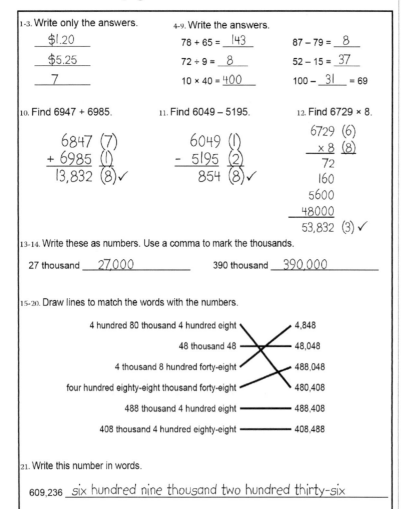

EXPLANATIONS:

267

ACTIVITIES FOR TEACHING:

EXPLANATIONS:

22-45. Find the products or quotients.

$6 \times 7 = 42$ $4 \times 8 = 32$ $9 \times 3 = 27$ $5 \times 8 = 40$

$7 \times 9 = 63$ $8 \times 8 = 64$ $6 \times 9 = 54$ $8 \times 9 = 72$

$1 \times 7 = 7$ $6 \times 6 = 36$ $0 \times 4 = 0$ $7 \times 7 = 49$

$36 \div 6 = 6$ $28 \div 4 = 7$ $54 \div 9 = 6$ $35 \div 5 = 7$

$56 \div 8 = 7$ $64 \div 8 = 8$ $81 \div 9 = 9$ $42 \div 7 = 6$

$49 \div 7 = 7$ $72 \div 9 = 8$ $36 \div 9 = 4$ $27 \div 3 = 9$

46-53. Complete the equations.

$589 + 17 - 17 = 589$

$34 + 56 = 90$

$6 \times 10 + 17 = 77$

$0 = 2 \times 0 \times 8$

$5 \times 9 \times 2 = 90$

$8 \times (4 + 6) = 80$

$(4 + 6) \times (3 + 7) = 100$

$24 - 19 = 5$

54-61. Write <, >, or = on the lines.

$30 \times 2 \underline{\ =\ } 3 \times 20$

$3 \times 4 \times 5 \underline{\ =\ } 5 \times 4 \times 3$

$46 + 57 \underline{\ <\ } 46 + 59$

$1 \times 1 \underline{\ <\ } 1 + 1$

$2 \times 2 \underline{\ =\ } 2 + 2$

$3 \times 3 \underline{\ >\ } 3 + 3$

$(8 \times 2) + (8 \times 8) \underline{\ =\ } (8 \times 10)$

$73 - 59 \underline{\ >\ } 72 - 59$

62-69. Write the next two terms for each pattern.

83	85	87	89	91
106	107	108	109	110
9	18	27	36	45
16	24	32	40	48
1	4	9	16	25
3	6	9	12	15
3	6	12	24	48
4	40	400	4000	40,000

70-73. Round 7465.

To nearest 10.	7470
To nearest 100.	7500
To nearest 1000.	7000

73-75. Round 37,908.

To nearest 10	37,910
To nearest 100.	37,900
To nearest 1000.	38,000

Worksheet solutions. Check the answers to the review worksheet with the child. Discuss the various methods for the solutions.

The next day will be a day of games. Games review and practice facts and skills in an enjoyable environment.

© Activities for Learning, Inc. 2015

LESSON 134: ARITHMETIC GAMES

OBJECTIVES:

1. To review skills by playing math card games

MATERIALS:

1. *Math Card Games* book, N46, P32, D6, and D12

ACTIVITIES FOR TEACHING:	EXPLANATIONS:
Rounding War game. Ask: What is 61 rounded to the nearest 10? [60] What is 68 rounded to the nearest 10? [70] What is 87 rounded to the nearest 10? [90] What is 35 rounded to the nearest 10? [40] Tell him 35 is in the middle and could go either way, but most of the time people round it up, to 40. Play a variation of the Rounding War game found in the *Math Card Games* book, N46. Instead of each player playing one card face up and rounding it, each person plays two cards face up. Add the two numbers together, then round the sum to the nearest ten. The player with the higher rounded value takes all four cards. When a war occurs, place two cards face down before laying two cards face up to determine the winner of that round. The winner then collects the twelve cards. ***Ring around the Products game.*** Ask: What is 6×6? [36] What is 7×5? [35] 5×7? [35] Ask: What is 7×7? [49] What is 8×6? [48] 6×8? [48] Ask: What is 8×8? [64] What is 7×9? [63] 9×7? [63] Ask: What is 9×9? [81] What is 8×10? [80] 10×8? [80] Play the Ring around the Products game found in the *Math Card Games* book, P32. ***Equal Quotients game.*** Write: $$1 \div 2 = \tfrac{1}{2}$$ and ask: Is this correct? [yes] Write: $$35 \div 5 = \tfrac{35}{5}$$ and ask: Is this correct? [yes] What is $35 \div 5$? [7] What is $\tfrac{35}{5}$? [7] What is $35 \div 7$? [5] What is $\tfrac{35}{7}$? [5]	

RightStart™ Mathematics Level D Second Edition

© Activities for Learning, Inc. 2015

ACTIVITIES FOR TEACHING:	EXPLANATIONS:

Write:

$$48 \div 8 =$$

and ask how it could be written as a fraction. [$\frac{48}{8}$] Ask: What is $48 \div 8$? [6] What is $\frac{48}{8}$? [6] What is $48 \div 6$? [8] What is $\frac{48}{6}$? [8]

Play the Equal Quotients game found in *Math Card Games* book, D6.

Division War game. If time permits, play the Division War game found in *Math Card Games* book, D12.

© Activities for Learning, Inc. 2015

Lesson 135: Time, Money, and Problem Solving Review

OBJECTIVES:
1. To review concepts learned during the year

MATERIALS:
1. Worksheet 111, Time, Money, and Problem Solving Review

ACTIVITIES FOR TEACHING:

Worksheet 111. Give the child the worksheet. Tell him that today will be a review for the upcoming final assessment. He will complete the worksheet, then discuss the solutions.

Have the child complete the worksheet. Solutions are below.

1-2. Write the time.

10:31   1:18

3-4. Draw the hands.

6:41   11:11

5-10. Solve the problems.

Plums cost $1.65 a pound and bananas cost 59¢ a pound. What is the total cost of 2 pounds of plums and 5 pounds of bananas?

C = 1.65 × 2 + 59¢ × 5
C = 3.30 + 2.95 = $6.25

Carrie is buying candles for a birthday cake for an aunt who is 73 years old. There are 8 candles in a package. How many packages does Carrie need?

73 ÷ 8 = 9 r 1
Carrie needs 10 packages.

At 9:30 Chelsea started to pick currants. It takes 20 minutes to fill a bucket. What will be the time when Chelsea finishes filling six buckets?

Minutes = 20 × 6 = 2 hr
9:30 + 2 hr = 11:30

Cody has 2 dollar bills, 3 quarters, 2 dimes, 4 nickels, and 7 pennies. How much more money does he need to have 5 dollars?

$2 + .25 × 3 + .10 × 2 + .05 × 4 + .01 × 7 = $3.22
$3.22 + m = 5
m = $1.78

Cameron pays 50¢ for a trolley ticket. How many tickets can he get for $5.50?

$5.50 ÷ 50¢ = 11 tickets

A rectangular pen for a cat is to be 42 sq. feet. One side of the pen is 7 ft. The fence is $4 per foot. What is the cost of the fence?

Other side = 42 ÷ 7 = 6
C = 2 × (6 + 7) × 4 = $104

EXPLANATIONS:

RightStart™ Mathematics Level D Second Edition   © Activities for Learning, Inc. 2015

ACTIVITIES FOR TEACHING:	EXPLANATIONS:
Worksheet solutions. Check the answers to the review worksheet with the child. Discuss the various methods for the solutions.	The next day will be a day of games. Games review and practice facts and skills in an enjoyable environment.

© Activities for Learning, Inc. 2015

Lesson 136: Time, Money, and Problem Solving Games

OBJECTIVES:
1. To review skills by playing math card games

MATERIALS:
1. Clock, Appendix p. 10
2. *Math Card Games* book, C23, M16, and A42
3. Math journal

ACTIVITIES FOR TEACHING:	EXPLANATIONS:
Fifteen Minutes Later game. Give the child the clock from the appendix. Say: If the time is 3:30, what time will it be 15 minutes later? [3:45] If the time is 5:25, what time will it be 15 minutes later? [5:40] If the time is 10:50, what time will it be 15 minutes later? [11:05]	
Play the Fifteen Minutes Later game, found in the *Math Card Games* book, C23.	
Counting Money game. Give the child the math journal. Play the Counting Money game, found in the *Math Card Games* book, M16. Have the child do his calculations in his math journal.	
The interesting point at the end of the game is that the two players' sum must equal $6.00. If it does not, the players need to check their work.	
Corners™ Puzzles game. Play the Corners™ Puzzles game, found in the *Math Card Games* book, A42.	This game is an exercise in problem solving. Perseverance is necessary for problem solving, whether it be a game, a word problem, or a real-life problem.
This game has puzzles that use addition facts to create a specified shape. Cards may be added or removed from the layout as desired.	

RightStart™ Mathematics Level D Second Edition

© Activities for Learning, Inc. 2015

ACTIVITIES FOR TEACHING:

Choose a method for joining the cards: either multiples of 5 or 4 with scoreless matching, or multiples of 3 with matching only. Scoreless matching is the same numbers joining that do not add up the desired multiple.

One shape is to make a line as long as possible, either horizontal or vertical. Another shape is to make "steps" by going over, then up, over and up and so on.

This game is not scored. The challenge is to use as many cards as possible and create the desired pattern.

EXPLANATIONS:

This game is an exercise in problem solving. Perseverance is necessary for problem solving, whether it be a game, a word problem, or a real-life problem.

The 9s are underlined.

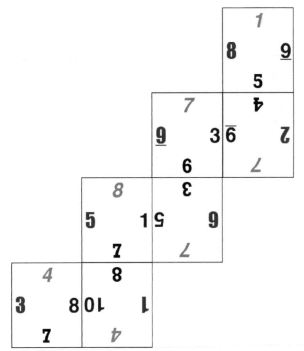

Making a line with multiples of 5.

Making steps with multiples of 3.

Lesson 137: Data, Fraction, and Geometry Review

OBJECTIVES:
1. To review concepts learned during the year

MATERIALS:
1. Worksheet 112, Data, Fraction, and Geometry Review

ACTIVITIES FOR TEACHING:

Worksheet 112. Give the child the worksheet. Tell him that today will be the last review for the upcoming final assessment. He will complete the two-page worksheet, then discuss the solutions.

Have the child complete the worksheet. Solutions are below and on the next page.

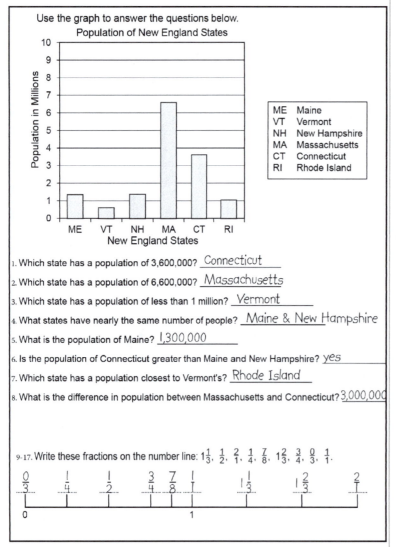

EXPLANATIONS:

The order of the states is not alphabetical, but geographical; north to south and west to east.

The answers may be given by the two-letter codes.

ACTIVITIES FOR TEACHING:

EXPLANATIONS:

18-21. Write <, >, or = on the lines.

$$\frac{1}{6} \; > \; \frac{1}{7}$$

$$\frac{2}{8} \; < \; \frac{3}{8}$$

$$\frac{3}{8} \; > \; \frac{3}{9}$$

$$\frac{2}{4} \; = \; \frac{3}{6}$$

22-24. Circle the fraction in each row that is nearest to one half.

$\frac{1}{6}$	$\boxed{\frac{1}{3}}$	$\frac{1}{4}$
$\frac{2}{8}$	$\frac{3}{8}$	$\boxed{\frac{4}{8}}$
$\boxed{\frac{4}{10}}$	$\frac{8}{9}$	$\frac{2}{2}$

25-27. Circle the greatest fraction in each row.

$\frac{1}{8}$	$\boxed{\frac{1}{3}}$	$\frac{1}{4}$
$\boxed{\frac{8}{8}}$	$\frac{7}{8}$	$\frac{6}{8}$
$\boxed{\frac{9}{10}}$	$\frac{8}{9}$	$\frac{7}{9}$

28-31. Circle the fractions in the rectangle that are needed to total to 1.

$\boxed{\frac{1}{6}}$	$\frac{2}{7}$	$\boxed{\frac{3}{6}}$	$\boxed{\frac{2}{6}}$	$\frac{4}{7}$
$\boxed{\frac{1}{8}}$	$\frac{2}{5}$	$\frac{1}{2}$	$\frac{1}{5}$	$\boxed{\frac{7}{8}}$

$\boxed{\frac{3}{10}}$	$\frac{2}{7}$	$\boxed{\frac{1}{10}}$	$\boxed{\frac{1}{10}}$	$\boxed{\frac{1}{2}}$
$\boxed{\frac{1}{8}}$	$\frac{2}{5}$	$\boxed{\frac{1}{2}}$	$\frac{4}{5}$	$\boxed{\frac{3}{8}}$

32-34. Fill in the blanks.

A quarter of an hour is __15__ minutes.

A half of a dollar is __50__ cents.

A quarter of an gallon is __1__ quarts.

35-37. Match angles and symbols.

90°

60°

30°

38-43. Use the letter in the figure to answer the questions below.

A   B   C   D   E   F

Which figure is an octagon? __C__

Which figures are quadrilaterals? __B, E, F__

Which figures are parallelograms? __B, E__

Which figure is a rectangle? __E__

Which figures have parallel lines? __B, C, E__

Which figures have right angles? __D, E__

44. Shade $\frac{3}{4}$.

45. Shade $\frac{2}{3}$.

There are other ways to shade the figures. Shading either the hexagon or hexagon and circle is acceptable.

Worksheet solutions. Check the answers to the review worksheet with the child. Discuss the various methods for the solutions.

The next day will be a day of games. Games review and practice facts and skills in an enjoyable environment.

© Activities for Learning, Inc. 2015

Lesson 138: Fraction Games

OBJECTIVES:
1. To review skills by playing math card games

MATERIALS:
1. Whole fraction charts and a 1-piece*
2. *Math Card Games* book, F9 and F18

ACTIVITIES FOR TEACHING:

Harder Fraction War game. Ask: What do you call the bottom number in a fraction? [denominator] What do you call the top number in a fraction? [numerator] What is the denominator in the fraction two thirds? [3] What is the numerator in the fraction two thirds? [2] How many more thirds are needed to make a whole? [1]

Distribute the fraction charts to the child. Write:

$$\frac{1}{3} \underline{\quad} \frac{3}{10}$$

and ask which is more. [$\frac{1}{3}$]

Use the whole fraction chart and the 1-piece to compare the two fractions. See the figure below.

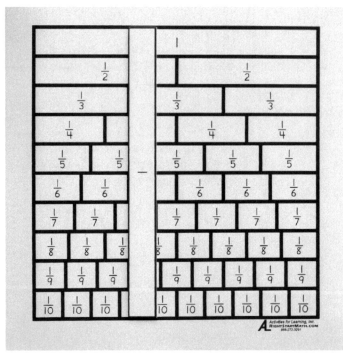

Using the left edge of the 1-piece to compare $\frac{1}{3}$ and $\frac{3}{10}$.

EXPLANATIONS:

*The 1-piece will be used for comparing fractions on the whole fraction chart. See the picture on the left. A 30-60 triangle or a ruler would also work.

ACTIVITIES FOR TEACHING:

Play the Harder Fraction War game, found in the *Math Card Games* book, F9. Tell him to use the fraction chart for comparisons.

One or Two game variation. Have the child play the One or Two game found in *Math Card Games* book, F18.

For a second game or to speed up the game, modify as follows:

> No need to remove the four fraction cards listed.
> The cards taken must total only 1 (not 2).
> Only one set of cards totaling 1 may be taken per turn.

EXPLANATIONS:

278

LESSON 139: FINAL ASSESSMENT

OBJECTIVES:

1. To assess concepts learned during the year

MATERIALS:

1. Worksheet 113, Final Assessment

ACTIVITIES FOR TEACHING:	EXPLANATIONS:

Worksheet 113. Give the child the worksheet. Tell him that today will be the final assessment.

Tell him to listen to the problems and write the answers. Read each problem twice.

$$80¢ \times 2 \qquad \tfrac{1}{2} \text{ of } \$8.40 \qquad 42 \div 6$$

Tell him to complete the five-page worksheet. Solutions are below and on the next four pages.

1-3. Write only the answers.

$\underline{\$1.60}$

$\underline{\$4.20}$

$\underline{\quad 7 \quad}$

4-9. Write the answers.

$84 + 39 = \underline{123}$

$72 \div 8 = \underline{9}$

$10 \times 70 = \underline{700}$

$78 - 69 = \underline{9}$

$64 - 18 = \underline{46}$

$100 - \underline{57} = 43$

10. Find 5839 + 8473.

$$\begin{array}{r} 5839 \;(7) \\ + 8473 \;(4) \\ \hline 14,312 \;(2) \checkmark \end{array}$$

11. Find 5095 − 3867.

$$\begin{array}{r} 5095 \;(1) \\ - 3867 \;(6) \\ \hline 1228 \;(4) \checkmark \end{array}$$

12. Find 5893 × 8.

$$\begin{array}{r} 5893 \;(7) \\ \times 8 \;(8) \\ \hline 24 \\ 720 \\ 6400 \\ 40000 \\ \hline 47,144 \;(2) \checkmark \end{array}$$

13-14. Write these as numbers. Use a comma to mark the thousands.

71 thousand $\underline{71,000}$

430 thousand $\underline{430,000}$

15-20. Draw lines to match the words with the numbers.

7 hundred 20 thousand 7 hundred two   722,072

72 thousand 72   7,272

7 thousand 2 hundred seventy-two   72,072

seven hundred twenty-two thousand seventy-two   702,722

722 thousand 7 hundred two   720,702

702 thousand 7 hundred twenty-two   722,702

21. Write this number in words.

870,603 _eight hundred seventy thousand six hundred three_

RightStart™ Mathematics Level D Second Edition

© Activities for Learning, Inc. 2015

279

ACTIVITIES FOR TEACHING:

EXPLANATIONS:

22-45. Find the products or quotients.

$8 \times 9 = 72$	$4 \times 8 = 32$	$7 \times 3 = 21$	$5 \times 8 = 40$
$9 \times 7 = 63$	$8 \times 8 = 64$	$6 \times 7 = 42$	$8 \times 6 = 48$
$1 \times 9 = 9$	$5 \times 8 = 40$	$8 \times 7 = 56$	$0 \times 9 = 0$
$42 \div 7 = 6$	$32 \div 8 = 4$	$64 \div 8 = 8$	$35 \div 5 = 7$
$56 \div 8 = 7$	$63 \div 7 = 9$	$81 \div 9 = 9$	$48 \div 6 = 8$
$49 \div 7 = 7$	$72 \div 9 = 8$	$36 \div 6 = 6$	$24 \div 3 = 8$

46-53. Complete the equations.

$435 + 19 - 19 = 435$

$28 + 42 = 70$

$7 \times 10 + 26 = 96$

$0 = 8 \times 0 \times 7$

$2 \times 7 \times 5 = 70$

$9 \times (3 + 7) = 90$

$(2 + 8) \times (1 + 9) = 100$

$23 - 17 = 6$

54-61. Write <, >, or = on the lines.

$40 \times 3 \underline{=} 3 \times 40$

$3 \times 2 \times 7 \underline{=} 7 \times 2 \times 3$

$53 + 78 \underline{<} 53 + 80$

$1 \times 1 \underline{<} 1 + 1$

$2 \times 2 \underline{=} 2 + 2$

$4 \times 4 \underline{>} 4 + 4$

$(6 \times 3) + (6 \times 7) \underline{=} (6 \times 10)$

$67 - 48 \underline{>} 66 - 48$

62-69. Write the next two terms for each pattern.

65	67	69	71	73
107	108	109	110	111
8	16	24	32	40
18	27	36	45	54
1	4	9	16	25
2	4	6	8	10
2	4	8	16	32
3	30	300	3000	30,000

70-72. Round 8258.

To nearest 10.	8260
To nearest 100.	8300
To nearest 1000.	8000

73-75. Round 28,602.

To nearest 10.	28,600
To nearest 100.	28,600
To nearest 1000.	29,000

The next three pages have the remaining solutions.

© Activities for Learning, Inc. 2015

Lesson 139: Final Assessment – Continued

ACTIVITIES FOR TEACHING:

76-77. Write the time.

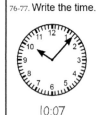 

10:07   8:27

78-79. Draw the hands.

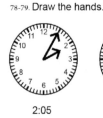 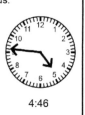

2:05   4:46

80-85. Solve the problems.

Apples cost 79¢ a pound and grapes cost $1.45 a pound. What is the total cost of 3 pounds of apples and 4 pounds of grapes?

C = 79¢ × 3 + 1.45 × 4
C = 2.37 + 5.80 = $8.17

Jamey is buying candles for a birthday cake for an aunt who is 65 years old. There are 8 candles in a package. How many packages does Jamey need?

65 ÷ 8 = 8 r 1
Jamey needs 9 packages.

At 8:30 Jordan started to pick berries. Each row takes 15 minutes to pick. What is the time when Jordan finished picking five rows?

Minutes = 15 × 5 = 1 hr 15 min
8:30 + 1 hr 15 min = 9:45

Jackson has 3 dollar bills, 2 quarters, 4 dimes, 2 nickels, and 5 pennies. How much more money does he need to have 5 dollars?

$3 + .25 × 2 + .10 × 4 + .05 × 2 + .01 × 5 = $4.05
$4.05 + m = 5
m = $0.95

Julie pays 50¢ for a bus token. How many tokens can she get for $4.50?

$4.50 ÷ 50¢ = 9 bus tokens

A rectangular pen for a dog is to be 48 sq. feet. One side of the pen is 6 ft. The fence is $3 per foot? What is the cost of the fence?

Other side = 48 ÷ 6 = 8
C = 2 × (6 + 8) × 3 = $84

EXPLANATIONS:

ACTIVITIES FOR TEACHING:

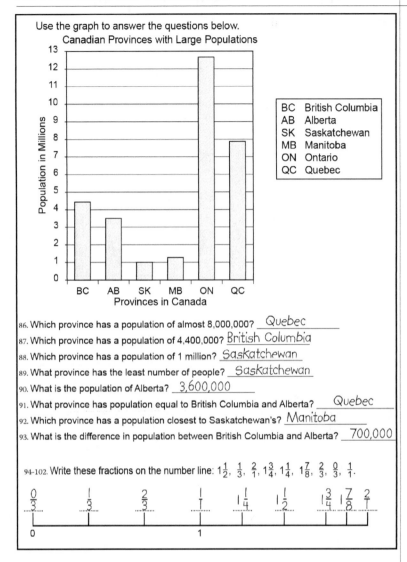

86. Which province has a population of almost 8,000,000? __Quebec__
87. Which province has a population of 4,400,000? __British Columbia__
88. Which province has a population of 1 million? __Saskatchewan__
89. What province has the least number of people? __Saskatchewan__
90. What is the population of Alberta? __3,600,000__
91. What province has population equal to British Columbia and Alberta? __Quebec__
92. Which province has a population closest to Saskatchewan's? __Manitoba__
93. What is the difference in population between British Columbia and Alberta? __700,000__

94-102. Write these fractions on the number line: $1\frac{1}{2}$, $\frac{1}{3}$, $\frac{2}{1}$, $1\frac{3}{4}$, $1\frac{1}{4}$, $1\frac{7}{8}$, $\frac{2}{3}$, $\frac{0}{3}$, $\frac{1}{1}$.

EXPLANATIONS:

The order of the provinces is not alphabetical, but geographical; west to east.

The answers may be given by the two-letter codes.

The next page has the remaining solutions.

LESSON 139: FINAL ASSESSMENT – CONTINUED

ACTIVITIES FOR TEACHING:

103-109. Write <, >, or = on the lines.

$\frac{1}{2} = \frac{3}{6}$

$\frac{6}{6} = \frac{3}{3}$

$\frac{3}{8} < \frac{3}{4}$

$\frac{7}{10} > \frac{5}{10}$

107-109. Circle the fraction in each row that is nearest to one half.

$\frac{3}{7}$	$\frac{3}{8}$	ⓐ$\frac{3}{6}$
ⓐ$\frac{4}{8}$	$\frac{2}{8}$	$\frac{3}{8}$
ⓐ$\frac{5}{10}$	$\frac{7}{8}$	$\frac{2}{2}$

110-112. Circle the greatest fraction in each row.

$\frac{2}{7}$	$\frac{2}{8}$	ⓐ$\frac{2}{2}$
$\frac{1}{6}$	ⓐ$\frac{1}{2}$	$\frac{2}{6}$
$\frac{5}{10}$	$\frac{6}{10}$	ⓐ$\frac{7}{10}$

113-116. Circle the fractions in the rectangle that are needed to total to 1.

| $\frac{9}{10}$ | $\frac{8}{3}$ | ⓐ$\frac{4}{8}$ | ⓐ$\frac{1}{8}$ | ⓐ$\frac{3}{8}$ |
| ⓐ$\frac{1}{4}$ | $\frac{4}{9}$ | ⓐ$\frac{1}{2}$ | ⓐ$\frac{1}{4}$ | $\frac{1}{7}$ |

| ⓐ$\frac{9}{10}$ | $\frac{8}{9}$ | $\frac{4}{8}$ | ⓐ$\frac{1}{10}$ | $\frac{3}{8}$ |
| $\frac{3}{2}$ | ⓐ$\frac{1}{4}$ | ⓐ$\frac{1}{2}$ | ⓐ$\frac{1}{4}$ | $\frac{1}{8}$ |

117-119. Fill in the blanks.

A half of an hour is __30__ minutes.
A quarter of a dollar is __25__ cents.
A half of an gallon is __2__ quarts.

120-122. Match angles and symbols.

45° — ∠ (acute)
60° — ∠ (obtuse)
90° — ∟

123-128. Use the letter in the figure to answer the questions below.

A (hexagon) B (trapezoid) C (triangle) D (rhombus) E (square/rhombus) F (right triangle)

Which figures are quadrilaterals? __B, D, E__
Which figures are rhombuses? __D, E__
Which figure is a trapezoid? __B__
Which figures have parallel lines? __A, B, D, E__
Which figures have right angles? __E, F__
Which figure is a rectangle? __E__

129. Shade $\frac{1}{2}$.

130. Shade $\frac{1}{4}$.

EXPLANATIONS:

There are other ways to shade the figures.

LESSON 140: GEOMETRY PANELS

OBJECTIVES:

1. To construct three-dimensional shapes

MATERIALS:

1. Geometry panels
2. RightStart™ Geometry Panels Instruction booklet

ACTIVITIES FOR TEACHING:	EXPLANATIONS:
Geometry panels. Give the child the geometry panels and instruction booklet. Tell him to construct pyramids, prisms, and any other figures he chooses. The instruction booklet will provide a picture of a shape, the name of the shape, and the net of the shape. Tell him that the net is a shape with some the sides connected but laid out flat.	Lesson 112 gives a brief description of how to attach the rubber bands.

© Activities for Learning, Inc. 2015

Congratulations!

Your child has completed RightStart™ Mathematics Level D and is now ready for Level E Second Edition.

Certificates of completion are in the back of the child's worksheets.

Certificate of Achievement
Presented to

_____

for completing

RIGHTSTART™ MATHEMATICS
LEVEL D
Second Edition

On this _____ *day of* _____

_____ *,Teacher*

Joan A. Cotter, Ph.D.
Kathleen Cotter Lawler

To move on to RightStart™ Mathematics Level E Second Edition, all you need is the Level E Book Bundle. This can be purchased at RightStartMath.com or by calling 888-272-3291.

APPENDIX

SHORT MULTIPLICATION TABLE

Appendix page 1

1									
2	4								
3	6	9							
4	8	12	16						
5	10	15	20	25					
6	12	18	24	30	36				
7	14	21	28	35	42	49			
8	16	24	32	40	48	56	64		
9	18	27	36	45	54	63	72	81	
10	20	30	40	50	60	70	80	90	100

Cut out the two squares at the left. Fold back on the heavy line to make the table stand up.

1									
2	4								
3	6	9							
4	8	12	16						
5	10	15	20	25					
6	12	18	24	30	36				
7	14	21	28	35	42	49			
8	16	24	32	40	48	56	64		
9	18	27	36	45	54	63	72	81	
10	20	30	40	50	60	70	80	90	100

© Activities for Learning, Inc. 2015

RightStart™ Mathematics Second Edition, D

Pascal's Triangle Part 1

Appendix page 2

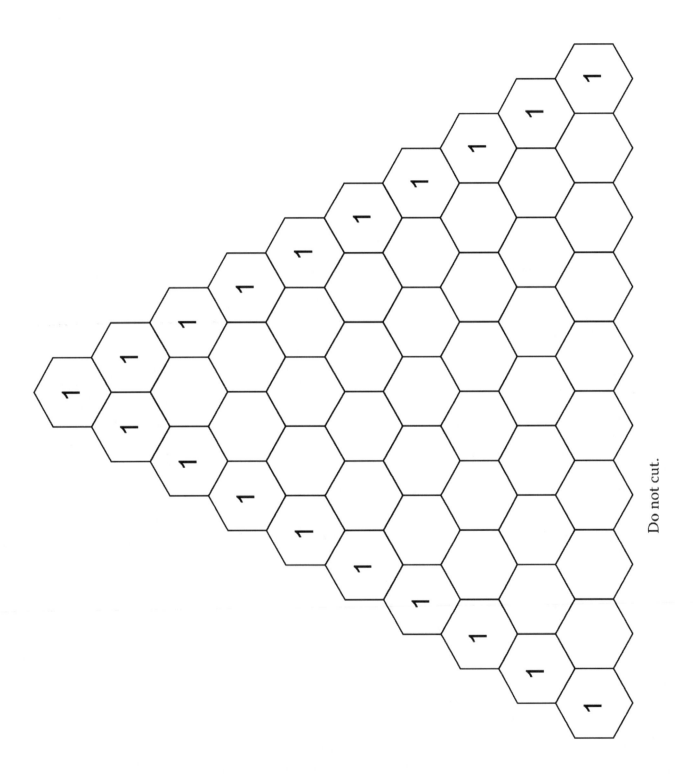

Do not cut.

Pascal's Triangle Part 2

Appendix page 3

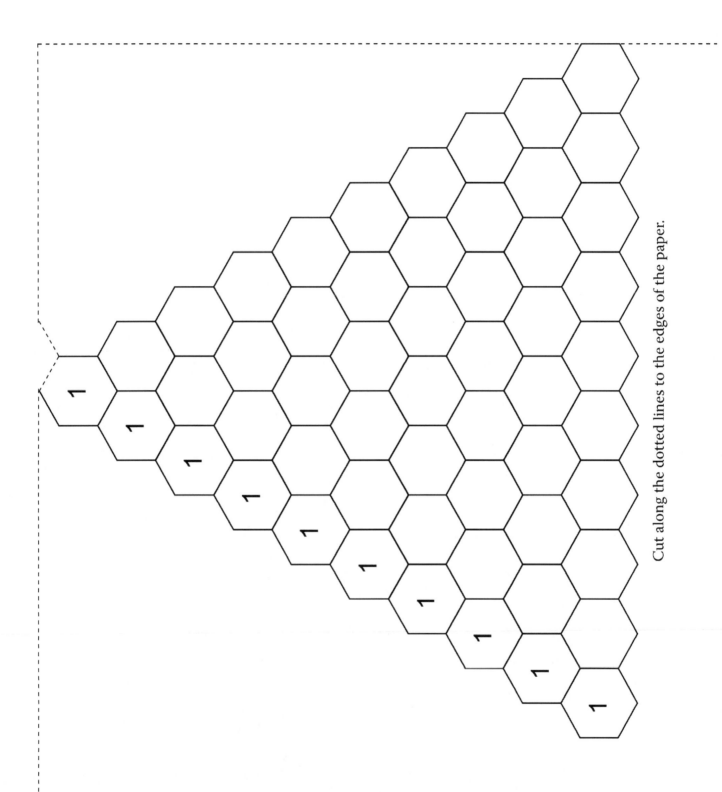

Cut along the dotted lines to the edges of the paper.

© Activities for Learning, Inc. 2015

RightStart™ Mathematics Second Edition, D

Pascal's Triangle Part 3

Appendix page 4

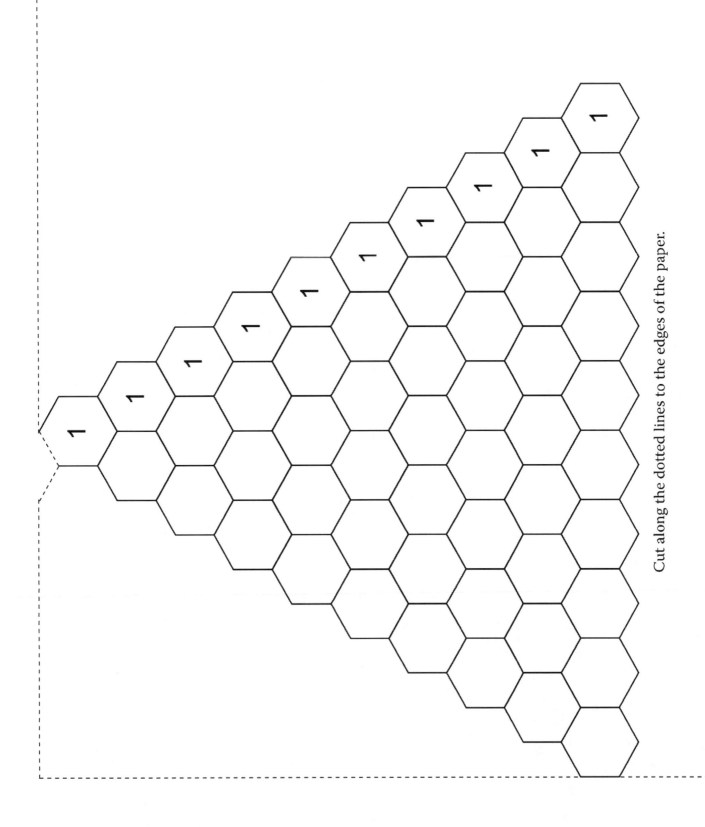

Cut along the dotted lines to the edges of the paper.

Pascal's Triangle Part 4

Appendix page 5

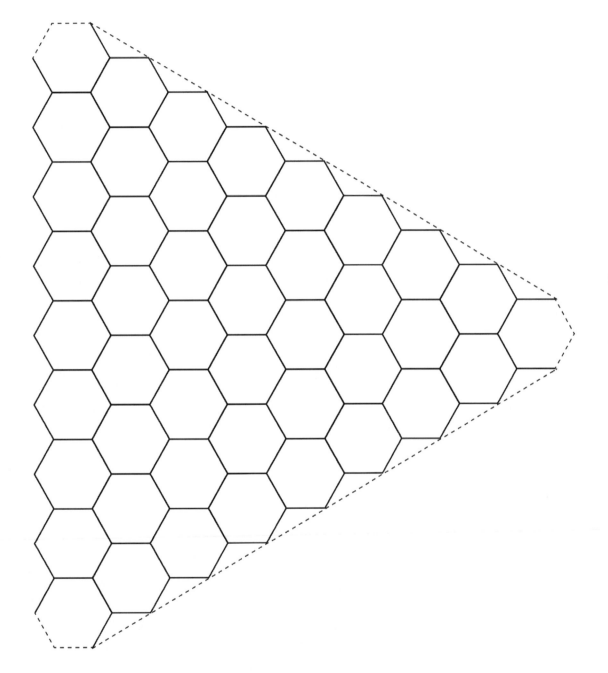

Cut out on the dotted lines.

Pascal's Triangle Part 4

Pascal's Triangle Pattern

Appendix page 6

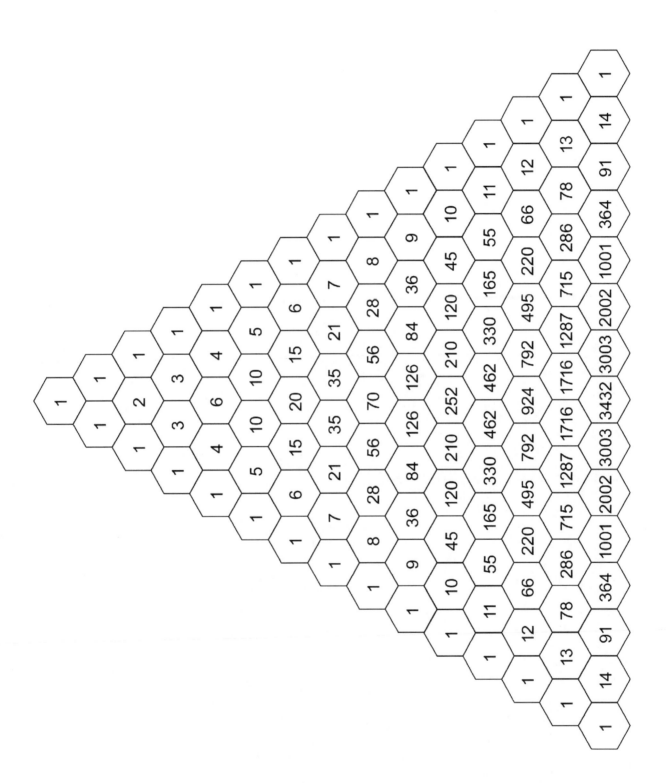

NON-UNIT FRACTIONS

Appendix page 7

Three 1-strips are needed per child.

1	1	1	1	1	1

© Activities for Learning, Inc. 2015

RightStart™ Mathematics Second Edition, D

ADDING HALVES AND FOURTHS

Appendix page 8

Four rectangles are needed per child.

© Activities for Learning, Inc. 2015

RightStart™ Mathematics Second Edition, D

Appendix page 9

2018

January
S	M	T	W	T	F	S
	1	2	3	4	5	6
	8	9	10	11	12	13
	15	16	17	18	19	20
	22	23	24	25	26	27
	29	30	31			

February
S	M	T	W	T	F	S
				1	2	3
4	5	6	7	8	9	10
11	12	13	14	15	16	17
18	19	20	21	22	23	24
25	26	27	28			

March
S	M	T	W	T	F	S
				1	2	3
4	5	6	7	8	9	10
11	12	13	14	15	16	17
18	19	20	21	22	23	24
25	26	27	28	29	30	31

April
S	M	T	W	T	F	S
	2	3	4	5	6	7
	9	10	11	12	13	14
	16	17	18	19	20	21
	23	24	25	26	27	28
	30					

May
S	M	T	W	T	F	S
		1	2	3	4	5
6	7	8	9	10	11	12
13	14	15	16	17	18	19
20	21	22	23	24	25	26
27	28	29	30	31		

June
S	M	T	W	T	F	S
					1	2
3	4	5	6	7	8	9
10	11	12	13	14	15	16
17	18	19	20	21	22	23
24	25	26	27	28	29	30

July
S	M	T	W	T	F	S
	2	3	4	5	6	7
	9	10	11	12	13	14
	16	17	18	19	20	21
	23	24	25	26	27	28
	30	31				

August
S	M	T	W	T	F	S
			1	2	3	4
5	6	7	8	9	10	11
12	13	14	15	16	17	18
19	20	21	22	23	24	25
26	27	28	29	30	31	

September
S	M	T	W	T	F	S
						1
2	3	4	5	6	7	8
9	10	11	12	13	14	15
16	17	18	19	20	21	22
23	24	25	26	27	28	29
30						

October
S	M	T	W	T	F	S
	1	2	3	4	5	6
	8	9	10	11	12	13
	15	16	17	18	19	20
	22	23	24	25	26	27
	29	30	31			

November
S	M	T	W	T	F	S
				1	2	3
4	5	6	7	8	9	10
11	12	13	14	15	16	17
18	19	20	21	22	23	24
25	26	27	28	29	30	

December
S	M	T	W	T	F	S
						1
2	3	4	5	6	7	8
9	10	11	12	13	14	15
16	17	18	19	20	21	22
23	24	25	26	27	28	29
30	31					

2019

Appendix page 9

January

S	M	T	W	T	F	S
	1	2	3	4	5	
6	7	8	9	10	11	12
13	14	15	16	17	18	19
20	21	22	23	24	25	26
27	28	29	30	31		

February

S	M	T	W	T	F	S
					1	2
3	4	5	6	7	8	9
10	11	12	13	14	15	16
17	18	19	20	21	22	23
24	25	26	27	28		

March

S	M	T	W	T	F	S
					1	2
3	4	5	6	7	8	9
10	11	12	13	14	15	16
17	18	19	20	21	22	23
24	25	26	27	28	29	30
31						

April

S	M	T	W	T	F	S
	1	2	3	4	5	6
7	8	9	10	11	12	13
14	15	16	17	18	19	20
21	22	23	24	25	26	27
28	29	30				

May

S	M	T	W	T	F	S
			1	2	3	4
5	6	7	8	9	10	11
12	13	14	15	16	17	18
19	20	21	22	23	24	25
26	27	28	29	30	31	

June

S	M	T	W	T	F	S
						1
2	3	4	5	6	7	8
9	10	11	12	13	14	15
16	17	18	19	20	21	22
23	24	25	26	27	28	29
30						

July

S	M	T	W	T	F	S
	1	2	3	4	5	6
7	8	9	10	11	12	13
14	15	16	17	18	19	20
21	22	23	24	25	26	27
28	29	30	31			

August

S	M	T	W	T	F	S
				1	2	3
4	5	6	7	8	9	10
11	12	13	14	15	16	17
18	19	20	21	22	23	24
25	26	27	28	29	30	31

September

S	M	T	W	T	F	S
1	2	3	4	5	6	7
8	9	10	11	12	13	14
15	16	17	18	19	20	21
22	23	24	25	26	27	28
29	30					

October

S	M	T	W	T	F	S
	1	2	3	4	5	
6	7	8	9	10	11	12
13	14	15	16	17	18	19
20	21	22	23	24	25	26
27	28	29	30	31		

November

S	M	T	W	T	F	S
					1	2
3	4	5	6	7	8	9
10	11	12	13	14	15	16
17	18	19	20	21	22	23
24	25	26	27	28	29	30

December

S	M	T	W	T	F	S
1	2	3	4	5	6	7
8	9	10	11	12	13	14
15	16	17	18	19	20	21
22	23	24	25	26	27	28
29	30	31				

Appendix page 9

2020

January

S	M	T	W	T	F	S
		1	2	3	4	
5	6	7	8	9	10	11
12	13	14	15	16	17	18
19	20	21	22	23	24	25
26	27	28	29	30	31	

February

S	M	T	W	T	F	S
						1
2	3	4	5	6	7	8
9	10	11	12	13	14	15
16	17	18	19	20	21	22
23	24	25	26	27	28	29

March

S	M	T	W	T	F	S
1	2	3	4	5	6	7
8	9	10	11	12	13	14
15	16	17	18	19	20	21
22	23	24	25	26	27	28
29	30	31				

April

S	M	T	W	T	F	S
		1	2	3	4	
5	6	7	8	9	10	11
12	13	14	15	16	17	18
19	20	21	22	23	24	25
26	27	28	29	30		

May

S	M	T	W	T	F	S
					1	2
3	4	5	6	7	8	9
10	11	12	13	14	15	16
17	18	19	20	21	22	23
24	25	26	27	28	29	30
31						

June

S	M	T	W	T	F	S
	1	2	3	4	5	6
7	8	9	10	11	12	13
14	15	16	17	18	19	20
21	22	23	24	25	26	27
28	29	30				

July

S	M	T	W	T	F	S
		1	2	3	4	
5	6	7	8	9	10	11
12	13	14	15	16	17	18
19	20	21	22	23	24	25
26	27	28	29	30	31	

August

S	M	T	W	T	F	S
						1
2	3	4	5	6	7	8
9	10	11	12	13	14	15
16	17	18	19	20	21	22
23	24	25	26	27	28	29
30	31					

September

S	M	T	W	T	F	S
		1	2	3	4	5
6	7	8	9	10	11	12
13	14	15	16	17	18	19
20	21	22	23	24	25	26
27	28	29	30			

October

S	M	T	W	T	F	S
				1	2	3
4	5	6	7	8	9	10
11	12	13	14	15	16	17
18	19	20	21	22	23	24
25	26	27	28	29	30	31

November

S	M	T	W	T	F	S
1	2	3	4	5	6	7
8	9	10	11	12	13	14
15	16	17	18	19	20	21
22	23	24	25	26	27	28
29	30					

December

S	M	T	W	T	F	S
		1	2	3	4	5
6	7	8	9	10	11	12
13	14	15	16	17	18	19
20	21	22	23	24	25	26
27	28	29	30	31		

2021

Appendix page 9

January

S	M	T	W	T	F	S
					1	2
3	4	5	6	7	8	9
10	11	12	13	14	15	16
17	18	19	20	21	22	23
24	25	26	27	28	29	30
31						

February

S	M	T	W	T	F	S
	1	2	3	4	5	6
7	8	9	10	11	12	13
14	15	16	17	18	19	20
21	22	23	24	25	26	27
28						

March

S	M	T	W	T	F	S
	1	2	3	4	5	6
7	8	9	10	11	12	13
14	15	16	17	18	19	20
21	22	23	24	25	26	27
28	29	30	31			

April

S	M	T	W	T	F	S
				1	2	3
4	5	6	7	8	9	10
11	12	13	14	15	16	17
18	19	20	21	22	23	24
25	26	27	28	29	30	

May

S	M	T	W	T	F	S
						1
2	3	4	5	6	7	8
9	10	11	12	13	14	15
16	17	18	19	20	21	22
23	24	25	26	27	28	29
30	31					

June

S	M	T	W	T	F	S
		1	2	3	4	5
6	7	8	9	10	11	12
13	14	15	16	17	18	19
20	21	22	23	24	25	26
27	28	29	30			

July

S	M	T	W	T	F	S
				1	2	3
4	5	6	7	8	9	10
11	12	13	14	15	16	17
18	19	20	21	22	23	24
25	26	27	28	29	30	31

August

S	M	T	W	T	F	S
1	2	3	4	5	6	7
8	9	10	11	12	13	14
15	16	17	18	19	20	21
22	23	24	25	26	27	28
29	30	31				

September

S	M	T	W	T	F	S
			1	2	3	4
5	6	7	8	9	10	11
12	13	14	15	16	17	18
19	20	21	22	23	24	25
26	27	28	29	30		

October

S	M	T	W	T	F	S
					1	2
3	4	5	6	7	8	9
10	11	12	13	14	15	16
17	18	19	20	21	22	23
24	25	26	27	28	29	30
31						

November

S	M	T	W	T	F	S
	1	2	3	4	5	6
7	8	9	10	11	12	13
14	15	16	17	18	19	20
21	22	23	24	25	26	27
28	29	30				

December

S	M	T	W	T	F	S
			1	2	3	4
5	6	7	8	9	10	11
12	13	14	15	16	17	18
19	20	21	22	23	24	25
26	27	28	29	30	31	

Appendix page 9

2022

January

S	M	T	W	T	F	S
						1
2	3	4	5	6	7	8
9	10	11	12	13	14	15
16	17	18	19	20	21	22
23	24	25	26	27	28	29
30	31					

February

S	M	T	W	T	F	S
		1	2	3	4	5
6	7	8	9	10	11	12
13	14	15	16	17	18	19
20	21	22	23	24	25	26
27	28					

March

S	M	T	W	T	F	S
		1	2	3	4	5
6	7	8	9	10	11	12
13	14	15	16	17	18	19
20	21	22	23	24	25	26
27	28	29	30	31		

April

S	M	T	W	T	F	S
					1	2
3	4	5	6	7	8	9
10	11	12	13	14	15	16
17	18	19	20	21	22	23
24	25	26	27	28	29	30

May

S	M	T	W	T	F	S
1	2	3	4	5	6	7
8	9	10	11	12	13	14
15	16	17	18	19	20	21
22	23	24	25	26	27	28
29	30	31				

June

S	M	T	W	T	F	S
			1	2	3	4
5	6	7	8	9	10	11
12	13	14	15	16	17	18
19	20	21	22	23	24	25
26	27	28	29	30		

July

S	M	T	W	T	F	S
					1	2
3	4	5	6	7	8	9
10	11	12	13	14	15	16
17	18	19	20	21	22	23
24	25	26	27	28	29	30
31						

August

S	M	T	W	T	F	S
	1	2	3	4	5	6
7	8	9	10	11	12	13
14	15	16	17	18	19	20
21	22	23	24	25	26	27
28	29	30	31			

September

S	M	T	W	T	F	S
				1	2	3
4	5	6	7	8	9	10
11	12	13	14	15	16	17
18	19	20	21	22	23	24
25	26	27	28	29	30	

October

S	M	T	W	T	F	S
						1
2	3	4	5	6	7	8
9	10	11	12	13	14	15
16	17	18	19	20	21	22
23	24	25	26	27	28	29
30	31					

November

S	M	T	W	T	F	S
		1	2	3	4	5
6	7	8	9	10	11	12
13	14	15	16	17	18	19
20	21	22	23	24	25	26
27	28	29	30			

December

S	M	T	W	T	F	S
				1	2	3
4	5	6	7	8	9	10
11	12	13	14	15	16	17
18	19	20	21	22	23	24
25	26	27	28	29	30	31

Clock

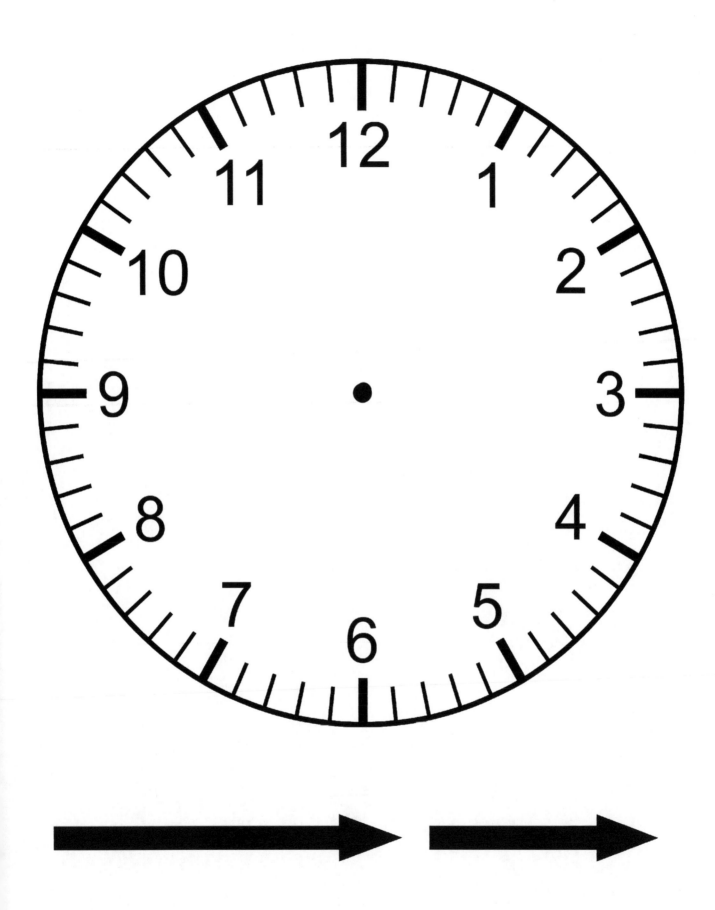